OPERA SIAM

2001-2018

THE FIRST SIXTY PRODUCTIONS

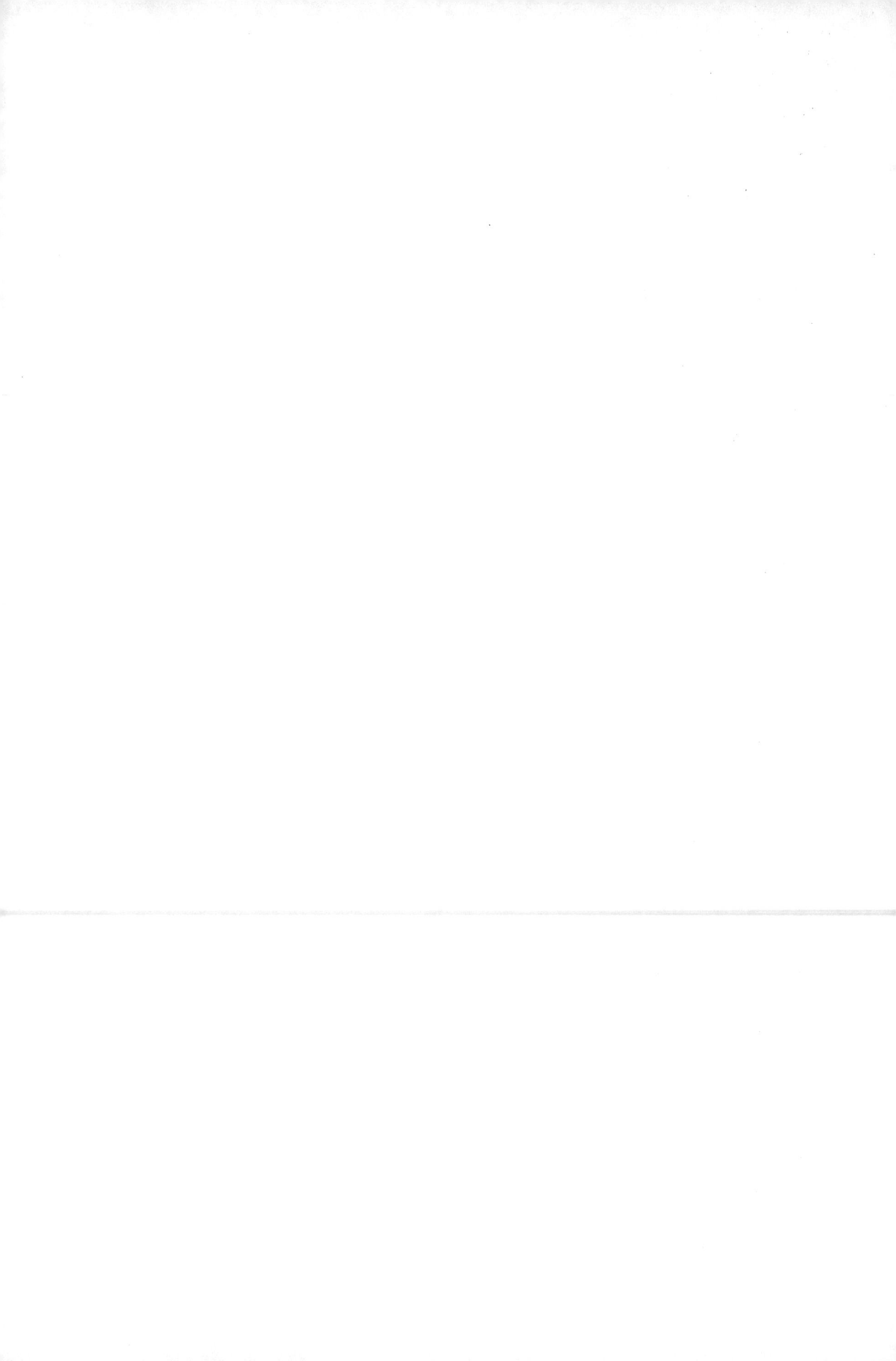

OPERA SIAM

2001-2018

THE FIRST SIXTY PRODUCTIONS

A PICTORIAL HISTORY

COMPILED BY S.P. SOMTOW

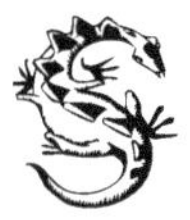

DIPLODOCUS PRESS
BANGKOK · LOS ANGELES

Opera Siam 2001-2018: THE FIRST SIXTY PRODUCTIONS
Diplodocus Press
Los Angeles • Bangkok

9781940999418 Trade Paperback
9781940999401 Hardcover
9781940999425 eBook

First Edition

0 9 8 7 6 5 4 3 2 1

OPERA SIAM 2001-2018

THE FIRST SIXTY PRODUCTIONS

A PICTORIAL HISTORY

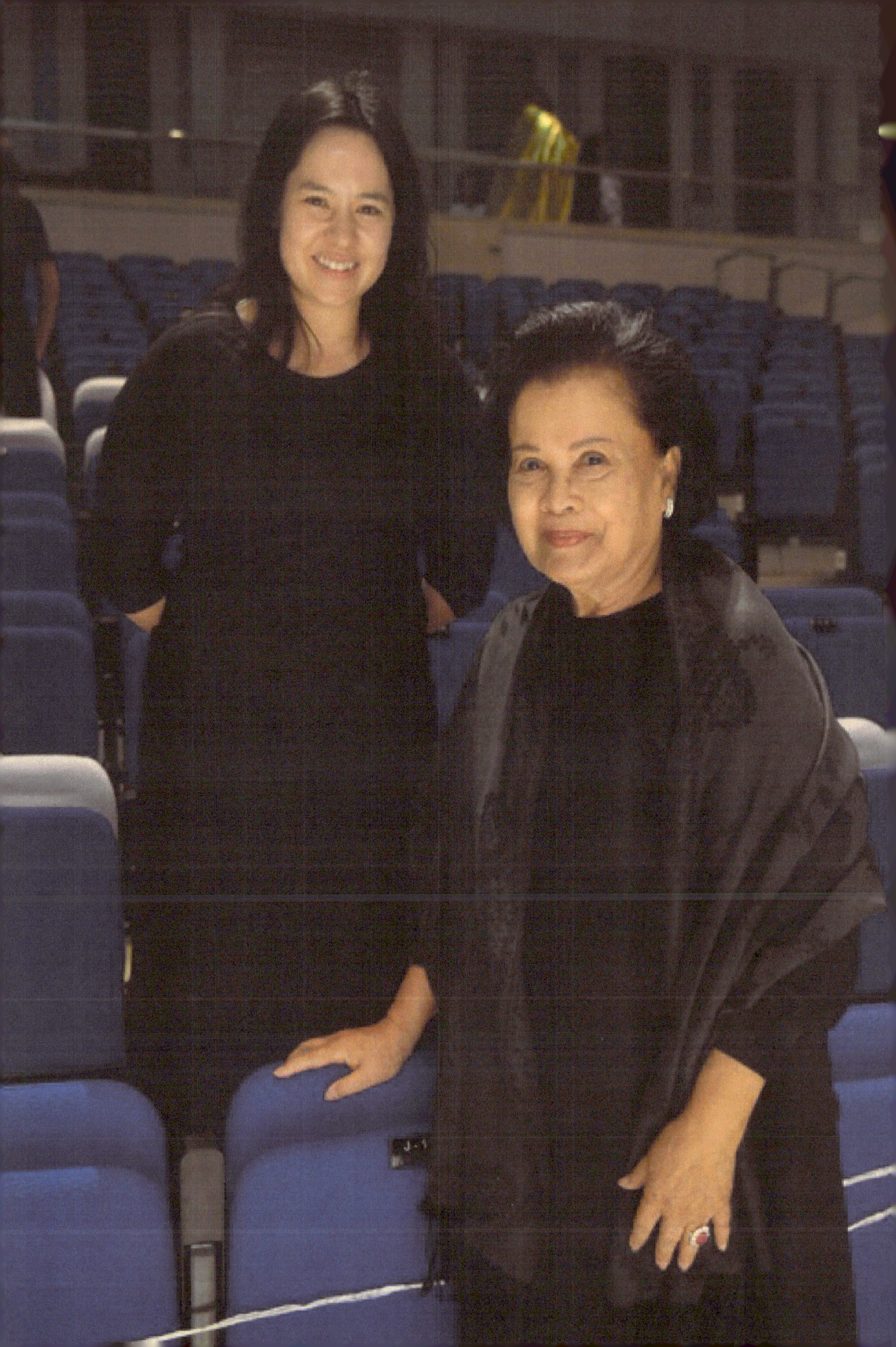

dedication

to *Khun Ploypailin Jensen*

a true musician who has been an inspiration
especially to Opera Siam's youthful musicians
and has always been willing
to lead the way by participating
in performances herself

and to

Thaithow Sucharitkul

who has supported Opera Siam from the very beginning
with tireless energy and dedication
sometimes known affectionately as
"The Dragon Lady" but
mostly frequently as "Grandma"

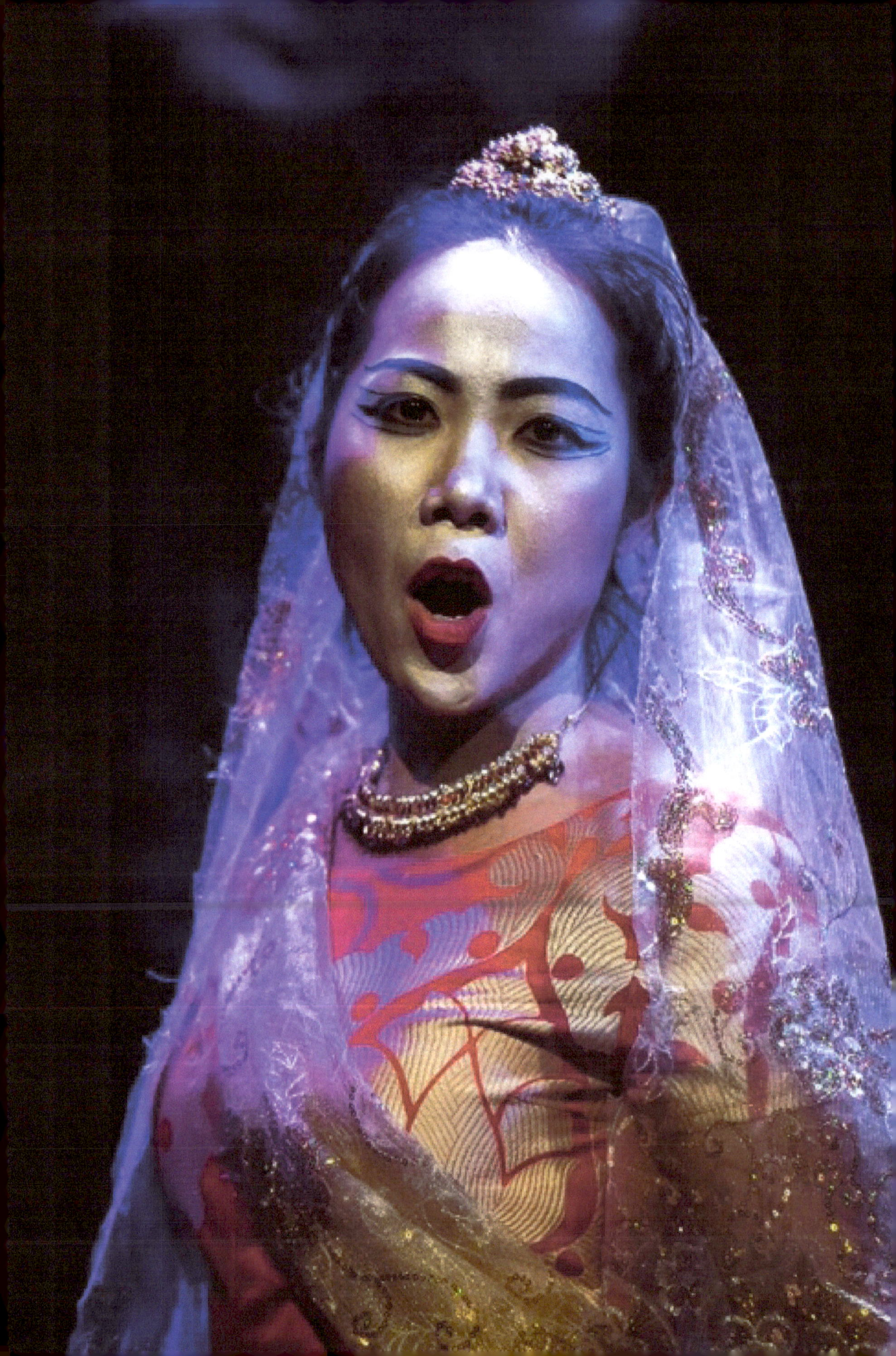

OPERA SIAM

Created in 2001. In five years time, the Bangkok Opera grew from a company which produced what *The Nation* once described to productions "akin to college or community theatre" to a company that created (to quote that same newspaper only one year later) "music put together with a vision and performed with an inspiration that are rarely found in the greatest opera houses of the world."

Now, eighteen years have gone by and the opera company rebranded itself as *Opera Siam.* It mounted ambitious works like *Bluebeard's Castle, The Flying Dutchman,* and *Otello,* as well as rarely performed masterpieces like *Thaïs;* it produced thought-provoking works like *The Diary of Anne Frank,* children's operas like *The Happy Prince* and *Brundibar,* and many of the operas by its founder, Somtow Sucharitkul, including the groundbreaking *Dan no Ura* and *The Snow Dragon,* and, still in progress, the ten-part music drama *DasJati, Ten Lives of the Buddha,* which when completed, according to *Opera Now,* will be the single largest integrated classical work in history.

Opera Siam has toured England, Germany, and the Czech Republic, scoring the kind of success that well-funded, nationally sponsored ensembles evince, and eventually leading to the distinction of being awarded the European Cultural Achievenent Award for 2017, the first time an Asian was ever granted this honour.

Despite its many successes, the company was basically still run out of a shoebox with massive deficits, eating up family resources and the resources of our friends. 2016 was a crisis year. I am putting together this book at a moment when, after our sixtieth production, our very survival is in doubt.

We've taken a few months to push the reset button and are about to unleash a whole new Opera Siam on the world. The 18th Season, I hope, will show a much expanded operation with wider outreach into all levels of society. Ten years ago, London's *Opera* magazine called Opera Siam "the operatic hub of Southeast Asia." In 2017, the same magazine said of our production of *La Bohème:* "a production as good as *any* by a European opera company."

From a "voice crying out in the wilderness," Opera Siam has come of age. Here are some pictures that tell the story.

THE PATRON SAINT OF CLASSICAL MUSIC

A NOTE BY S.P. SOMTOW

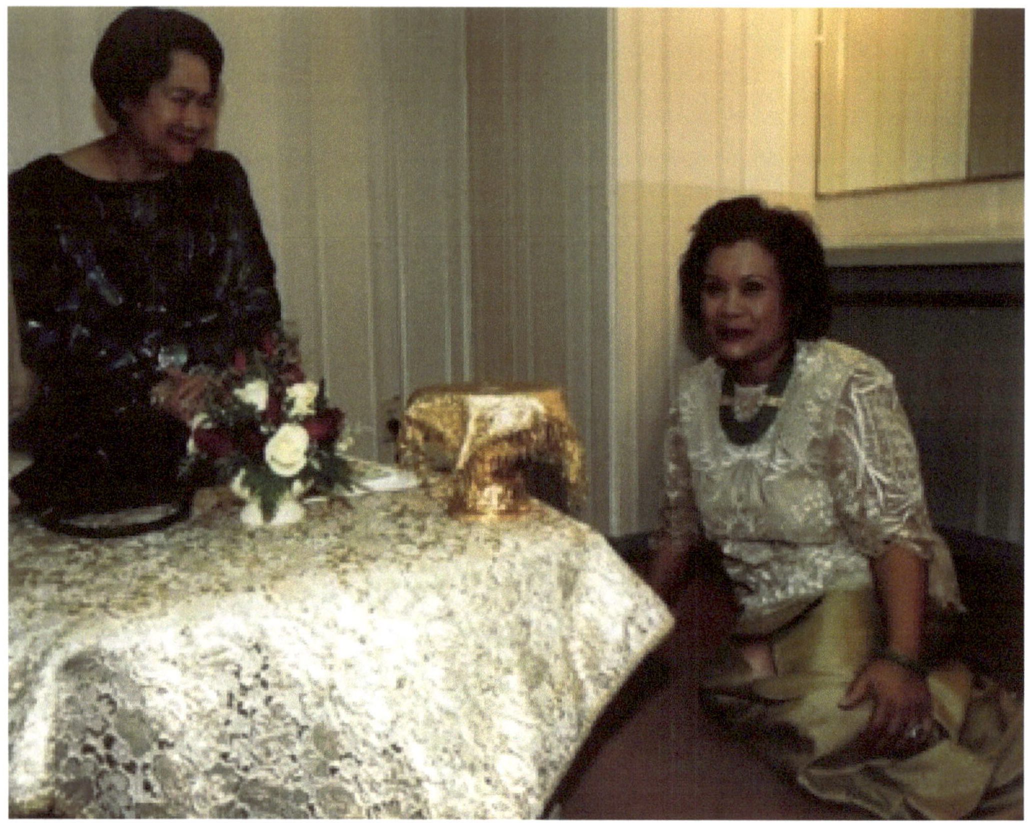

In the years that I have been involved in music in Thailand, the most supportive figure has always been the late HRH Princess Galyani Vadhana. I called her the princess of a thousand smiles. During her lifetime she attended dozens of our events.

I'm sometimes a stranger in my own land, having moved away at the age of six months and having lived my entire life, and had my whole career, in the west, I've been known to fumble in the elaborate world of Thailand's hierarchy.

When I received a fax from Her Royal Highness thanking me for a recording of the *Mahajanaka Symphony* which I had sent to the palace, I was too uneducated in the ways of protocol to realize that one didn't just send a fax back to the return fax number on the fax sheet. I simply didn't realize that it is customary to go through channels.

Her Royal Highness was not offended by this appalling breach of protocol and instead there began an occasional correspondence as a result of which she accepted the role of Patron of the Bangkok Opera, a role which she fulfilled with dignity, humor, and compassion for five years, lending a sympathetic ear to our many problems, appearing at many of the opera performances when she was able to.

Her Royal Highness was a pioneer in getting classical music heard in this country and in encouraging youthful artists. Her passing was a profound loss for the classical music world in Thailand.

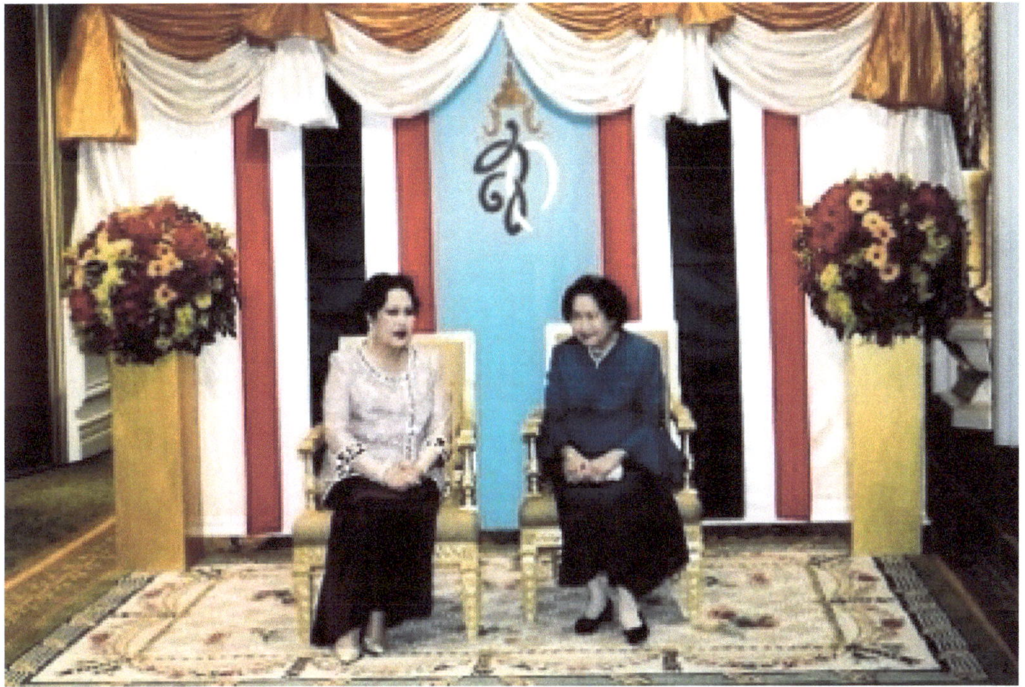

In the photograph above, Her Royal Highness is seen with Her Majesty the Queen, when both royals graciously presided over the world premiere of my *Sirikit Concerto,* composed in honour of Her Majesty's birthday and performed at a charity gala to raise funds for Her Majesty's Breast Cancer Centre.

— S.P. Somtow

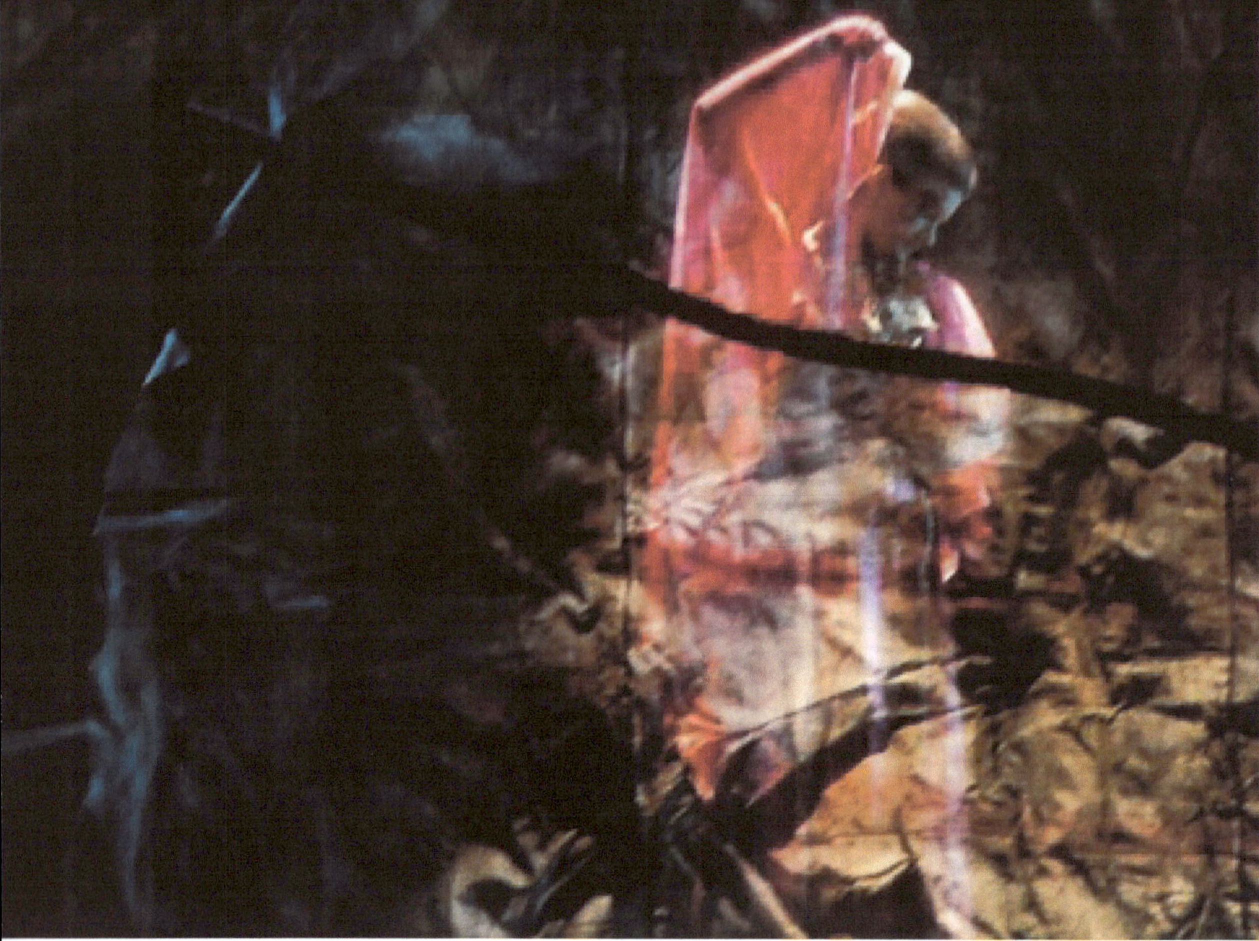

1. MADANA (2001) - WORLD PREMIERE

Madana was conceived as a one-shot; there was an invitation from an organization devoted to restoring H.M. King Rama VI's Phyathai Palace. The idea was to compose an opera to help raise money for the restoration, and I was approached. This was to be the first full-scale grand opera by a Thai composer and to me the most fitting subject was a play authored by the king himself and dedicated originally to my great-aunt, H.M. Queen Indrakdisachi.

Madanabada is a very romantic story and the musical treatment was correspondingly lush. The idiom was overwhelmingly late-romantic because I wanted to create a period piece, with a musical language that would have been accessible to the Thai court of the 1920s.

For the title role I was lucky enough to have bagged the very young Stacey Tappan, whom I had known as a teenager in Los Angeles. I had known, ever since she nonchalantly sailed through Mozart's *Come scoglio* at a computer nerds' get-together at my house, that she was going to be an important opera singer. I don't think she took me seriously when I told her this, but it seemed only a blink of an eye before she was taking Juillard by storm.

The opera was commissioned by opera lover Dr. Suprija Mokkhavesa. To everyone's amazement, performances were packed; the final night, extra seats had to be brought in. It was clear that Bangkok had a hunger for this kind of performance. Dr. Suprija's idea to commission the first "grand opera" by a Thai composer proved to be one of great visionary import and was the seed from which all the other operatic achievements in Bangkok germinated.

Lars Mellander, the tenor who created the role of King Jayasena, has recently reinvented himself as a baritone. Barbara Smith Jones, who sang Queen Chanti, has returned to the Bangkok Opera numerous times — as Fricka in *Das Rheingold,* and to sing the role of the governess in *The Turn of the Screw.*

What *Madana* proved to us was that there is a real market for opera in Thailand. Every performance was packed and there were not only glitterati present but members of at least two royal families: the Crown Princess and Princess of Belgium graced us with their presence in addition to numerous representatives of the Thai royal family.

— *S.P. Somtow*

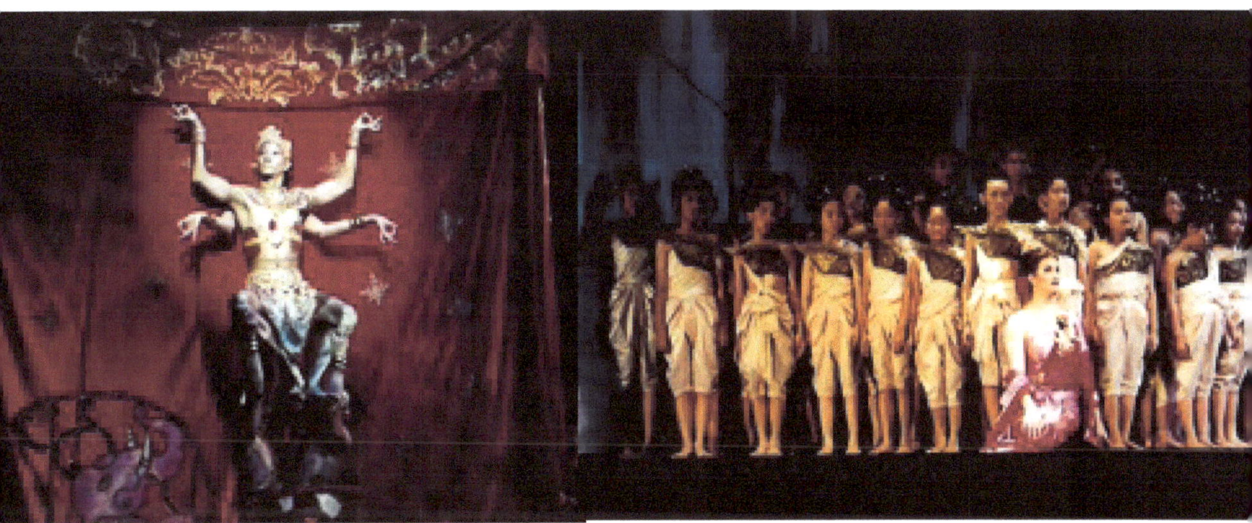

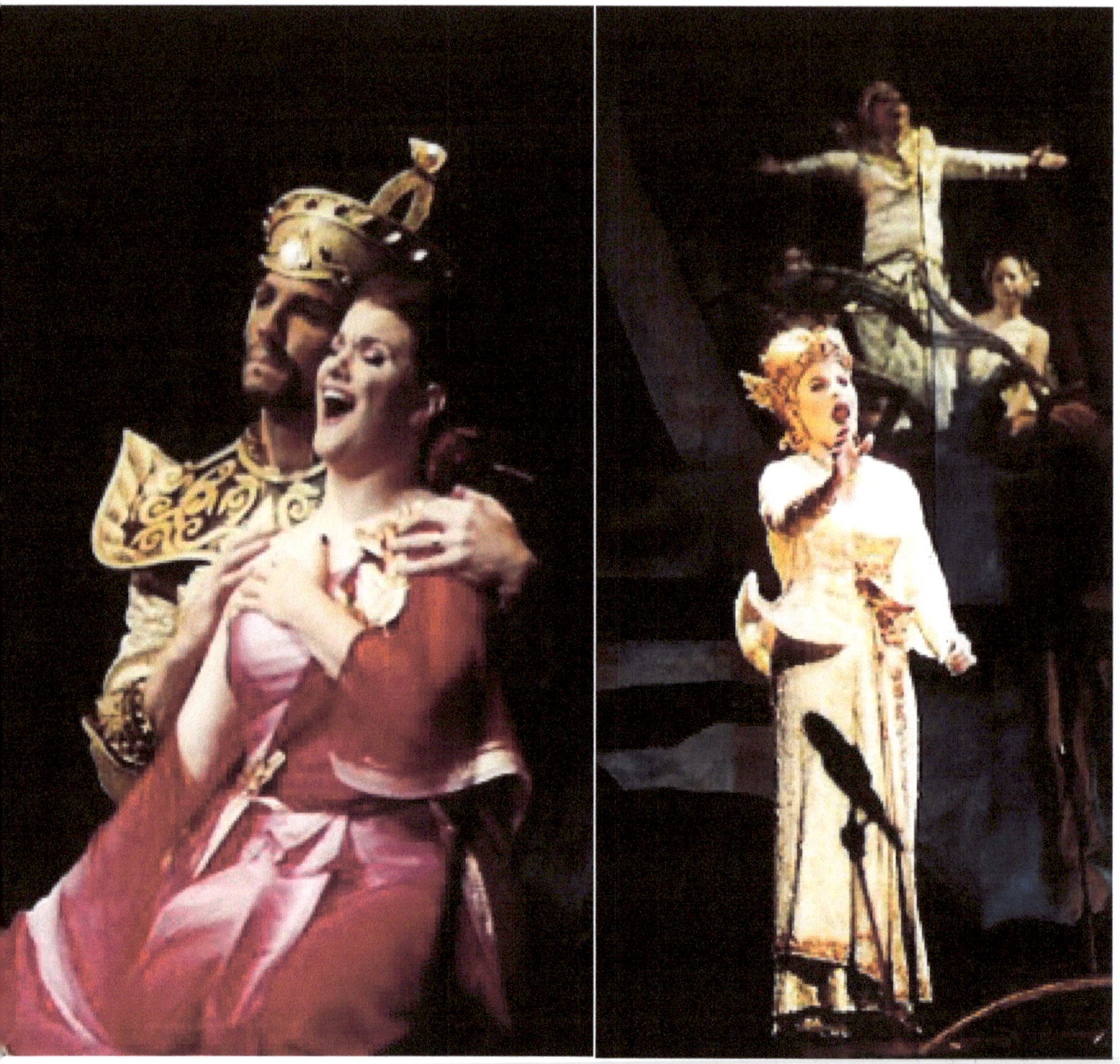

— Main cast: Stacey Tappan, Lars Mellander, Barbara Smith Jones, Ralph Schatzki, Dusdi Banomyong, Pradichaya Poonyarit

— Bangkok Symphony Orchestra, conducted by Somtow Sucharitkul

— Chatvichai Prohmadattavedi, designer

— Somtow Sucharitkul, director

2. DIDO AND AENEAS (2002)

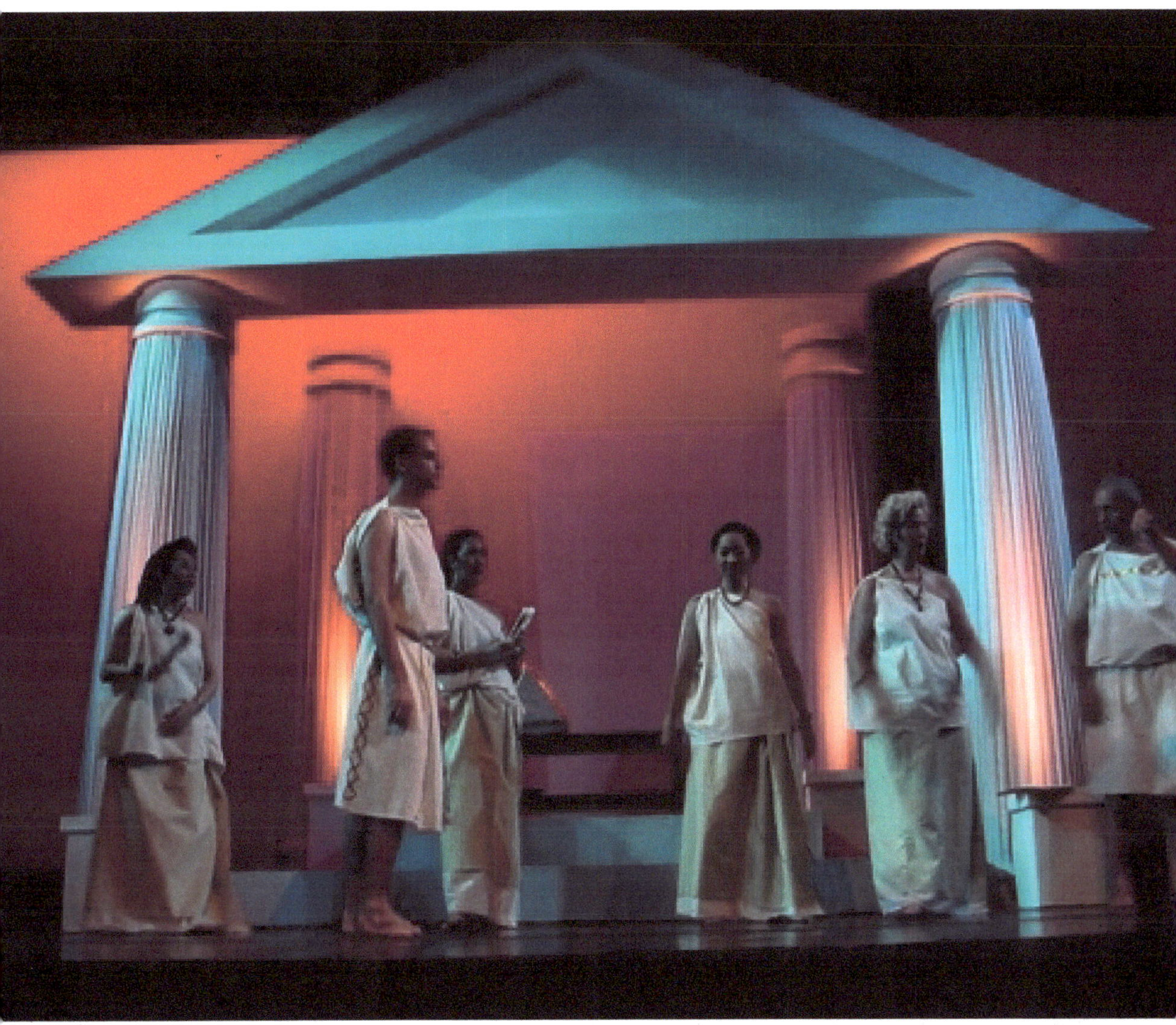

Dido — a nice safe opera, perhaps, with a very small orchestra, was the Bangkok Opera's first production as an independent opera company. In an attempt to provide an experience for as many local artists as possible, the opera was double cast and there was also a school matinée in the afternoon.

The production was rustled together for only 700,000 baht, with only a string quartet and harpsichord as accompaniment, in the Small Hall of the

Thailand Cultural Centre. It proved to be a historical orchestra in that Trisdee na Patalung, who was later to found the Bangkok Baroque Ensemble and to direct Monteverdi from the harpsichord at the Concertgebouw in Amsterdam, played continue for the first time in an opera, on a Roland electronic harpsichord which had been generously donated by the Roland representative.

The concept was to try to replicate the atmosphere of the 17th Century court, so the performance featured a chorus members such as Richard Henderson beginning the opera as "footmen", announcing the arrival of prominent members of the audience. The conductor and orchestra were costumed (though the orchestra refused to wear powdered wigs!) and participated in the action in a number of ways.

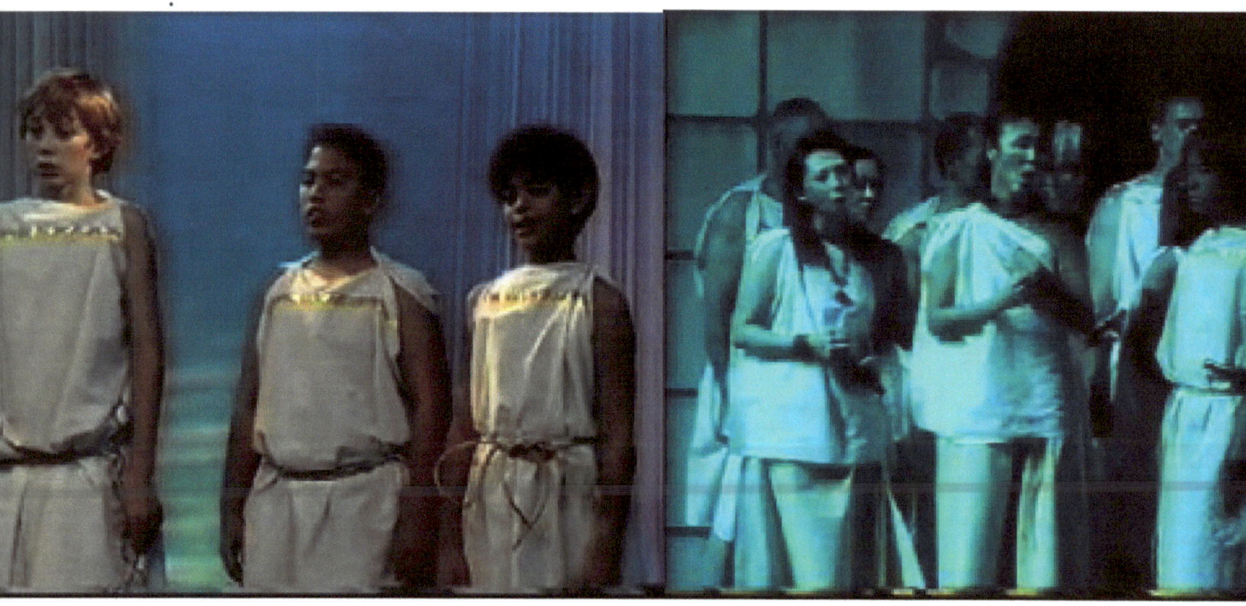

— Main Cast: Pradichaya Poonyarit, Ralph Schatzki, Ema Naito, Audrey Vallance,

— I Musicini, Trisdee na Patalung, continuo

— Somtow Sucharitkul, director and conductor

3. PORGY AND BESS (2002)
CONCERT VERSION

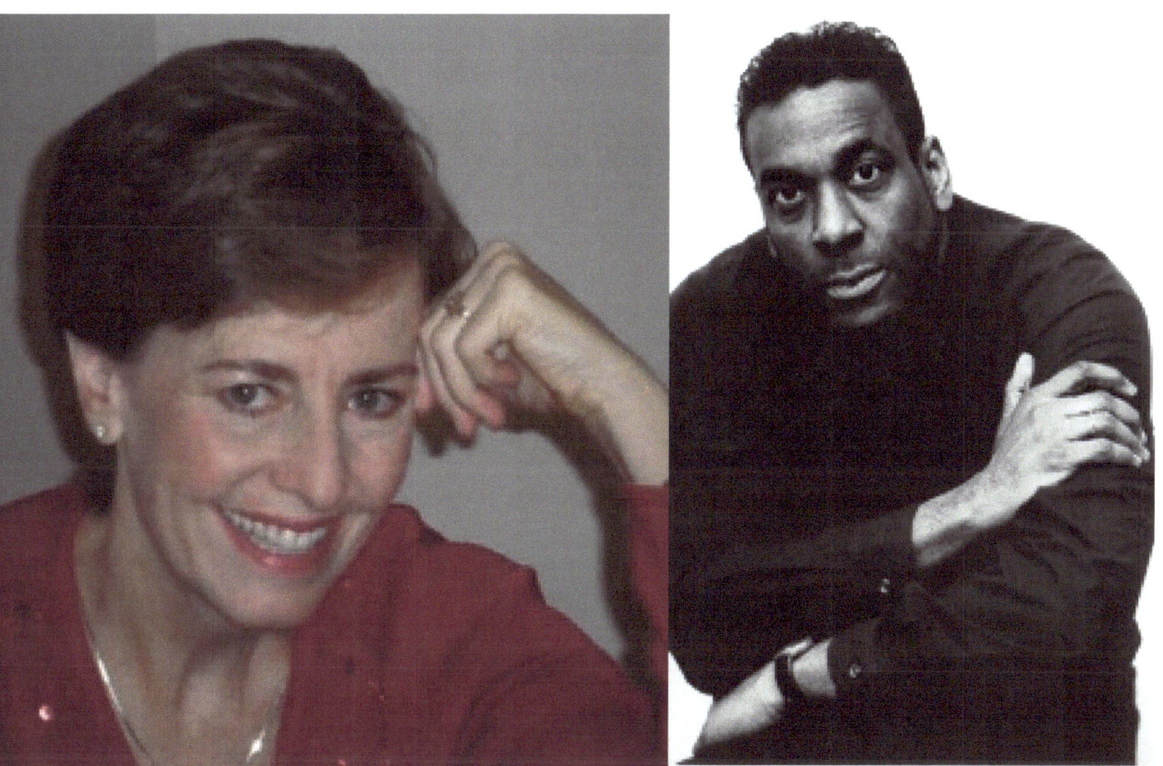

Coordinated by Audrey Vallance with *American Voices* and sponsored by UnoCal, this was a performance that included members of the Orpheus Choir of the Bangkok Opera.

The event was conducted by Ira Spaulding, a prominent baritone and choral conductor. The Opera's archives have failed to produce any photos of this event, but perhaps they can be found in time for a second printing.

4. DIE ZAUBERFLÖTE (2003)
THAILAND PREMIERE

The Bangkok Opera's first "mainstream classic" was attended by no less a figure than Her Majesty the Queen in addition to HRH Princess Galyani Vadhana. This was the debut of the "Thai-sci-fi" look which became a feature of many productions at the Bangkok Opera. It was also

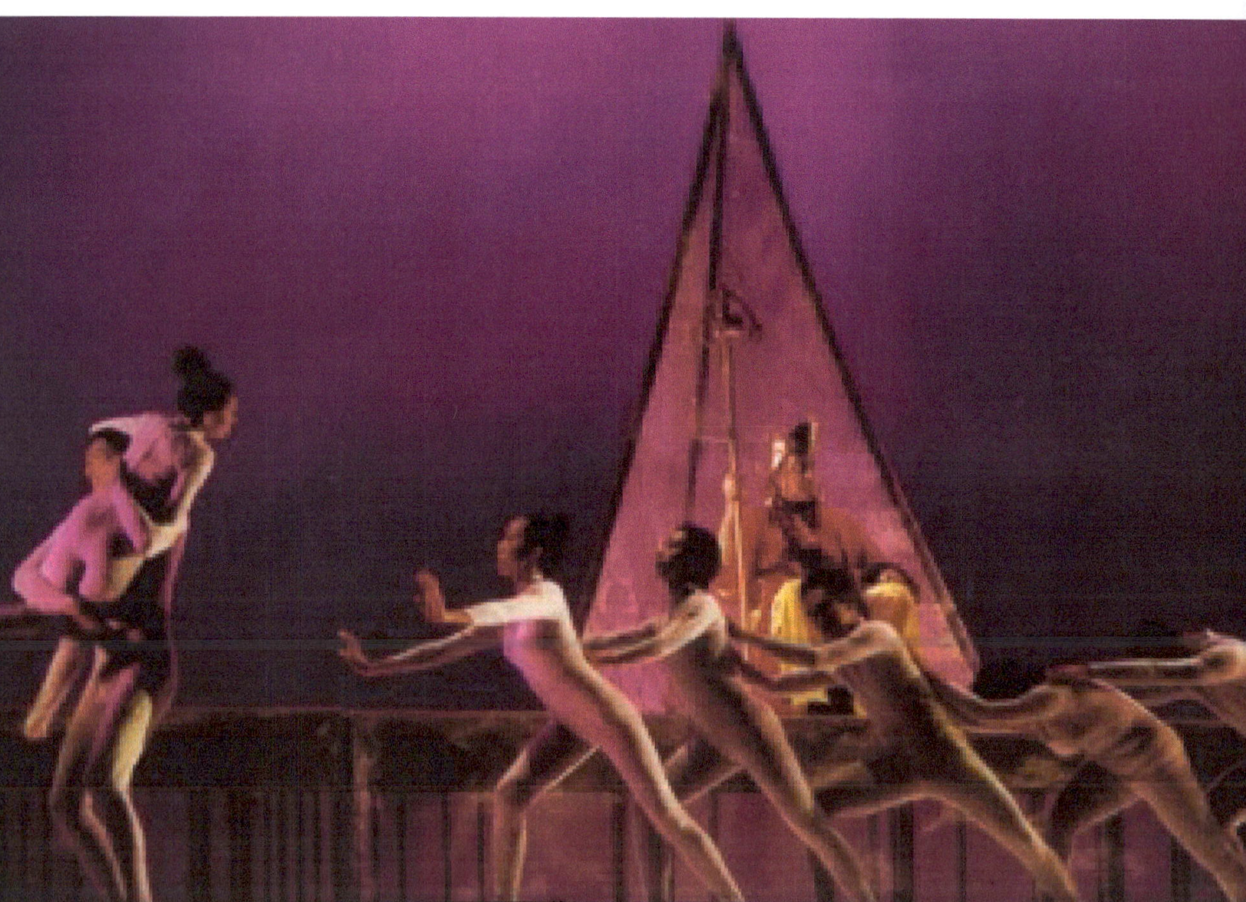

the debut in a major role of Saran Suebsantiwongse, who went on to become one of the leading baritones in the region.

This production also marked the beginning of Opera Siam's involvement with the children of Father Joe's Mercy Center, who have been invited to every performance since then and who very much enjoy our special backstage tours and our meet-the-stars moments.

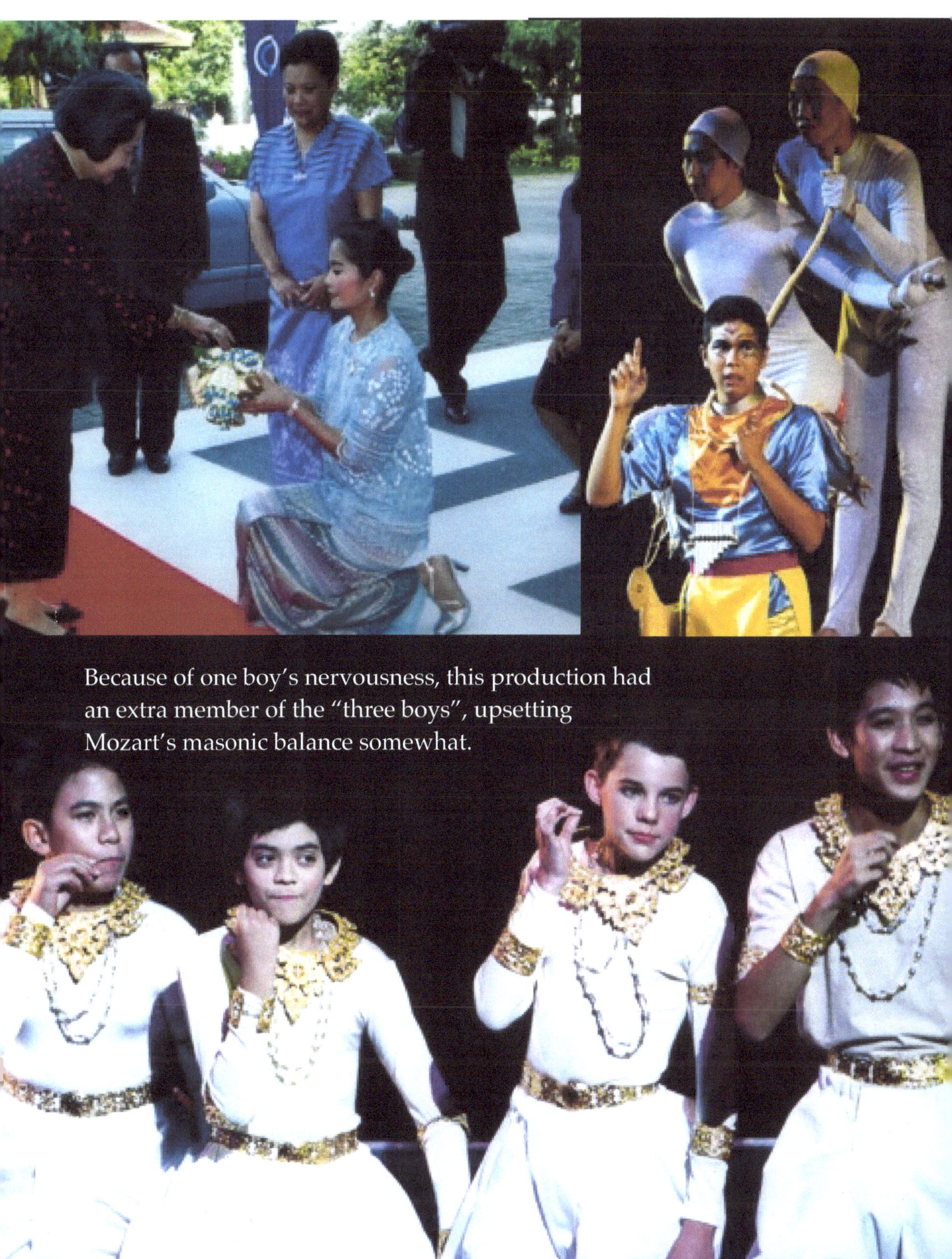

Because of one boy's nervousness, this production had an extra member of the "three boys", upsetting Mozart's masonic balance somewhat.

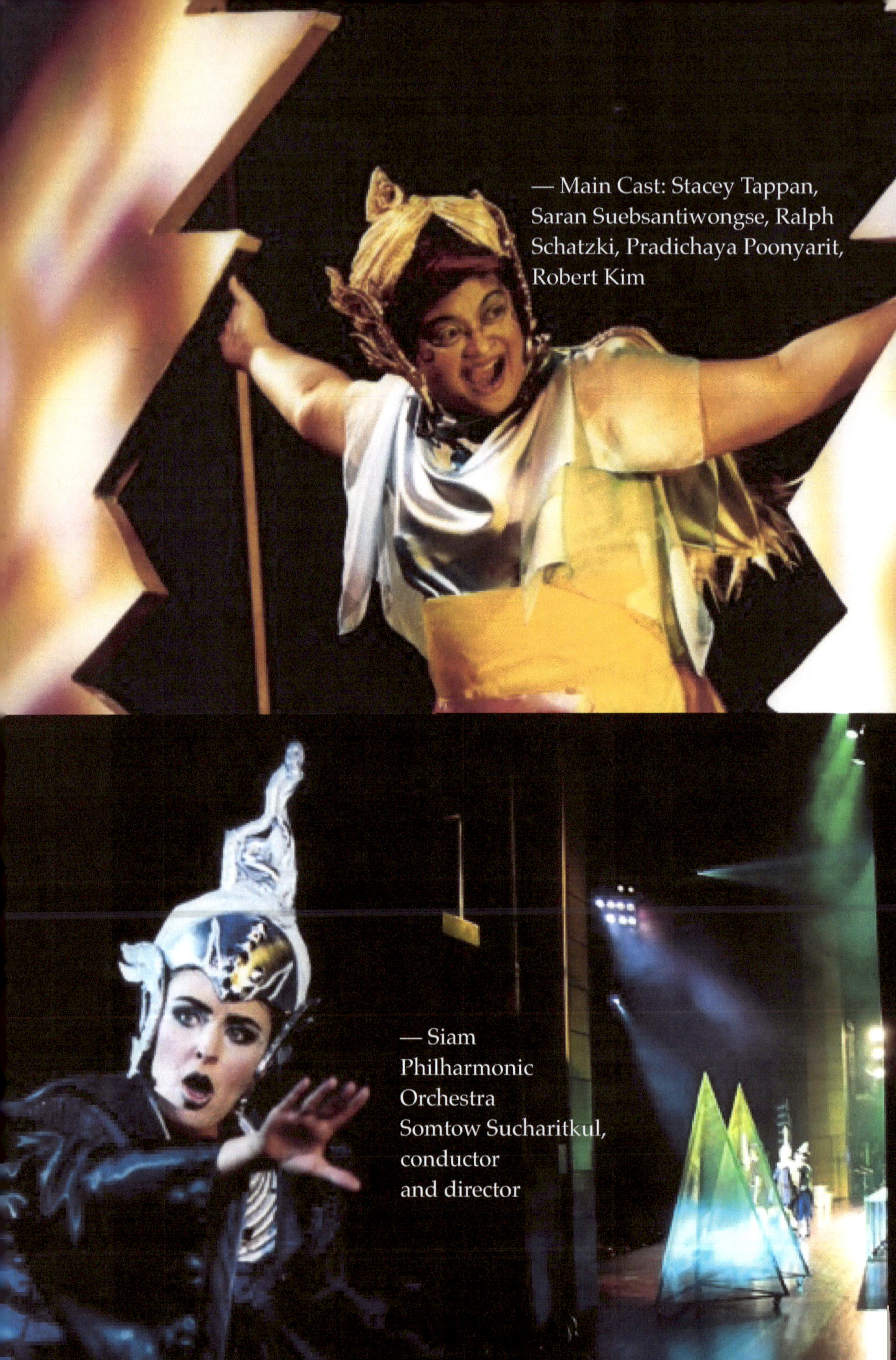

— Main Cast: Stacey Tappan, Saran Suebsantiwongse, Ralph Schatzki, Pradichaya Poonyarit, Robert Kim

— Siam Philharmonic Orchestra
Somtow Sucharitkul, conductor and director

5. MAE NAK (2003) WORLD PREMIERE

The concept for this opera, to take Thailand's most popular ghost story, as familiar to Thais as *Dracula* might be to an American, and turn it into an opera with Sumet Jumsai's avant-garde designs, was not Somtow's; it was M.R. Pandis Diskul who convinced him that this would be the perfect subject for an opera, and by then he had met the perfect soprano for the role: Nancy Yuen, whose unearthly pianissimo high tones could, he knew, be as chilling as they were beautiful, and who nevertheless possessed a histrionic ability that allowed her to play such parts as Tosca convincingly.

Frederic Chaslin, resident conductor of the Vienna State Opera, was to call *Mae Naak* "an important landmark in today's music."

Dr Sumet Jumsai, the daring Thai architect and painter, produced the basic designs for *Mae Naak.* The designs were brought to life by the well known stage designer Chatvichai Promadhattavedi.

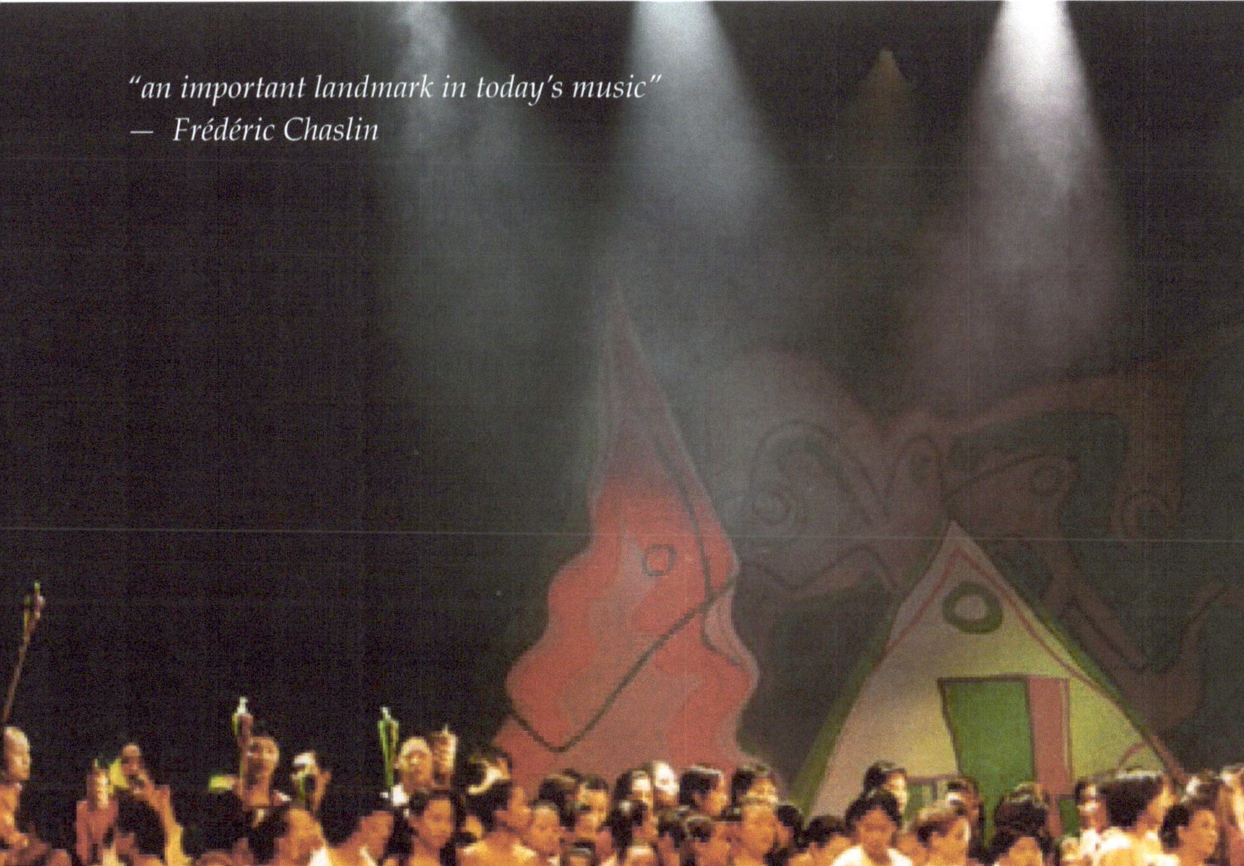

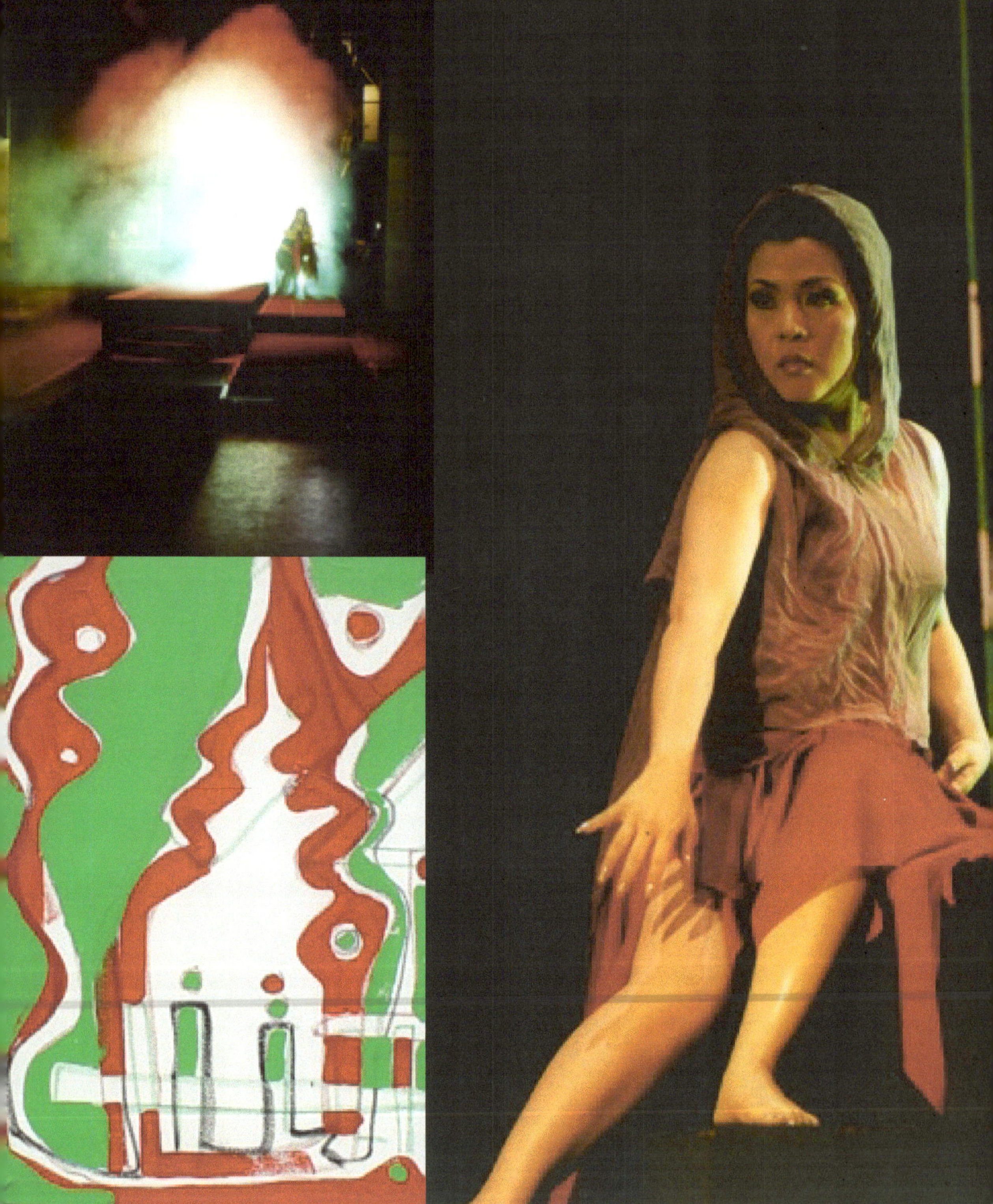

— Main Cast: Nancy Yuen, Ralph Schatzki, Pradichaya Poonyarit, Dusdi Banomyong

— Design: Sumet Jumsai na Ayuthaya, Chatvichai Promadhattavedi

— Siam Philharmonic Orchestra, Somtow

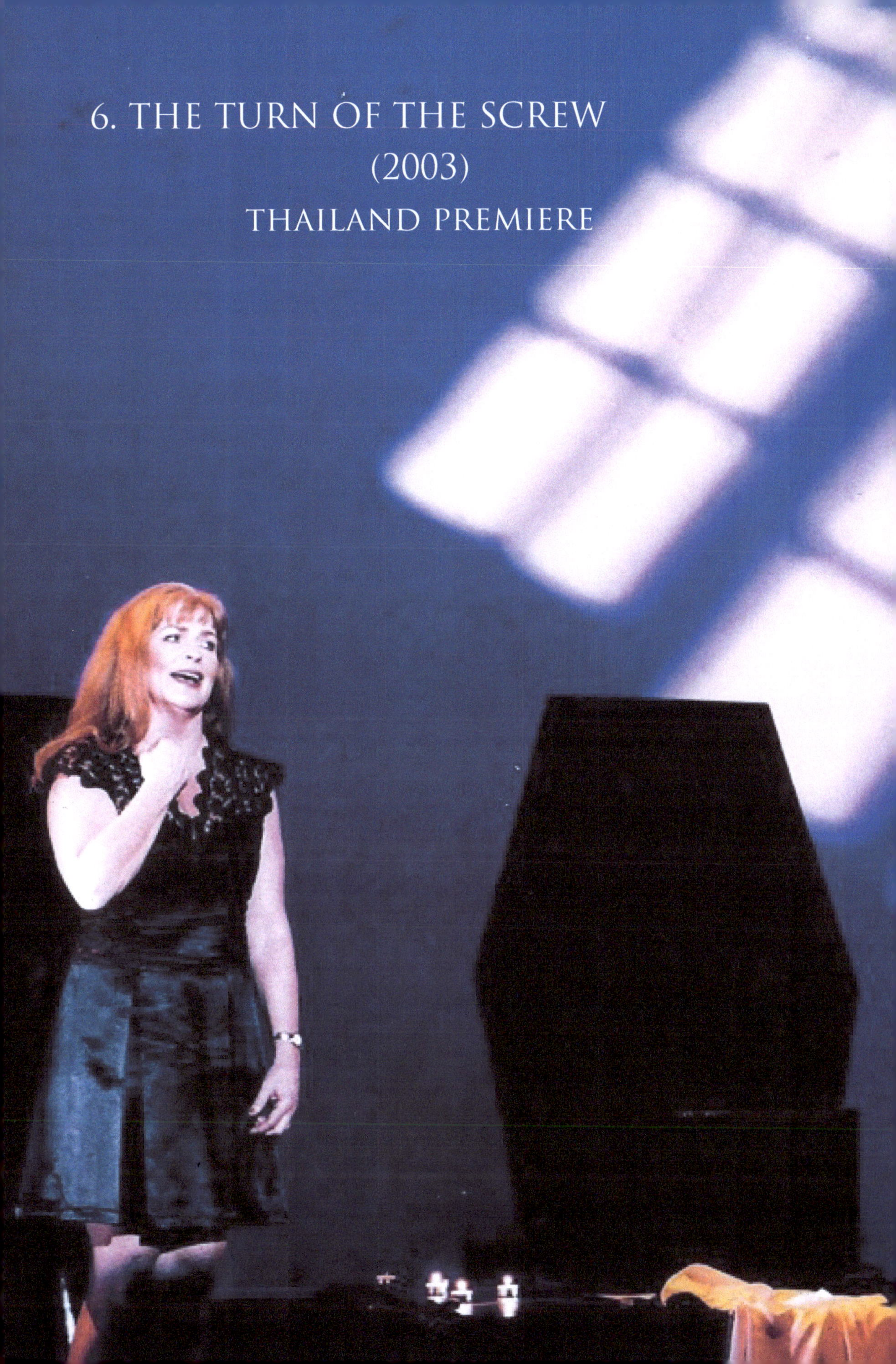

6. THE TURN OF THE SCREW
(2003)

THAILAND PREMIERE

Main Cast: Linda Cummings, Nadlada Thamtanakom, Brendan Schatzi, Barbara Smith Jones, Pradichaya Poonyarit

Siam Philharmonic, conducted by Leo Phillips

directed by Somtow Sucharitkul

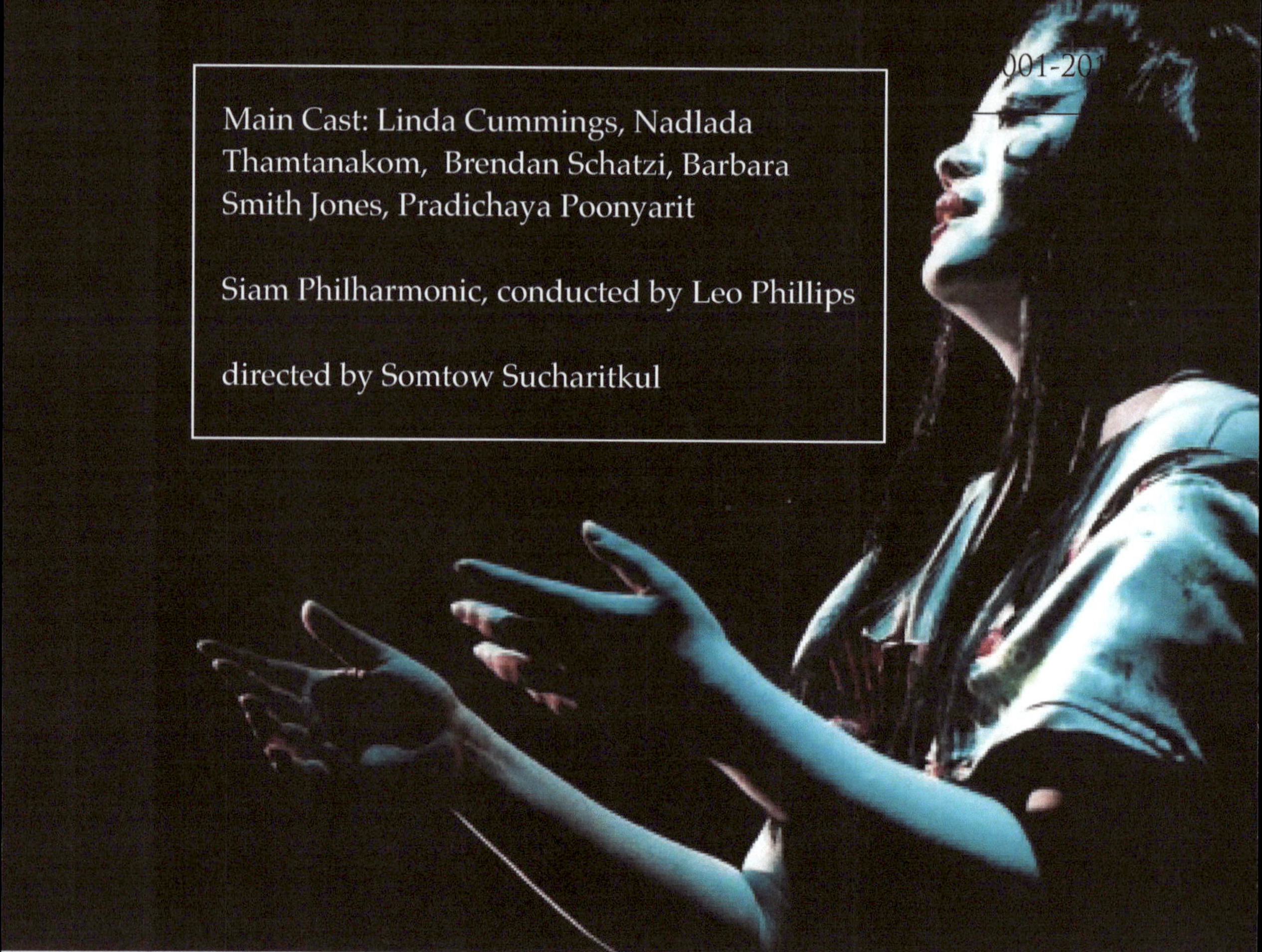

Bangkok Opera's production of *The Turn of the Screw* was an adventure in which we experimented with the use of kabuki techniques to tell the story. Leo Phillips conducted a very energetic and eager young ensemble. This was the major role debut of young Brendan Schatzki, son of two opera singers, who performed the role of Miles with great imagination and insight. The production was attended by the legendary Wolfgang Wagner and his wife, seen in the photographs below.

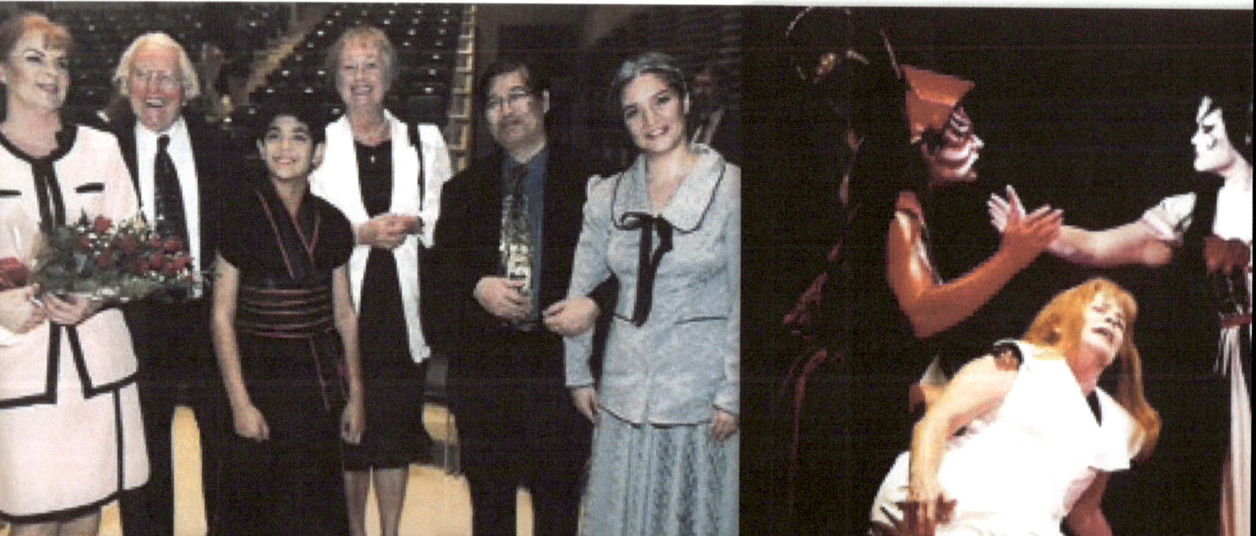

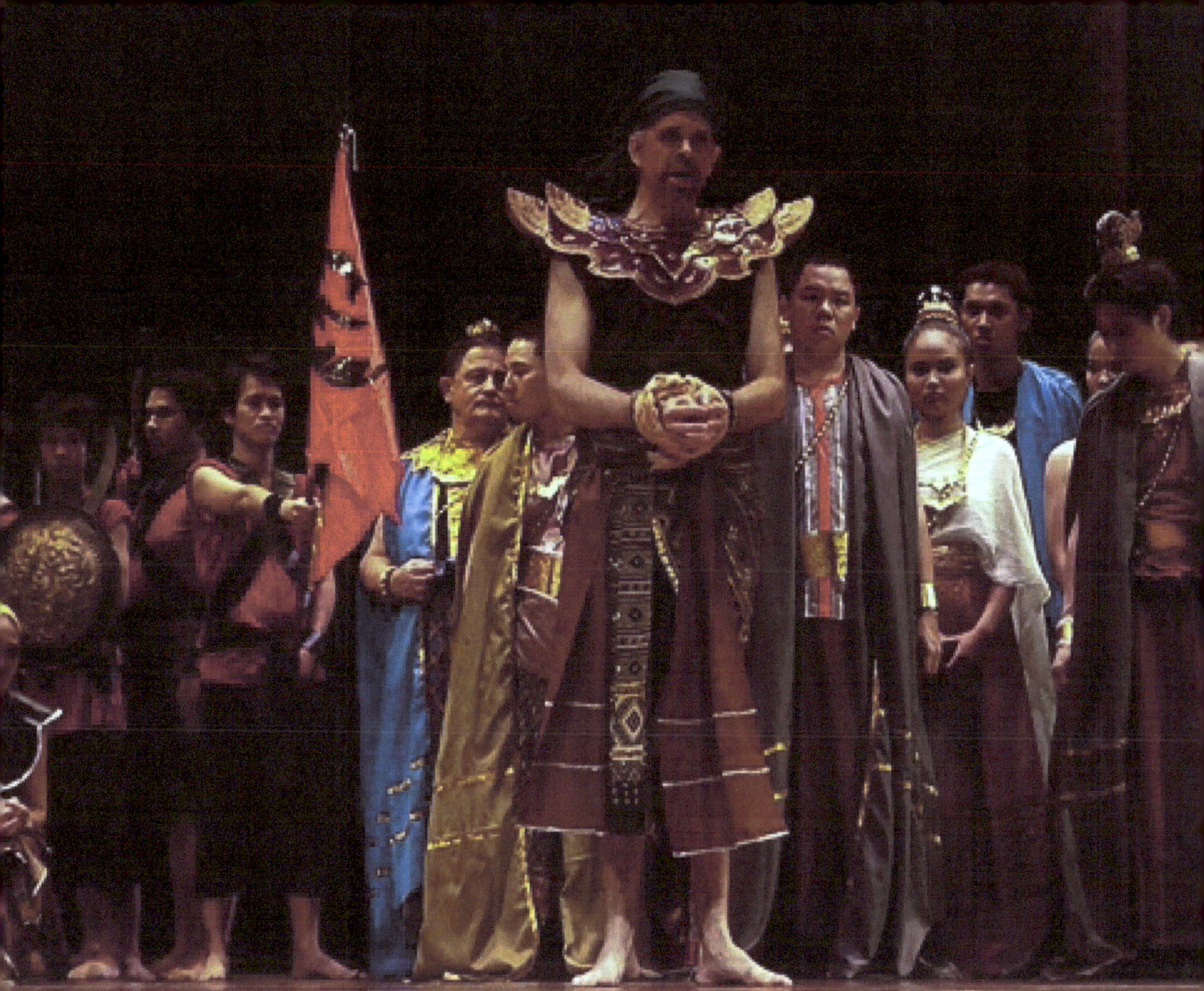

7. AIDA (2004) THAILAND PREMIERE

RIchard Harrell's production of Verdi's *Aida* moved the setting to the Siamese-Burmese wars of the Sixteenth Century, which was an ideal way to make the story feel real to a Thai audience. Unfortunately, the elephant hired to open the show by performing an obeisance to HRH Princess Galyani Vadhana before the opera opened did a disappearing act on the morning of the performance! It turned out that he was an unlicensed elephant, and the police had done a big sweep the night before.

Elephants, like any immigrants, need work permits....

The production was a breakthrough for the opera company, garnering international attention owing to its exotic setting.

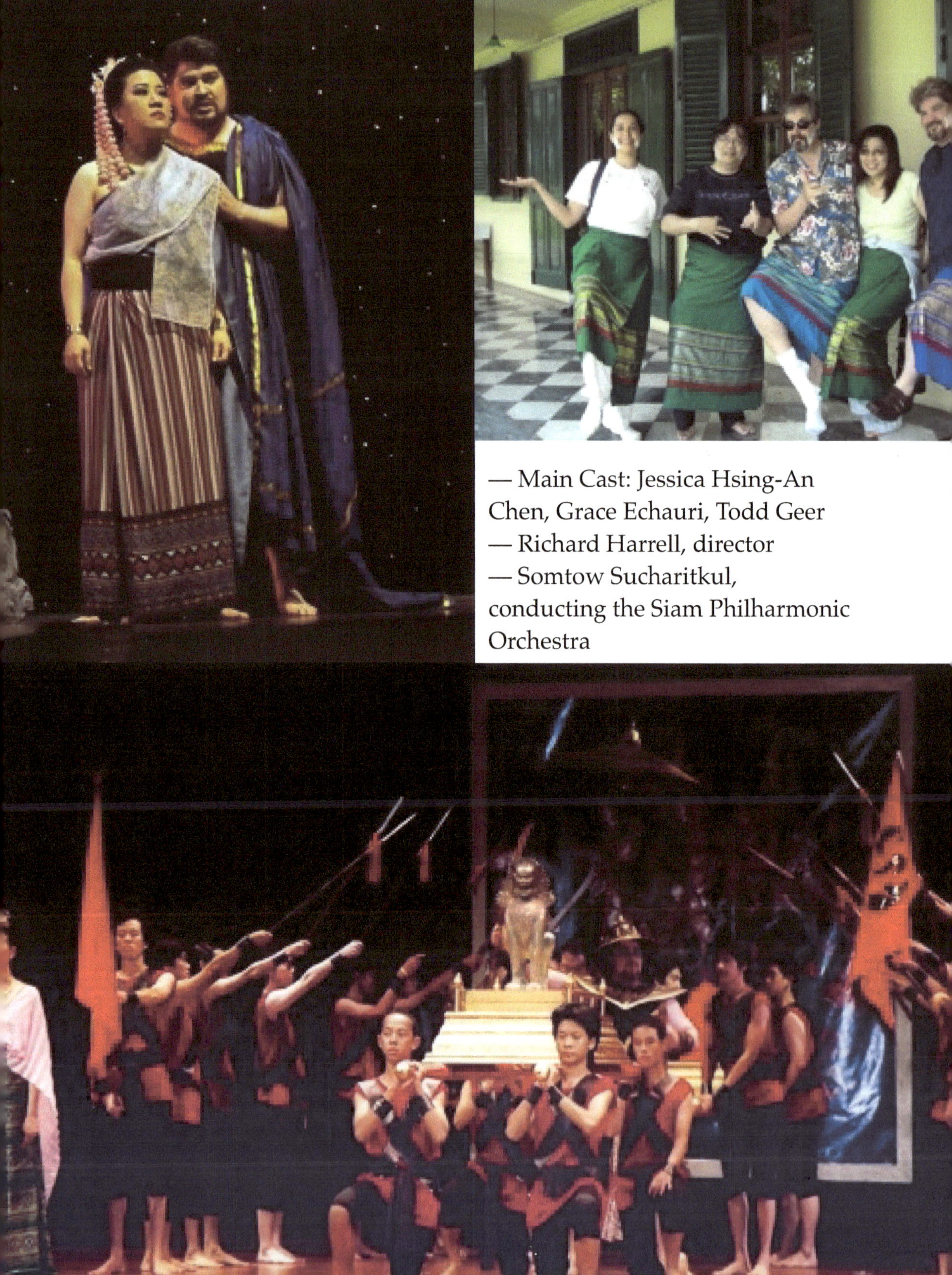

— Main Cast: Jessica Hsing-An Chen, Grace Echauri, Todd Geer
— Richard Harrell, director
— Somtow Sucharitkul, conducting the Siam Philharmonic Orchestra

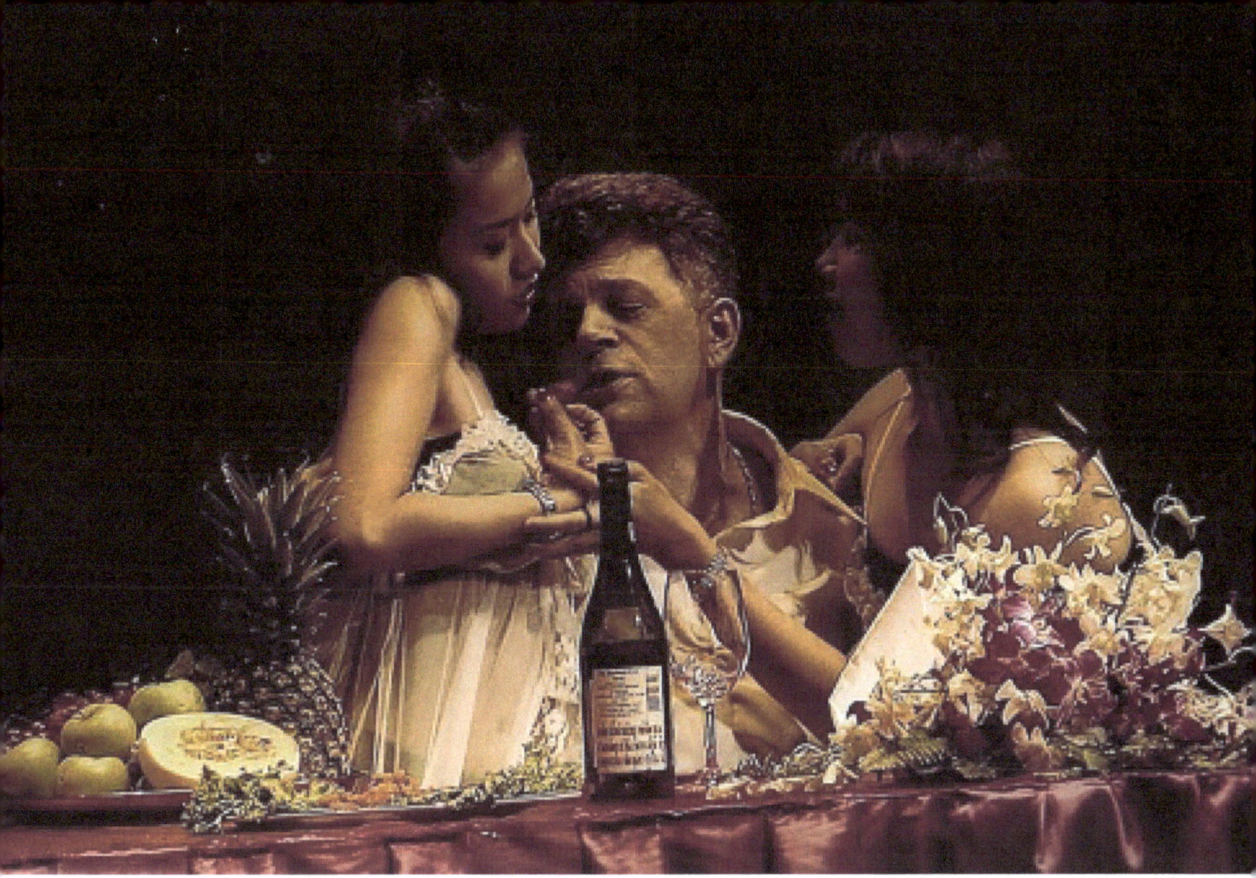

8. DON GIOVANNI (2004)
THAILAND PREMIERE

Directed by Richard Harrell of San Francisco, Mozart's Don Giovanni was moved to modern Bangkok, with the delicious subtext of the Don as predatory sex tourist added to the mix.

Later, reviewer Jonathan Richmond was to rave about this production in London's *Opera* magazine, making it one of the first times that the Bangkok Opera drew notices in a major international opera publication. One of Bangkok's favorites, Ralph Schatzki, played the role of the Don before moving back to the United States to continue his operatic career. Nancy Yuen played Donna Anna and Pradichaya Poonyarit Donna Elvira, with Peter Ong, Korawit Devahastin na Ayudhya, and a gorgeous young "Bow" as Zerlina, her first role on the big stage.

Richard Harrell directed.

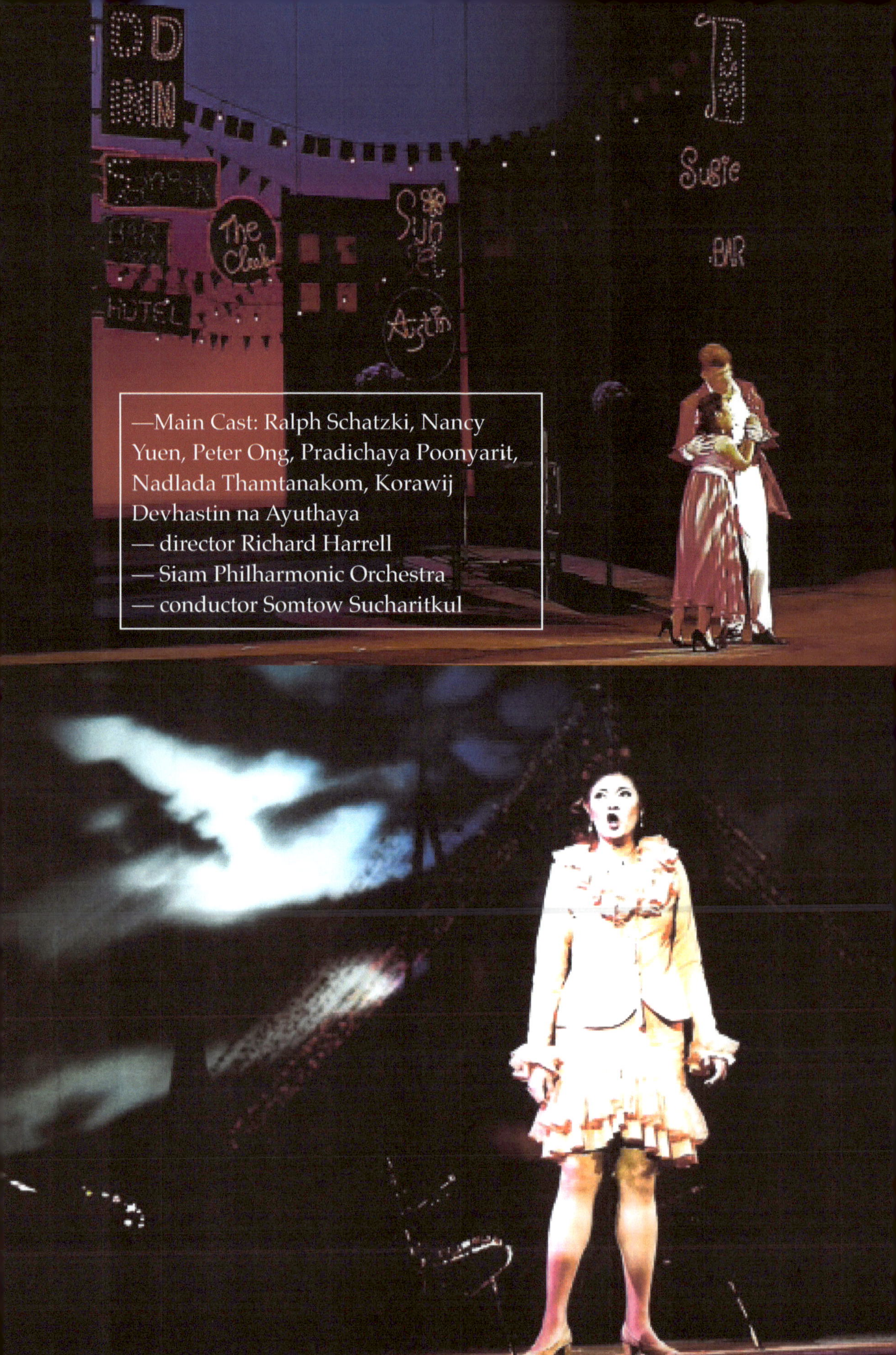

—Main Cast: Ralph Schatzki, Nancy Yuen, Peter Ong, Pradichaya Poonyarit, Nadlada Thamtanakom, Korawij Devhastin na Ayuthaya
— director Richard Harrell
— Siam Philharmonic Orchestra
— conductor Somtow Sucharitkul

9. TURANDOT (2004)
THAILAND PREMIERE

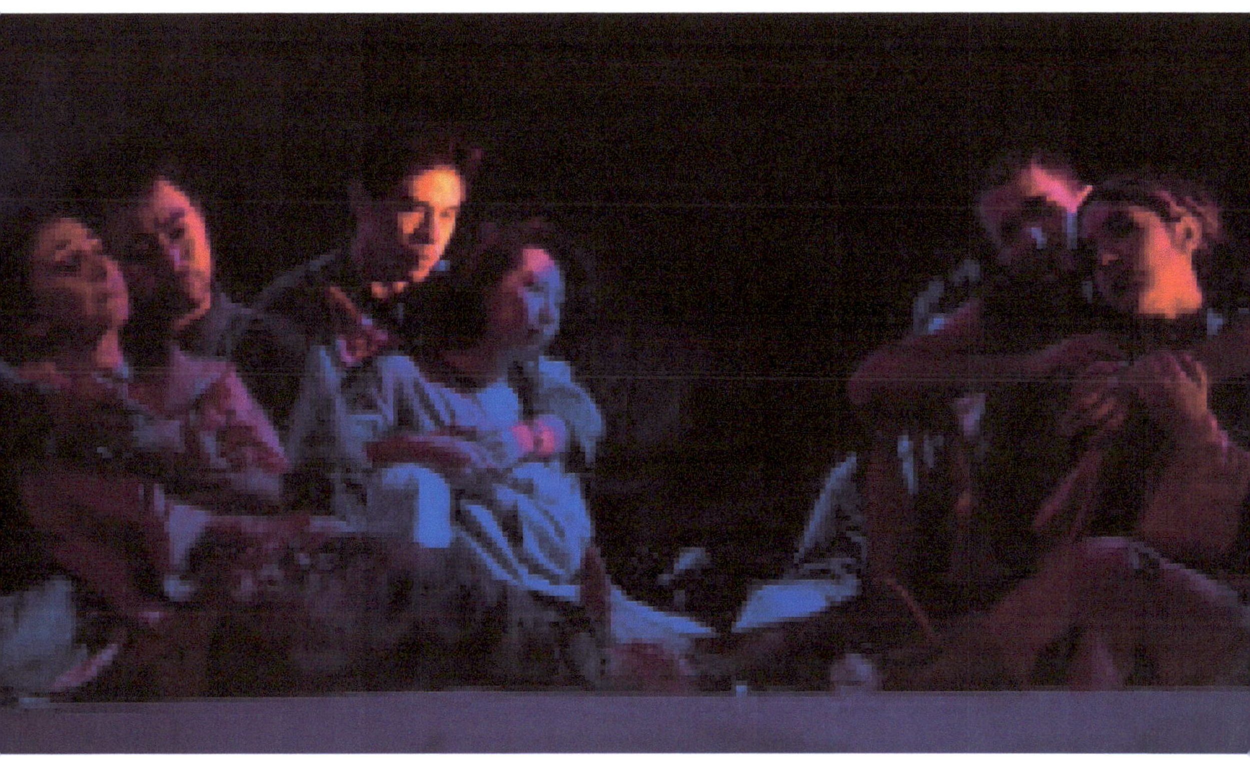

Puccini's last opera was performed in Thailand with a new twist; another ending, supplied by Maestro Somtow and the fourth ending to Puccini's unfinished opera ever to be performed. Jessica Hsing-An Chen proved a fabulous Turandot and Chang Beer made a great splash as the first all-Thai company to fully sponsor a production of the Bangkok Opera. Anette Pollner directed this production.

— Main Cast: Jessica Hsing-Ann Chen, Marc Deaton, Nancy Yuen

— Anette Pollner, director

— Siam Philharmonic Orchestra, conducted by Somtow Sucharitkul

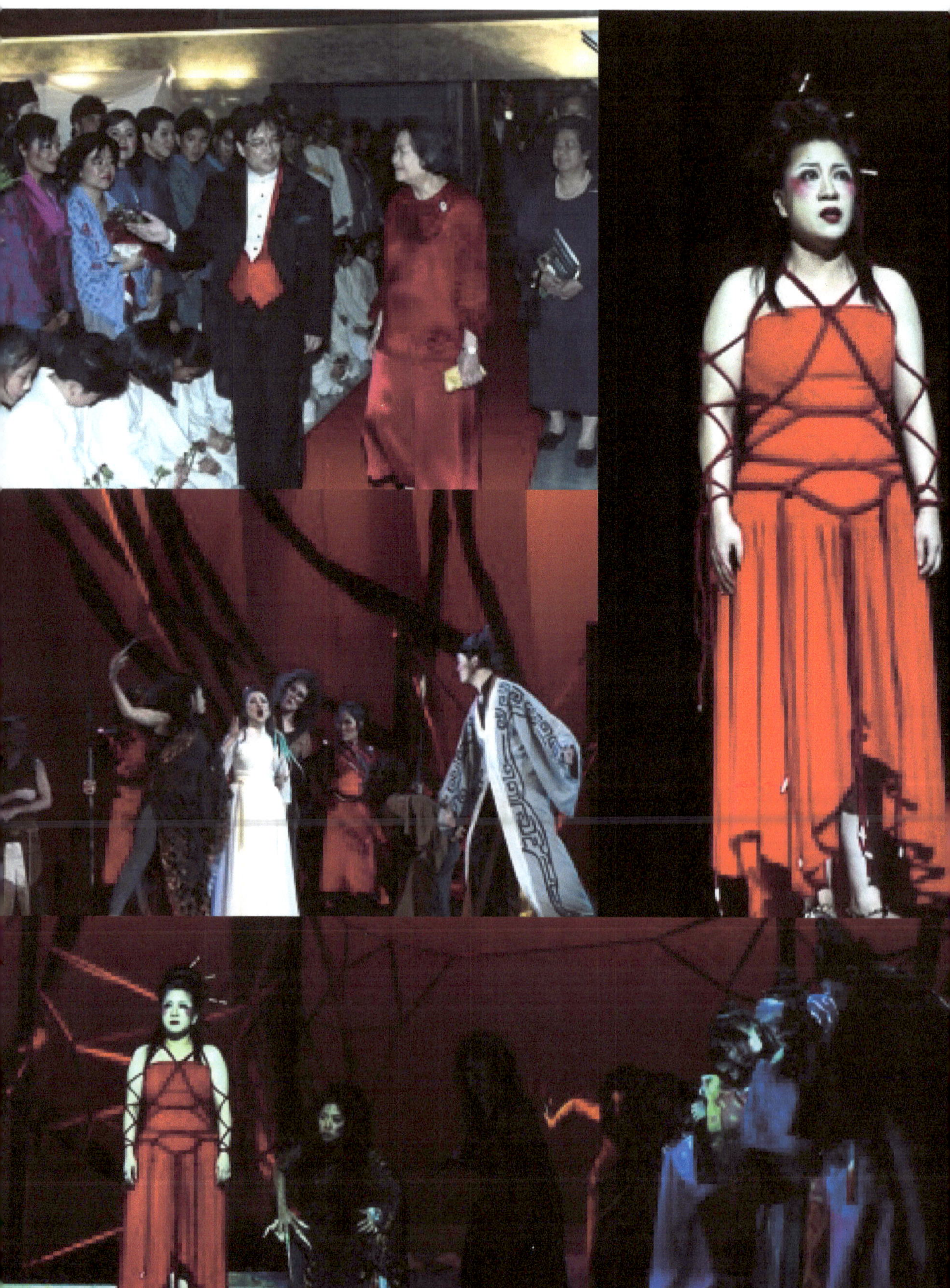

10. MAE NAAK (2005)
REVIVAL

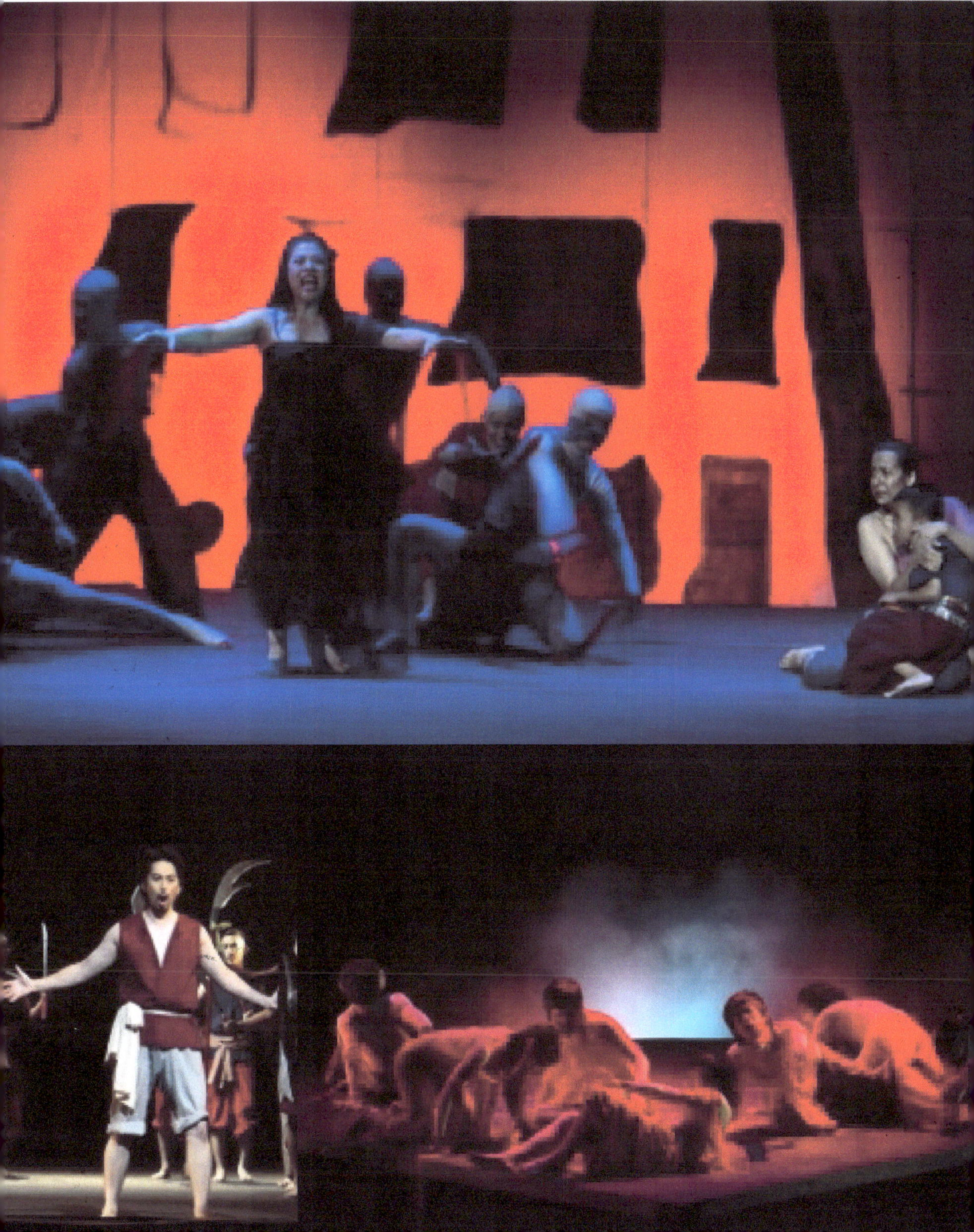

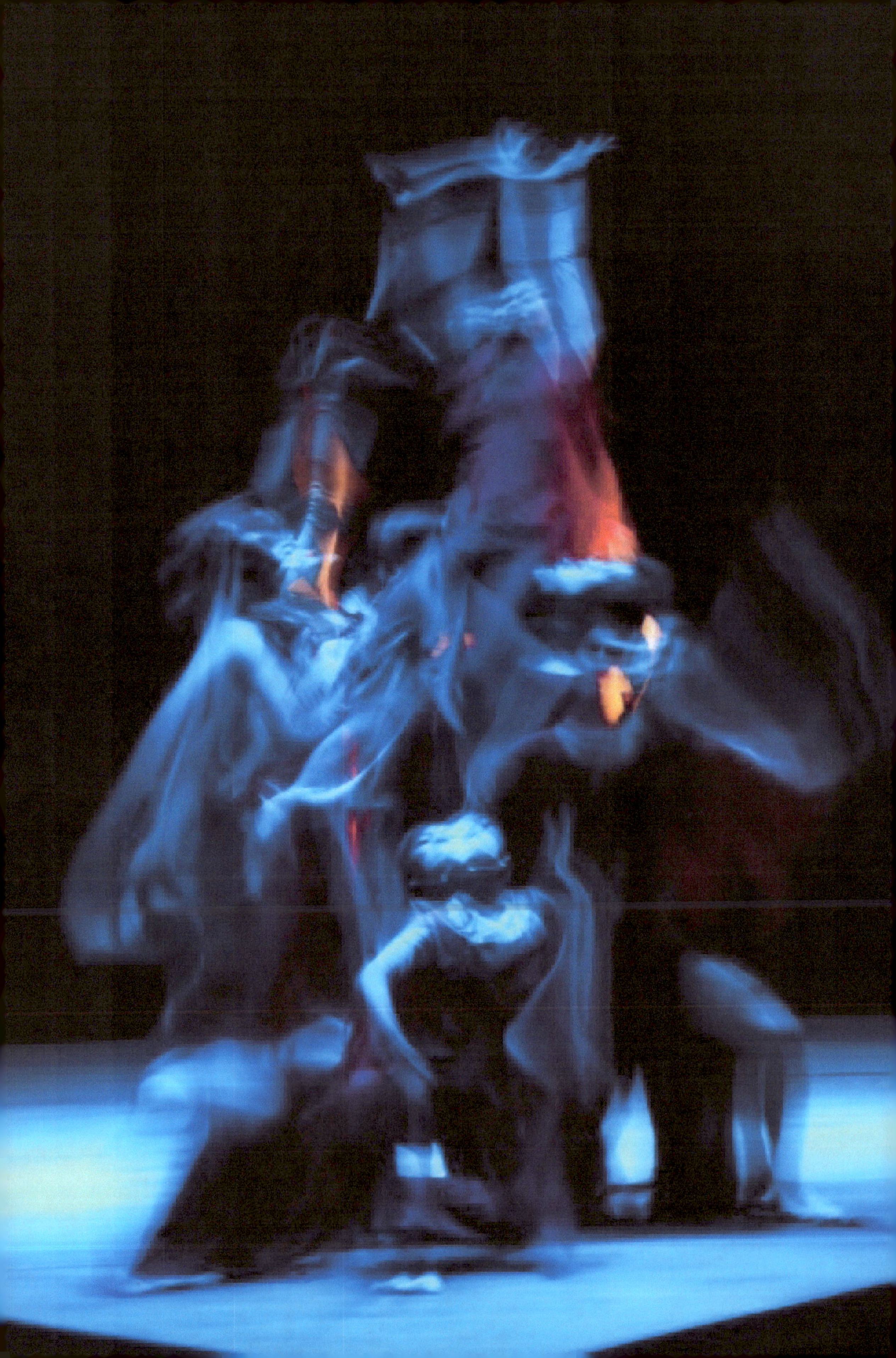

The revival of *Mae Naak* in 2005 was more a complete rethinking of the opera courtesy of well known Hawaiian director Henry Akina. The stark two-color imagery of Sumet's original designs was exchanged for a riot of exotic colors. Naak was now attended by a troupe of dancers and the cast underwent dramatic changes, including many more international stars. It was this version of *Mae Naak* that first attracted the attention of international opera magazines.

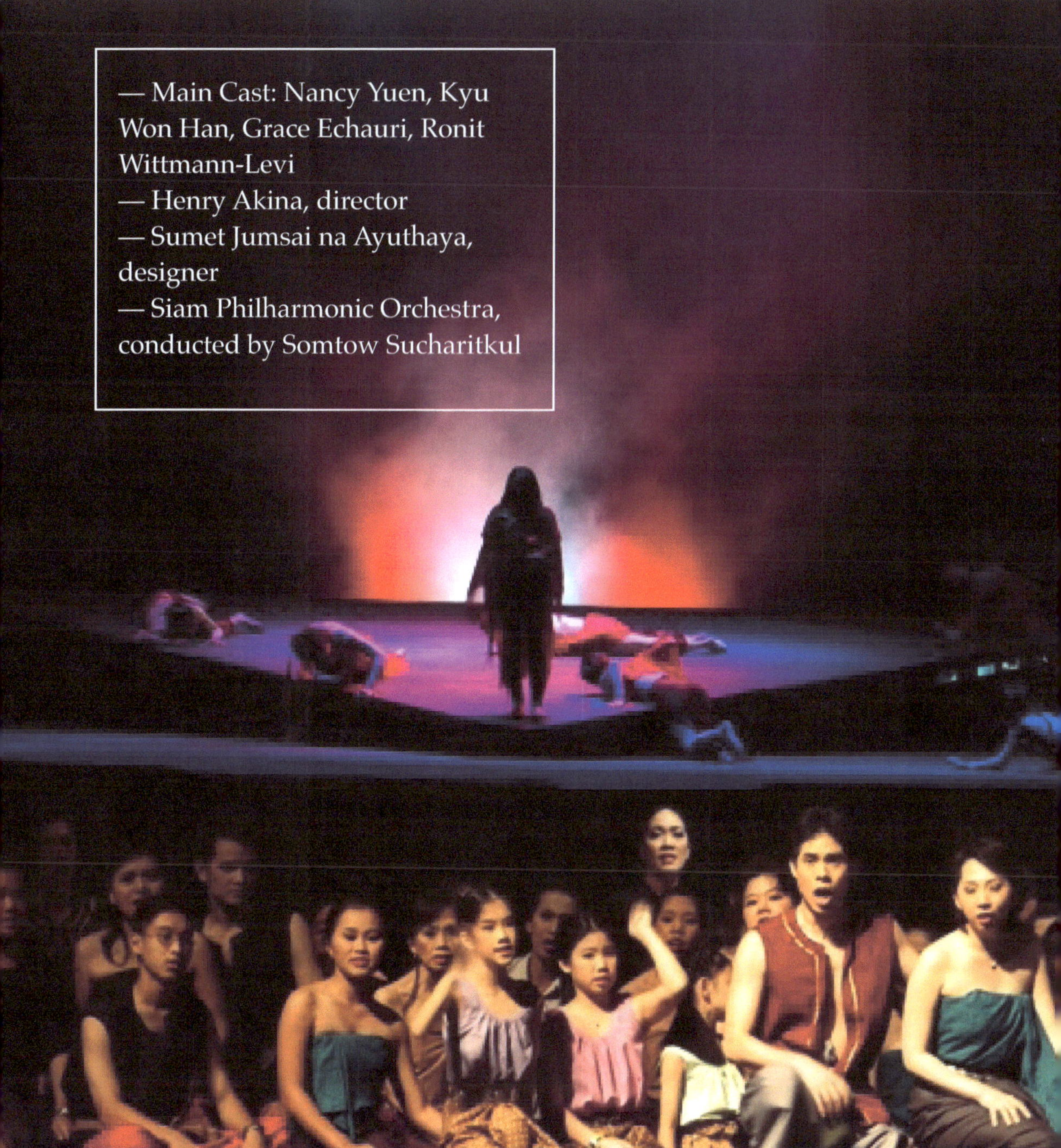

— Main Cast: Nancy Yuen, Kyu Won Han, Grace Echauri, Ronit Wittmann-Levi
— Henry Akina, director
— Sumet Jumsai na Ayuthaya, designer
— Siam Philharmonic Orchestra, conducted by Somtow Sucharitkul

11. THE MAGIC FLUTE (2006)

The operatic conducting debut of Trisdee na Patalung was an auspicious one and the 2006 revival of my Thai-sci-fi production of *Zauberflöte* was one of the happiest productions we've done together. It's the magic of Mozart as well. 2006 was of course the big Mozart year and we planned two Mozart operas, this one and *Così.* Although some of the props and costumes from 2003 did reappear, this was essentially a new version of the opera, keeping only the English (and sometimes Thai) dialogue of the first.

Somtow redesigned the 2003 design using Lego elements for a dreamlike "toy" setting.

London's *Opera* was very impressed with Trisdee's debut and said, "If the word 'genius' still has any meaning in this age of rampant hyperbole, Trisdee is truly a living example."

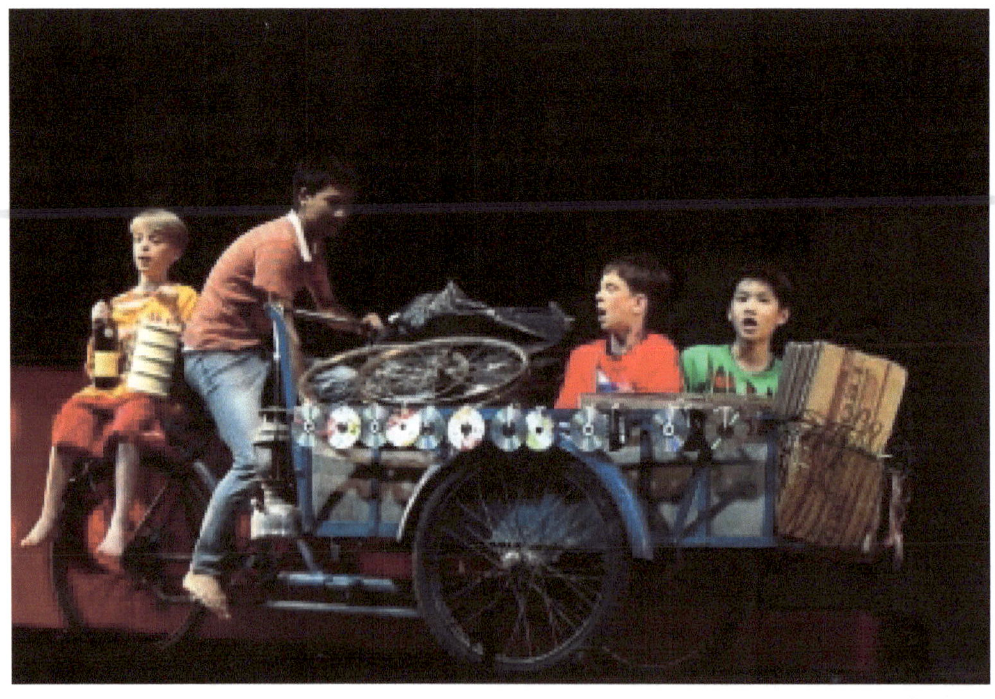

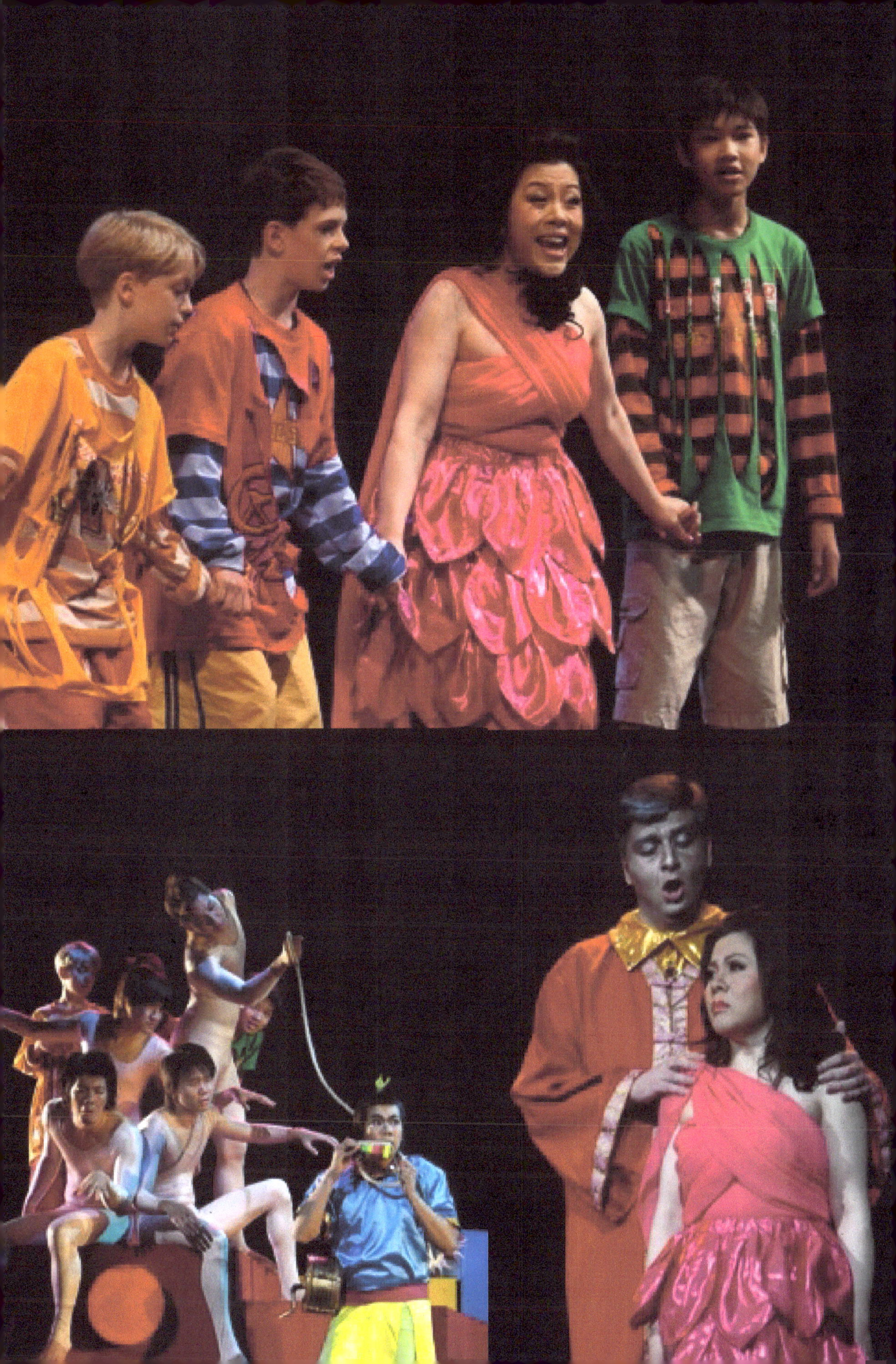

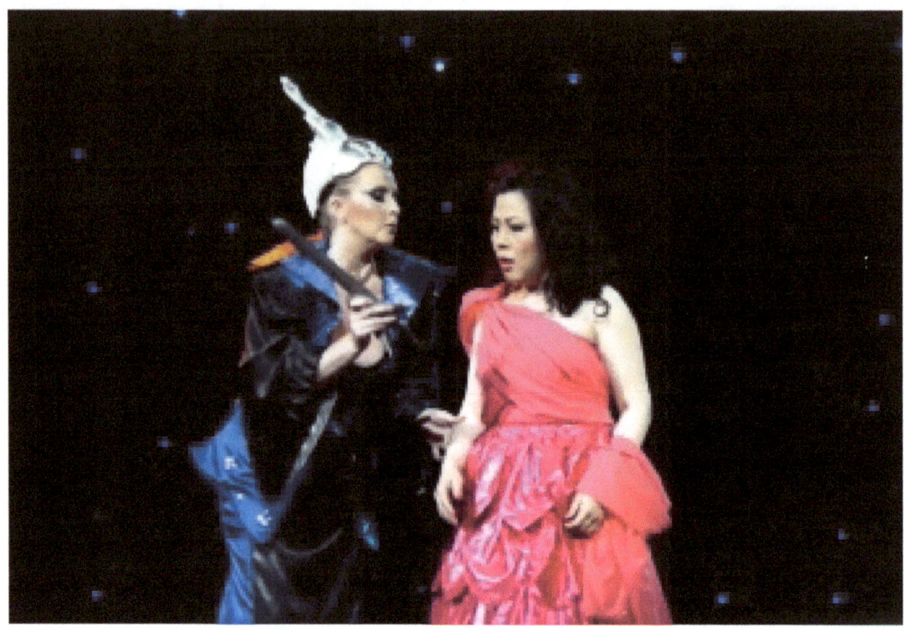

Cast members were delighted when the highly popular Linda Cummings, choir master during the period of the Orpheus Choir's greatest extra-operatic activity, flew back from Colorado to perform as one of the Three Ladies along with current choir master Karen TenBrink. Ema Naito completed the trio.

The combination of a Lego-inspired set with many Thai motifs such as tuk-tuks proved popular with the crowd.

This was also the production that made Trisdee's reputation as an opera conductor, because the international reviewers referred to him as a genius. It led to his being invited to conduct all over Europe.

— Main Cast: Nancy Yuen, Sandra Partridge, Saran Suebsantiwongse, Harold Meers, Vassilis Konstatinopoulos
— Somtow Sucharitkul, director
— Trisdee na Patalung conducting the Siam Philharmonic Orchestra

12. DAS RHEINGOLD (2006)
THAILAND PREMIERE

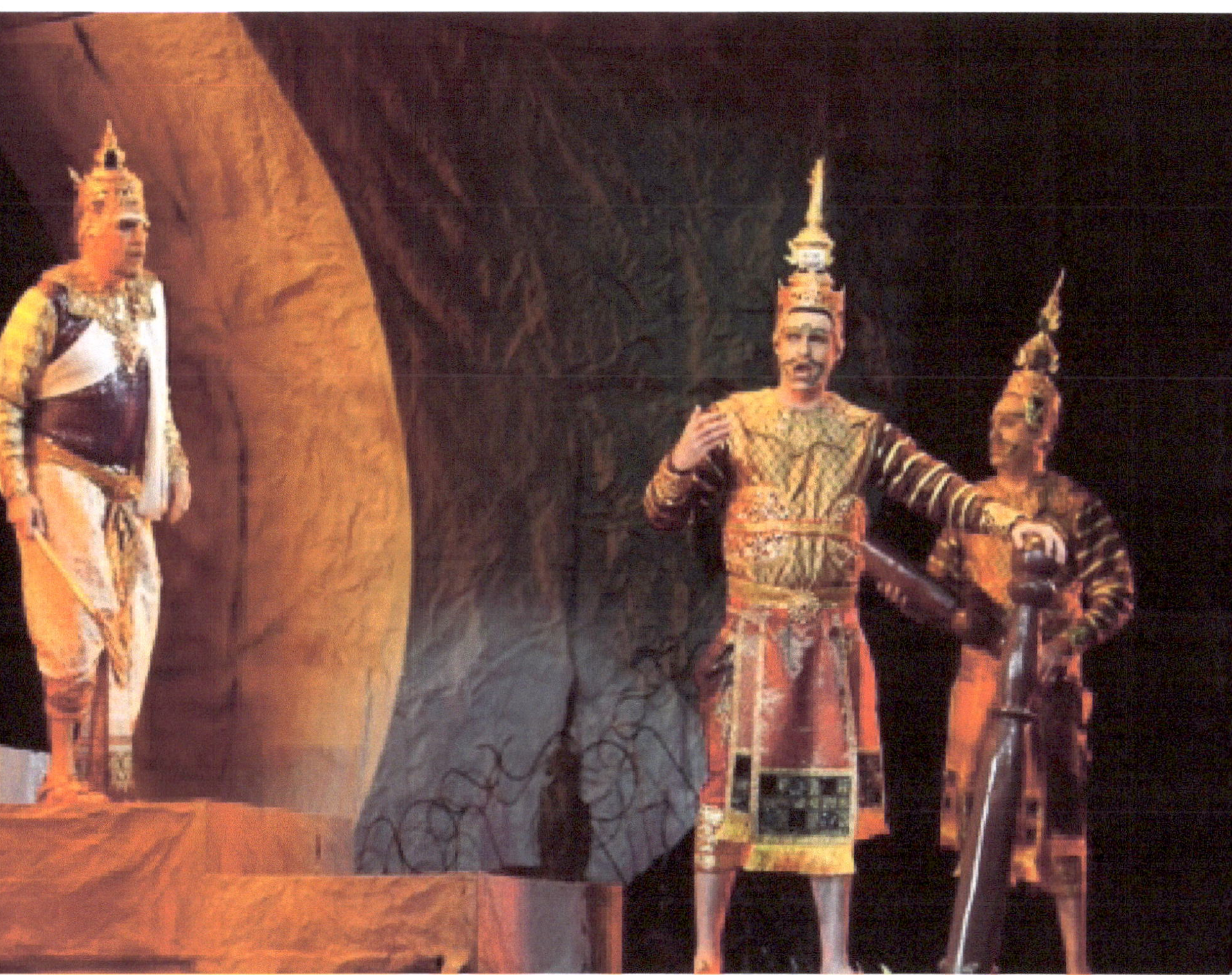

Taking a huge risk, we decided to go ahead with what was, for Somtow, a lifelong dream: to do a whole *Ring Cycle* from a brand-new Asian perspective. "It was, for me personally, a disaster in that I ended up losing my house in L.A. and pretty much everything I owned. And yet, I suspect, I would do it again if I could. *Opera Now* (whose critic came to the opening night) didn't much care for it. *Opera,* whose critic came to the second night, raved. Both, I think, were right. The second night was *much* better." Somtow said.

One of the major surprises of *Rheingold* was that there was an audience; indeed, there was a higher per-night ticket sale than for any previous production. And there was a heartwarming reception amongst Wagnerites worldwide, who publicized the event in numerous Wagner newsletters and magazines throughout the world. It meant that there was a built-in audience for Part Two, which will now become the opener for the Bangkok Opera's Seventh Season.

The excitement was not only musical. There was political upheaval in the background as well. As this production dwelt on the very Buddhist message of karma and the results of attachment to material things, the people of Thailand were also gathering to protest the rapacity of certain political figures. Of course, productions are conceived months, years in advance, so this was really an accident. But one cannot help wonder about the nature of karma.

"The theft of a golden ring, traditionally portrayed as a kind of Christian original sin, in Somtow's version launches the Buddhist cycle of karma, fueled by attachment or greed, that creates life and all its beautiful imperfections."

— *Seattle Times*

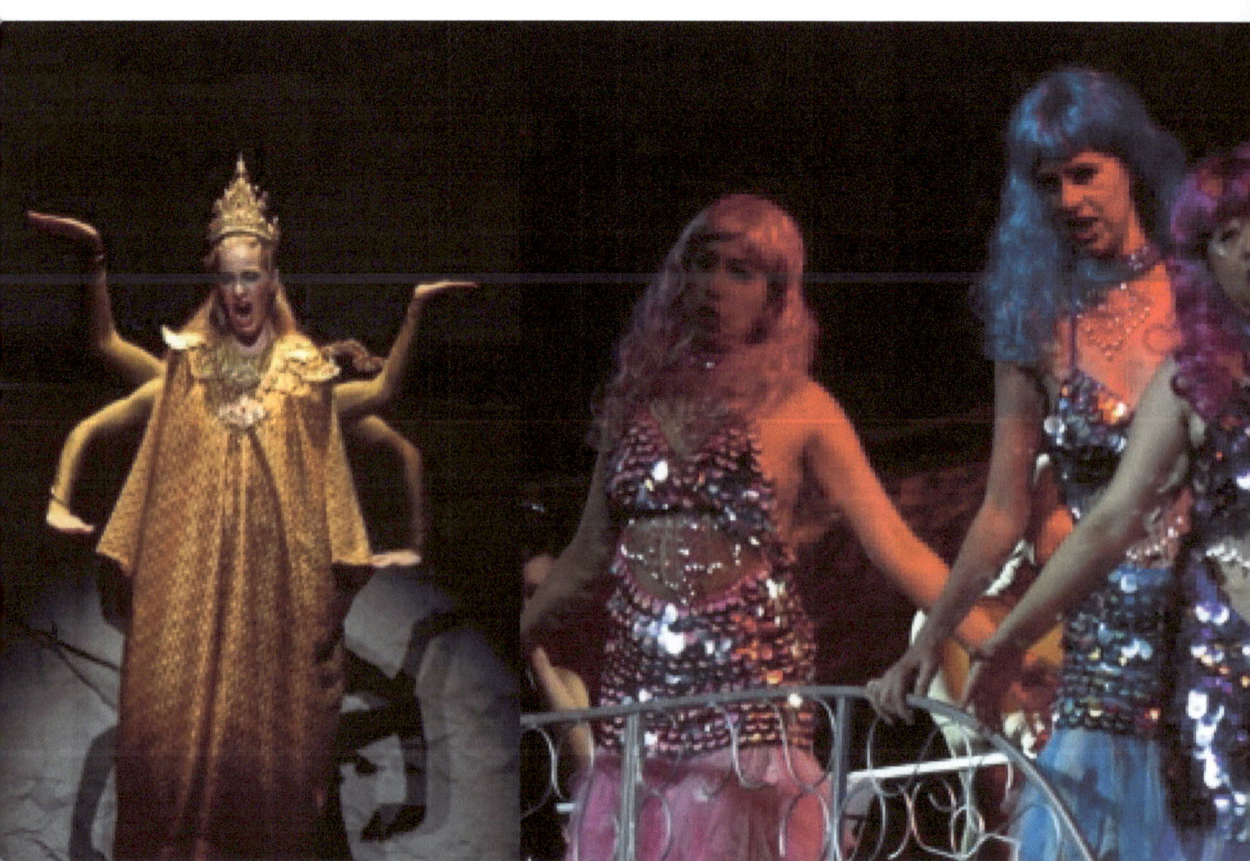

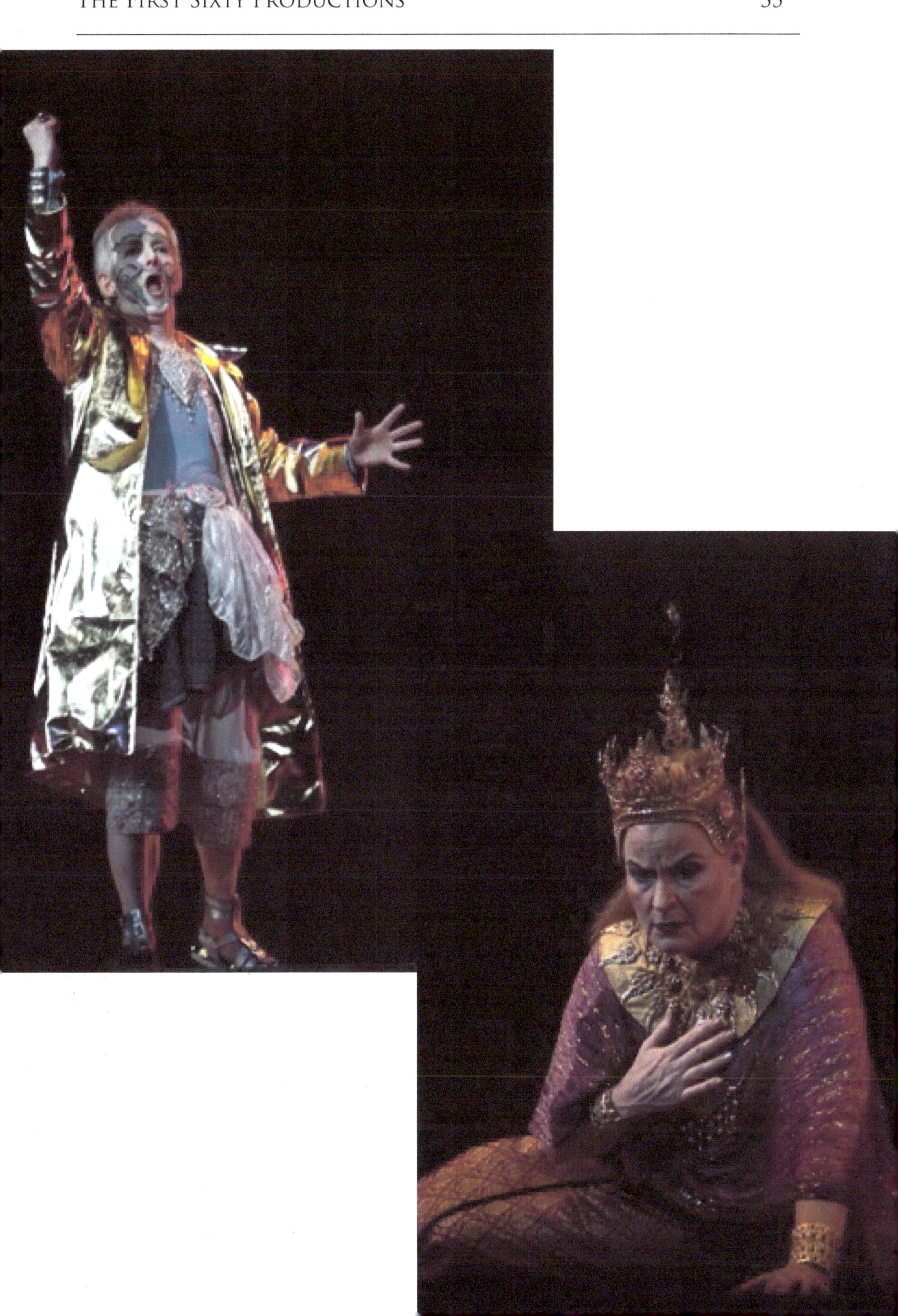

— Main Cast: Lars Waage, Barbara Smith Jones, Marc Deaton, Colin Morris, Ronit Widmann-Levy, Grace Echauri, John Ames, Ralph McDonald, Grace Lin, Julia Oesch
— Siam Philharmonic Orchestra
— conducted, directed and designed by Somtow Sucharitkul

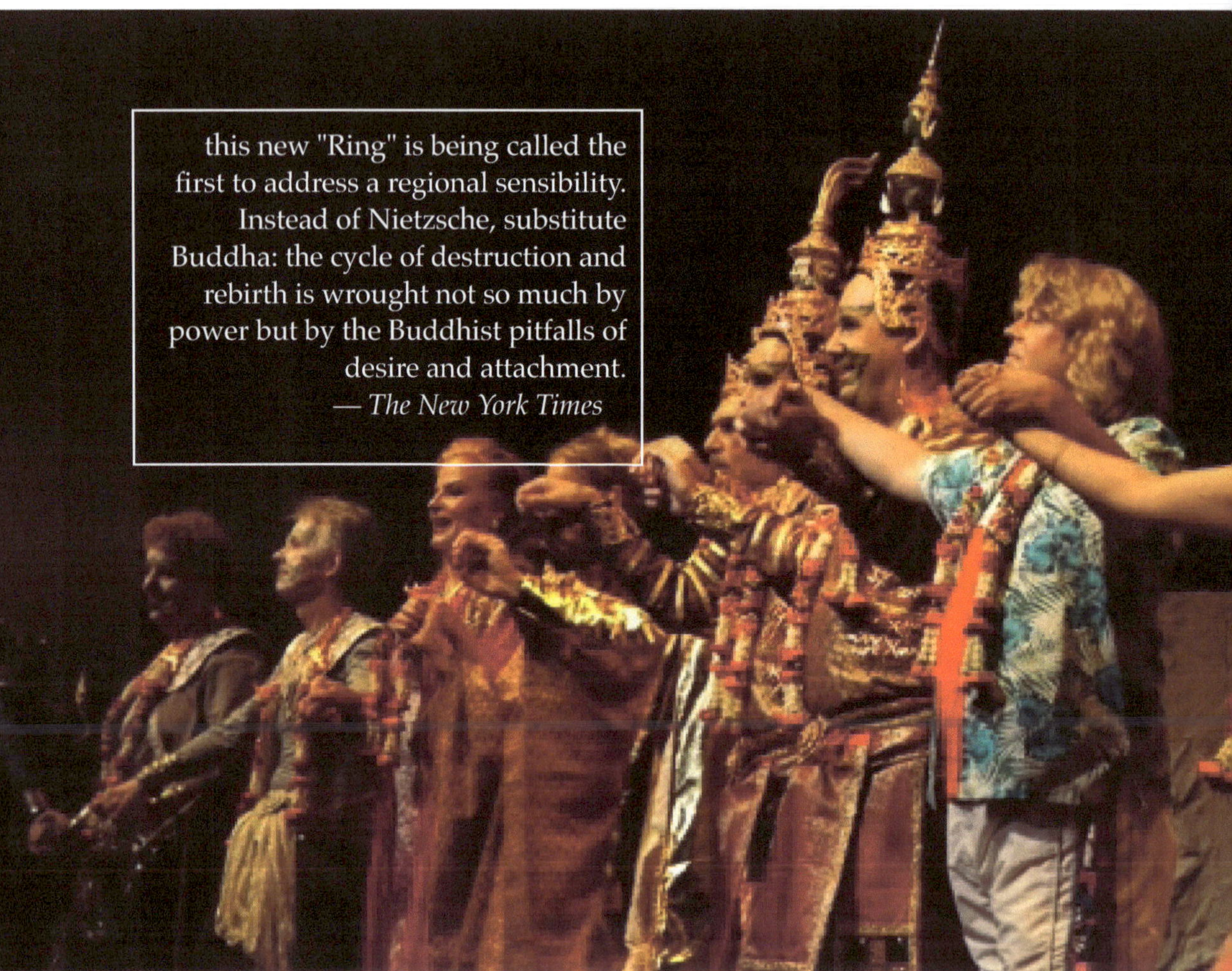

this new "Ring" is being called the first to address a regional sensibility. Instead of Nietzsche, substitute Buddha: the cycle of destruction and rebirth is wrought not so much by power but by the Buddhist pitfalls of desire and attachment.
— *The New York Times*

"One of the show's most memorable moments is when the giants Fafner and Fasolt
push Freia onto the stage in a shopping cart."
— *International Herald Tribune*

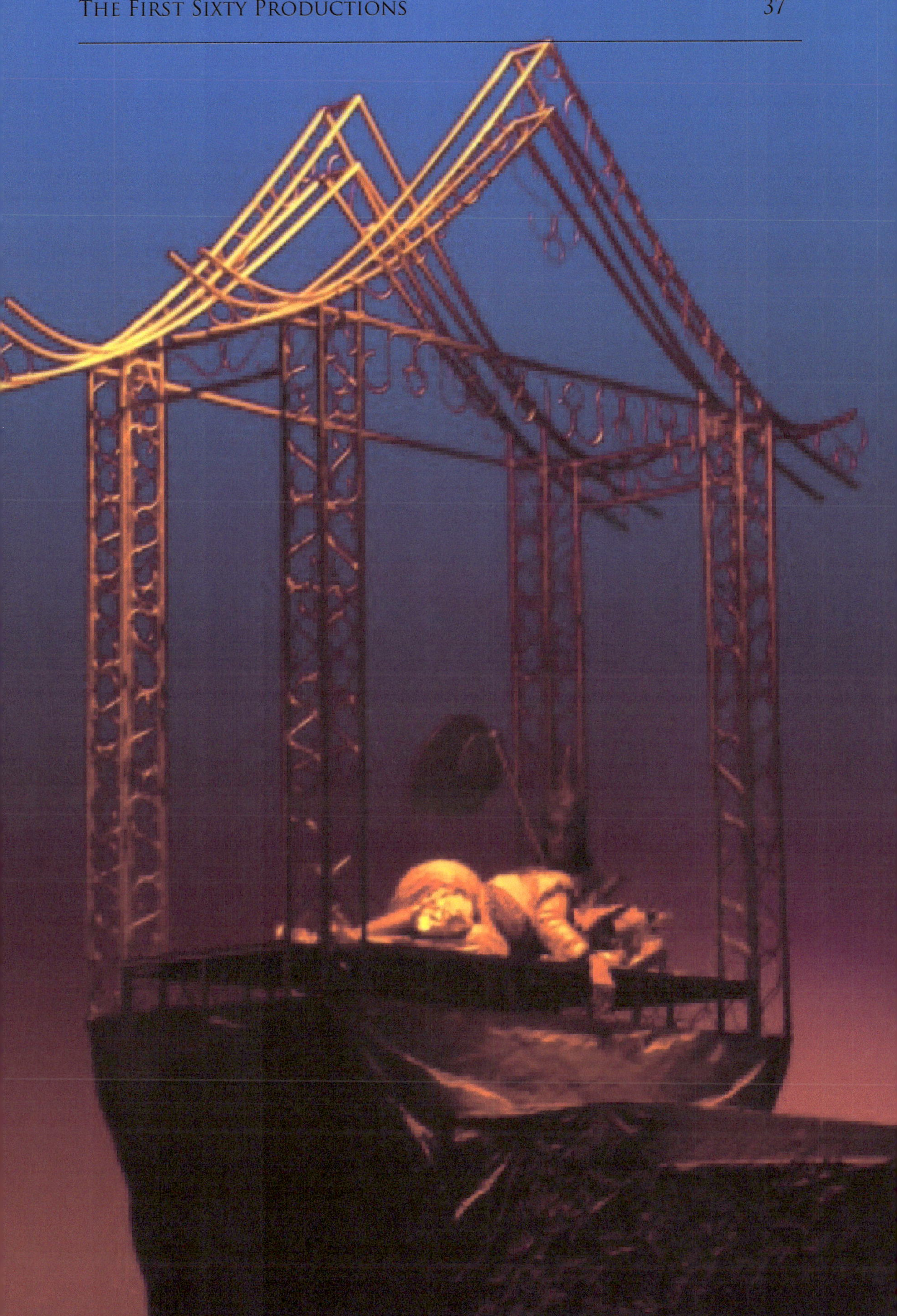

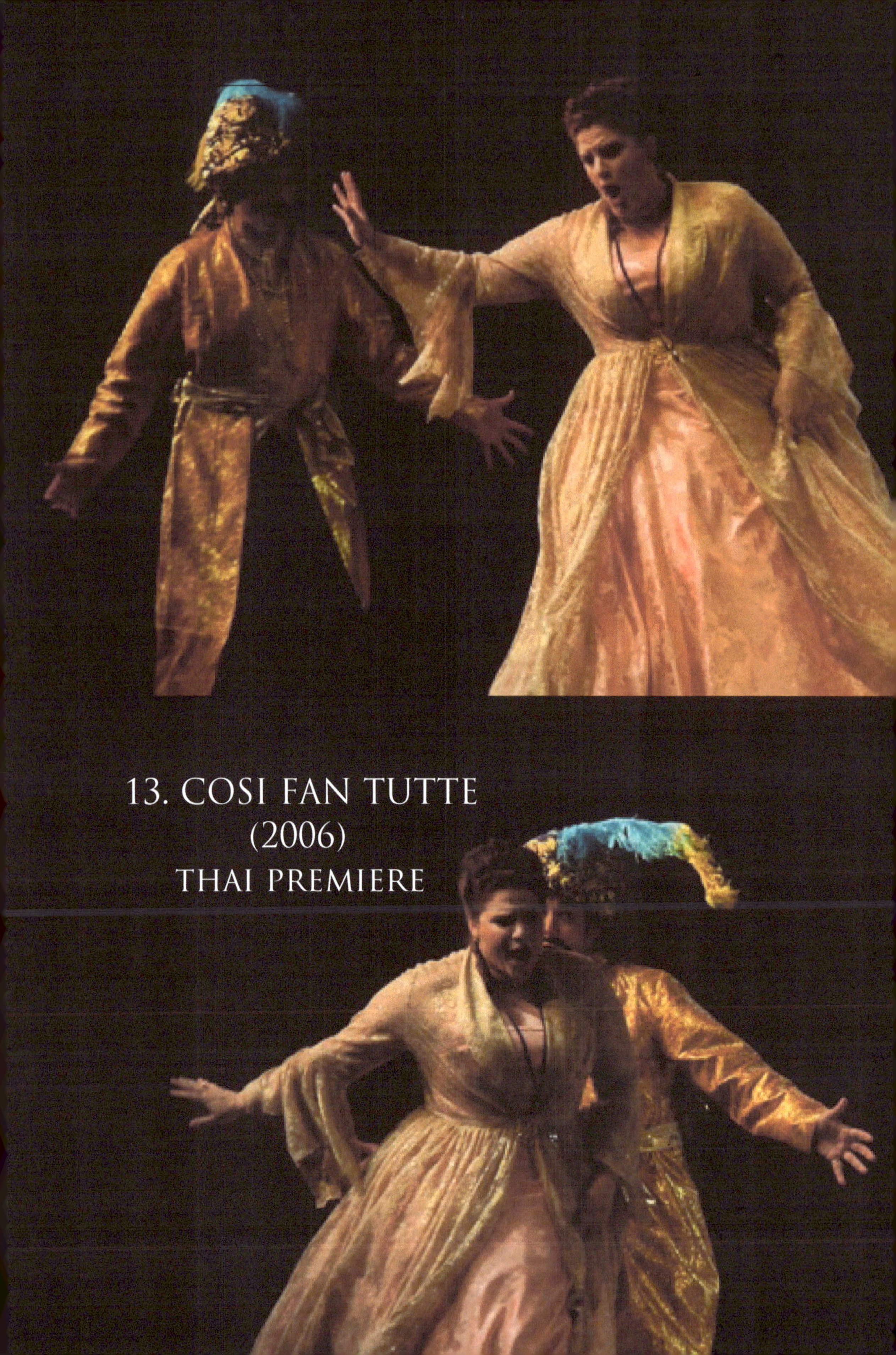

13. COSI FAN TUTTE
(2006)
THAI PREMIERE

The second operatic entry in the Mozart year was a production of *Così fan Tutte* which was the third production to be directed by Richard Harrell here in Bangkok.

It was perhaps the first "traditional"production we had done; it was my idea that one production per season should be done "straight" just to show that we were not really going the way of "Eurotrash".

Così had a cast that was mostly introduced by Richard Harrell. Iyt was interestying in that there was an Asian pair of lovers and a Caucasian one, and the way they swapped back and forth seemed to some in the audience to speak to Thai-farang relationships.

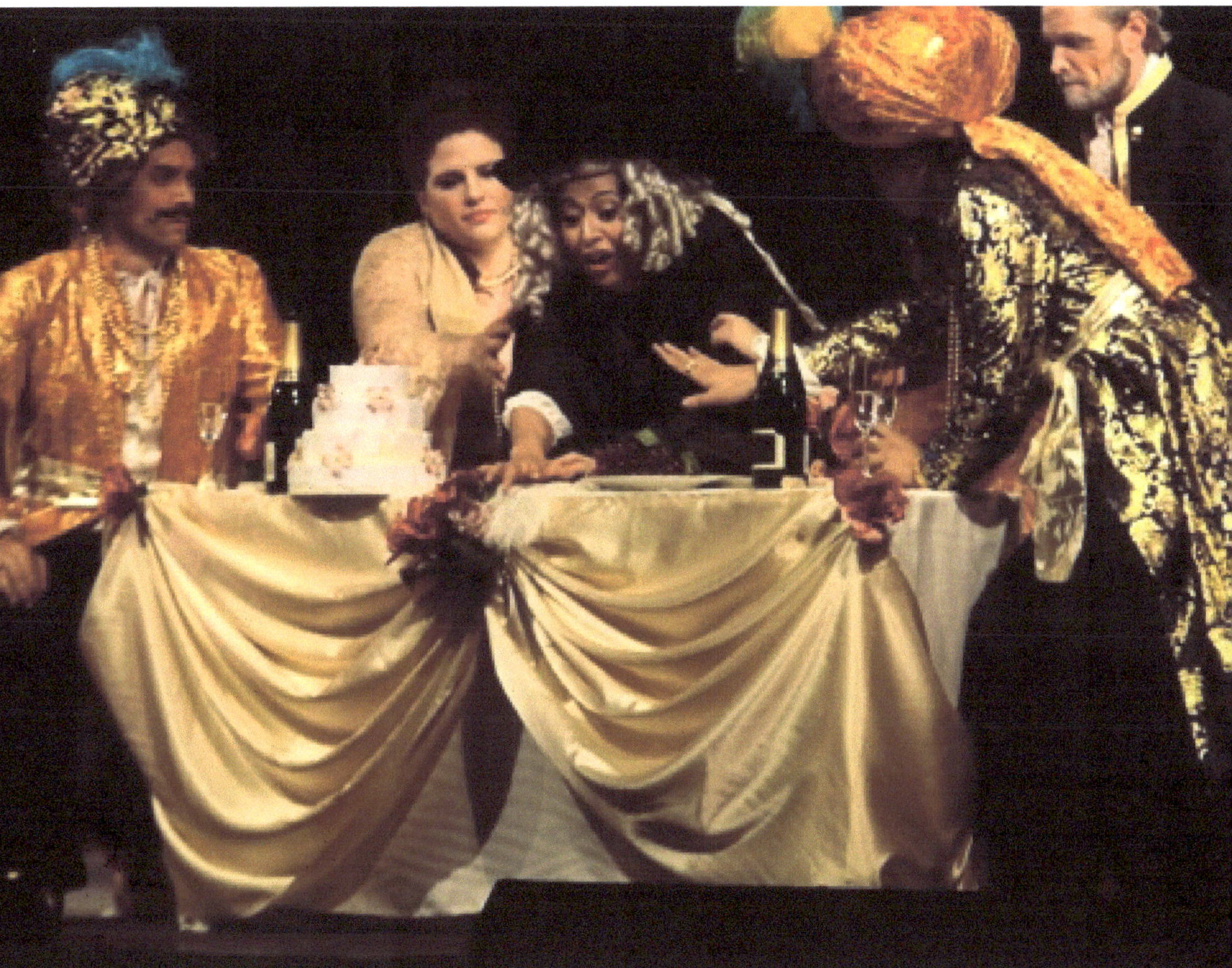

—Main Cast: Lori Decter, Grace Lin, Paul Murray, Saran Suebsantiwongse
— Siam Philharmonic Orchestra, conducted by Somtow Sucharitkul
— directed by Richard Harrell

14. AYODHYA (2006)
WORLD PREMIERE

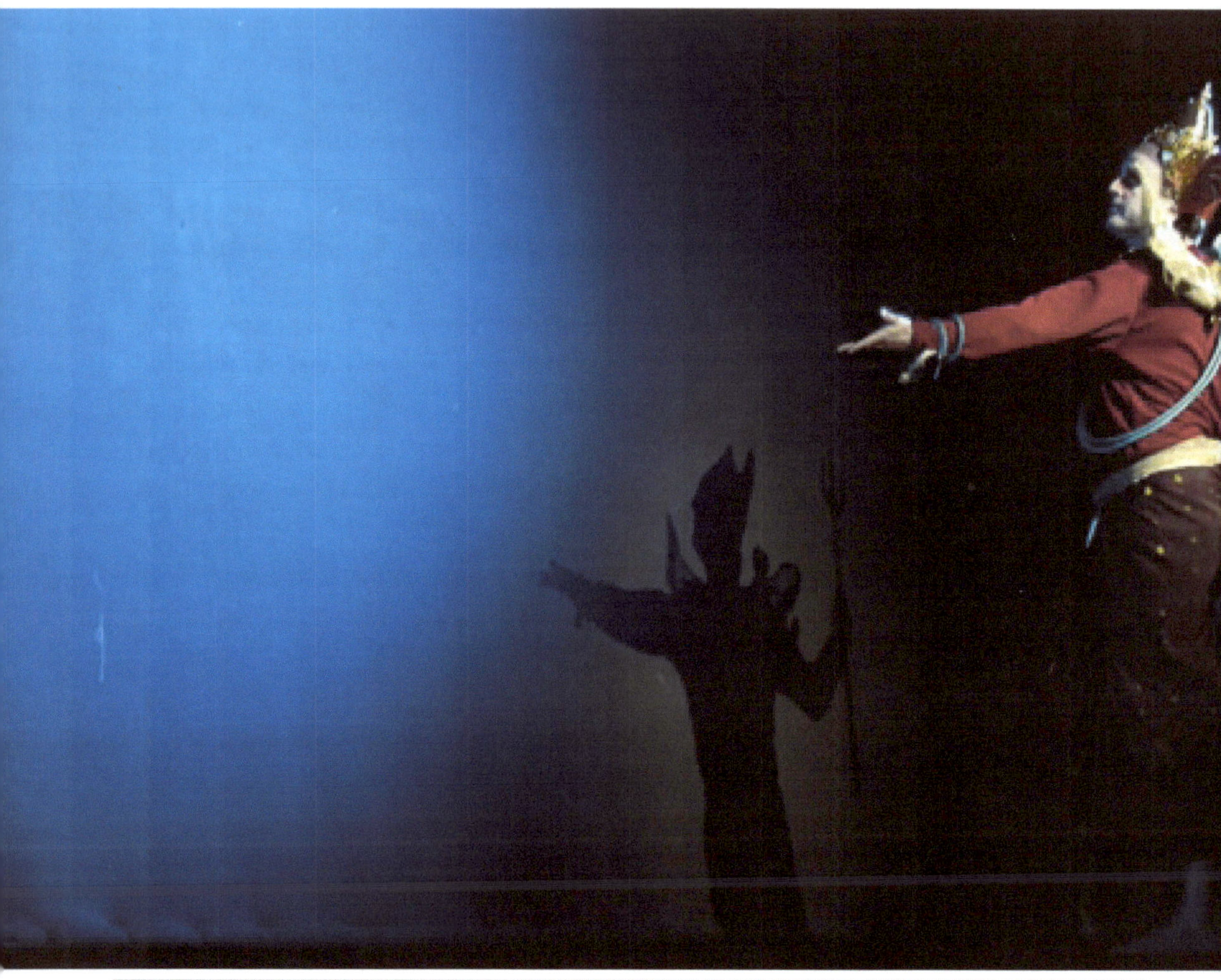

"Opera Siam has already accomplished more than companies many times its age. Founded by present director Somtow Papinian Sucharitkul, it has mounted operas ranging from chamber works such as Dido and Aeneas and Turn of the Screw to full-blown productions of Madama Butterfly and Turandot. Among other ventures, it has embarked on a Ring cycle (Das Rheingold was presented last February; Die Walküre is due in July 2007), the first to be fully staged and produced by an Asian company. Bangkok Opera is the only company in southeast Asia operating with a full season (five productions per year)" — *Opera News, New York*

HRH Princess Maha Chakri Sirindorn was the guest of honor at the world premiere of Ayodhya, composed on the occasion of the Sixtieth Regnal Year of His Majesty the King of Thailand.

Ayodhya proved to be the opera that would make the Bangkok Opera truly world- famous, and one cannot therefore avoid mentioning the censorship scandal. There has been a lot of fallout from this, from bizarre anonymous letters faxed to members of the royal family to SPAM emails sent across the internet accusing me of malfeasance (as though anyone could ever choose to try to get rich off opera.)

The press did get one thing very wrong, and that's because when the international community thinks *junta,* it starts to think about prison camps and so on, and we are convinced that Thailand's government had very little to do with trying to censor the opera; it was a few bureaucrats, terrified that they'd get into trouble, overreacting. In any case no one censored the opera. An opera is words and music, and every note of the music, and every word of the libretto, got played.

It was so obvious from the words and the music that the demon king was dead that changing the staging really made no difference to the opera's emotional impact.

With the reviews this opera has had, perhaps the scandal will in time be more of a footnote.

Help from the Gods came, because in true Thai fashion, the singers all performed a propitiatory ritual to make sure the gods of the Ramayana approved of the entire operation.

"*Ayodhya* remains in this writer's memory as a work greater than the sum of its parts, a feast for both the eye and the ear, a throwback to the era of grand opera that featured stirring choruses, theatrical effects, lavish costumes, big voices, sumptuous orchestration, lyrical melodies and an aura of magic. " — *Opera News, New York*

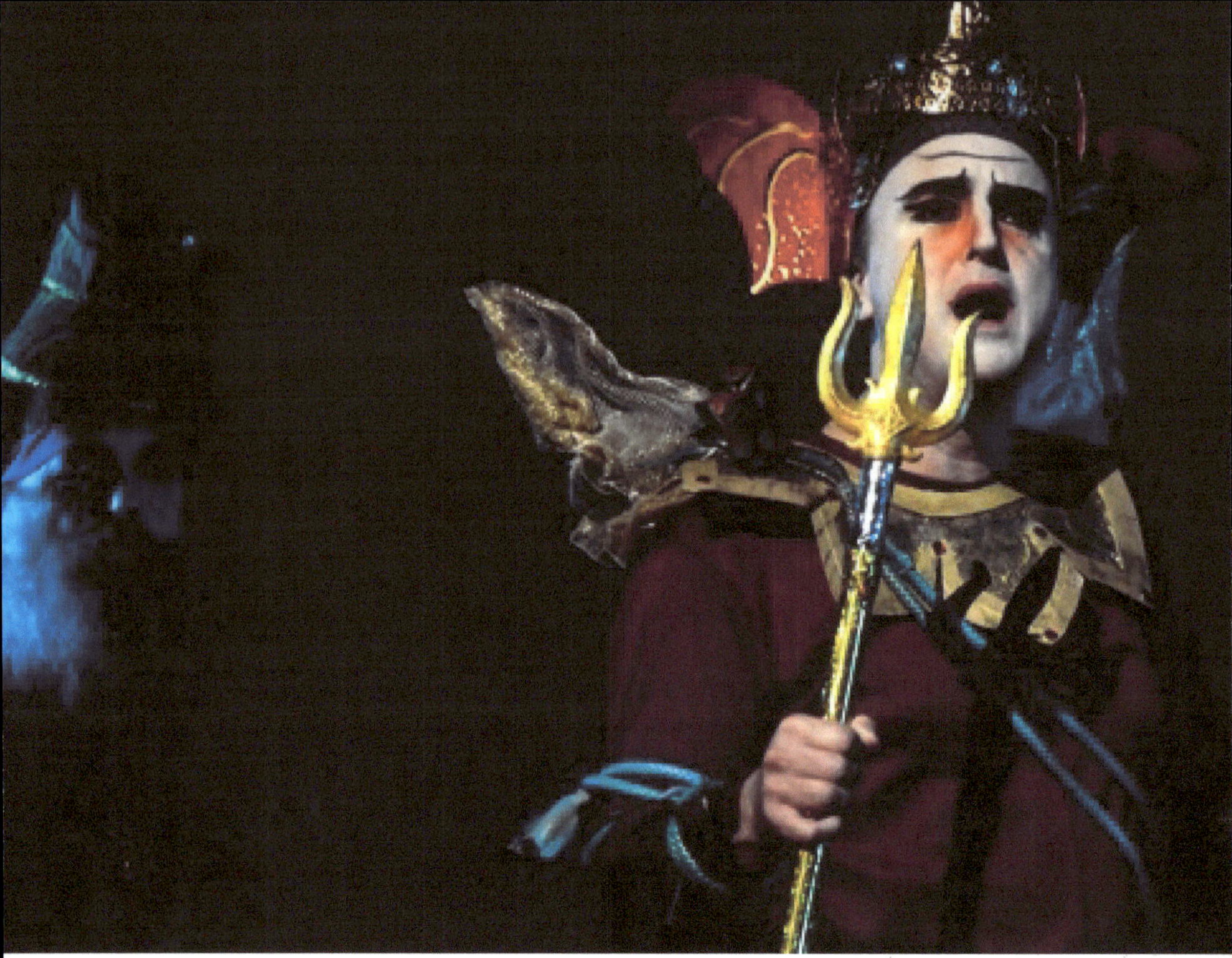

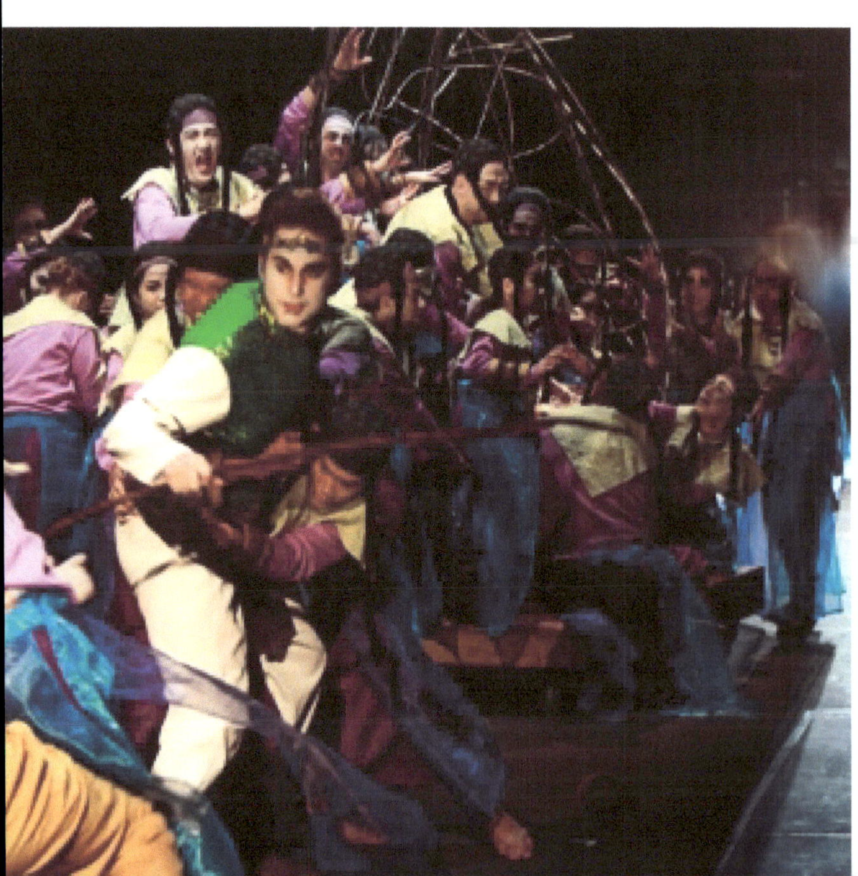

— Main Cast: Nancy Yuen, Michael Chance, John Ames, Ellen van Beek, Saran Suebsantiwongse, Marina Zytkova
—Hans Nieuwenhuis, director
— Jubilee Orchestra, conducted by Somtow Sucharitkul

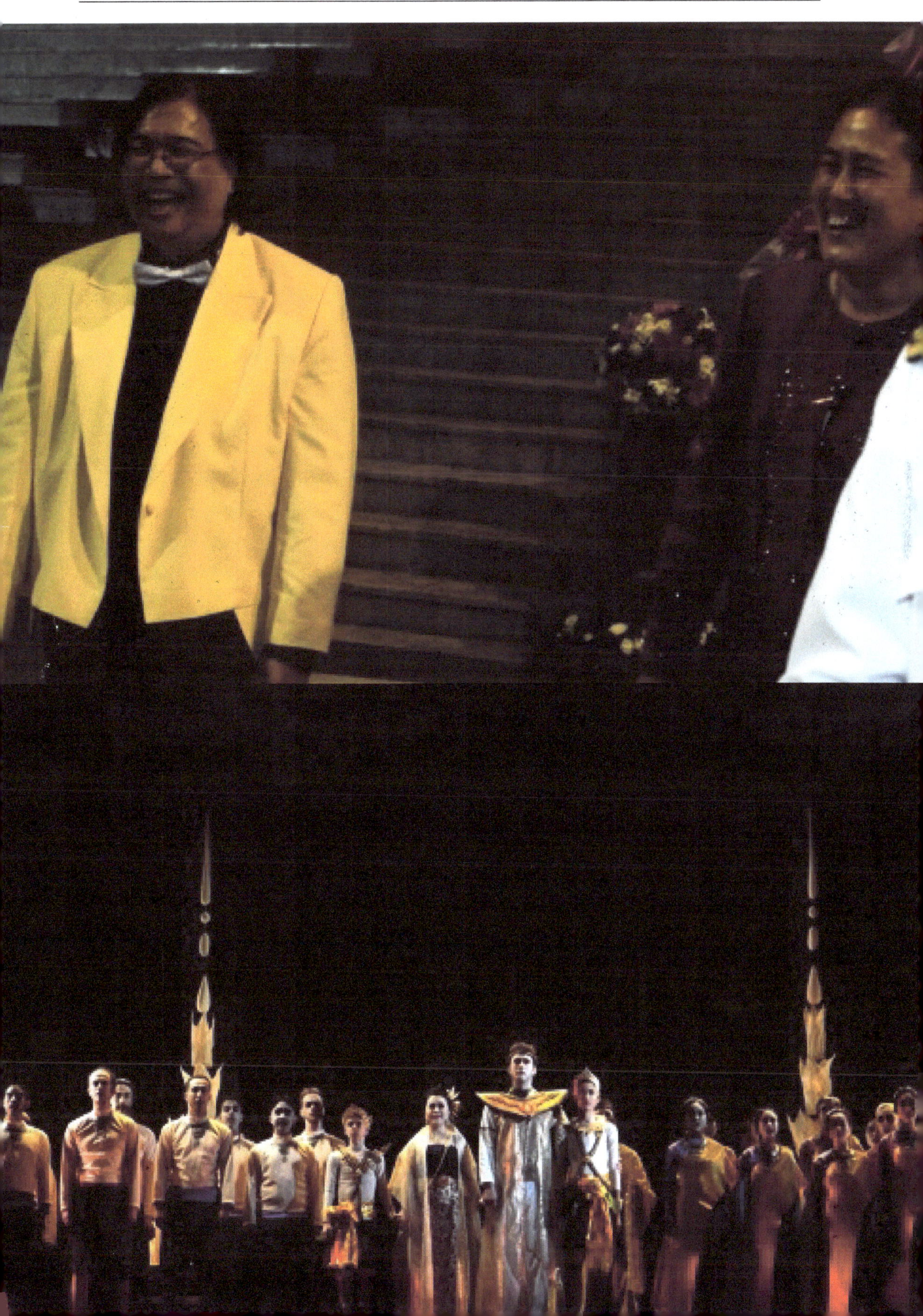

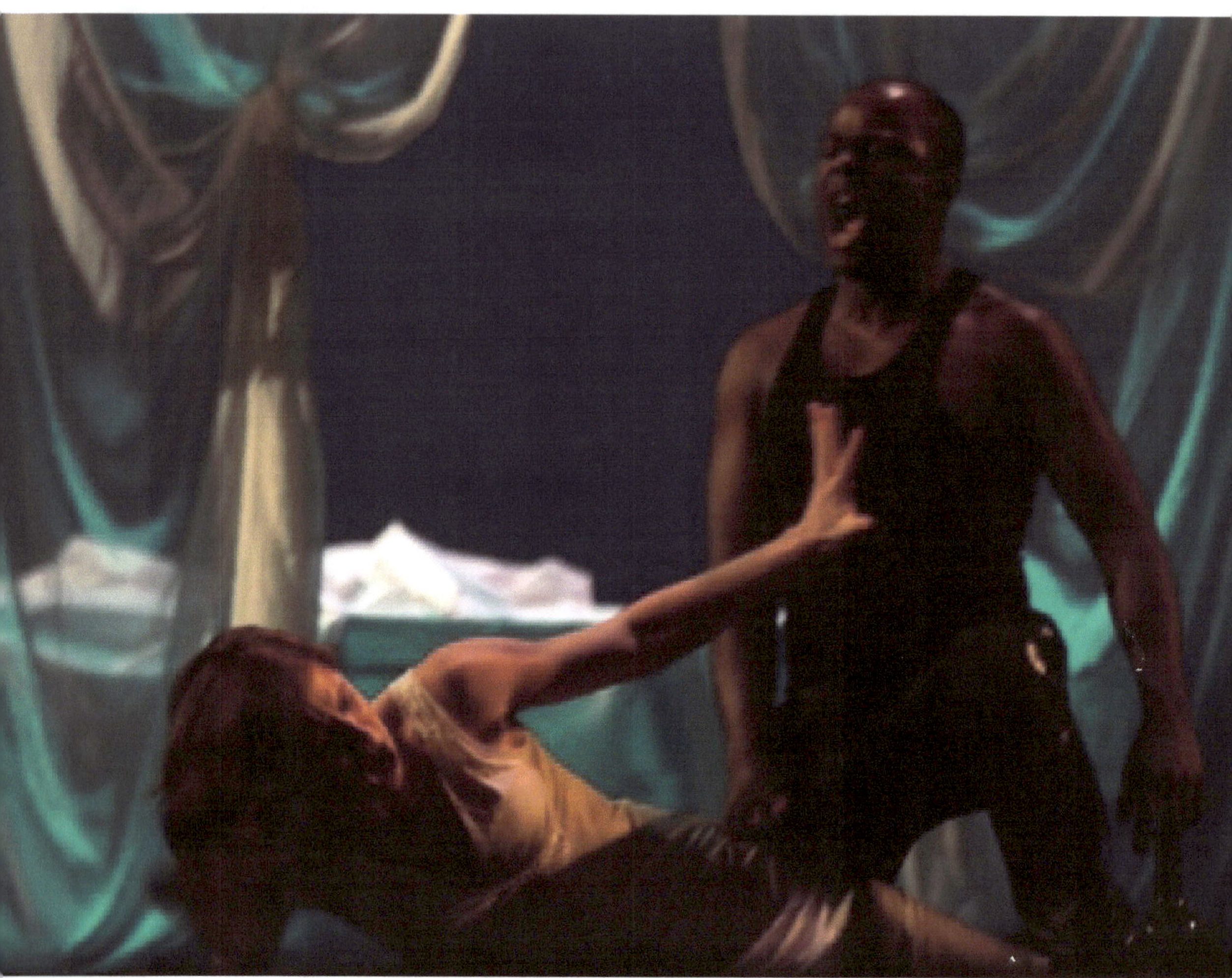

15. THE RAPE OF LUCRETIA (2007)
THAILAND PREMIERE

The Bangkok Opera's first international tour was also the first time a twentieth century opera had ever been staged in Vietnam, as well as our first performance at the historic Chalerm Krung Theatre. The Vietnamese authorities were wary of using the word *rape* in the title, and so at the Hanoi Opera House we just called it "Lucretia".

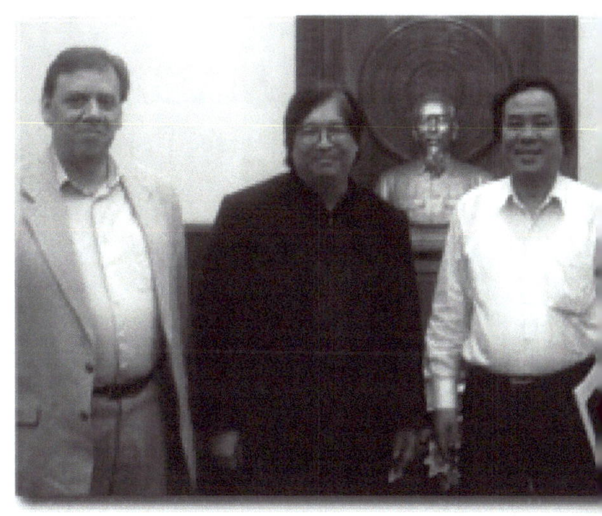

Director Hans Nieuwenhuis and Somtow called on the Deputy Minister of Culture in Hanoi in order to discuss long-term cooperation. Here, they are seen with Pham Hong Hai of the Vietnam National Opera and Ballet, at the Ministry, with a striking bust of Ho Chi Minh in the background.

A clip from the Rape of Lucretia was the Bangkok Opera's most popular excerpt on youtube, garnering three quarters of a million hits in only a few months.

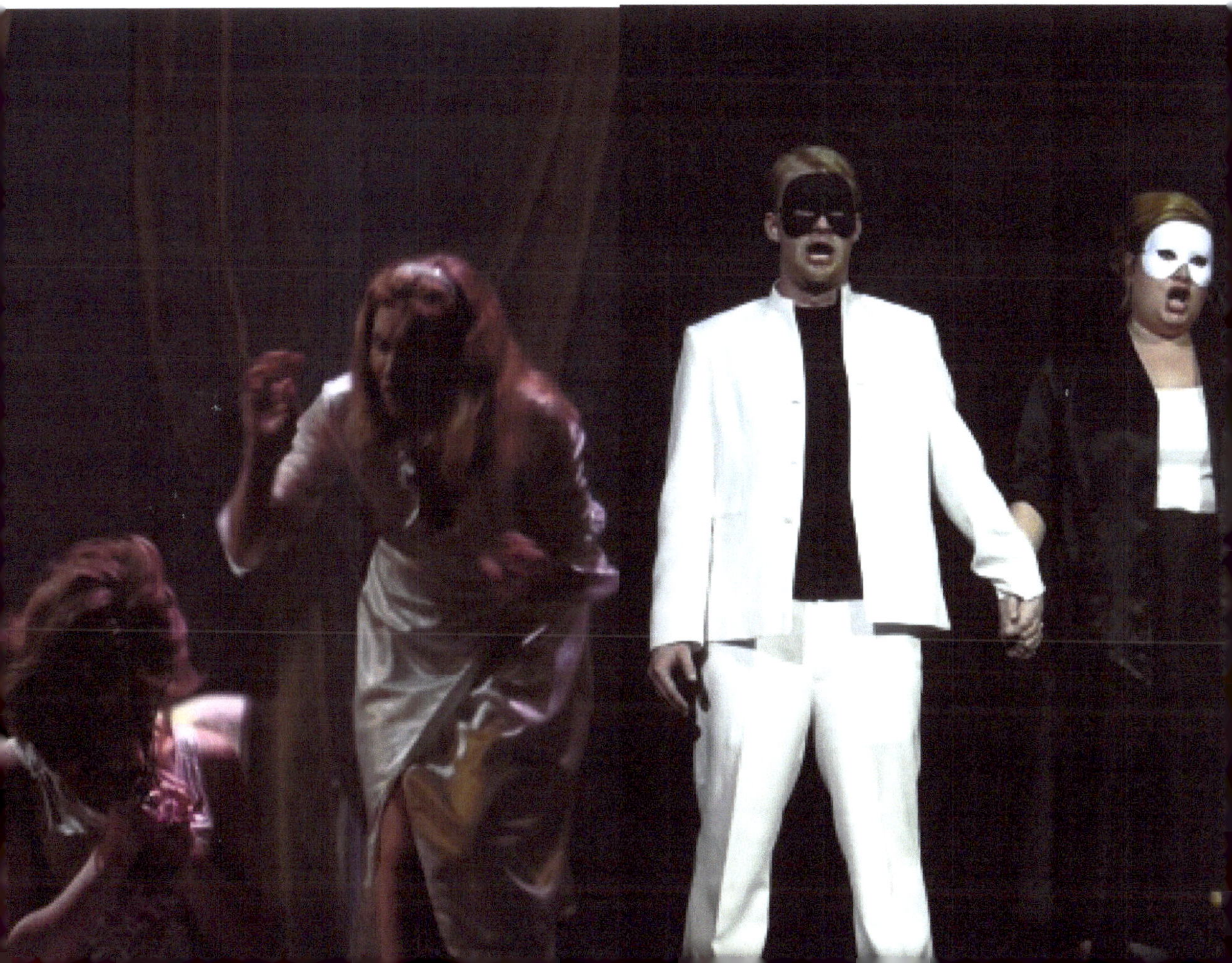

16. MADAMA BUTTERFLY (2007)
FIRST LOCAL PRODUCTION

Bangkok Opera's most recent production as of the publication of this book, Henry Akina's austere, kabuki-inspired staging of *Madama Butterfly* had record attendance. Stars included Israel Lozano, new to Bangkok, and Yun Deng, veteran of the Met as well as old favorites like Peter Ong, Pitchaya Kemasingki, and the much-loved Nancy Yuen in her signature role. For the first time, government funding played a major role in the production with a grant from the Ministry of Tourism and Sport.

This production design by Dean Shibuya was so well-liked that it was later recreated at the Savonlinna Festival in Finland, and then travelled to Hawaii as well as being revived numerous times in Finland.

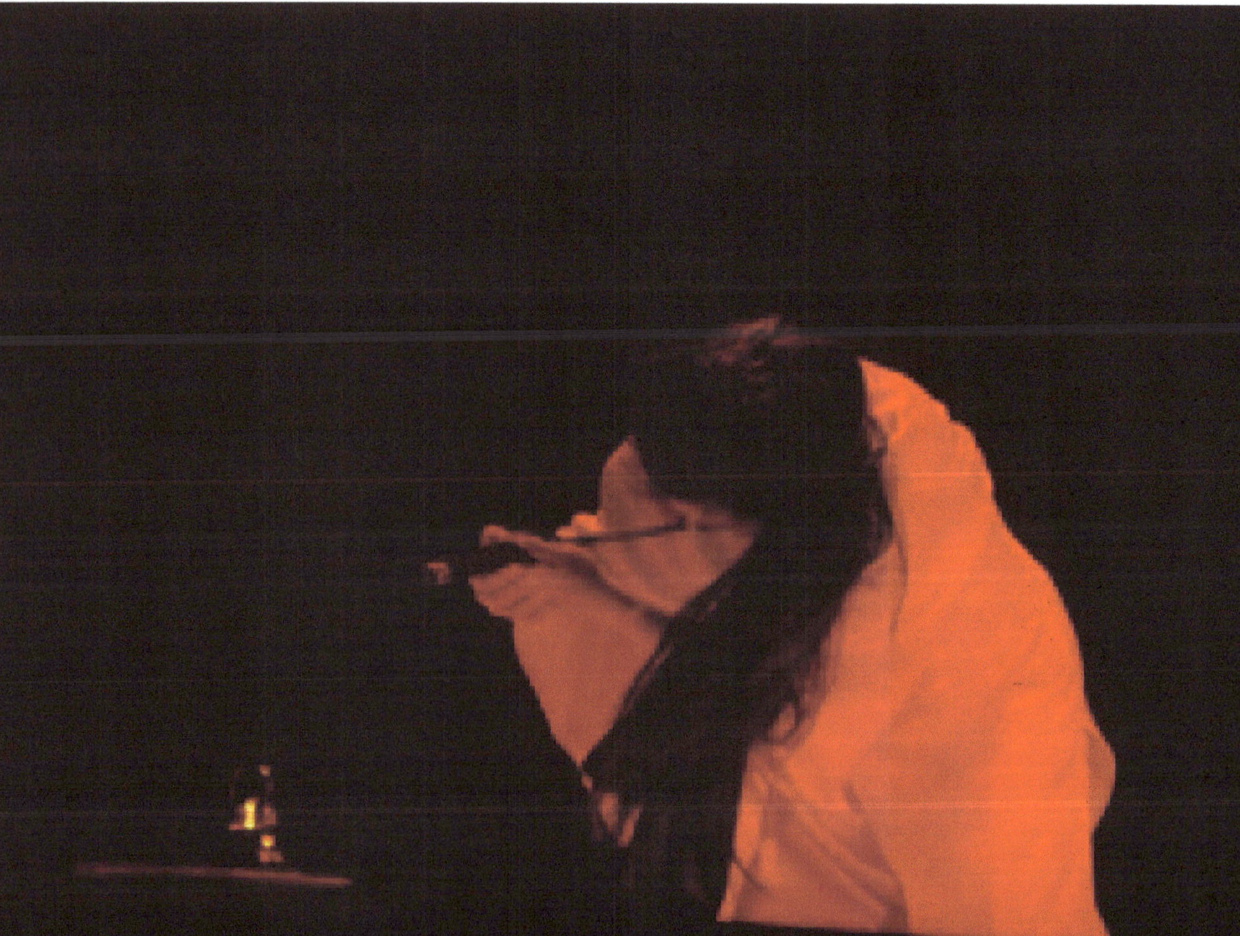

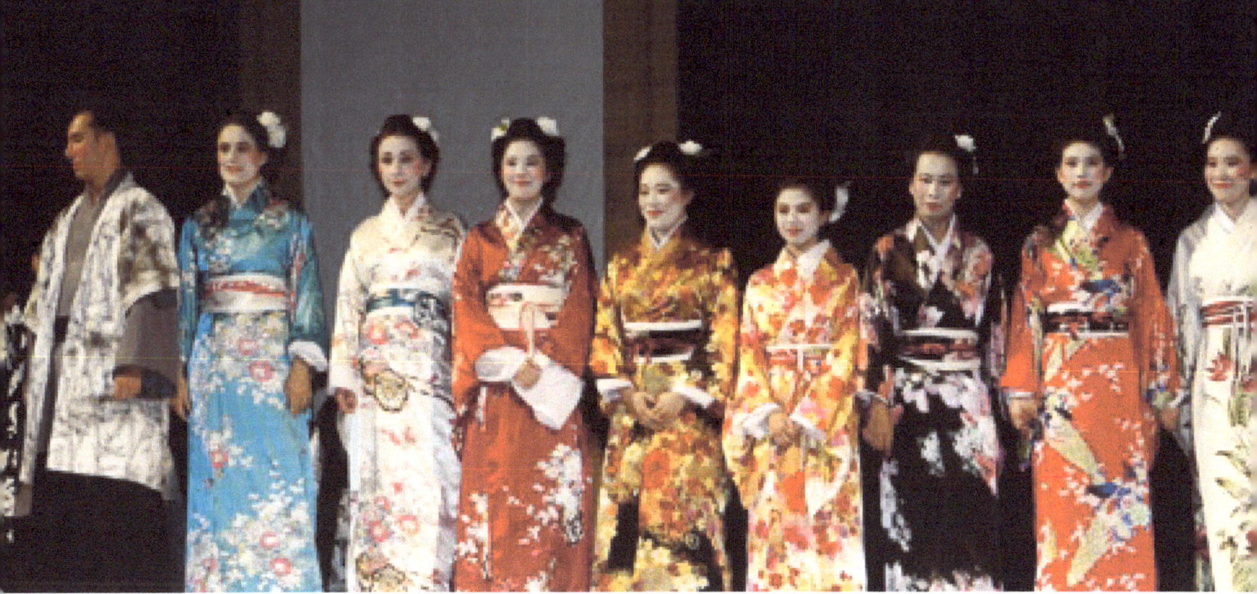

> This time around, Bangkok has earned itself the position as the center of Southeast Asian Opera! A truly exciting production!
>
> — *The Nation*

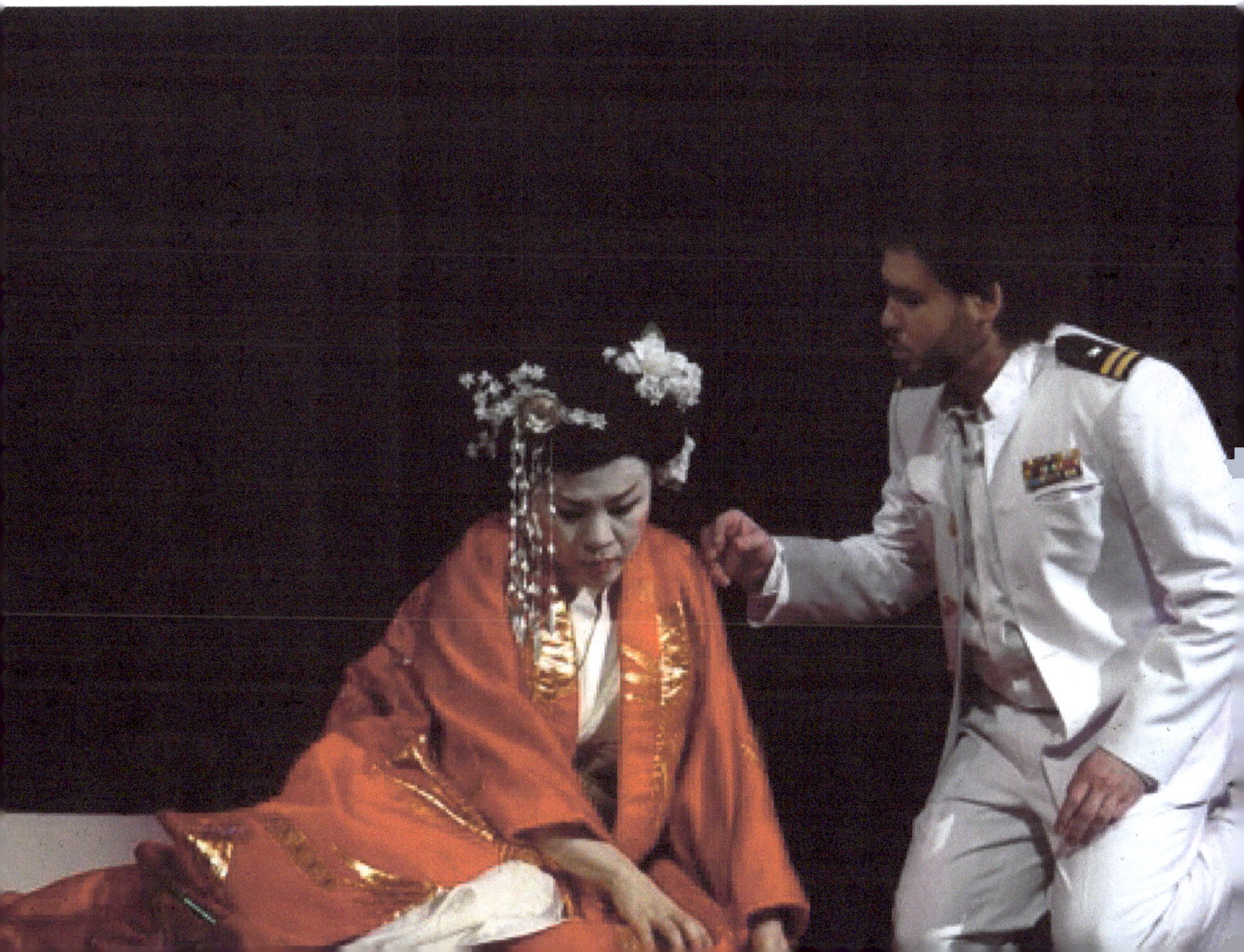

17. DIDO AND AENEAS (2007) CONCERT PERFORMANCE

Dido and Aeneas opened at the Pridi Hall and was repeated at the Regent Hotel with a banquet. A lovely, upscale dinner theater event, directed by Trisdee na Patalung with the Bangkok Baroque Ensemble.

— Main Cast: Catherine Harsono, Pitchaya Khemasinki, Susheilagh Angpiroj. Sandra Partridge

— Bangkok Baroque Ensemble, directed by Trisdee na Patalung

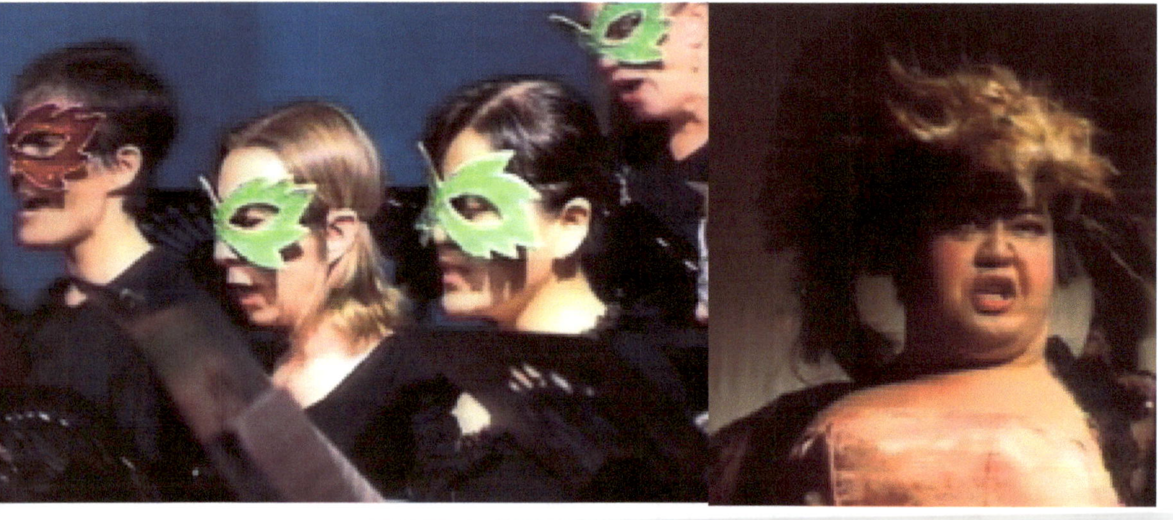

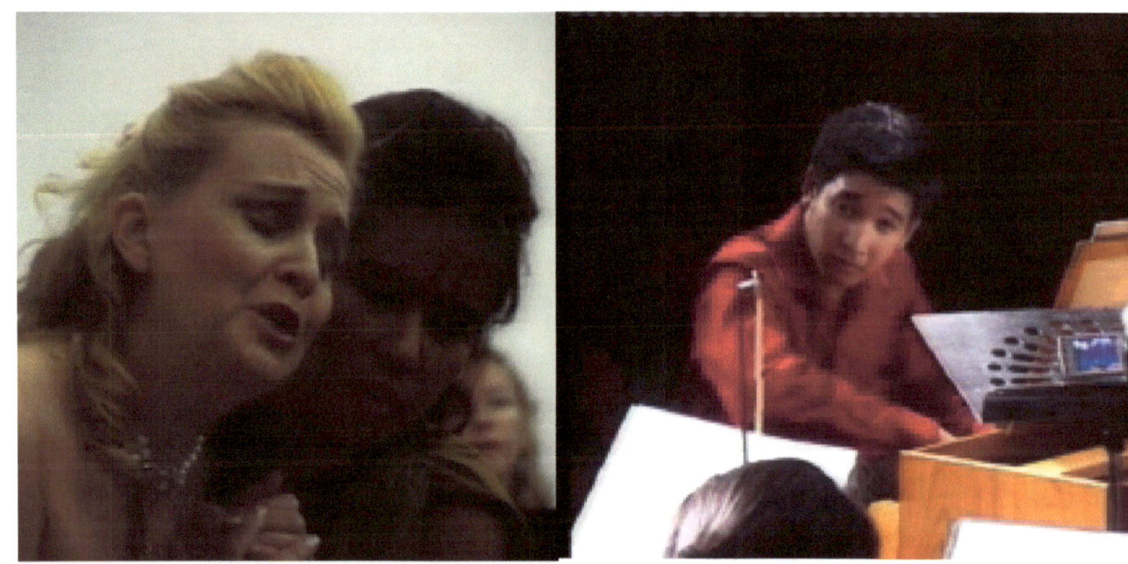

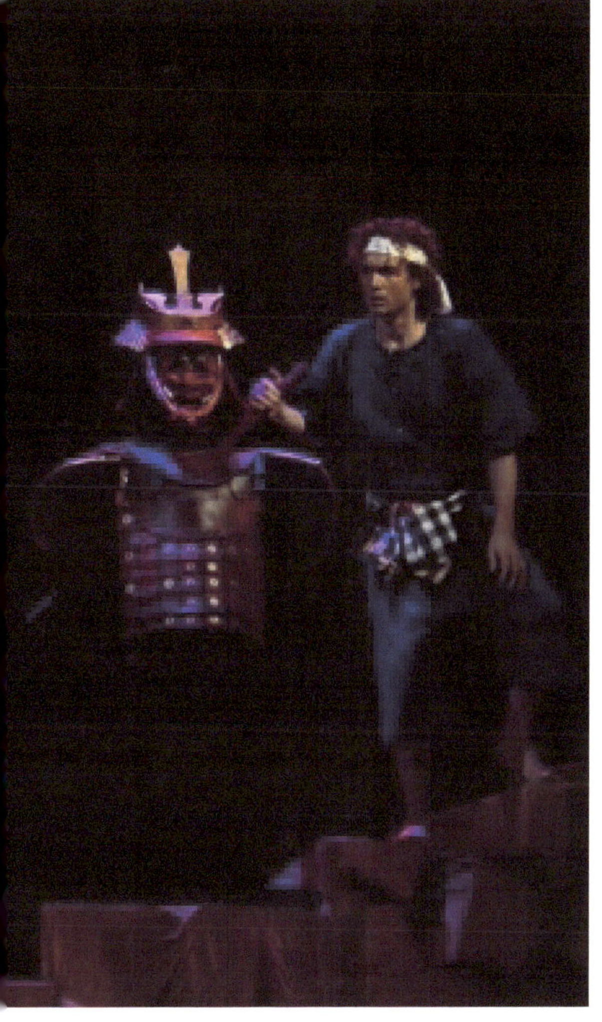

18. DIE WALKÜRE (2007) ASEAN PREMIERE

The second part of *Der Ring des Nibelungen* was performed with special orchestral guest Hans Pfizka from the Bavarian State Orchestra as first horn; he came to help train the Siam Philharmonic's brass. Somtow's continuation of his *Rheingold* interpretation moved from Thailand's mythic past to a more recent period of Thai history — his *Walküre* takes places during the Japanese occupation of Thailand, in the era of the Second World War.

The intention was the *Siegfried* would take place during Thailand in the 1990s, the age of financial boom and bust, and that the "jungle" would be a concrete jungle (with the dragon as a gigantic wrecking crane) ... and then Siegfried would eventuall take the elevator to the uppermost penthouse of the most upscale office building in Bangkok to meet Wotan. *Götterdämmerung* would in this interpretation be set in a futuristic space age Bangkok.

As of 2018, we only have the first two *Ring* operas; a curse seems to have settled on our *Ring* because every time we schedule *Siegfried,* something happens to the tenor. More when we discuss *The Flying Dutchman.*

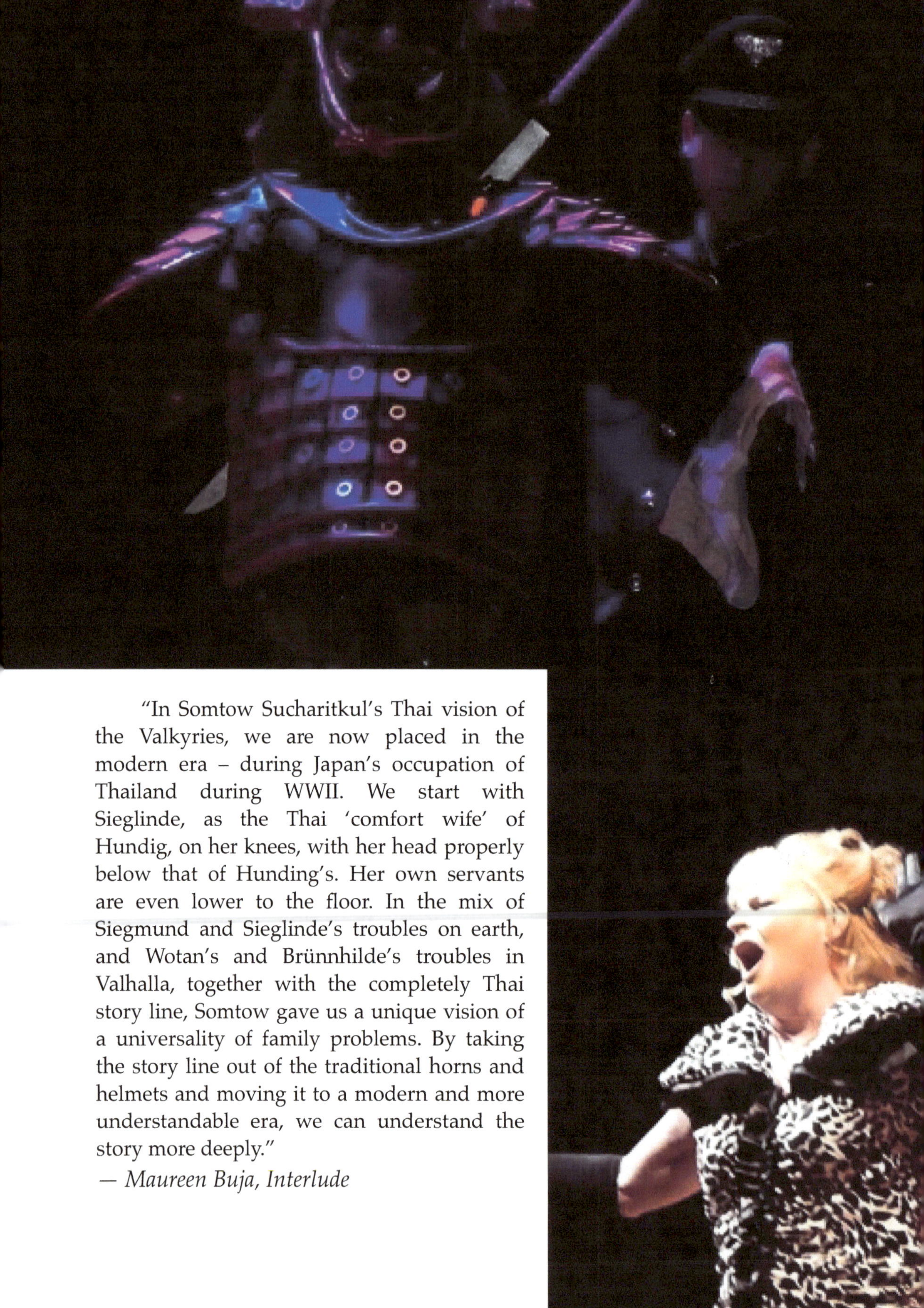

"In Somtow Sucharitkul's Thai vision of the Valkyries, we are now placed in the modern era – during Japan's occupation of Thailand during WWII. We start with Sieglinde, as the Thai 'comfort wife' of Hundig, on her knees, with her head properly below that of Hunding's. Her own servants are even lower to the floor. In the mix of Siegmund and Sieglinde's troubles on earth, and Wotan's and Brünnhilde's troubles in Valhalla, together with the completely Thai story line, Somtow gave us a unique vision of a universality of family problems. By taking the story line out of the traditional horns and helmets and moving it to a modern and more understandable era, we can understand the story more deeply."

— Maureen Buja, Interlude

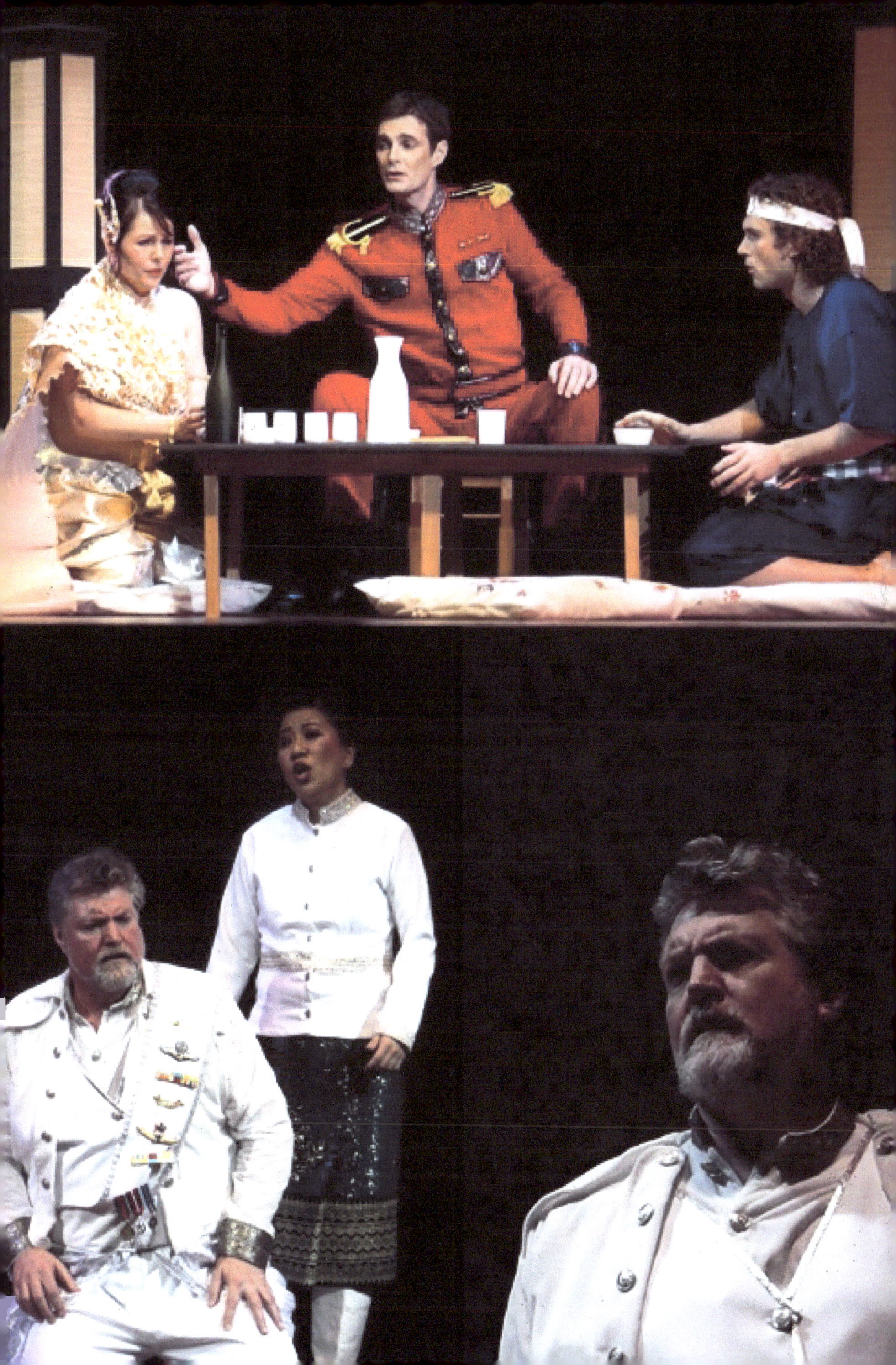

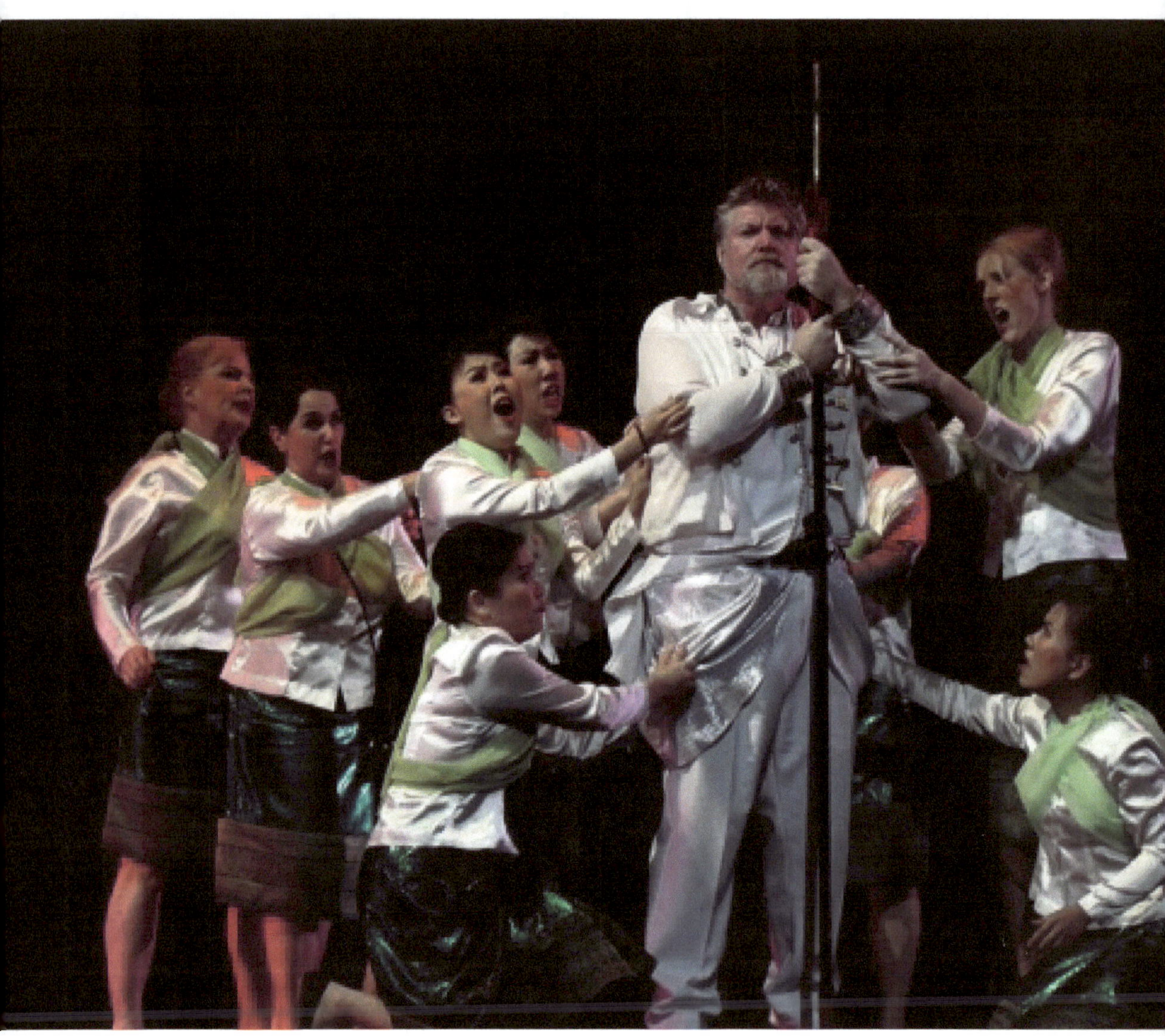

— Main Cast: Phillip Joll, John Ames, Jessica Hsing-An Chen, Barbara Smith Jones, Charles Hens, Jany Zomer

— Siam Philharmonic Orchestra

— Somtow Sucharitkul, director and conductor

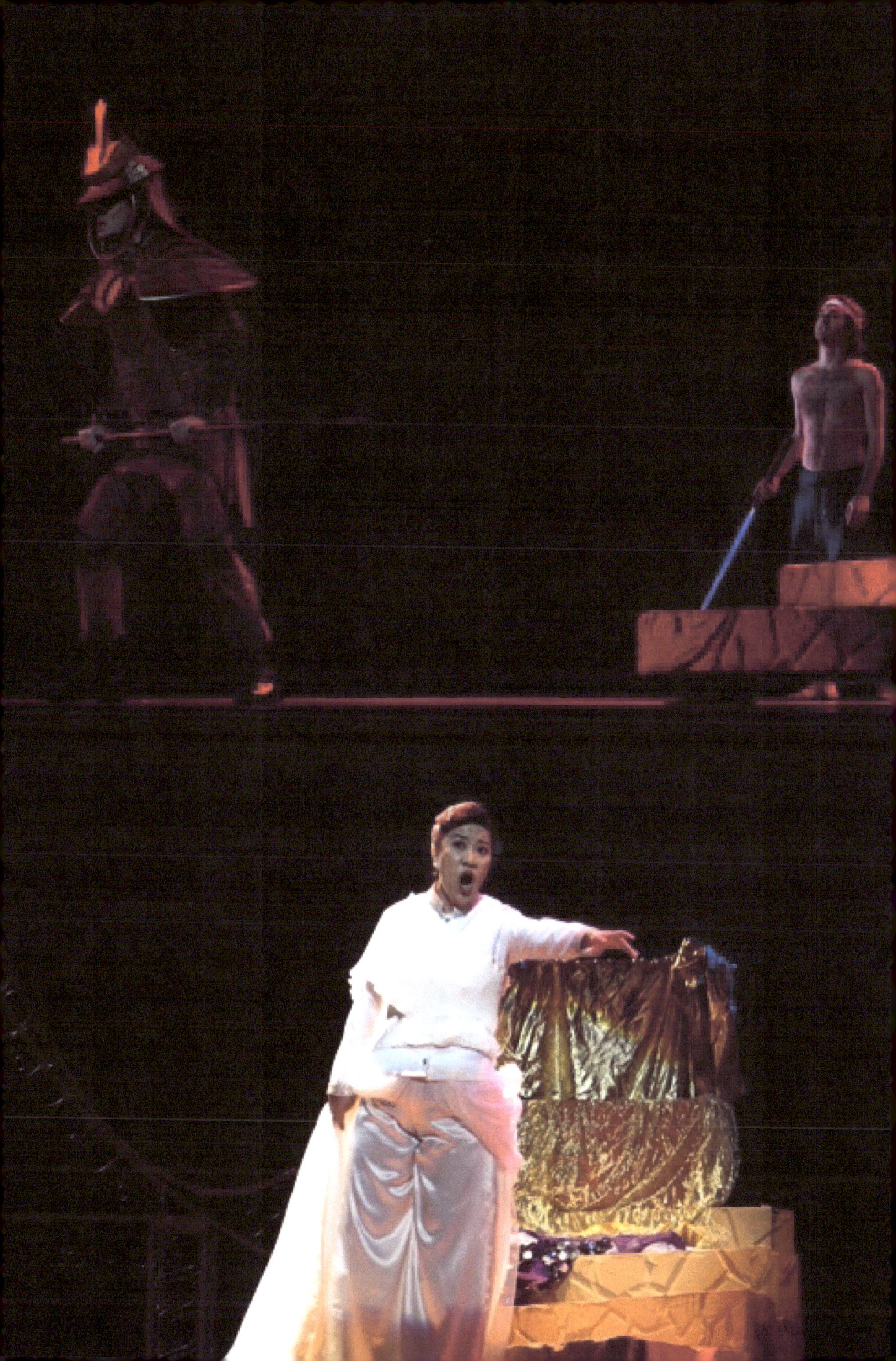

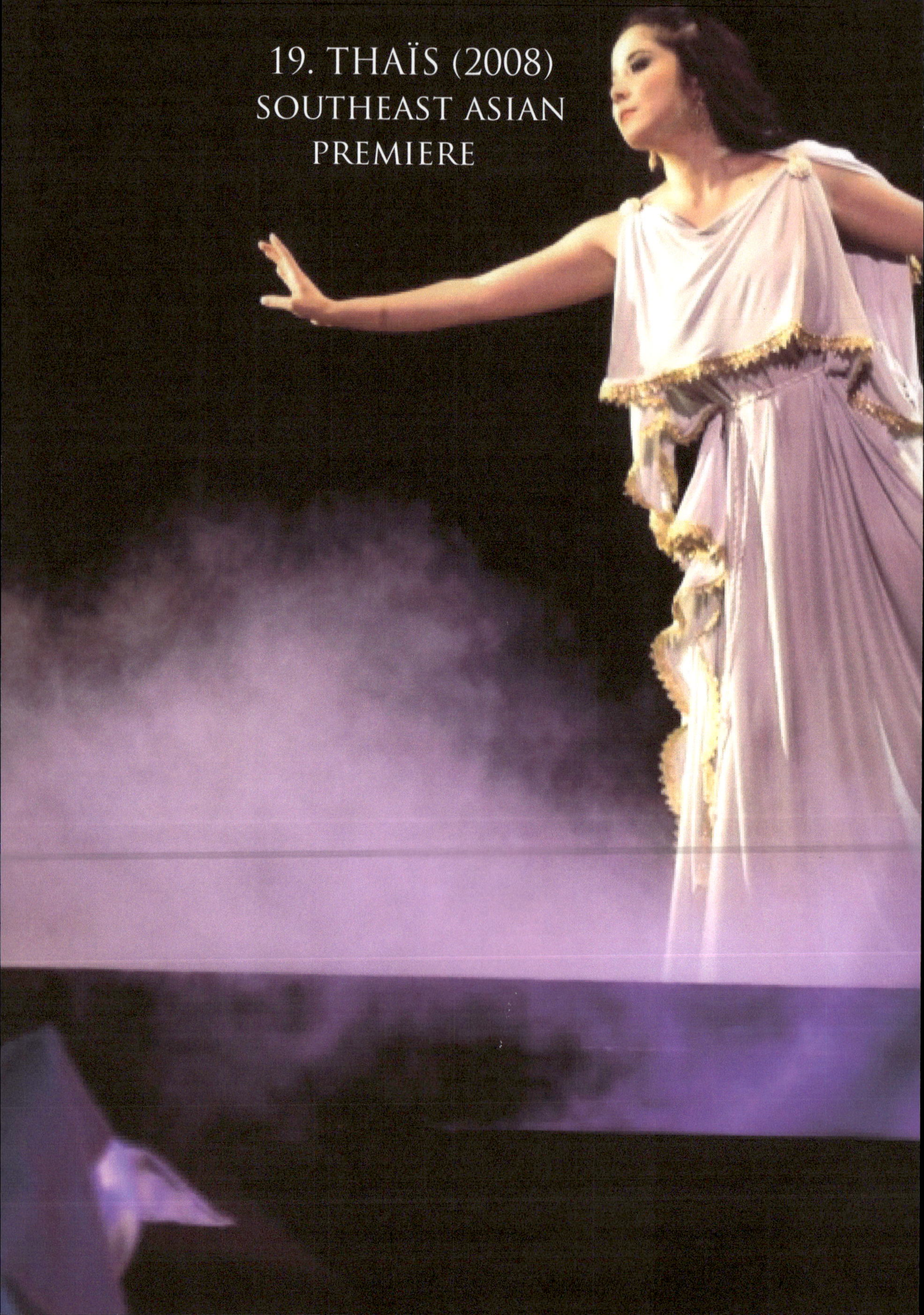

19. THAÏS (2008)
SOUTHEAST ASIAN PREMIERE

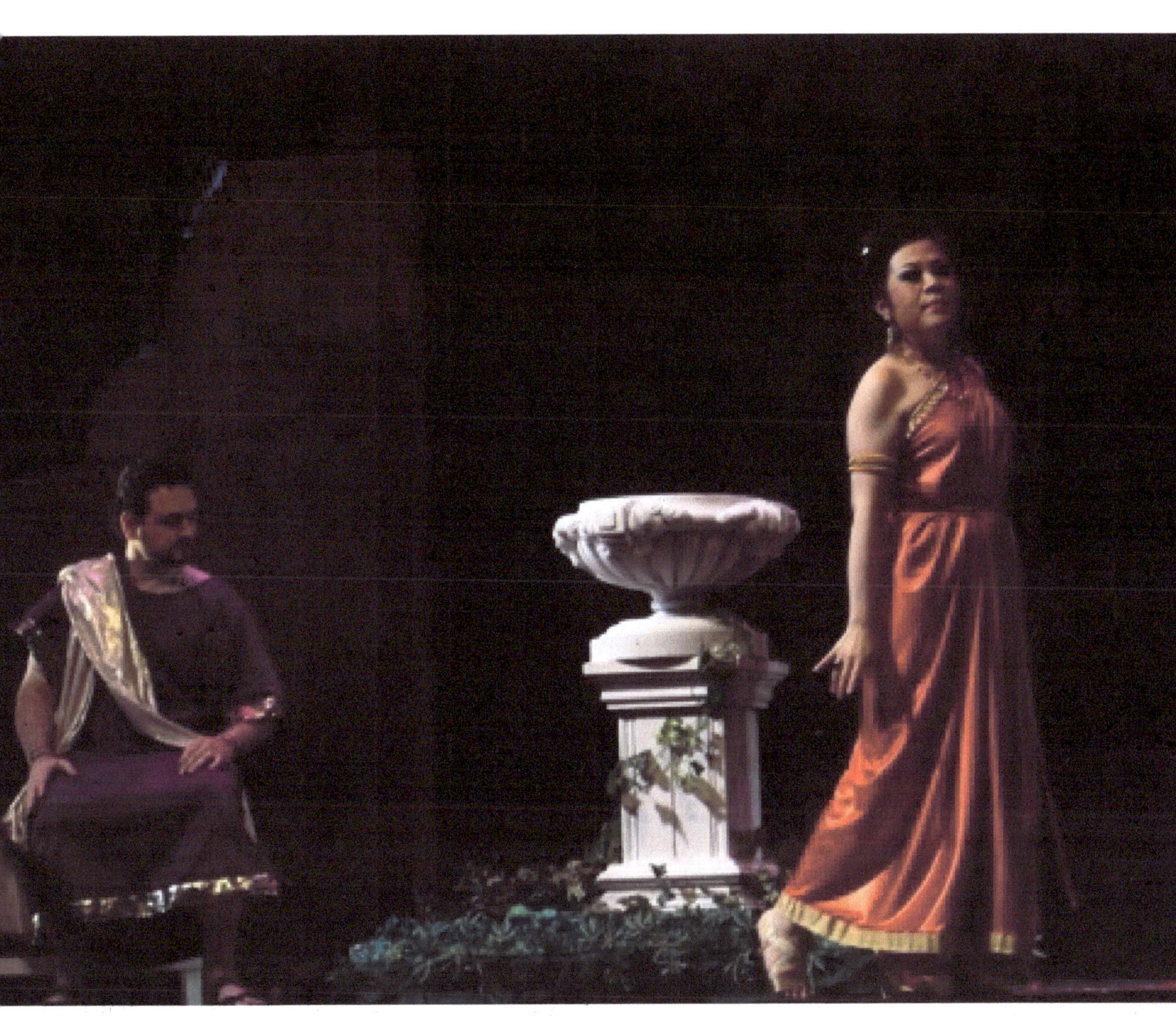

Opera Siam's first foray into the French romantic repertoire, this production was directed by famed dancer Darren Royston, and was therefore one of the only productions to feature the full-length version of the ballet in Act II, which is generally presented in a cut version.

The conductor's niece Vanina did a much admired turn as a dancer during the famous *Meditation* sequence, and HRH Princess Soamsawali attended; this was her first visit to an Opera Siam production. This was a "traditional" production, gorgeously conceived in a holistic, dance-like way by the British director. It was Nancy Yuen's first Thaïs and her command of the French idiom was breathtaking.

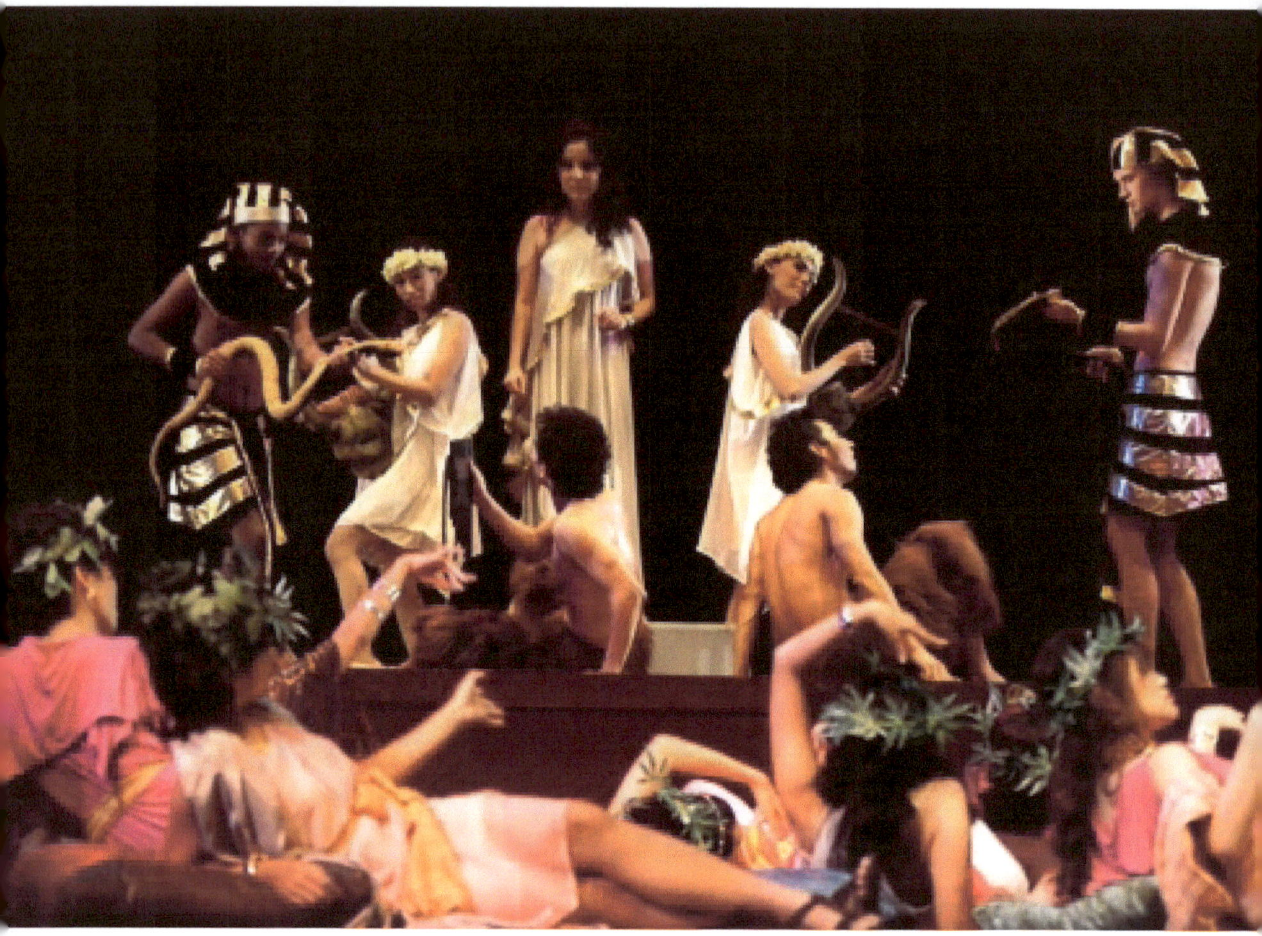

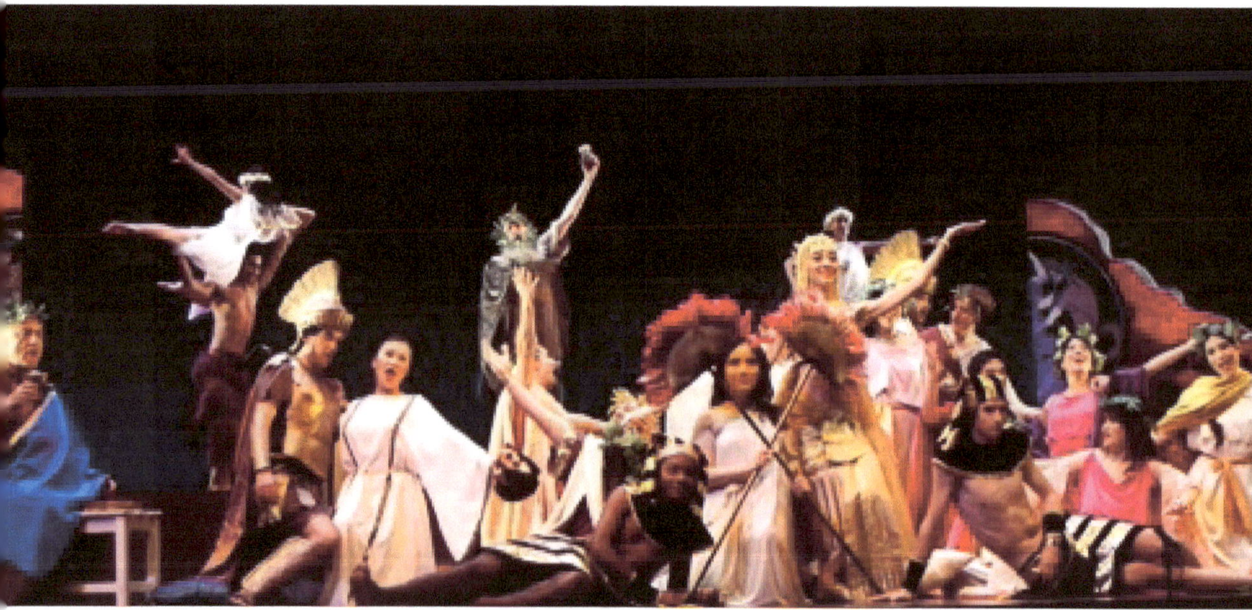

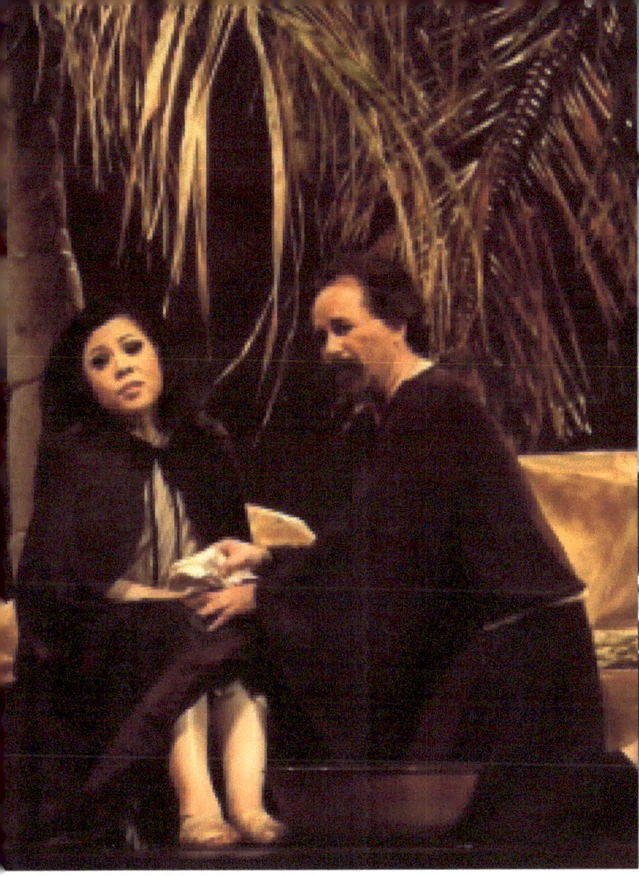

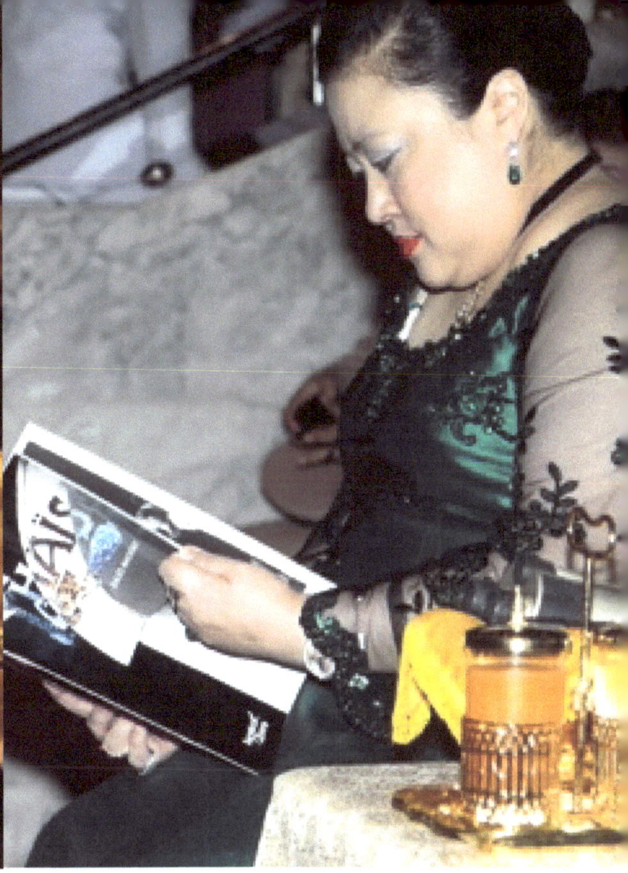

— Main Cast: Nancy Yuen, Javier Agulló, Stefan Sanchez, Susheilagh Angpiroj, Jak Cholvijarn, Ema Naito, Monique Klongtruadroke
— Darren Royston, director and choreographer
— Siam Philharmonic Orchestra, conducted by Somtow Sucharitkul

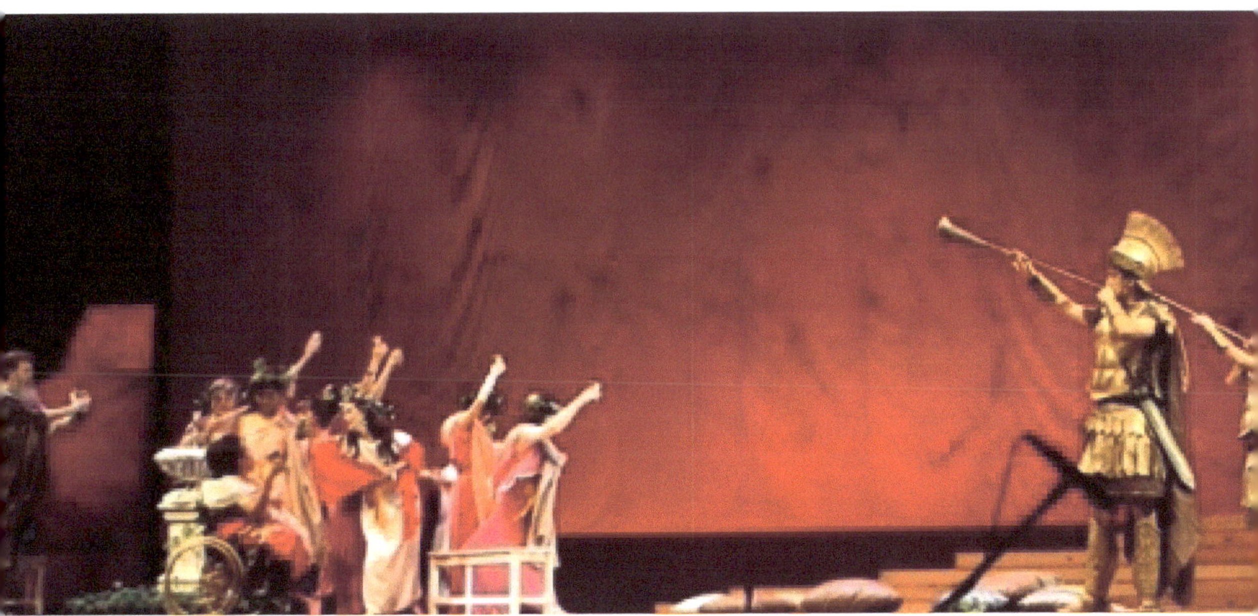

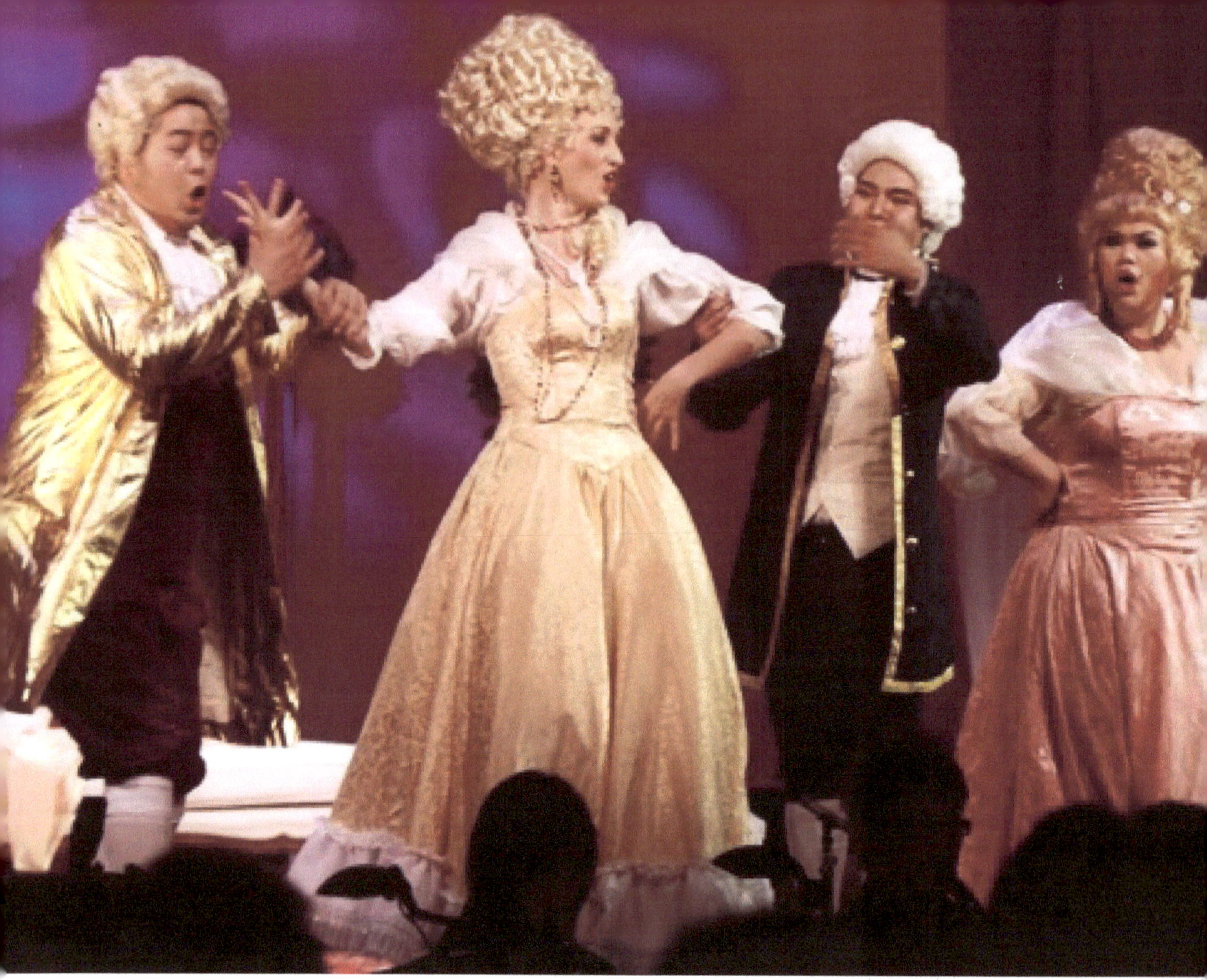

20. PRIMA LA MUSICA (2008)
THAILAND PREMIERE

This may well have been the first Salieri opera done in the entire region. It was with a double bill with Mozart's *Der Schauspieldirektor.* Nancy Yuen directed and Trisdee conducted.

— Main Cast: Barbara Zion, Korawij Devahastin na Ayuthaya, Pitchaya Khemasinki
— directed by Nancy Yuen
— conducted by Trisdee na Patalung

21. THE IMPRESARIO (2008)
THAILAND PREMIERE

This was in fact the same double bill ordered by the Emperor of Austria in which two comedies, by Mozart and Salieri, were played off against one another. These productions took place in the Small Hall of the Cultural center which was redecorated to create an intimate space with the orchestra placed very close to the audience.

— Main Cast: Sandra Patridge, Pitchaya Khemasinki, Vanina Sucharitkul
— directed by Somtow Sucharitkul
— conducted by Trisdee na Patalung

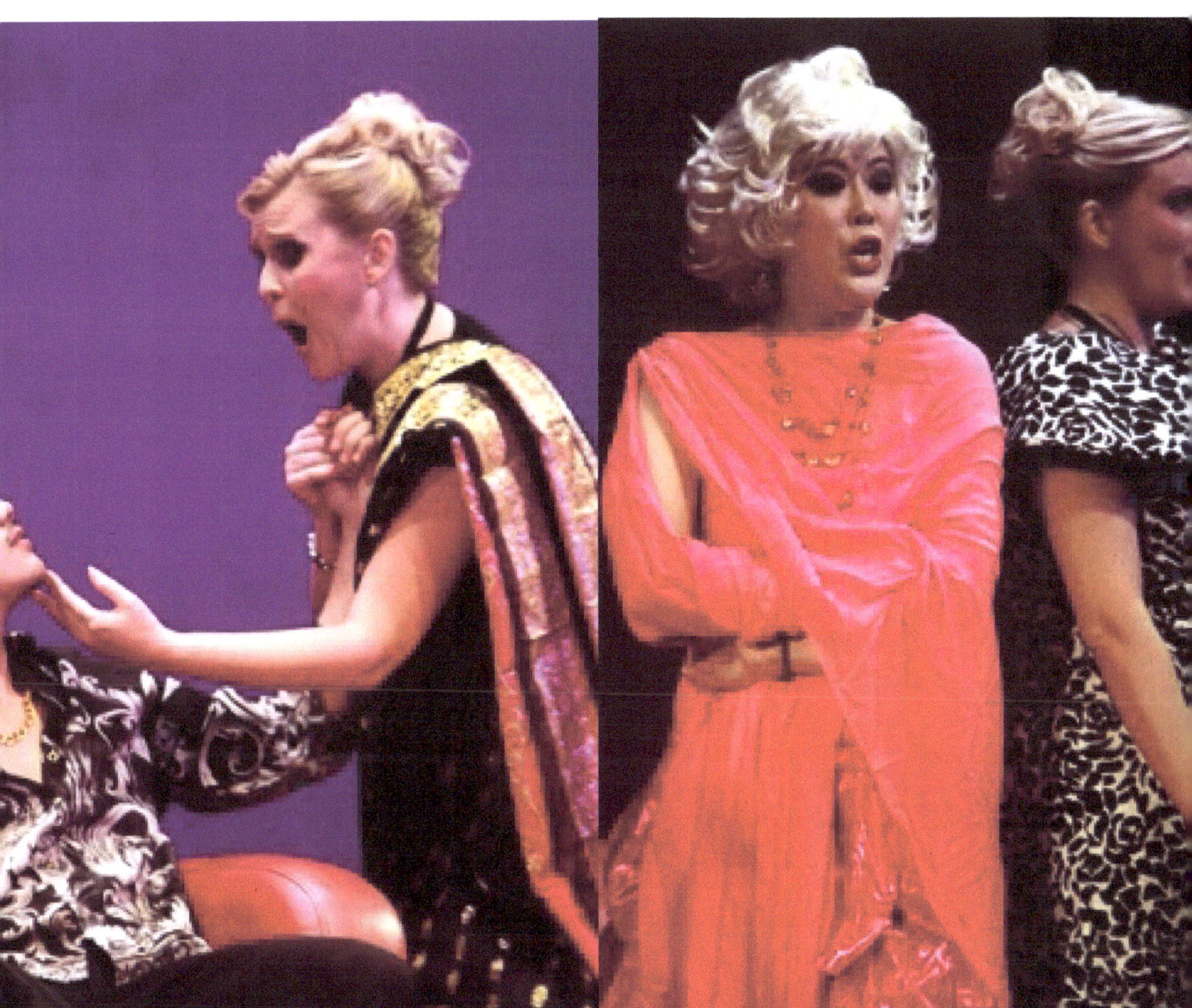

22. LA BOHÈME (2008)
REDUCED VERSION

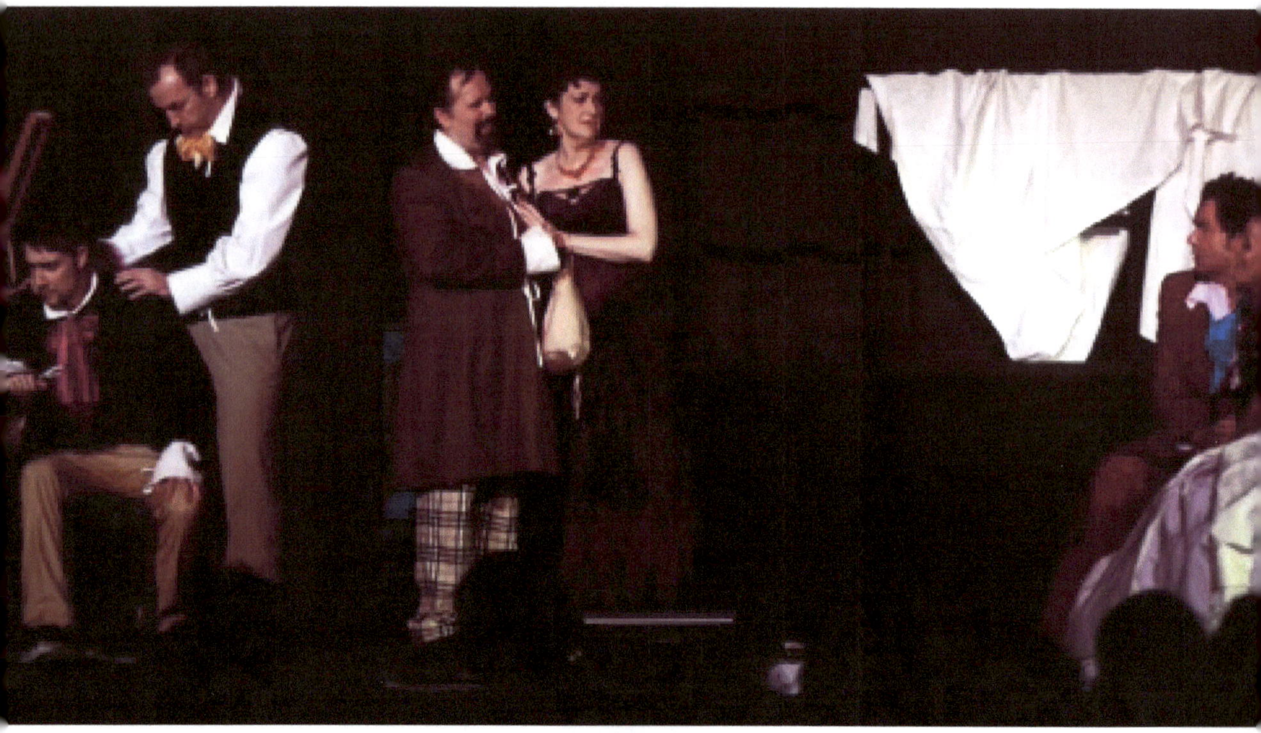

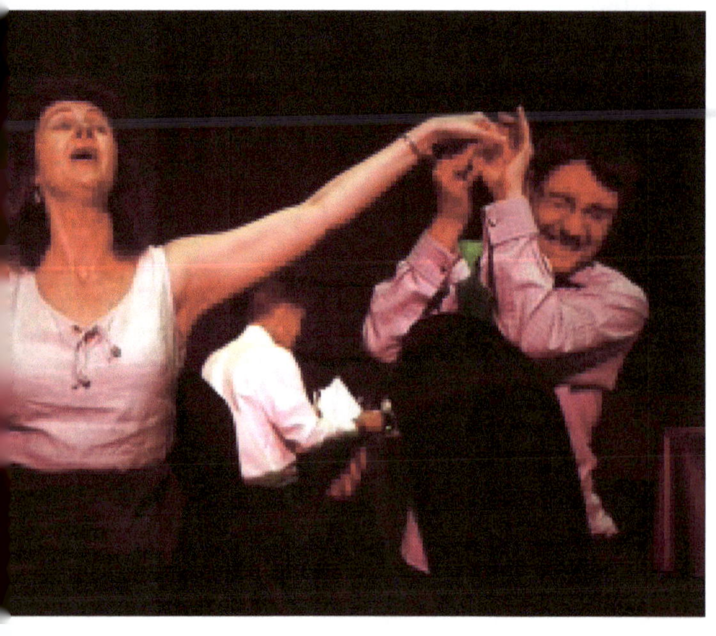

A dinner theater version of *La Bohème* with a reduced orchestra and young singers from the United Kingdom was brought to the Sheraton Grande by travelling impresario Stefan Sanchez. Somtow Sucharitkul conducted the ensemble of about twenty young musicians and the cast. Stefan Sanchez directed and performed the role of Marcello.

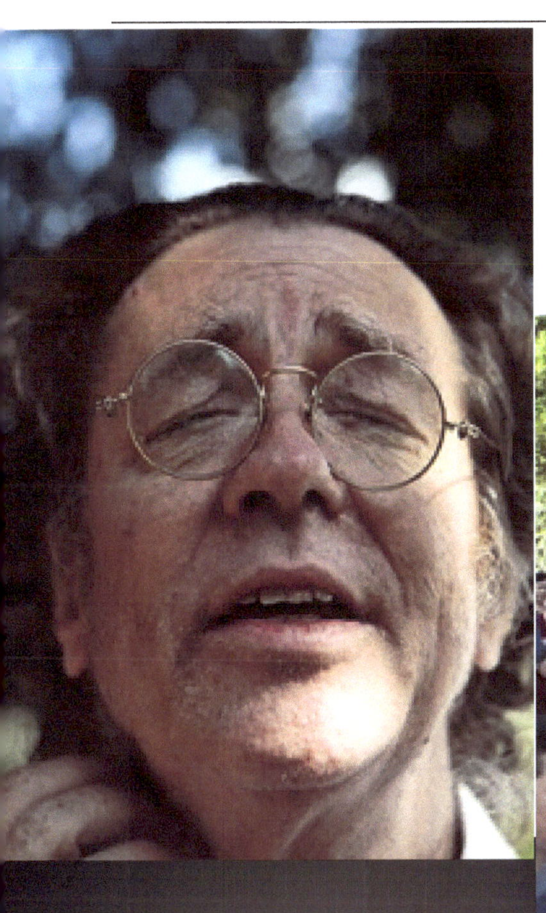

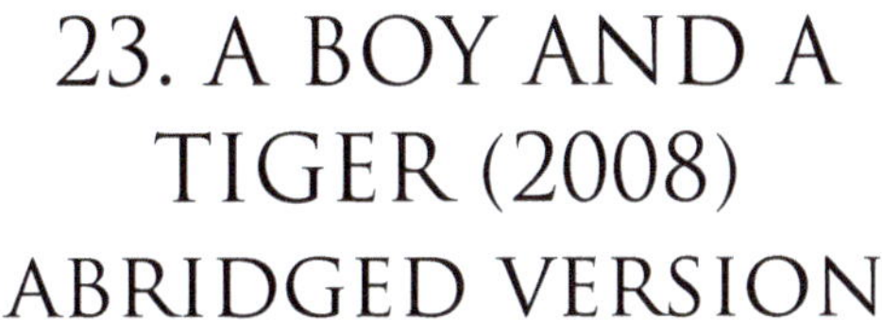

23. A BOY AND A TIGER (2008) ABRIDGED VERSION

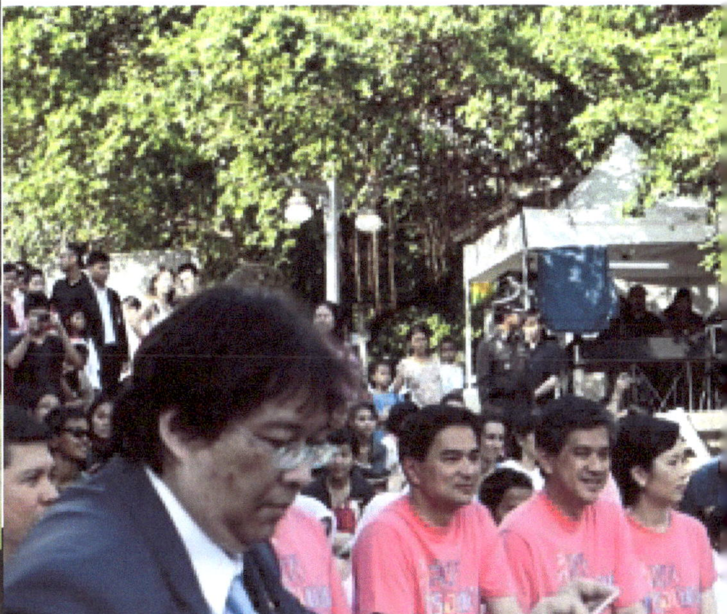

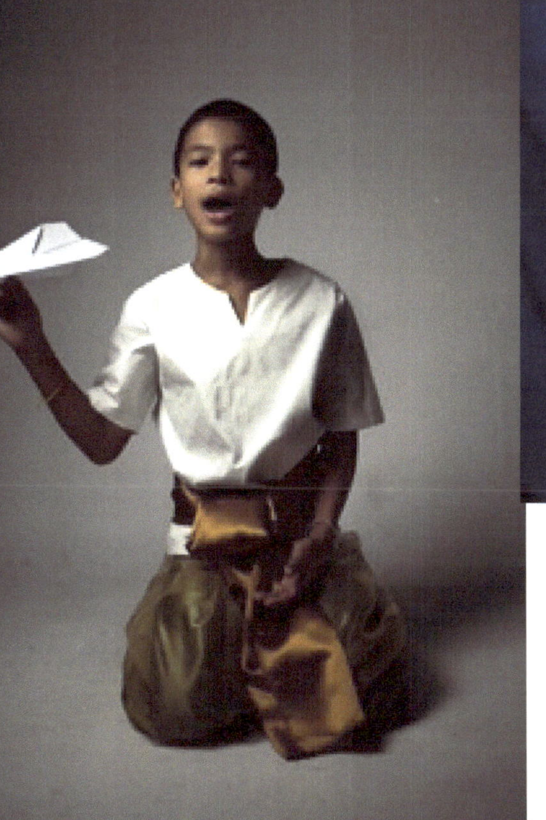

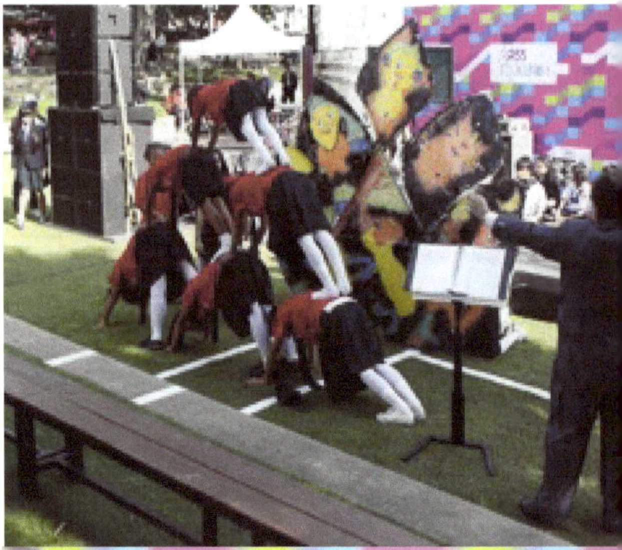

Bruce Gaston's opera performed by children and inspired by the bestselling novel *The Life of Pi*. Gaston worked with the children of Baan Gerda for many years. In the opera the tiger becomes a metaphor for the AIDS virus. Several abridged versions were performed with Somtow Sucharitkul conducting a group of very young musicians. The abridged version was performed in Lumphini Park for an audience that included then prime minister Abhisit.

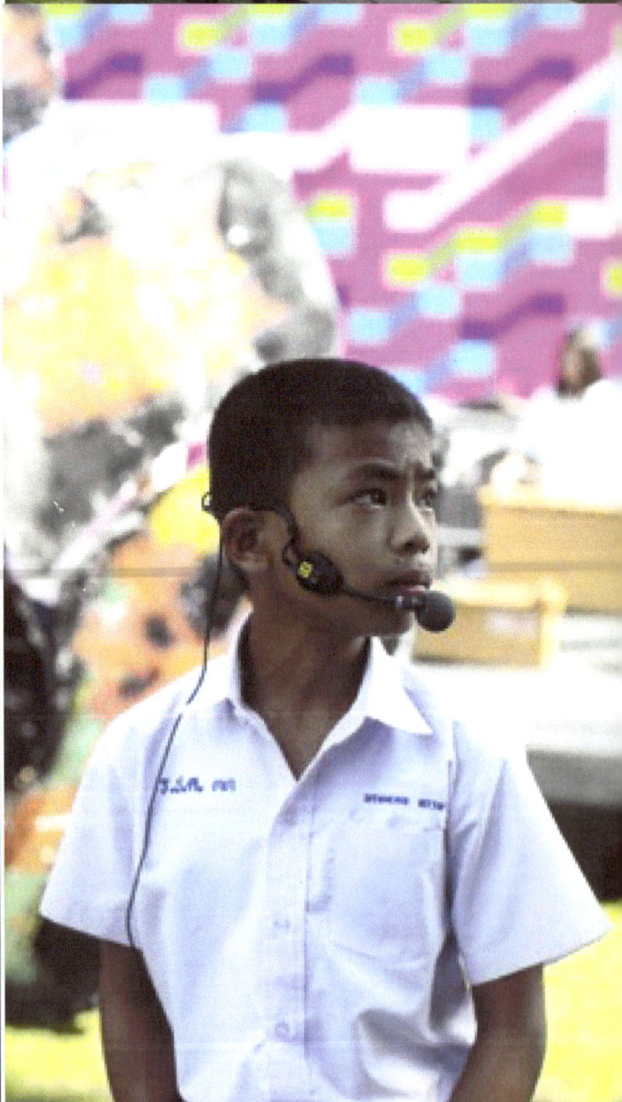

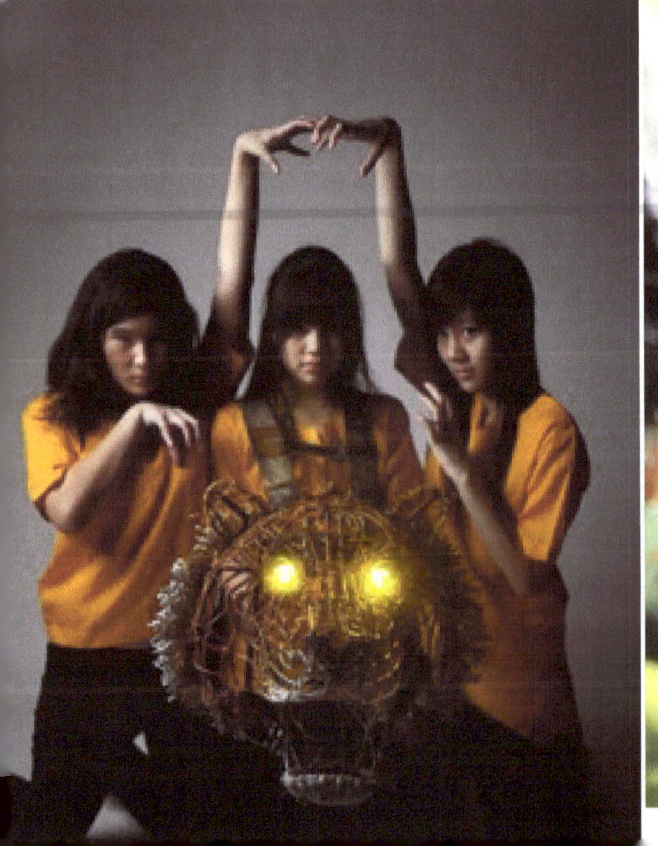

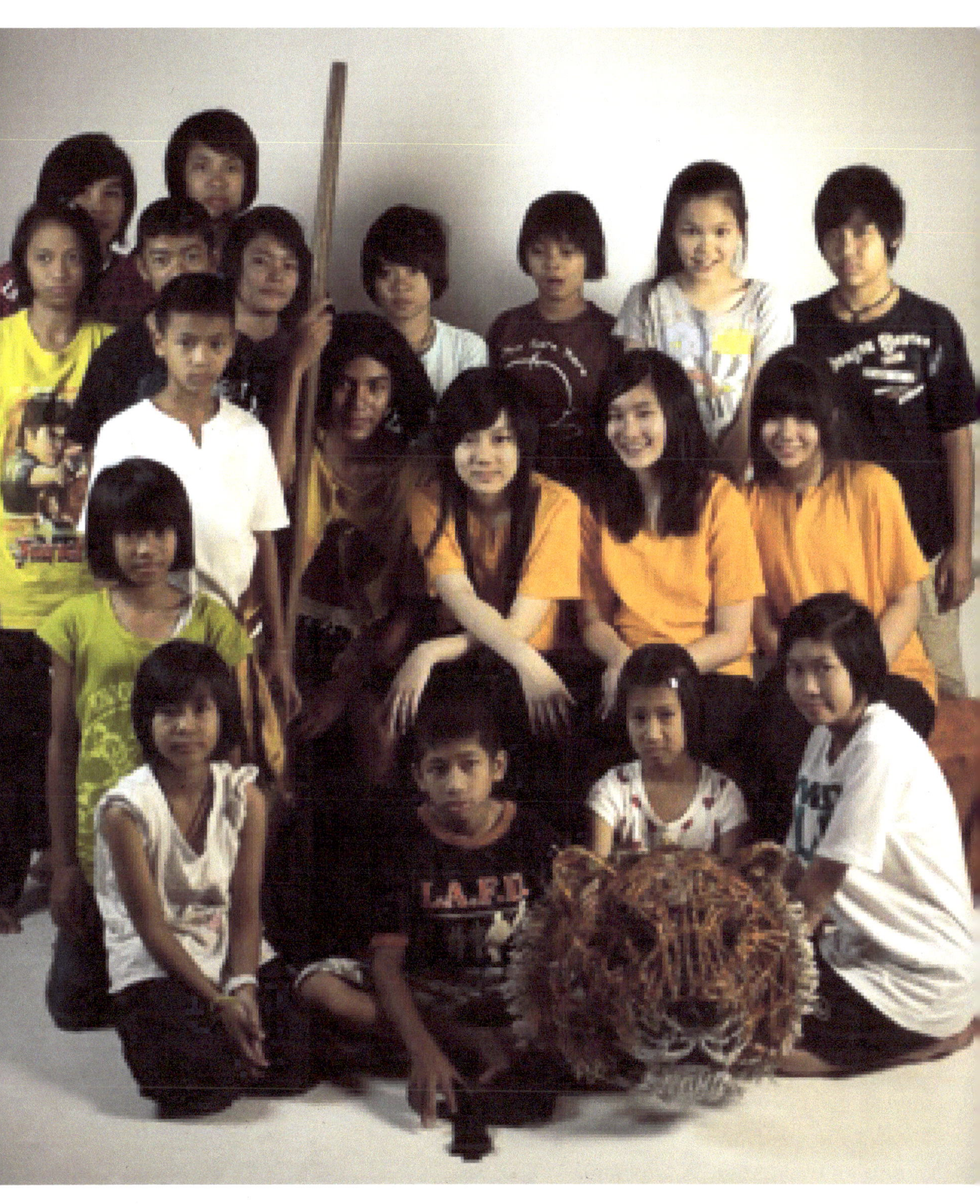
L.A.F.D.

24. CARMEN (2009)
FIRST PERFORMANCE BY A LOCAL COMPANY

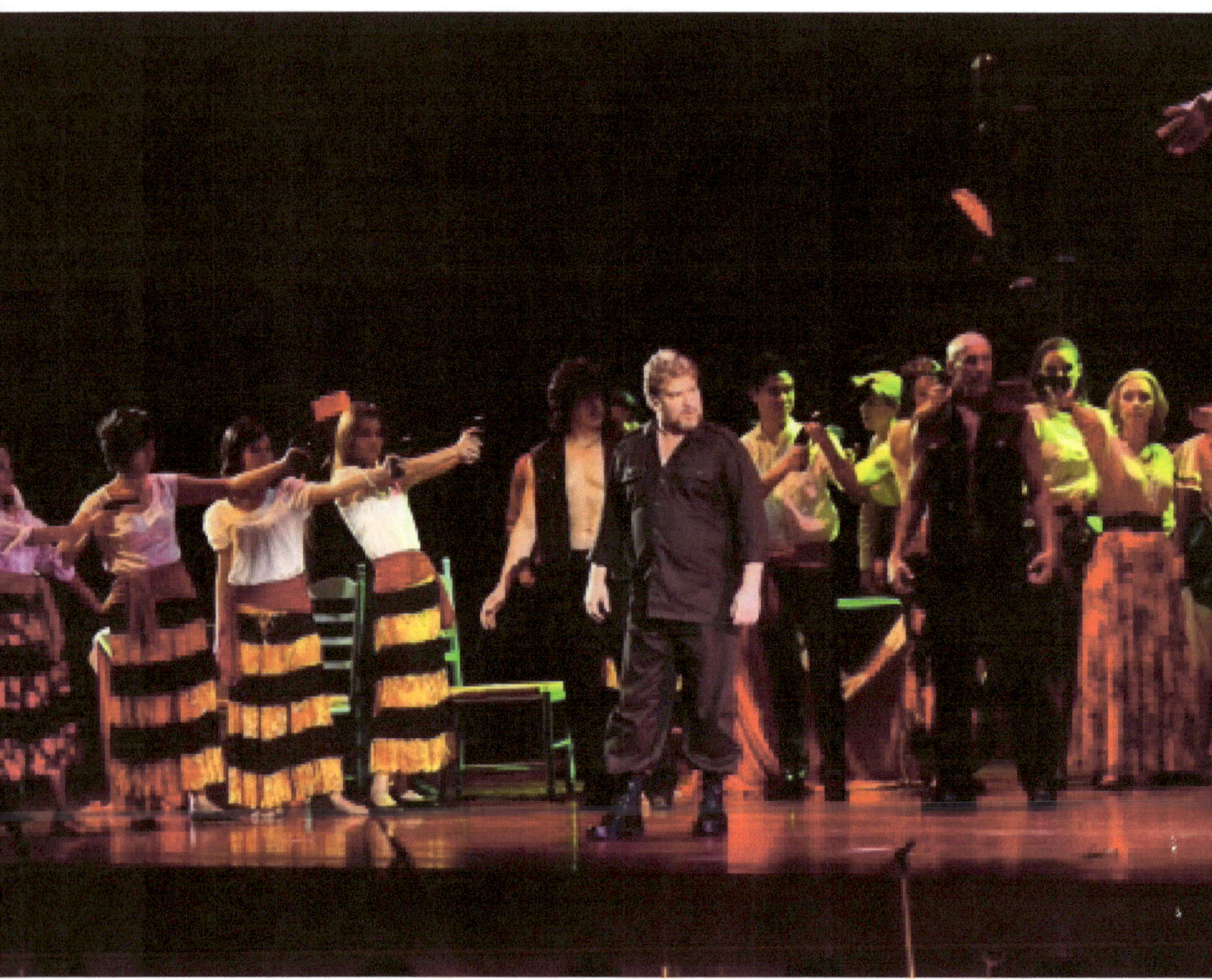

Darren Royston's fabulous production of *Carmen* was set in Mexico instead of the traditional Spanish setting, allowing for even more exoticism. Grauce Echauri who is Mexican herself performed with panache and great sensuality

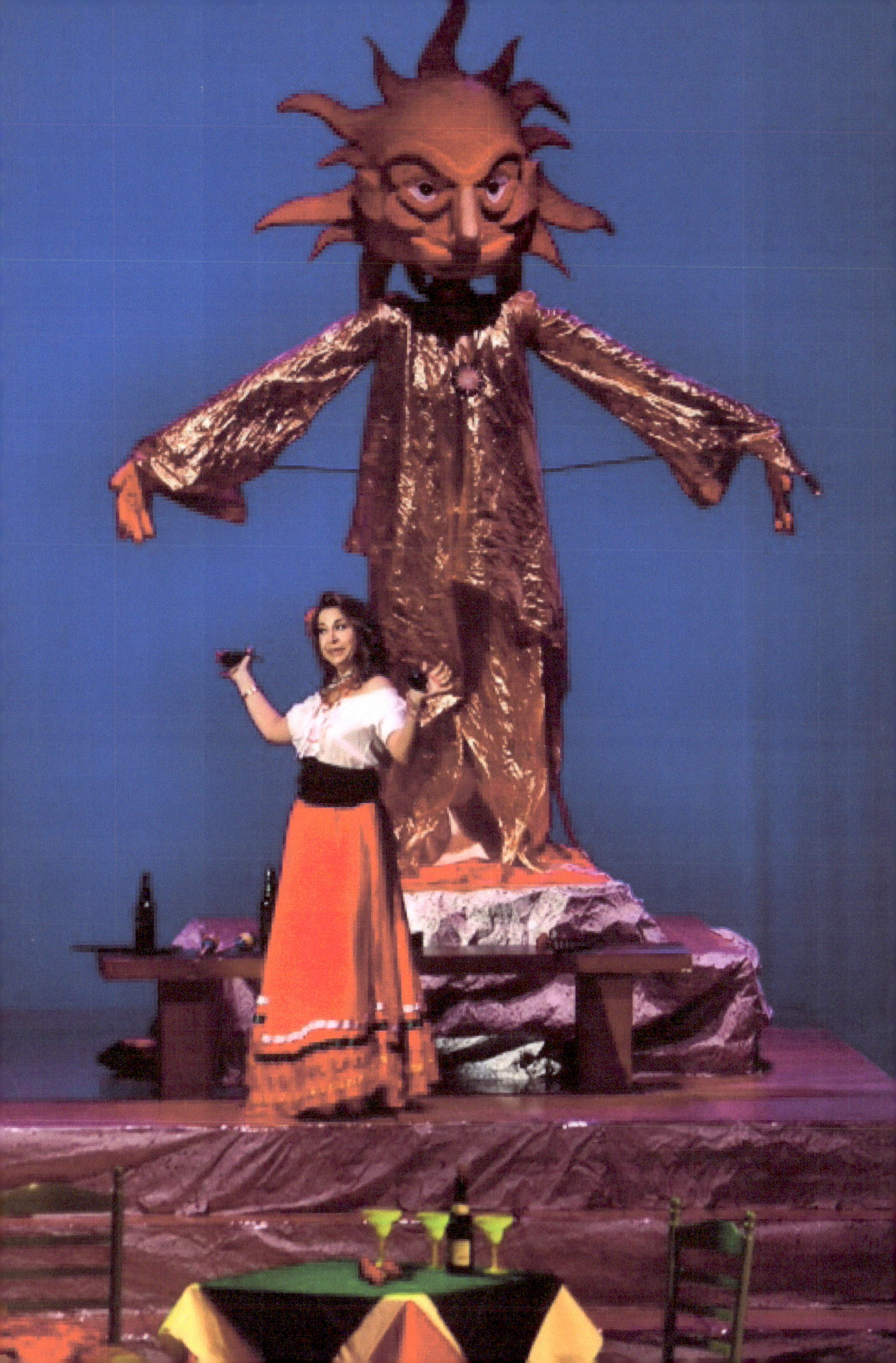

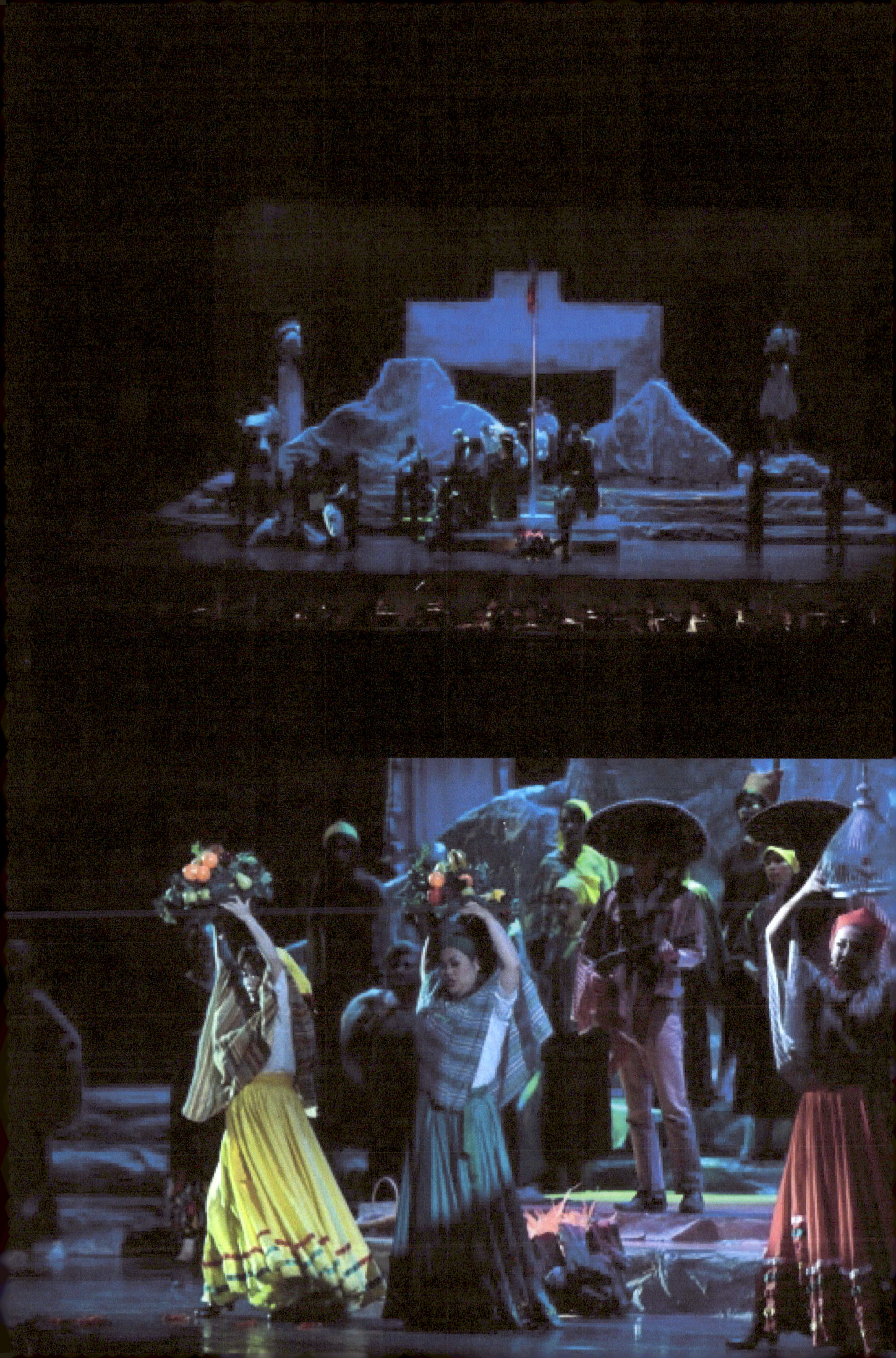

— Main Cast: Grace Eachuri, Stefan Sanchez, Todd Geer, Nancy Yuen, Barbara Zion, Saran Senavinin
— directed by Darren Royston
— Siam Philharmonic Orchestra conducted by Somtow Sucharitkul

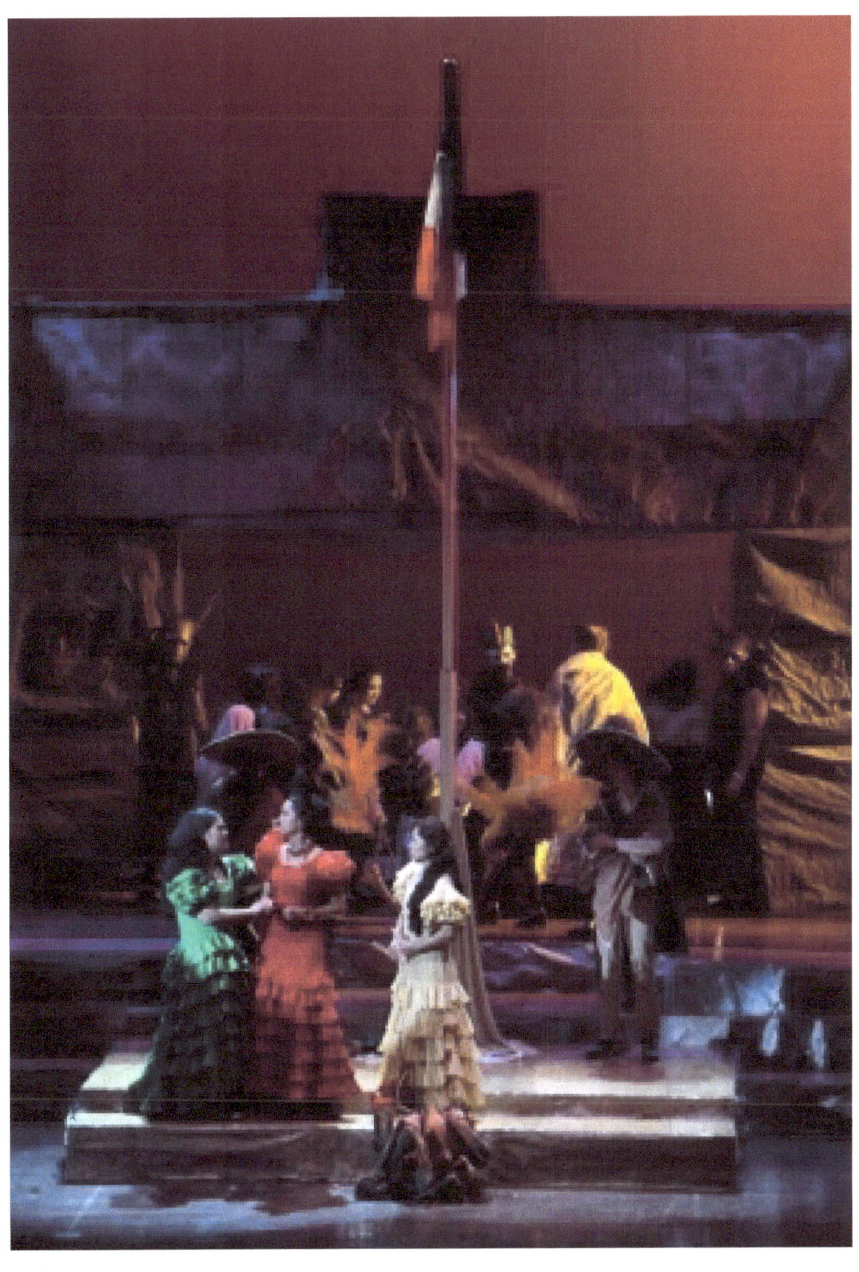

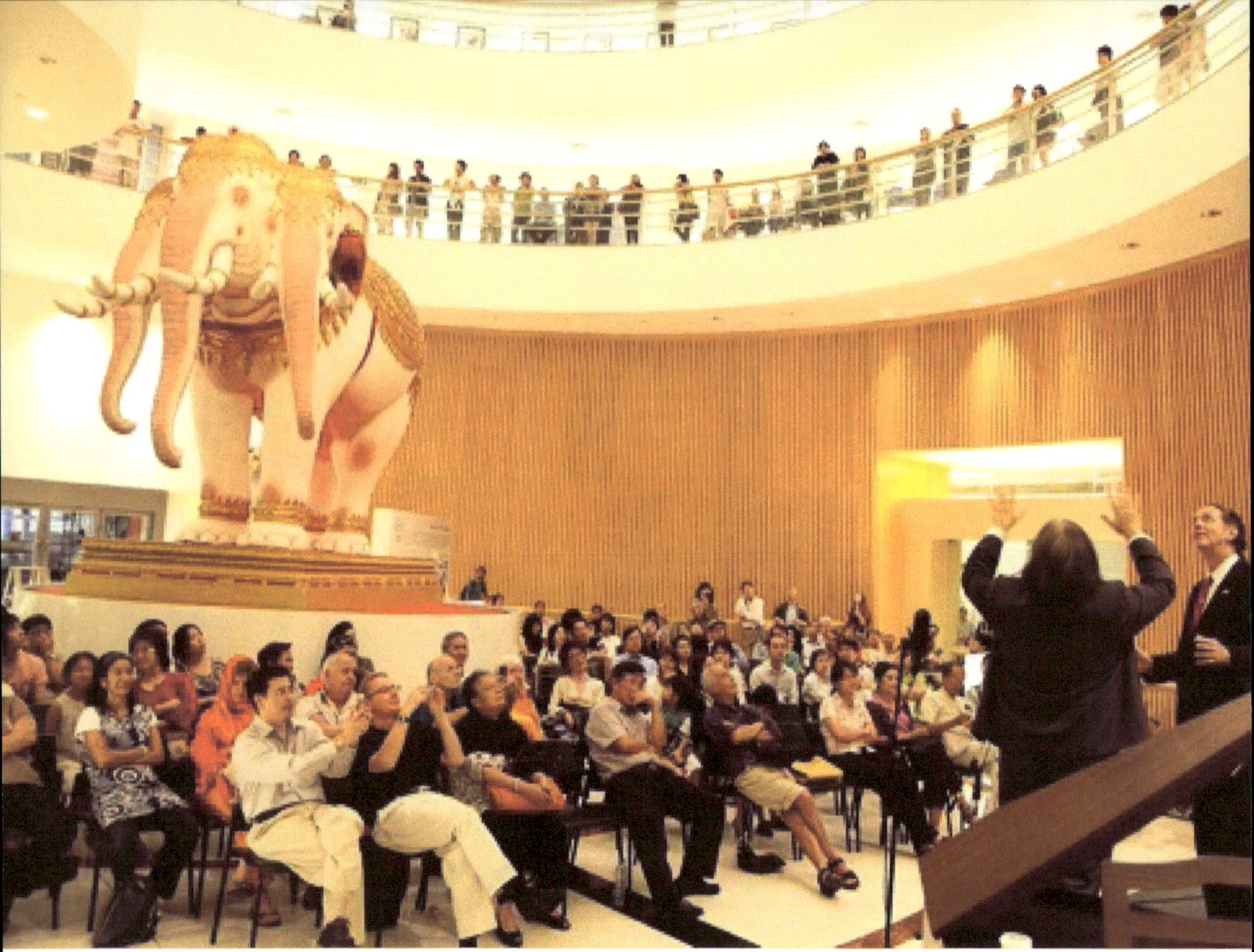

25. AVATAR DVADAS: THE ALIEN OPERA

IMPROVISED OPERA

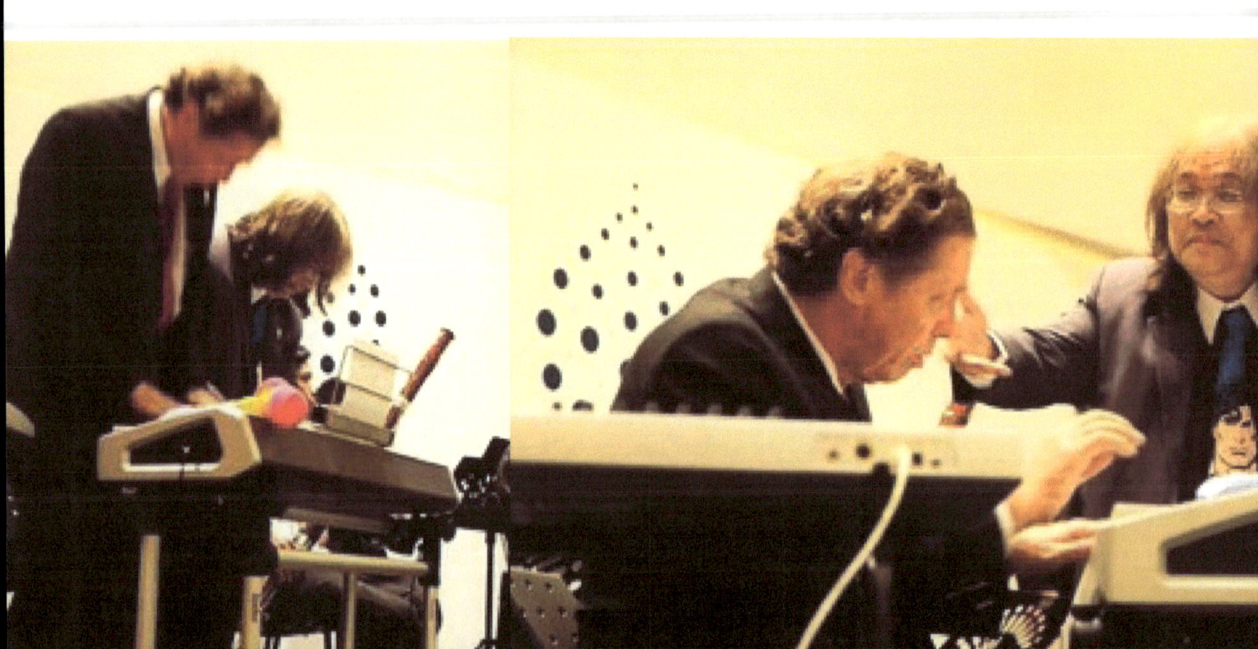

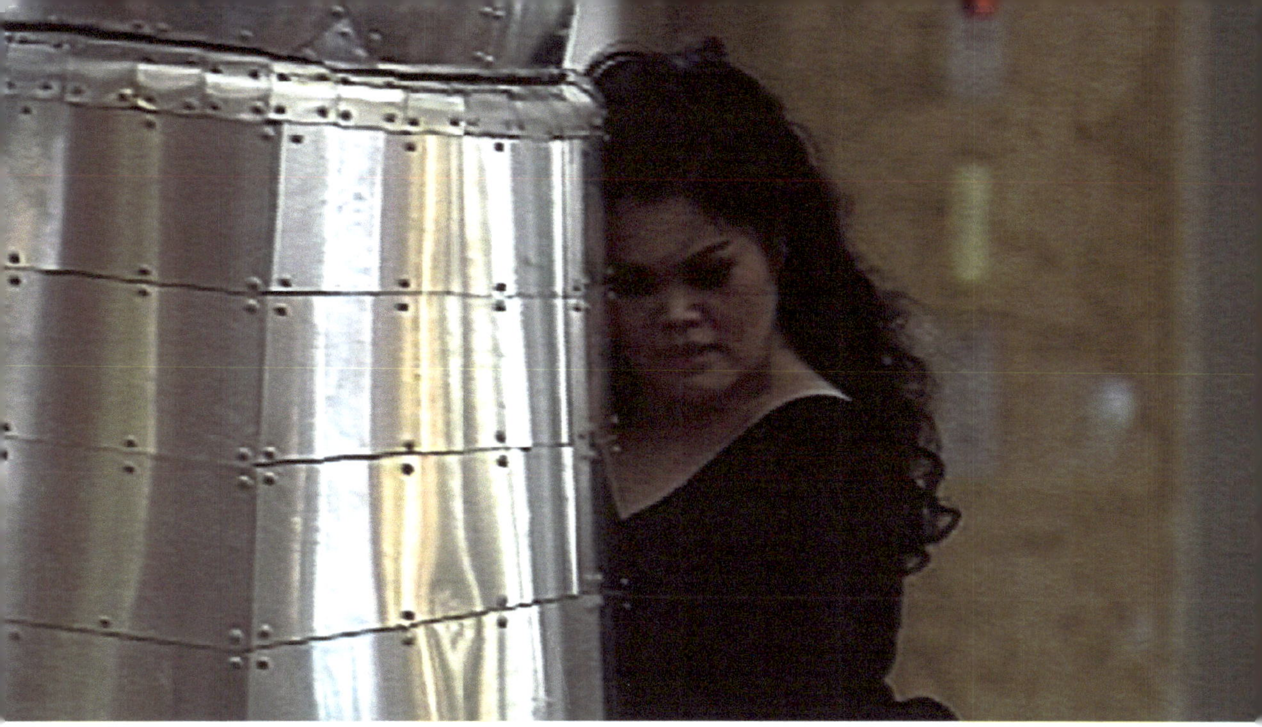

Bruce Gaston's ensemble Fong Naam worked with Opera Siam to create a multi-part "meta-symphony" which produced a total of seven installments. The third istallment was "an alien opera" which was improvised by performance artist Barbara Zion while an orchestra of Thai and western instruments improvised. A gigantic robot, one of the exhibits in the museum, provided an unintended duet partner in the opera.

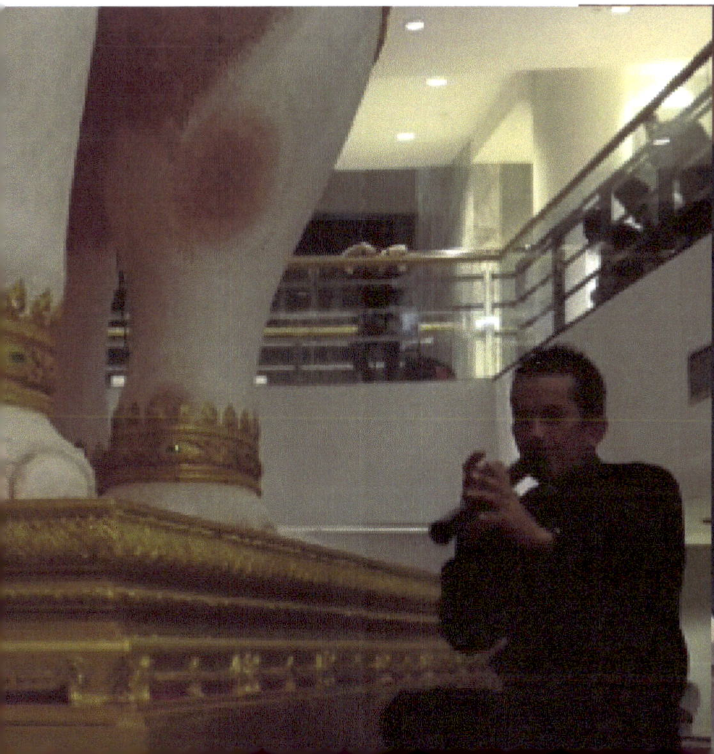

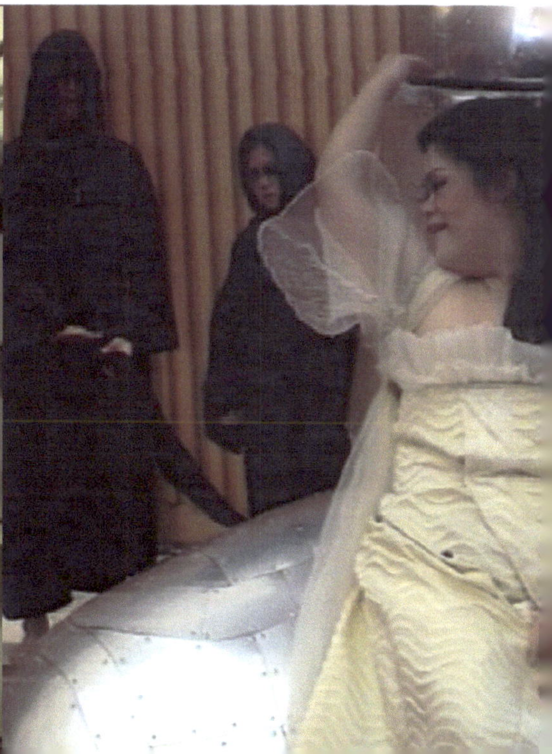

26. LA BOHÈME (2010)
FULL VERSION

Opera Siam's third full production of a Puccini opera was *La Bohème,* one of the world's most popular pieces. This production by Darren Royston added dance to many scenes. The setting was the traditional Left Bank of Paris setting. The amazing pairing of Nancy Yuen with Israel Lozano turned out to be long-lasting; since then they have bee collaborating for more than ten years and have become a perfectly matched duo. At the time, this *Bohème* was felt to be Opera Siam's best production ever.

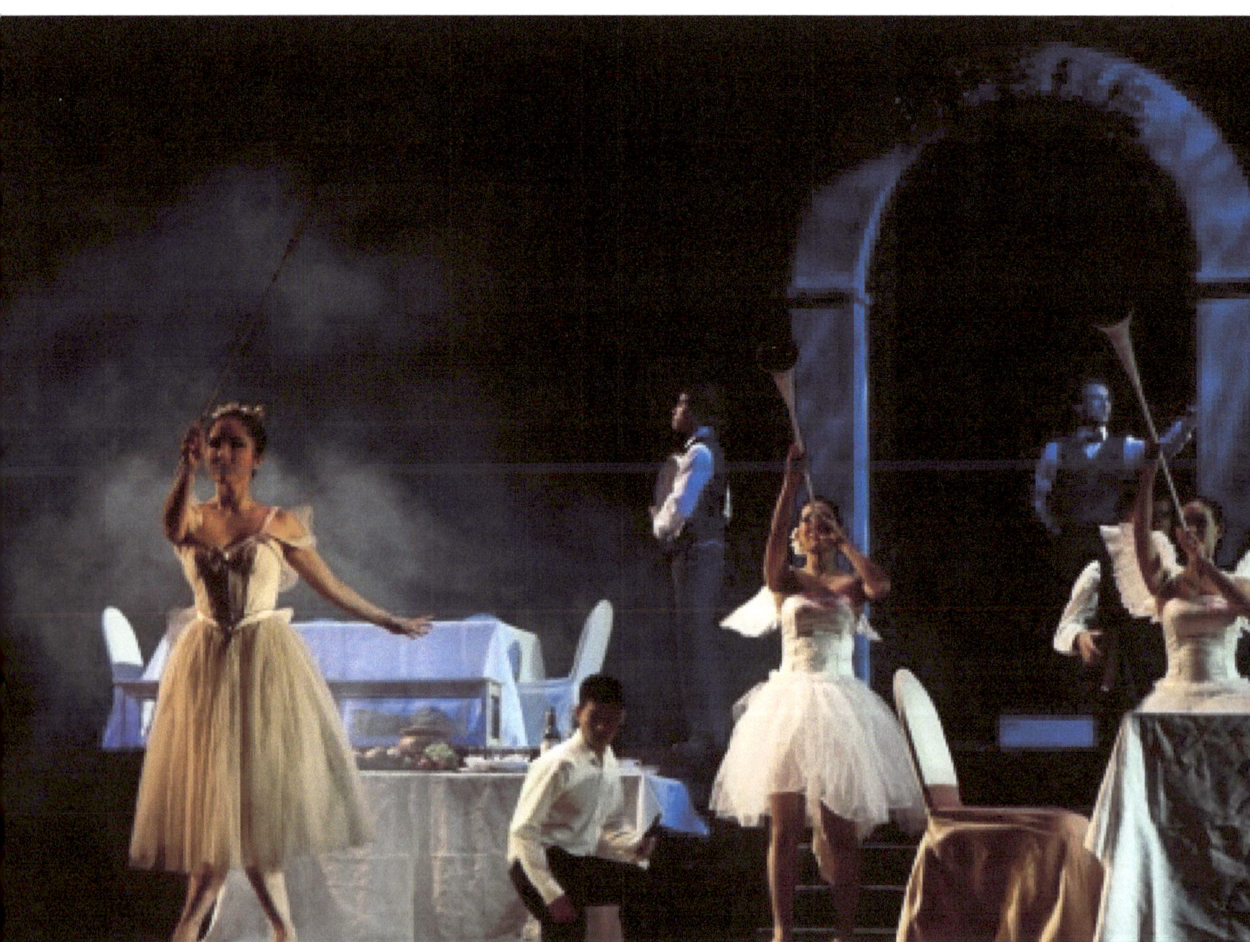

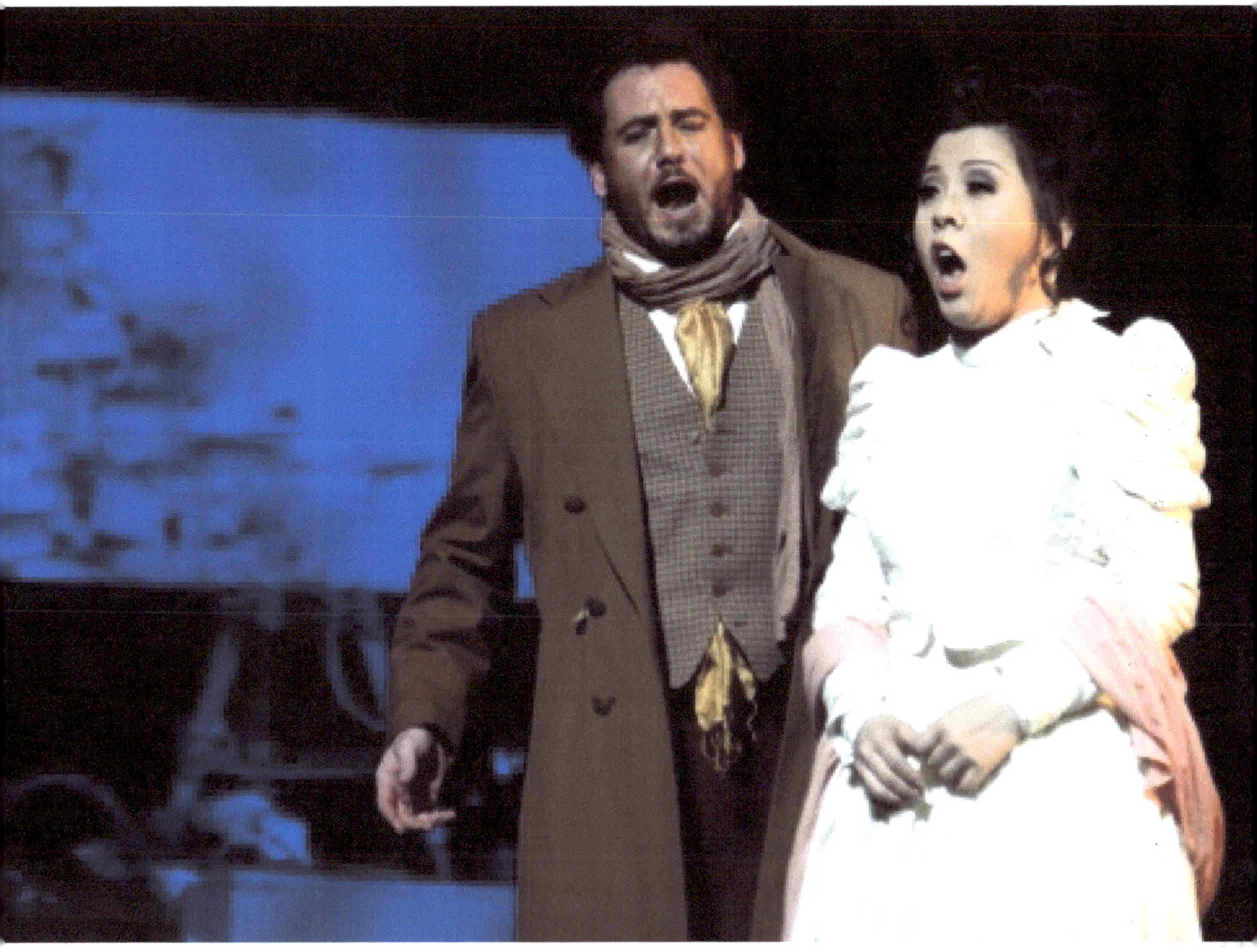

— Main Cast: Nancy Yuen, Israel Lozano, Stefan Sanchez, Barbara Zion — directed by Darren Royston — Siam Philharmonic Orchestra, conducted by Somtow Sucharitkul

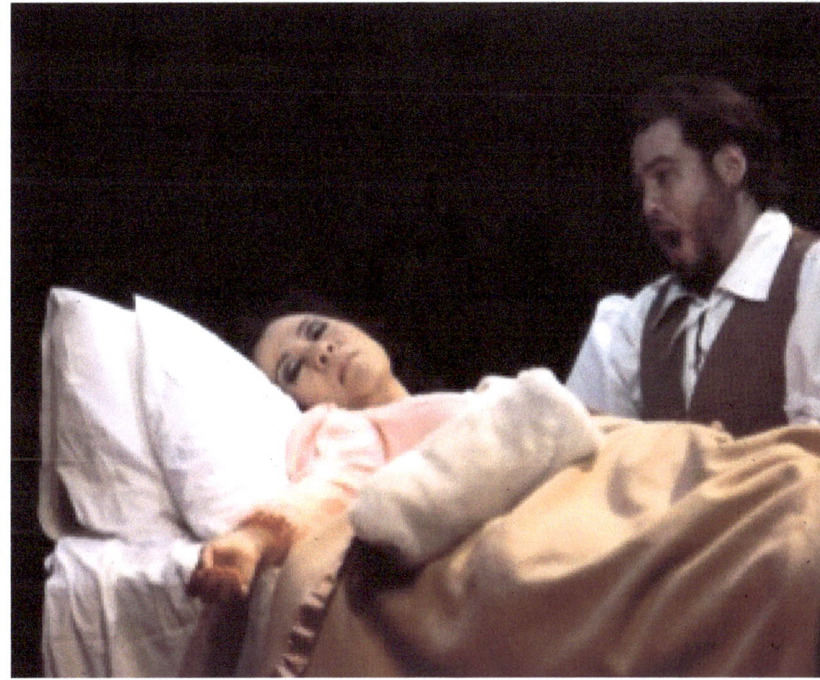

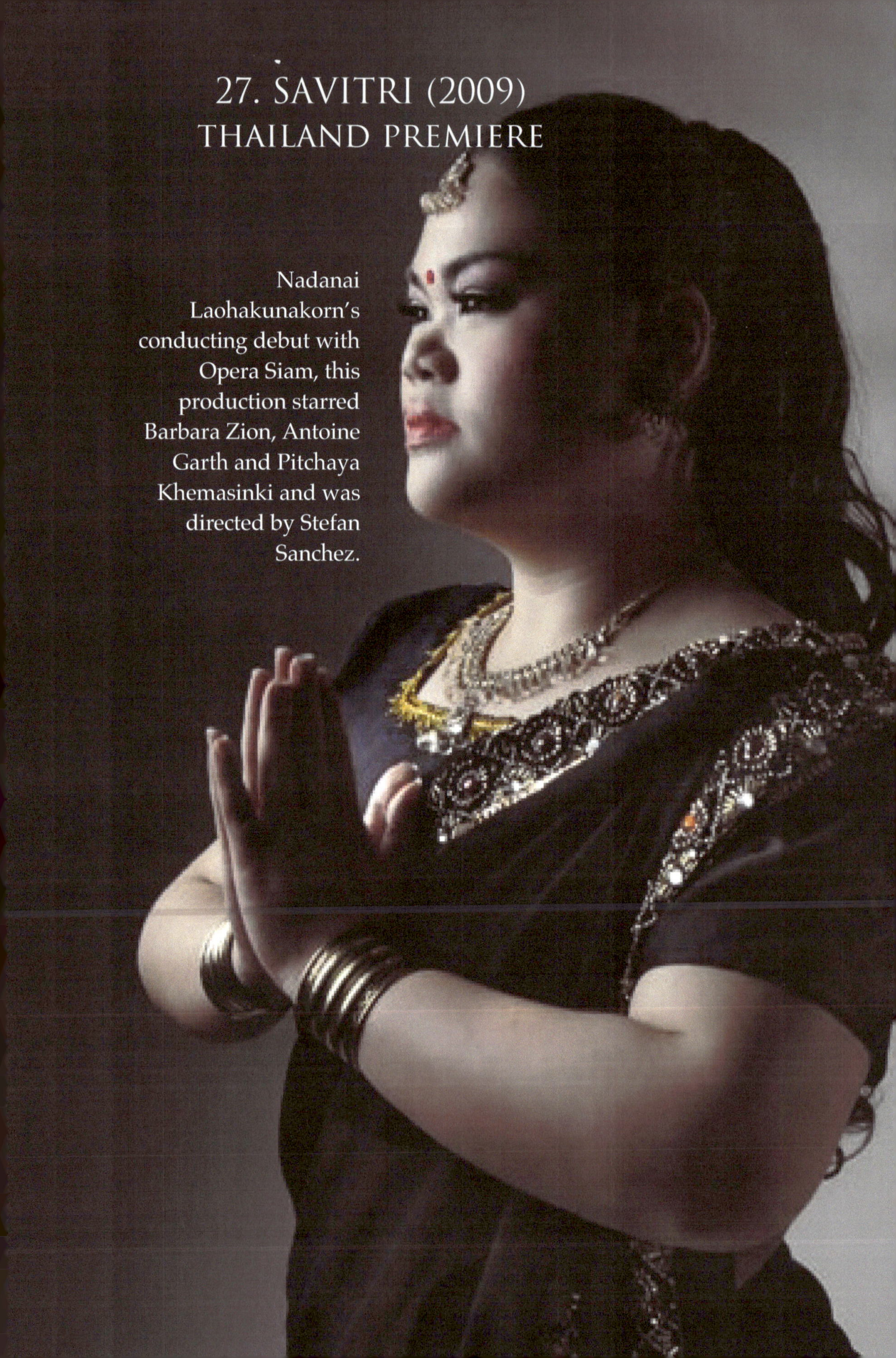

27. SAVITRI (2009)
THAILAND PREMIERE

Nadanai Laohakunakorn's conducting debut with Opera Siam, this production starred Barbara Zion, Antoine Garth and Pitchaya Khemasinki and was directed by Stefan Sanchez.

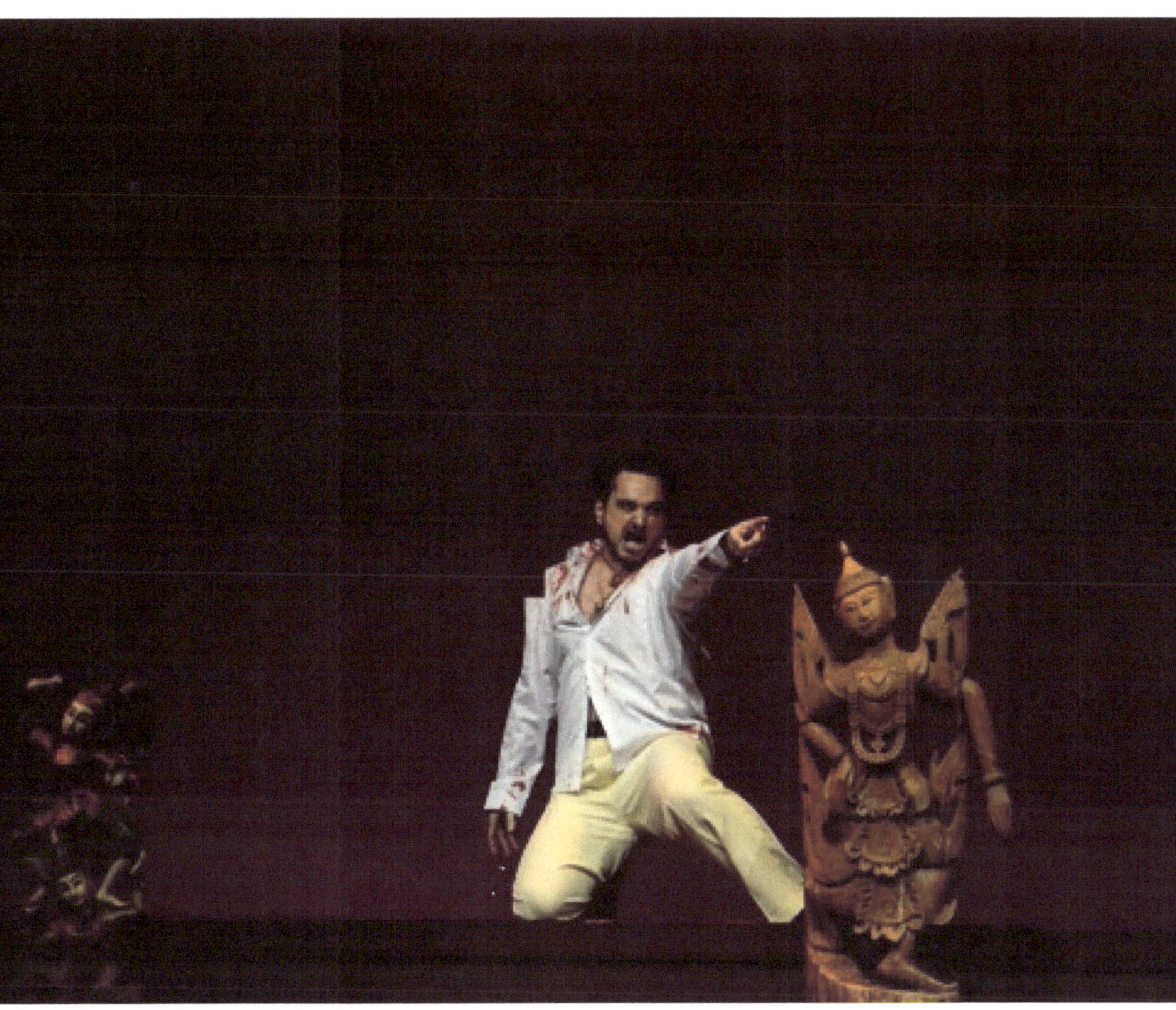

28. TOSCA (2010)

Opera Siam's *Tosva* began with the union of two contrasting concepts: Somtow Sucharitkul had long wanted to create a *Tosca* set during the French occupation of Indochina, which would have all sorts of meaningful resonances; Stefan Sanchez on the other hand already had directed *Tosca* and had a concept in his mind already, one based on the Spanish Civil War.

The twain did meet, in a manner of speaking and this production which garnered standing ovations was the result.

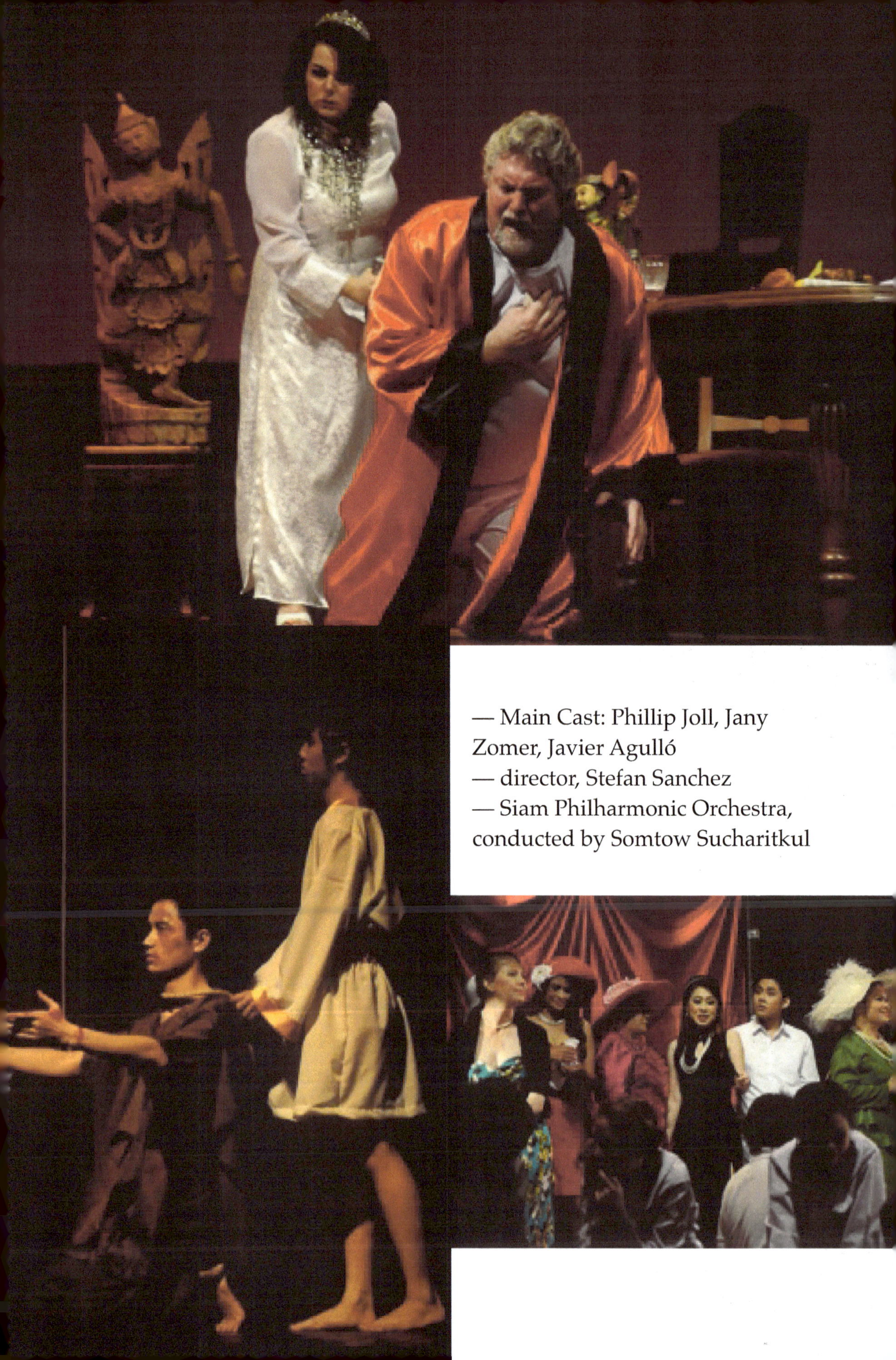

— Main Cast: Phillip Joll, Jany Zomer, Javier Agulló
— director, Stefan Sanchez
— Siam Philharmonic Orchestra, conducted by Somtow Sucharitkul

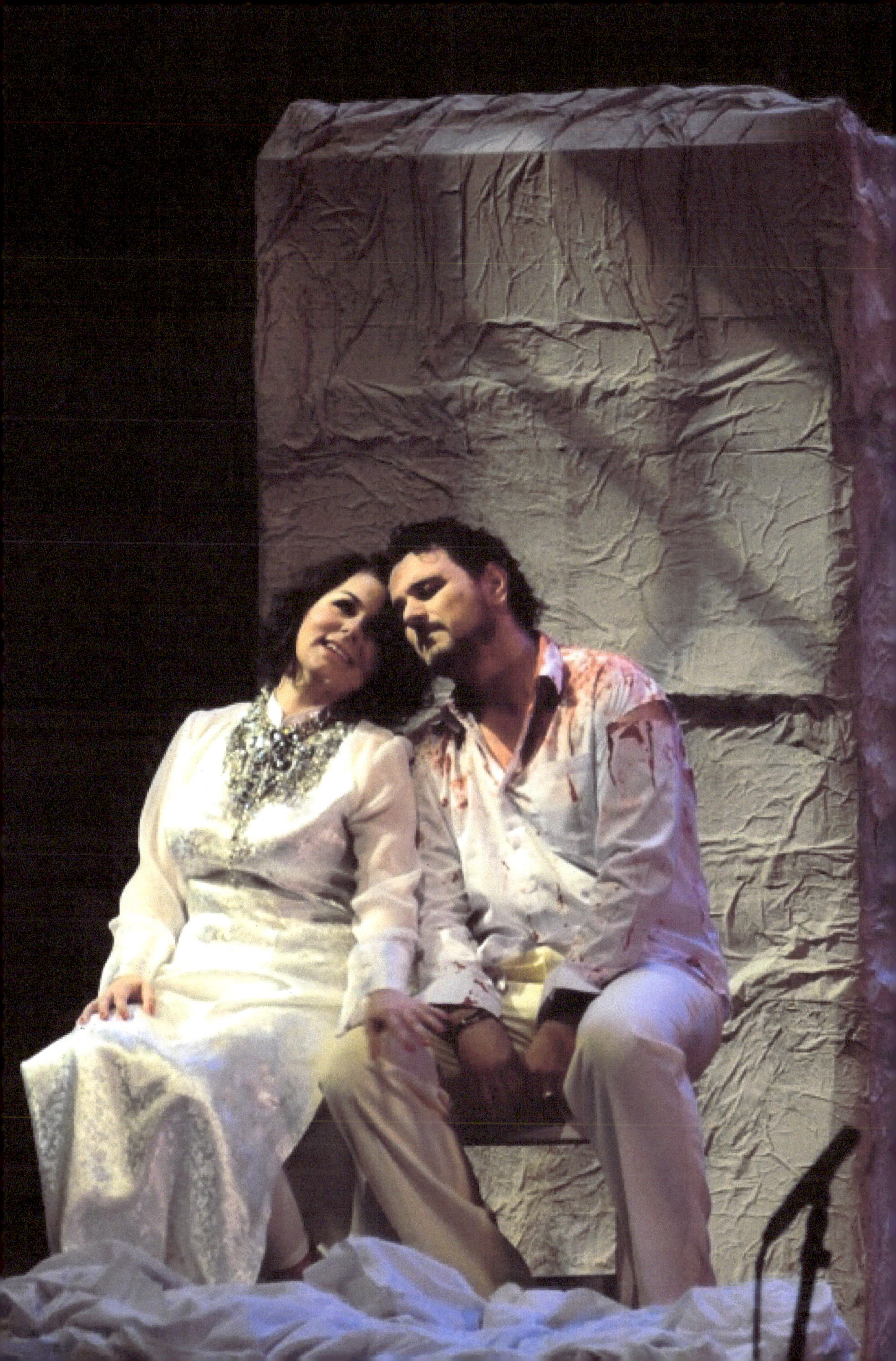

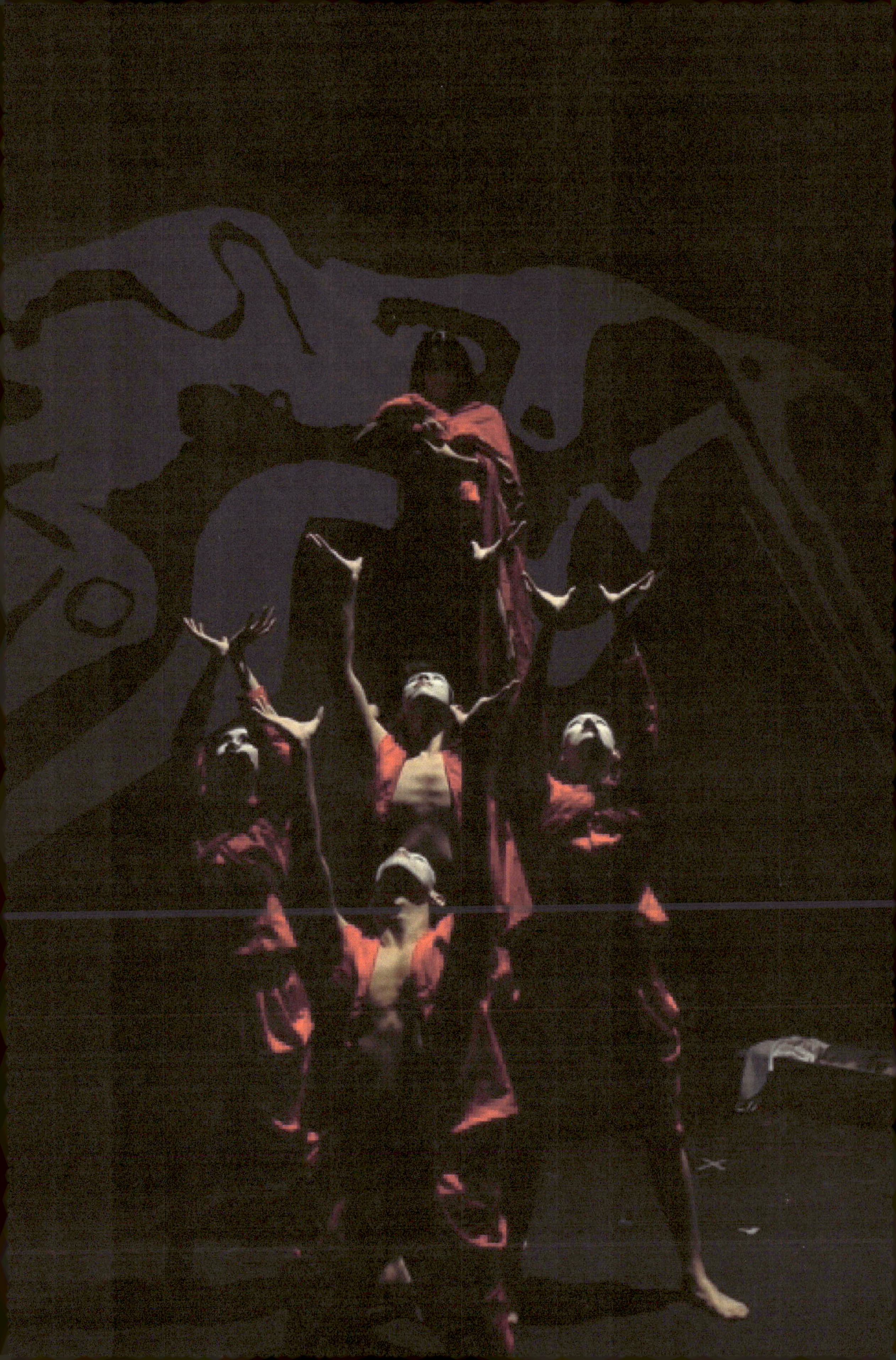

29. MAE NAAK (2010)
SECOND REVIVAL

Somtow Sucharitkul's most popular opera has always been *Mae Naak* and this production was revived in order to prepare for taking the opera to Britain. The revival director was Stefan Sanchez. The production was conducted by Trisdee na Patalung.

The production was downsized to fit into the Chalermkrung Theater. Most of the artists were the same as in the 2005 production directed by Henry Akina, but this version was more faithful to the colour schemes created by the original designer, Sumet Jumsai.

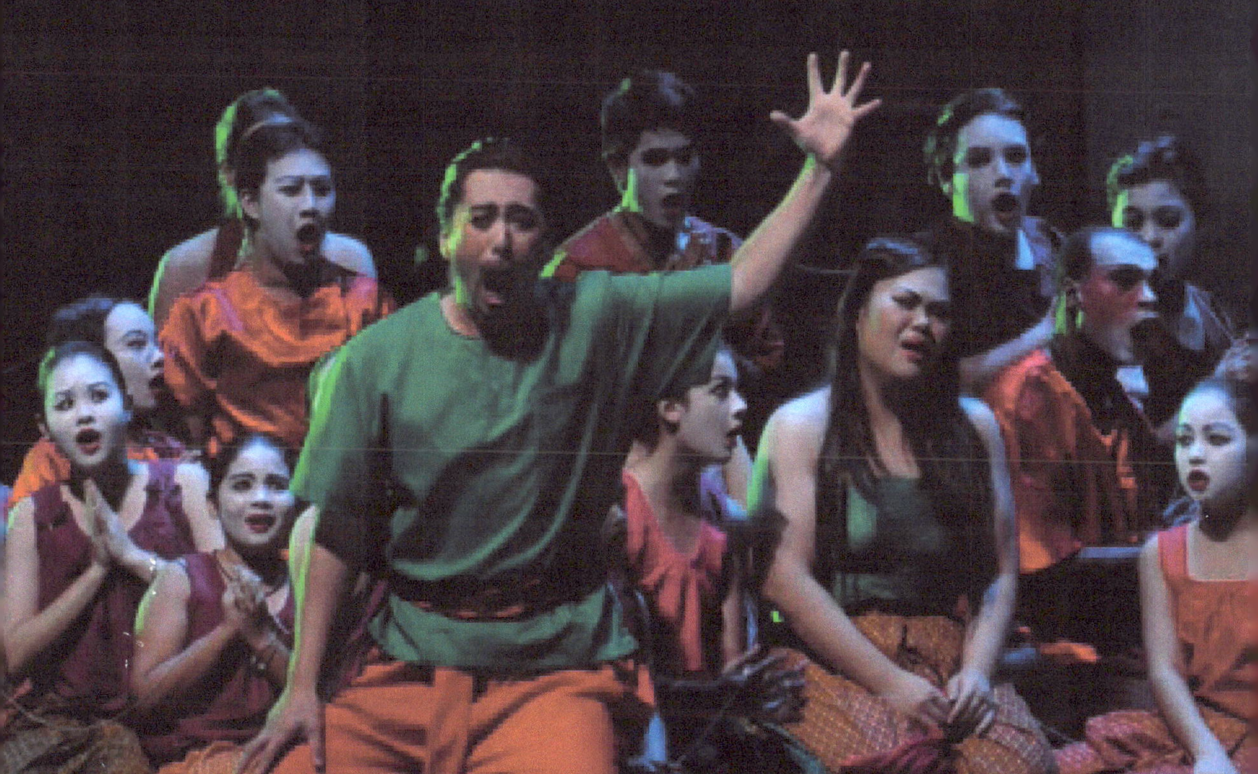

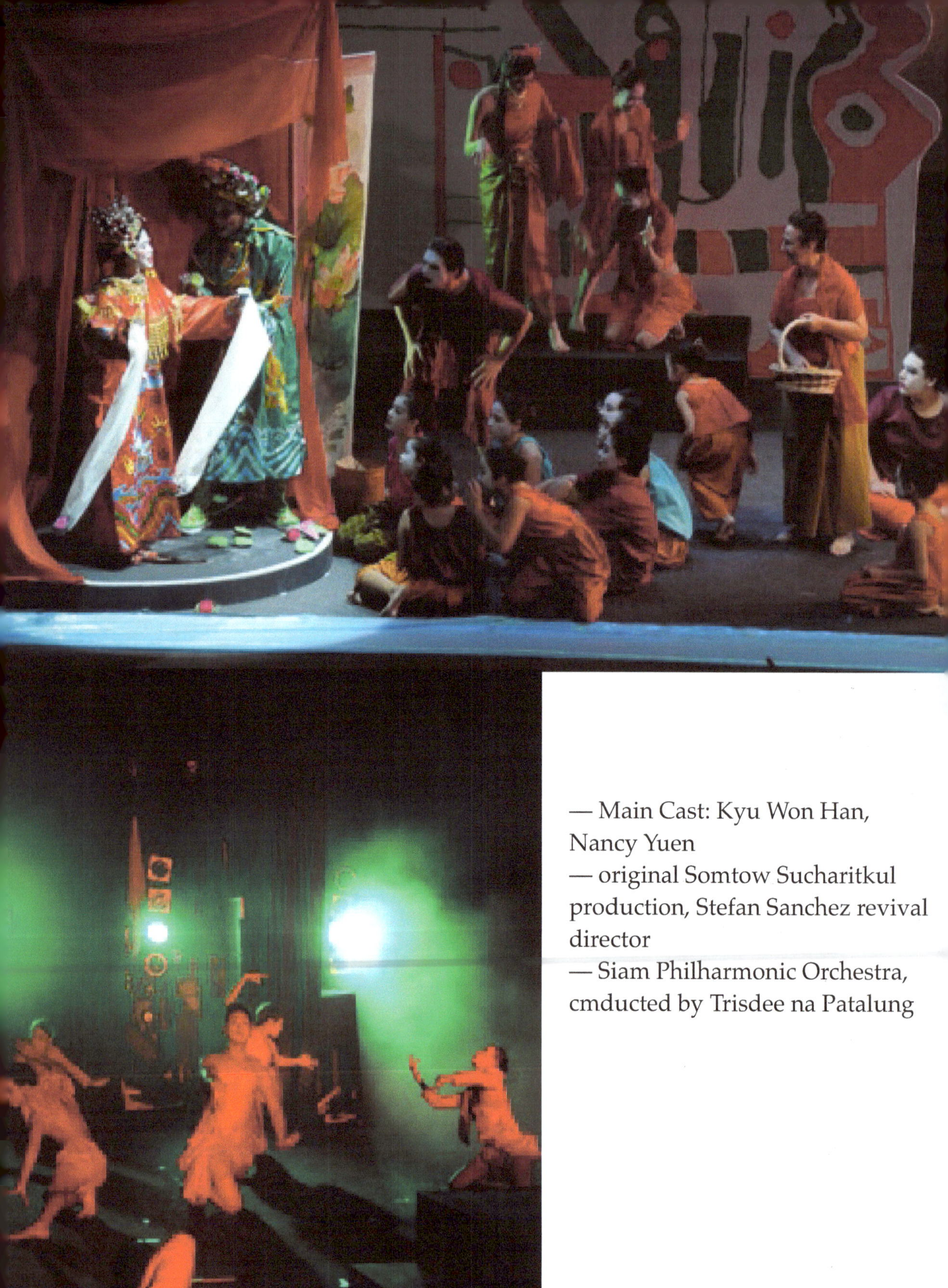

— Main Cast: Kyu Won Han, Nancy Yuen
— original Somtow Sucharitkul production, Stefan Sanchez revival director
— Siam Philharmonic Orchestra, cmducted by Trisdee na Patalung

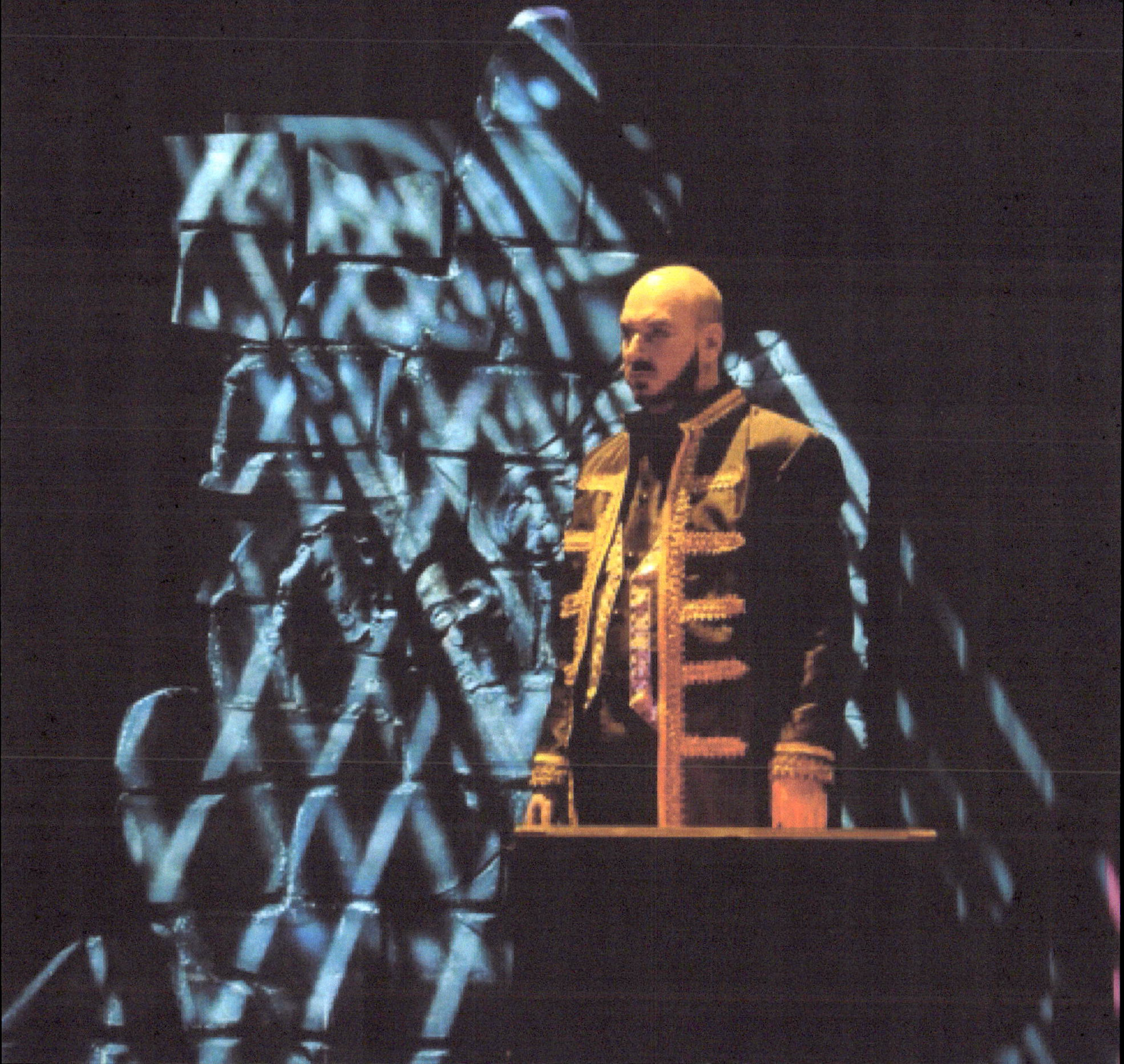

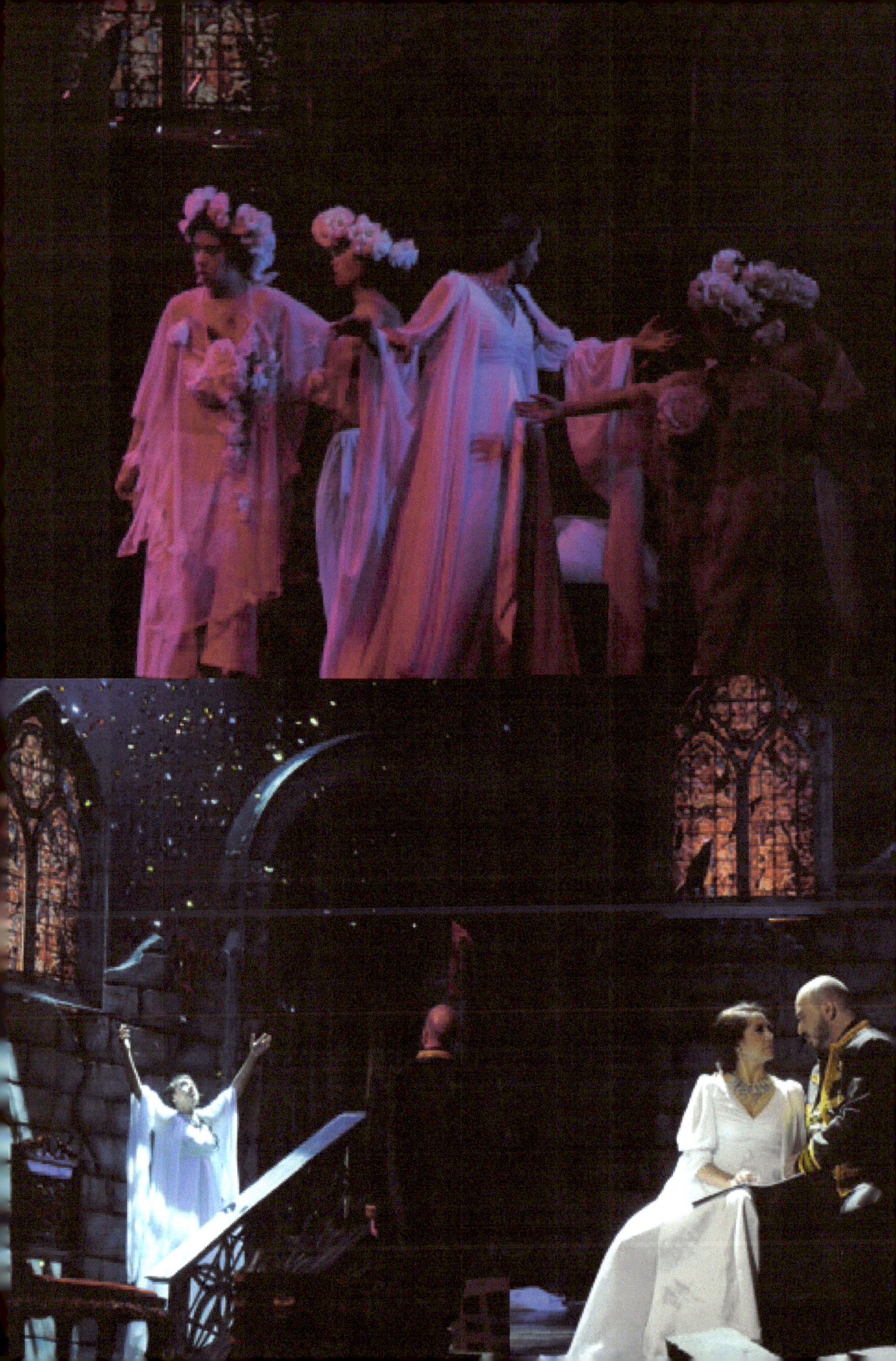

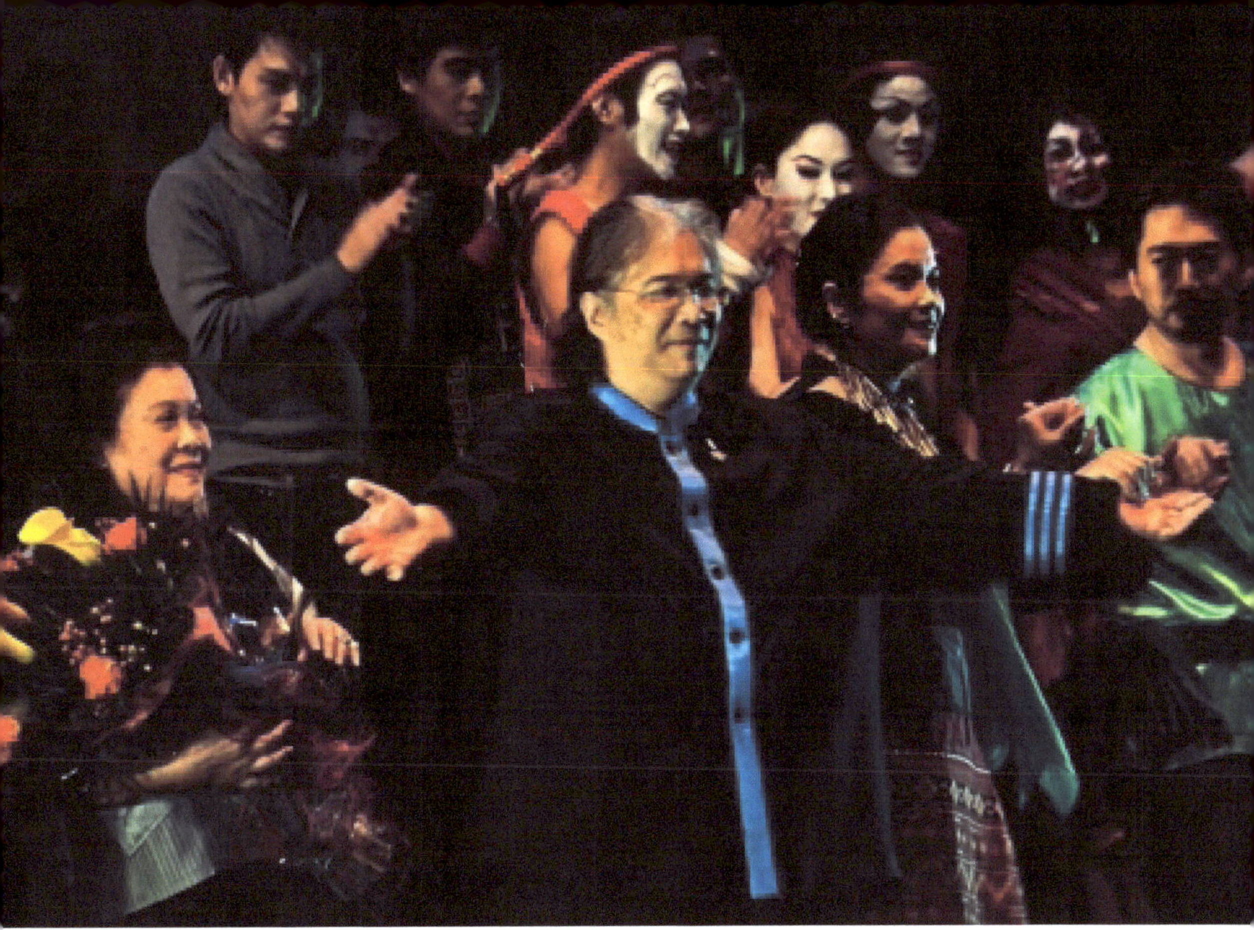

31. MAE NAAK (2011)
EUROPEAN PREMIERE - LONDON

Somtow Sucharitkul became the first Thai to have an opera premiered in Europe when Opera Siam took the production of *Mae Naak* to the Bloomsbury Theatre in London.

The production was fraught with drama. A week before departure, we were still trying to raise money so that some chorus members could travel to London. The set didn't fit on the plane. One of the cast members got stalled at immigration in Britain. Many things, such as the accommodation scouted by the British partners, came as a shock to the musicians.

And yet, miraculously, it came together.

In fact, every seat was sold for the final night.

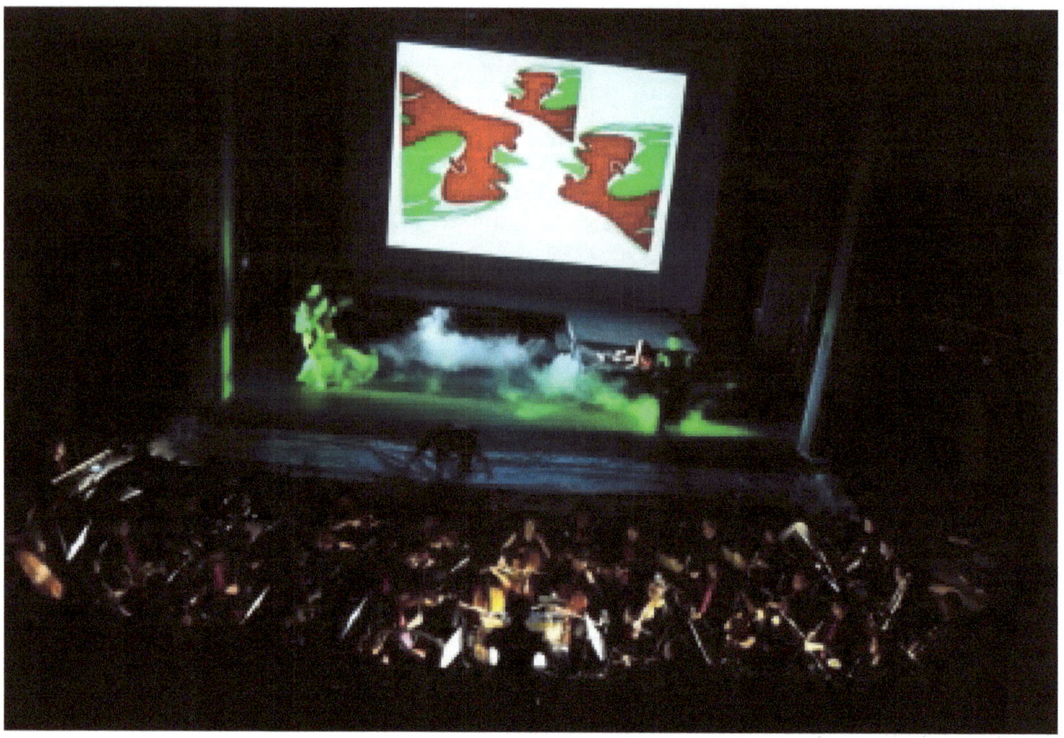

"a stunning work that fuses a European operatic style with Thai folkloric music. It deserves to be shown for far more than a short three-night season I recommend that it return to London again."

— *London Fringe Review*

"Best of all is the committed playing of the mainly young musicians of the Siam Philharmonic Orchestra, and the perfect control obtained by conductor Trisdee na Patalung."

— *The Stage*

— Main Cast: Nancy Yuen, Kyu Won Han, Emma McNairy, Vassilis Kostopoulos, Pimluck Sukswasti, Barbara Zion, Grace Echauri

— directed by Stefan Sanchez

— Siam Philharmonic Orchestra, conducted by Somtow Sucharitkul

32. REYA - THE MUSICA
WORLD PREMIERE

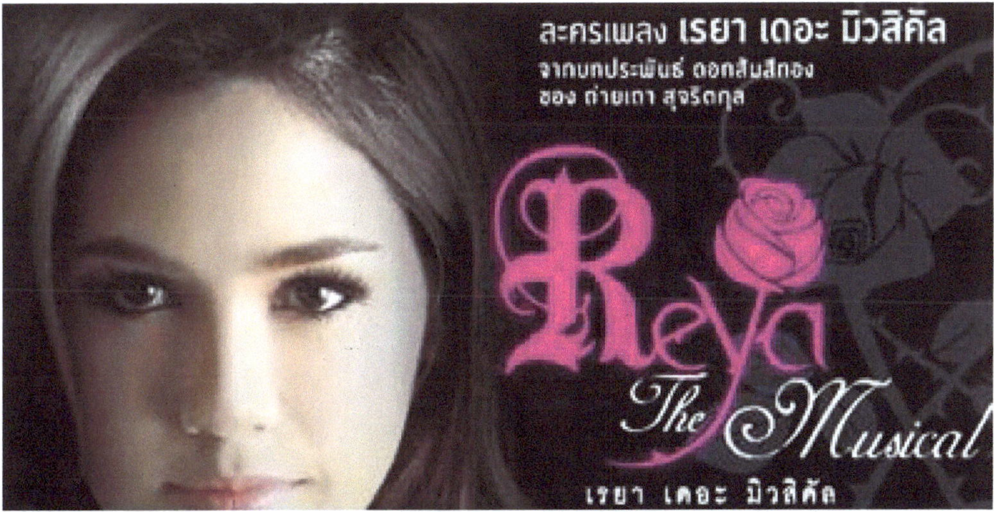

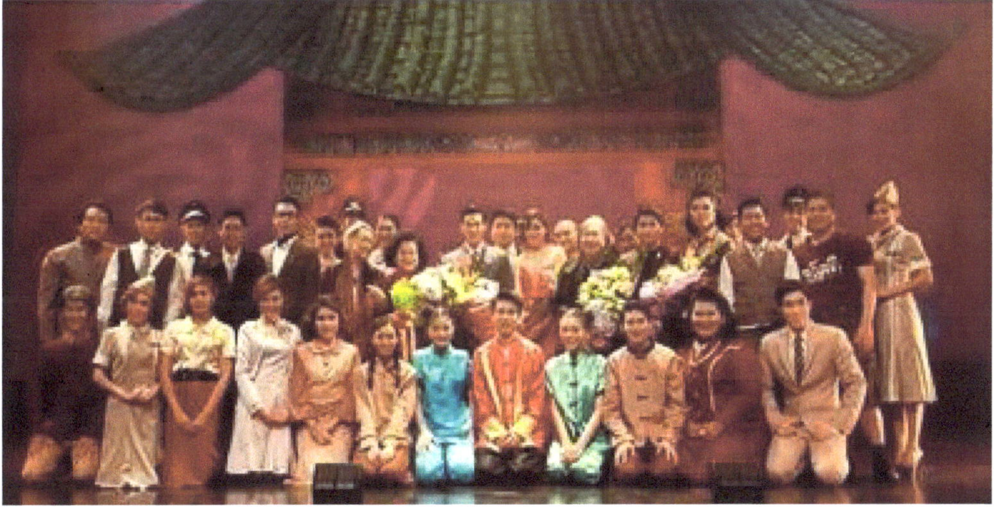

After the huge drama of the British tour, Opera Siam coproduced the musical *Reya,* based on Thaithow Sucharitkul's best-selling novel, with *The Nation.* The musical played for around twenty performances and was voted one of the top ten all-time Thai musicals.

33. THE SILENT PRINCE (2012)
THAILAND PREMIERE

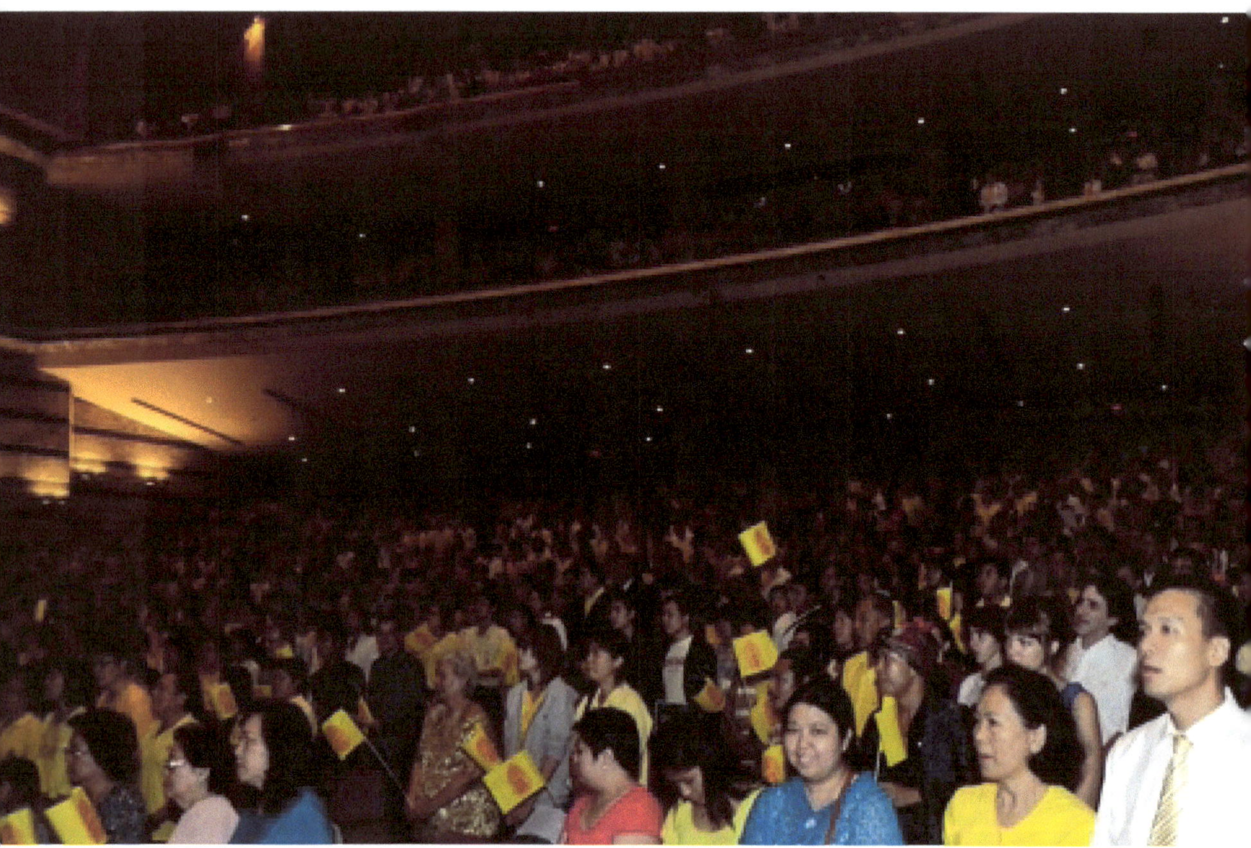

The Thailand premiere of *The Silent Prince,* which was the first Buddhist opera and which had two years earlier premiered to a completely full house in Houston under the baton of Viswa Subbaraman, was the first instance of a completely full house for an opera in Thailand. The production celebrated the birthday of H.M. King Rama IX, and the audience helped to celebrate by participating in one of the first "mass singalongs" of the Royal Anthem, which because a major feature of Opera Siam's performances.

At the time of this premiere, the idea of *DasJati* was still very far from the composer's mind. The opera was written as a one-off. The nine sequels were not in anyone's concept until considerably later.

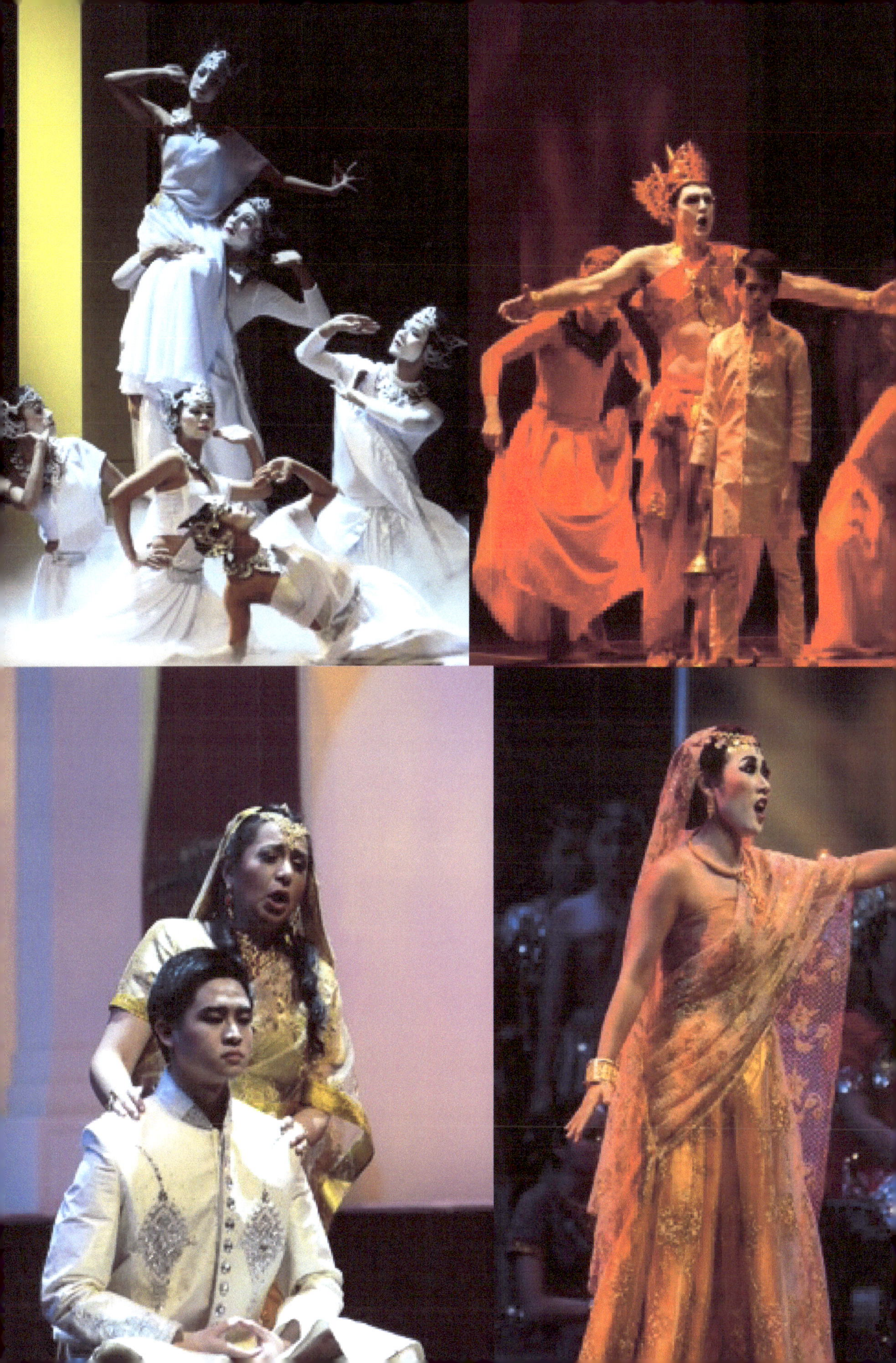

"Somtow Sucharitkul's sumptuous and marvellously lyrical score is enchanting,with the use of traditional Indian instruments in the orchestra - tamburas, celeste and harmonium. The show is moving and intriguing and always retains a deep sense of mystery and spirituality. His rich and beautiful orchestrations are masterful, meaningful and mesmerising."

— *The Houston Chronicle*

"Sucharitkul disperses a misconception that contemporary opera is esoteric and impertinent."

— *Joel Luks on the website CultureMap.*

As a tribute to His Majesty, on the very day the King exhorted his devoted people to follow the dharma and hold harmony in their hearts, Somtow could not have come up with a better endorsement of the triumphant power of the path to love and truth. "The Silent Prince" is an extraordinary achievement for Thailand, and a gift to the world."

— *The Nation*

— Main Cast: Jak Cholvijarn, Nadlada Thamtanakom, Grace Echauri, John Ames, Barbara Zion, Kyu Won Han, Rom Parnichkun

— Siam Philharmonic Orchestrra

— conductor, Trtisdee na Patalung

— director, Somtow Sucharitkul

— designer, Dean Shibuya

— lighting, Ryan Attig

34. OTELLO (2013)
THAILAND PREMIERE

Somtow's production of *Otello,* produced both in the Verdi year and the year commemorating H.M. King Rama VI, had a fascinating take on the story that simultaneously honoured both those figures.

Somtow stated that the story is really about an "honor killing" and that during the Srivijaya period of Southeast Asian history, when a major Buddhist kingdom existed but there were already merchants from the Islamic world. Conditions in the Mediterranean of the Renaissance were echoed perfectly in the islands of Southeast Asia.

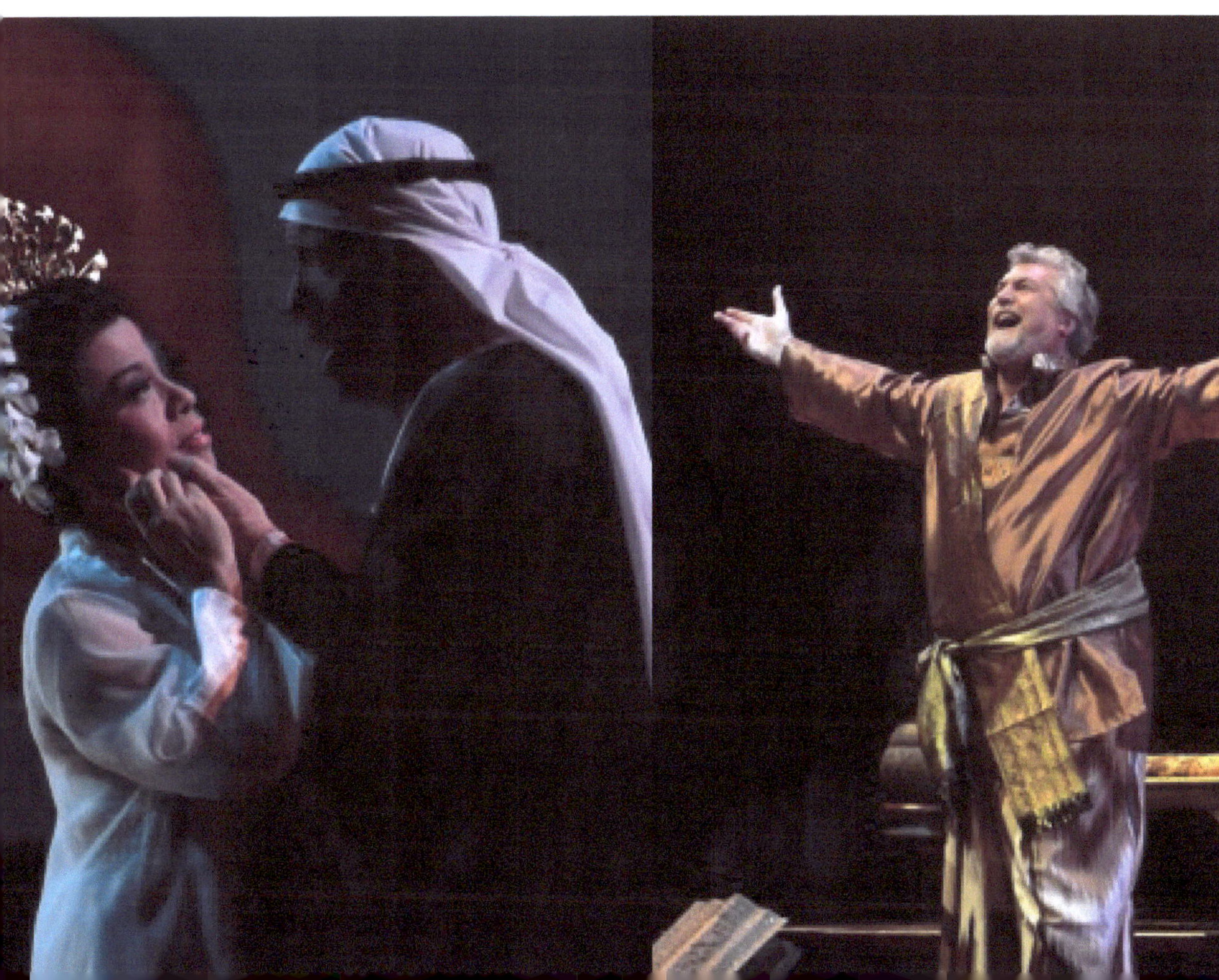

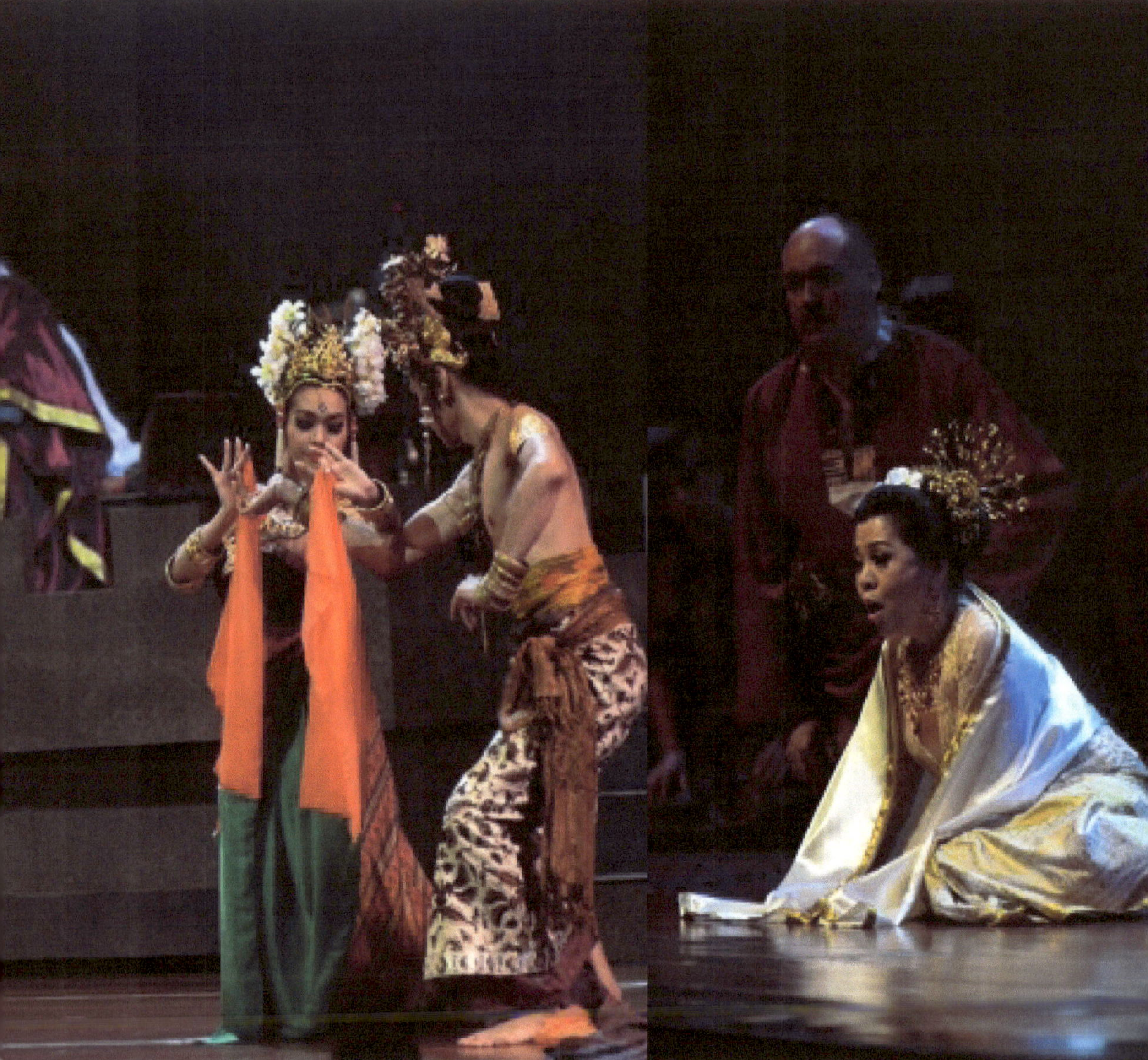

— Main cast: Nancy Yuen, Phillip Joll, Javier Agulló, Jeffrey Springer, Emanuela Barazia
— Puwarate Wongatichote, choreography
— Ryan Attig, lighting
— Somtow Sucharitkul, conductor and director

"Those in the know have started to realize that Bangkok has a genuine operatic presence, thanks to the uniquely bicultural presence of artistic director Somtow Sucharitkul who both directed and conducted the Thai premiere of *Otello* in February. Aware that in this Verdi year, he needed a new twist, Somtow drew on *Phya Rachawangsan*, a play by King Rama VI which is adapted from Shakespeare's *Othello* and which just happens to be having its own 100th anniversary in 2013.

"Opera Siam's production became as much a celebration of Thailand's new creative confidence as a performance of a classic. If you closed your eyes, you would hear an excellent performance of Verdi's opera — but if you closed your *ears*, you would see King Rama VI's play, in which the setting has moved from the Mediterranean to the Straits of Malacca, and in which the Islamic outsider Otello isn't having jealous fits on Christian Cyprus but in the Buddhist kingdom of Srivijaya, circa 700 AD.

"Into this setting he places a conventional, indeed, "by the book" *Otello*. Yet every traditional gesture, every cliché trope becomes informed with this cultural duality and forces you to examine every moment of the opera as though it were completely new. WIth honor killings in the news these days, this concept makes *Otello* contemporary and relevant.

"But the real star of the evening was the orchestra. Having gone through most of Mahler's symphonies, the Siam Philharmonic has emerged as an orchestra that could belong in any major western city. They played with passion and followed the twists and turns of Somtow's authentic Italianate rubato with nary a hitch."

— Stan Gayuski, *The Bangkok Post*

35. THE SILENT PRINCE (2013)
REVIVAL

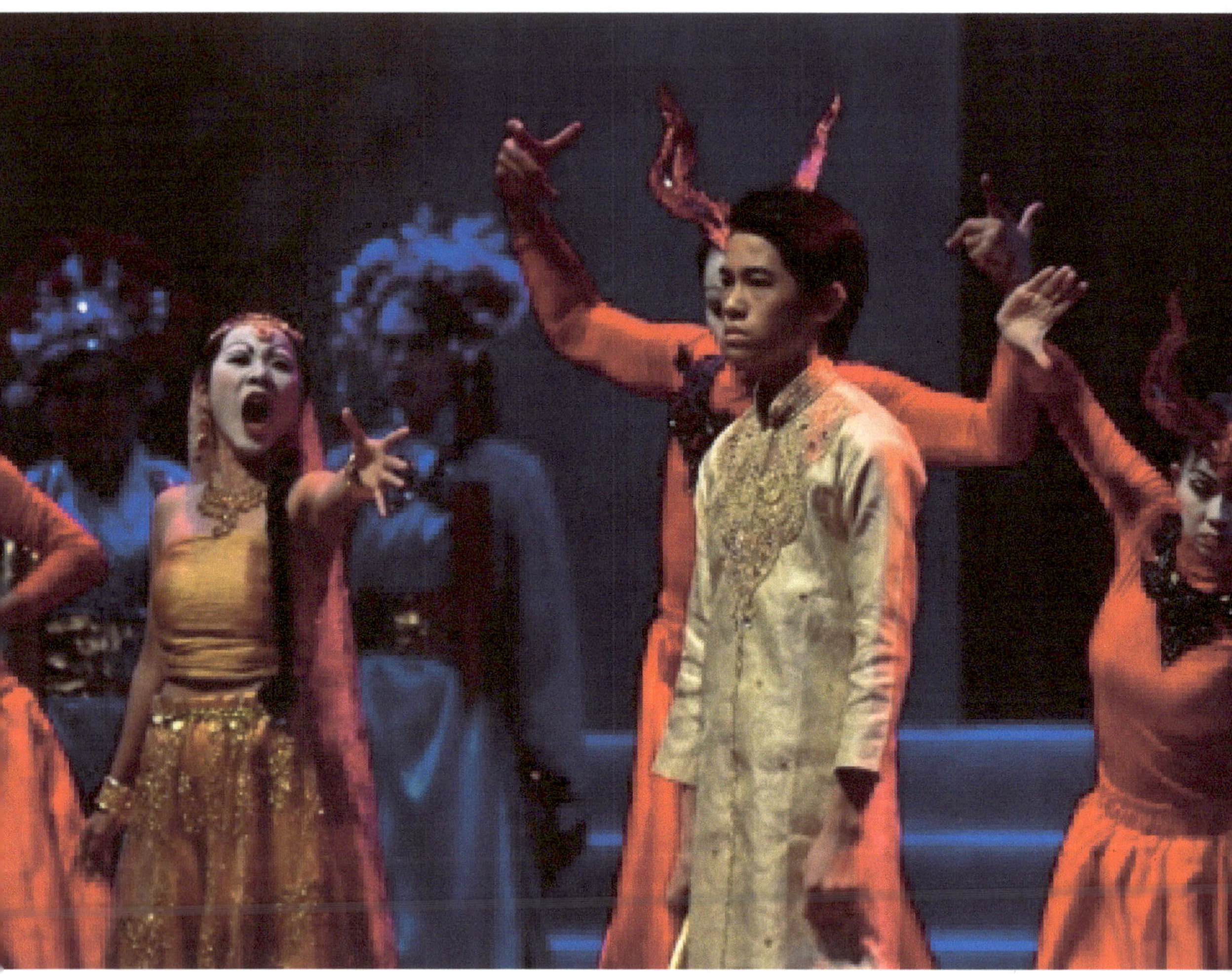

Basically a return to the 2012 production, which had had only had a single performance. The very impressive New Zealand artist Martin Snell, from the Bayreuth Festival, stepped in for an indisposed John Ames.

There was still no thought that this, this first of the *Ten Lives of the Buddha,* would actually evolved into a project to dramatize all ten of the *Lives.* The late Princess Sukhumabinanda, mother of the then governor of Bangkok, was present to bestow flowers on the performers at the end.

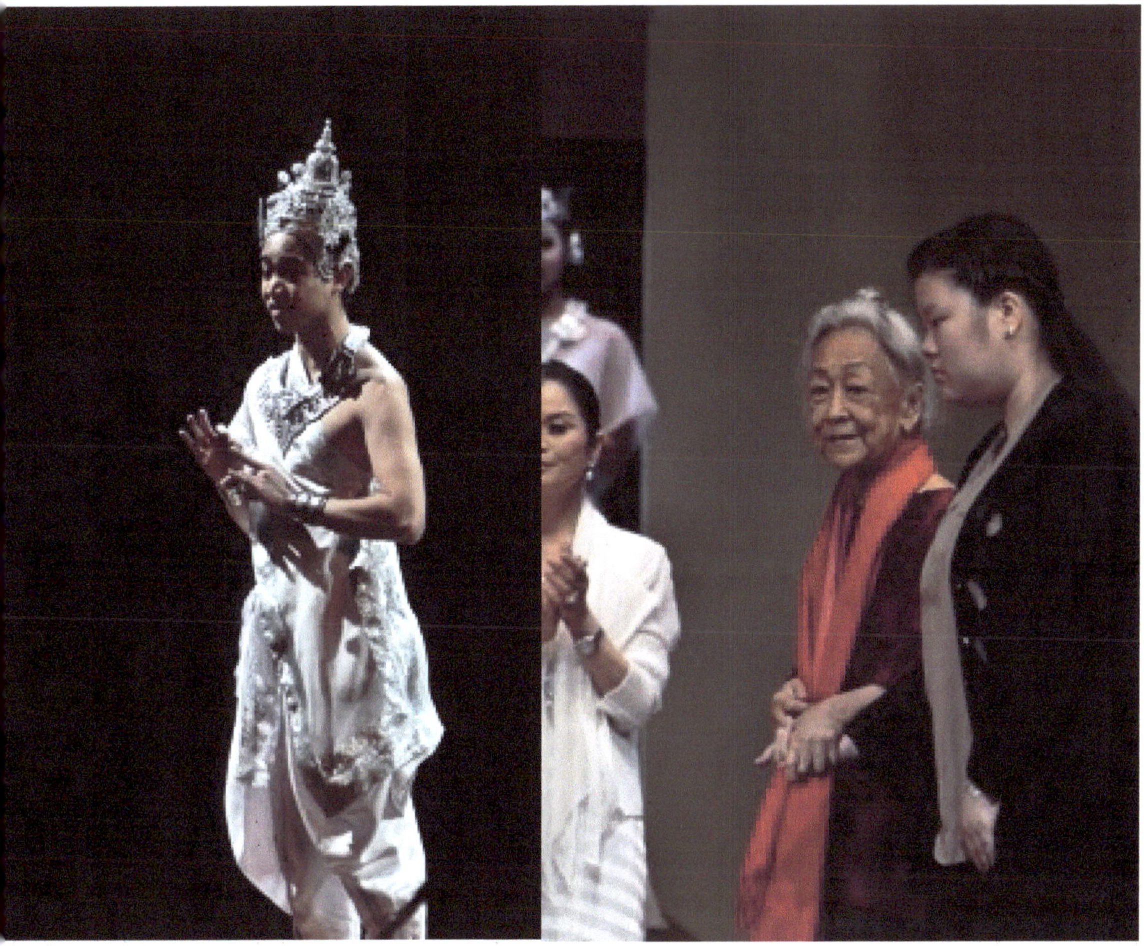

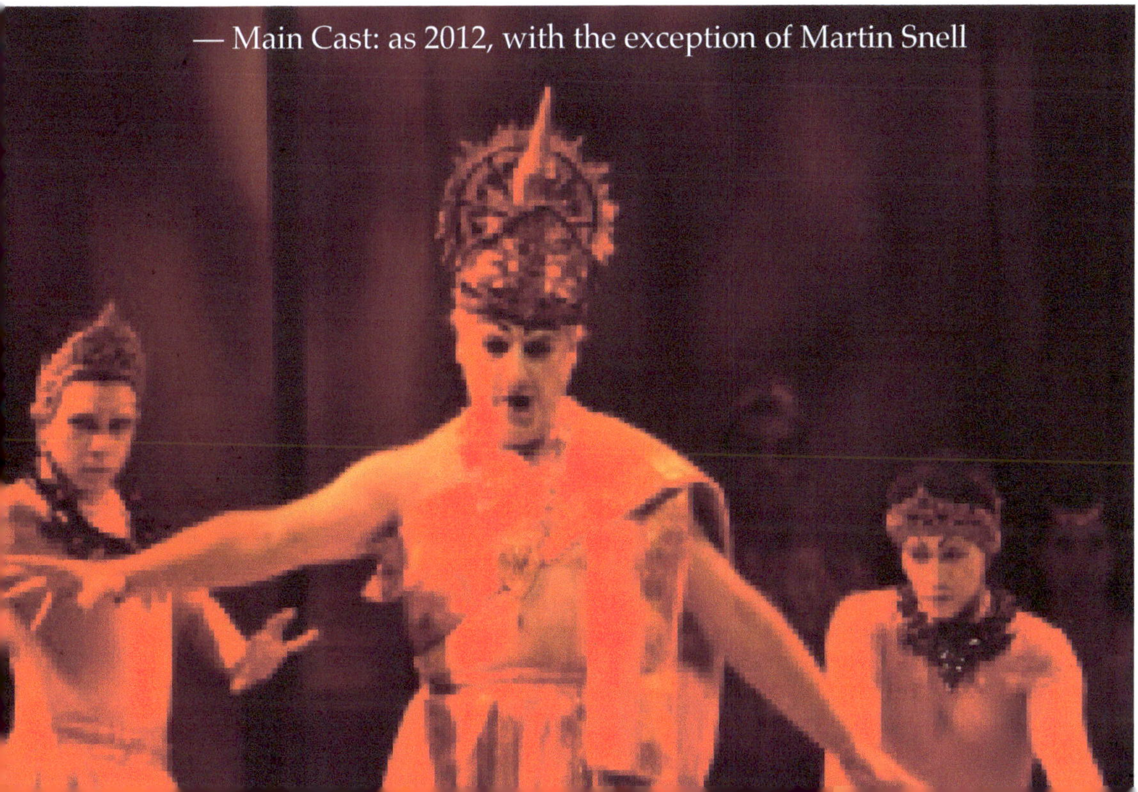

— Main Cast: as 2012, with the exception of Martin Snell

36. AND 37. SURIYOTHAI (2013) FOLLOWED BY IMMEDIATE RERUN - WORLD PREMIERE

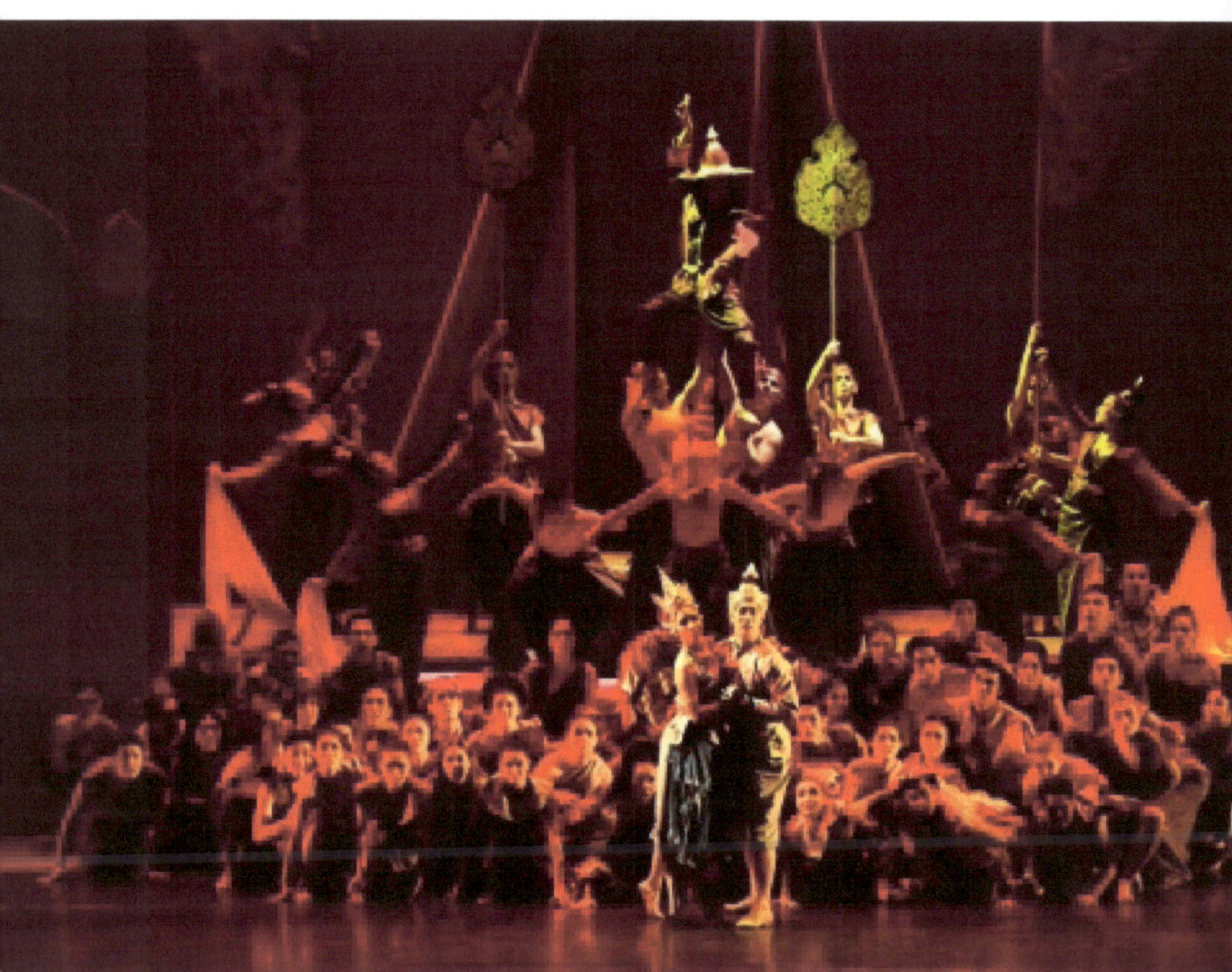

Suriyothai – a ballet-opera was a breakthrough work for Opera Siam. In creating a ballet that contained operatic sections, Somtow discovered that this was an effect entirely opposite to having a ballet inside an opera. Whereas in the former, the ballet tends to be a moment of repose, giving the characters a break in the action — i.e. a divertissement, for example — in the reverse situation the ballet *is* the action. So opera comes in when the emotion becomes so heightened that the human voice must break in.

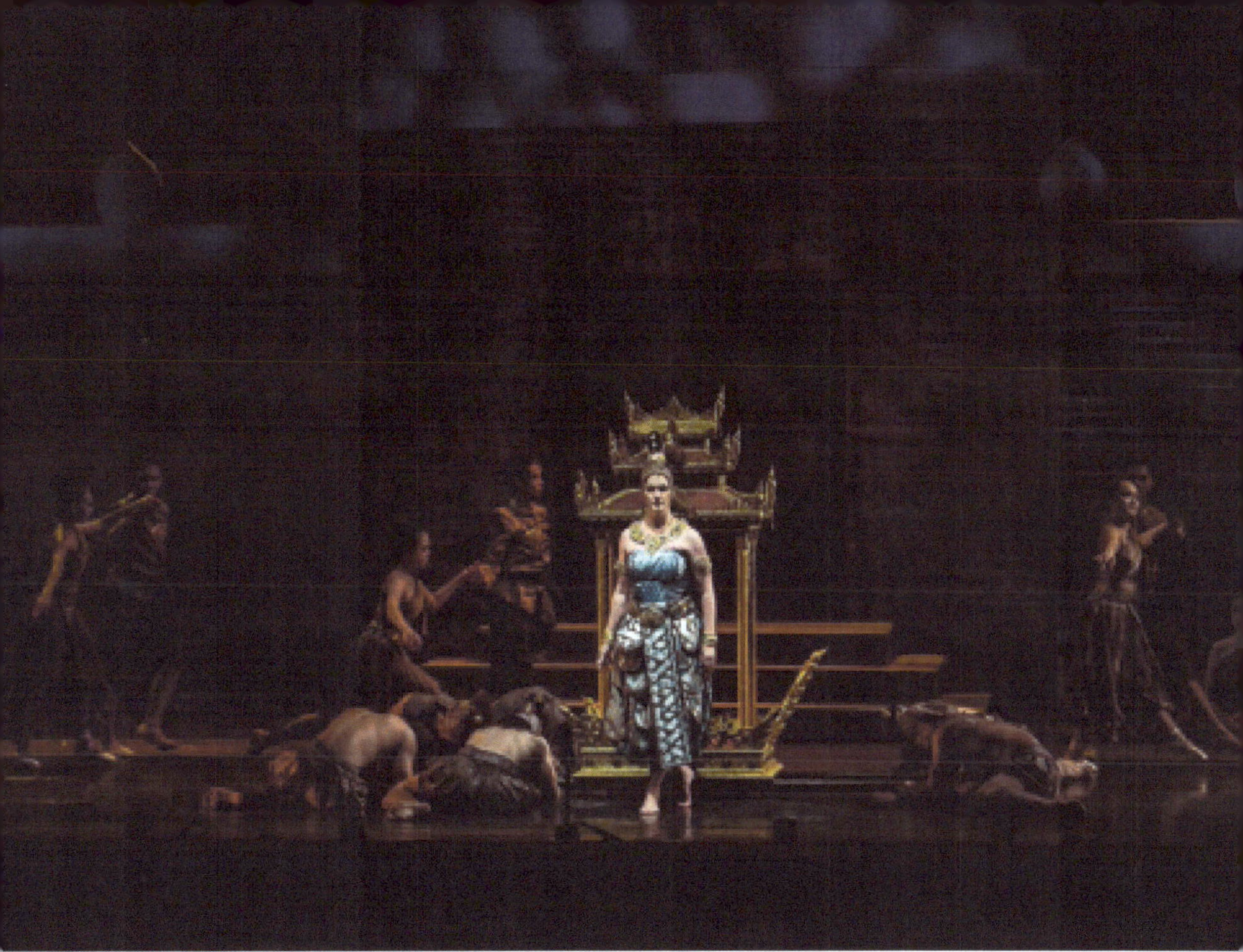

Suriyothai as a soprano was sung by Stacey Tappan — who is now a regular at the Met.

Recreating a Renaissance era culture that had substantial links to Europe while existing in a quintessentially Asian world-view meant using not only Southeast Asian musical tropes but the styles that were prevalent in Europe of the 16th Century. The war been Pegu and Ayudhya that forms the historical background of the work is an iconic part of the history of the region, told very differently in different countries, so the world constructed in *Suriyothai* draws on the dance traditions of Pegu, Siam *and* Europe. This is especially seen in the courtroom sequence when the French ambassadors presents dances from the court of Versailles to the Thai King and the dances are interrupted by Thai performers who are trying to interpret them in their own way.

The performances were unprecedently successful and with the Ministry of Culture's encouragement was immediately revived a few months later.

— Main Cast: Stacey Tappan, Jak Cholvijarn — choreographed by Puwarate Wongatichat — Siam Philharmonic Orchestra, conducted by Trisdee na Patalung

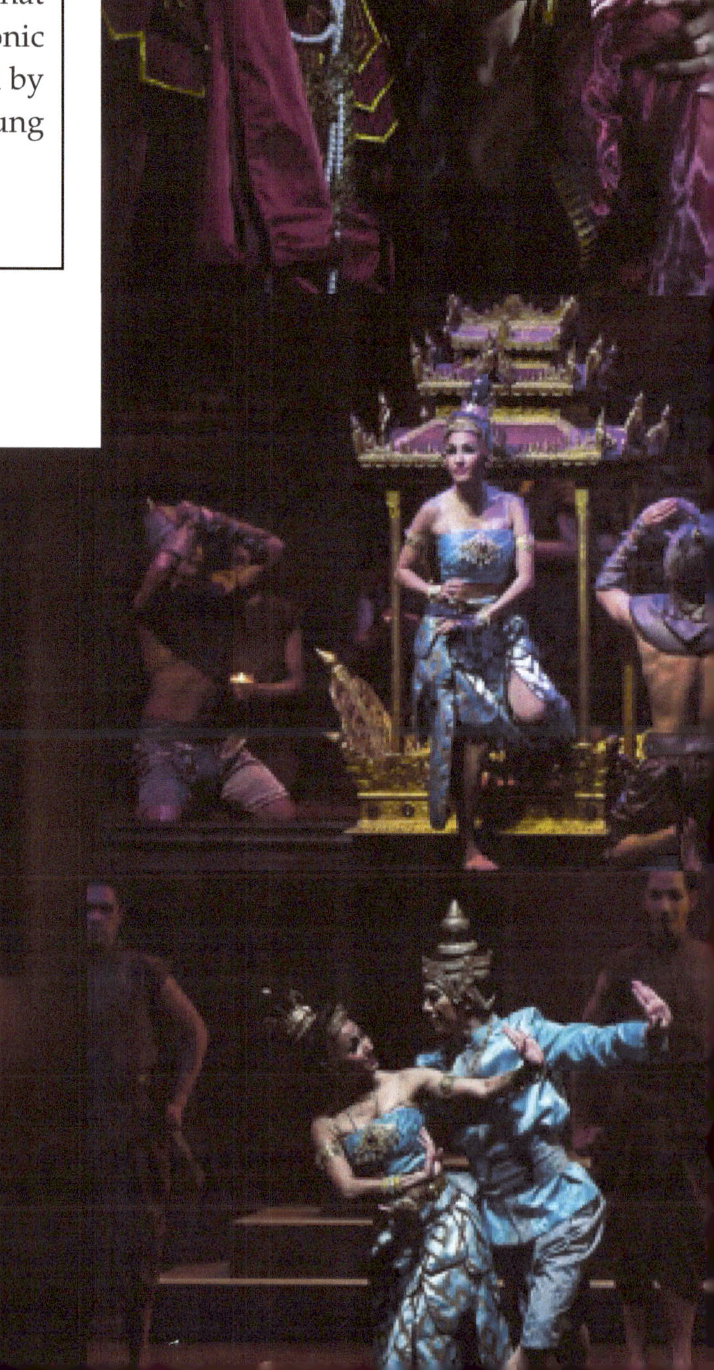

38. THE FLYING DUTCHMAN (2013)
THAILAND PREMIERE

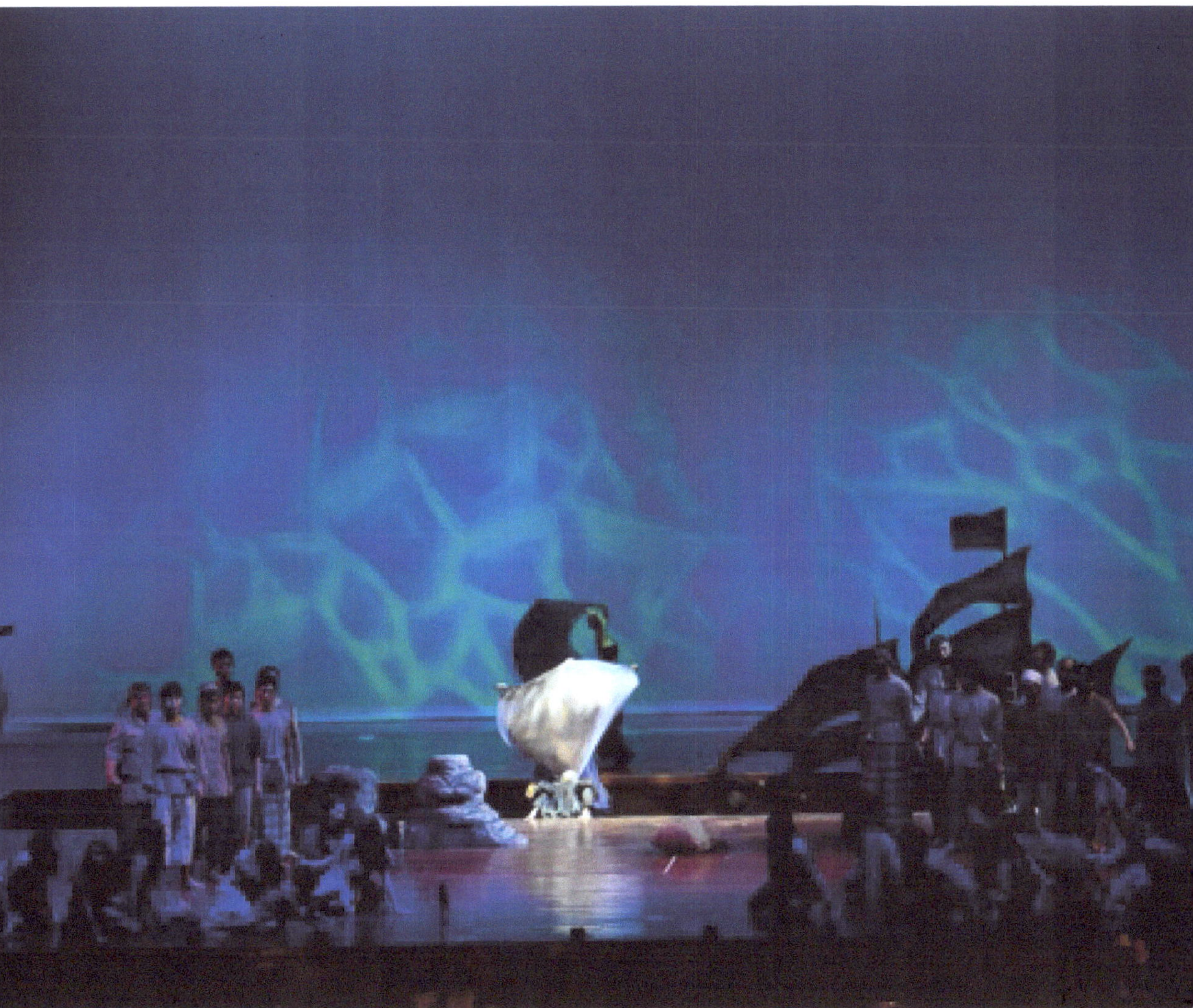

This opera was decided on only a month before its performance, because Somtow received a message from his contracted Siegfried saying that he was unable to perform the role from memory as he thought it would be a concert performance. This was the third time that the planned *Siegfried*, third part of *The Ring* cycle, had been scuttled at the last minute. A quick search through the cast's resume found that *Dutchman* was the one work that many of them had in common, so a production was hastily scheduled.

As Somtow needed to come up with a concept very quickly, he hit upon the idea that if the Flying Dutchman were indeed wandering the seas, able to emerge only once on a while and only to find the love of a pure woman, it made sense that the ocean would eventually bring him to Southeast Asia.

Setting the opera beside a *kelong* or fishing platform, in modern times yet very remote from "civilization" allowed elements of the plot to make sense — such as the idea that a village headman would not think twice about selling his daughter. It also allowed references to contemporary problems like trafficking and exploitative labor (the village women are now part of a thankless clothing combine and watched over by a stern matron.)

Stacey Stofferahn's brilliant debut in this role was a revelation. The overture was choreographed in order to tell the entire story in mime, allowing those who couldn't understand German or didn't know the plot in advance to grasp the entire tale in miniature.

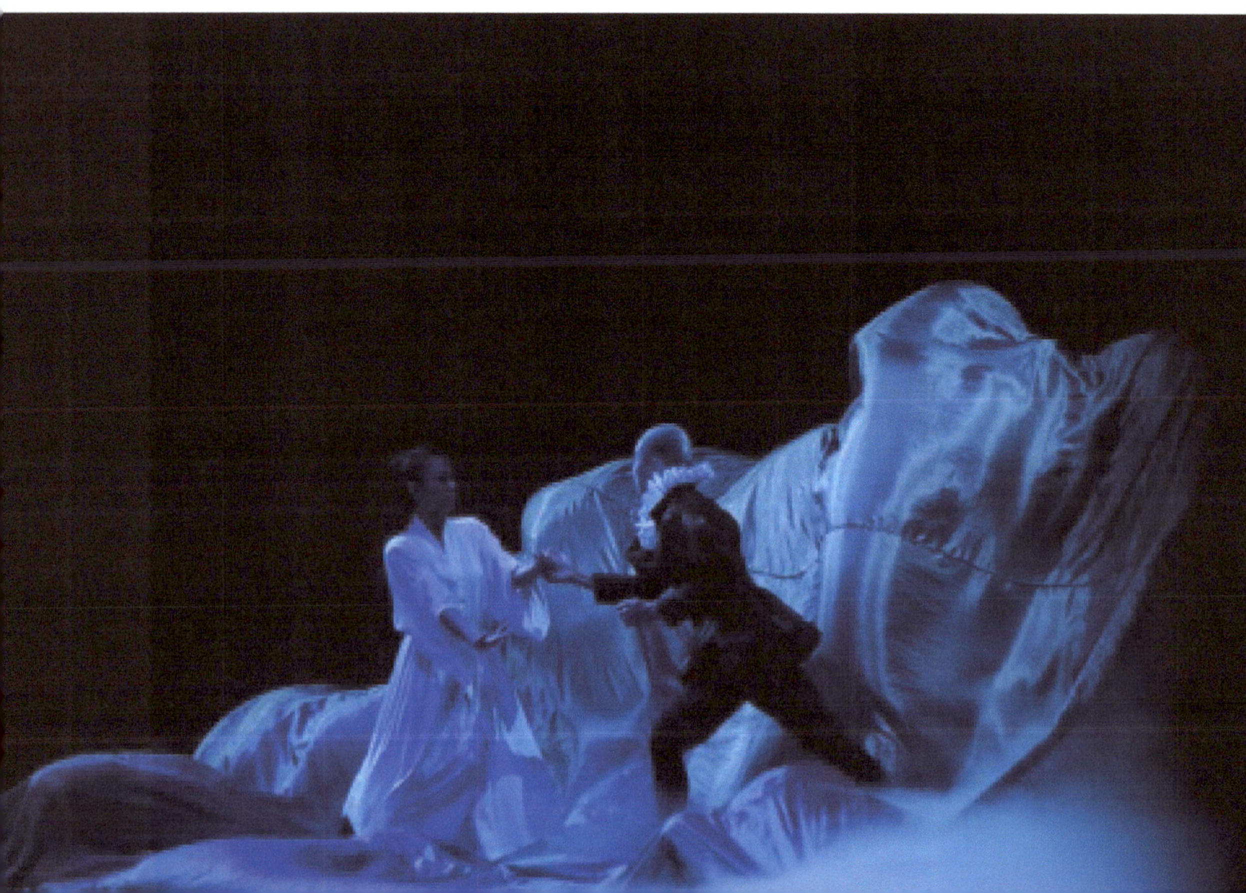

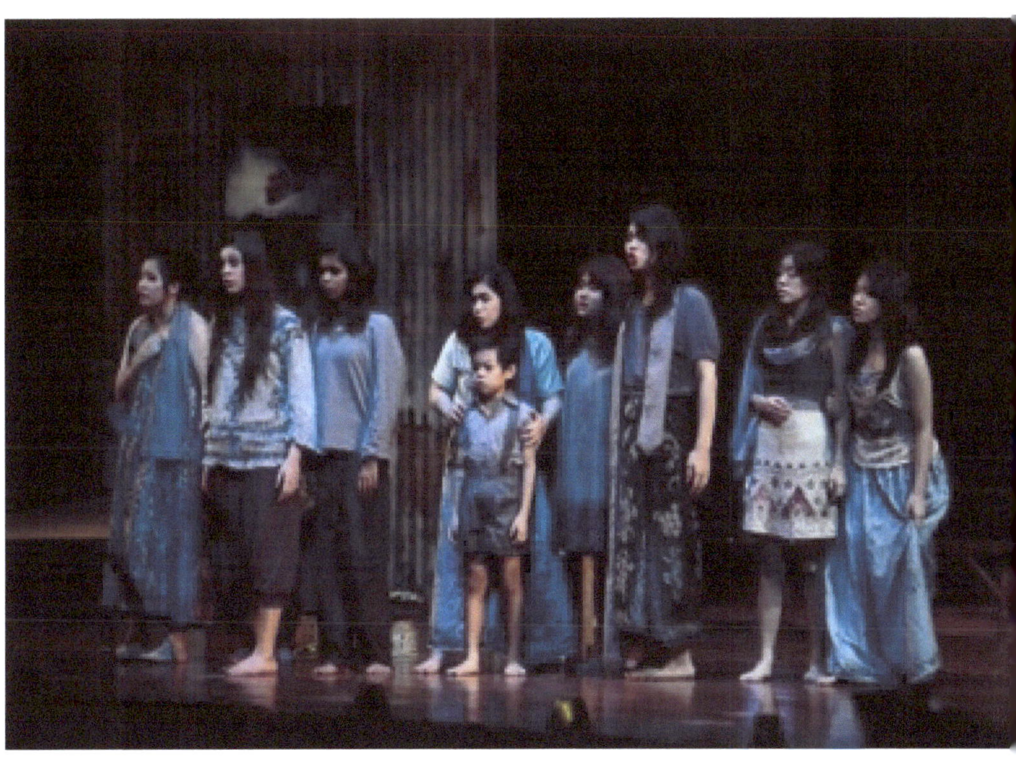

—Main Cast: Stacey Stofferahn, Kyu Won Han, Martin Snell, Arnold Bezuyen, Joseph Hu, Emanuela Barazia

— Siam Philharmonic Orchestra

— directed, designed and conducted by Somtow Sucharitkul

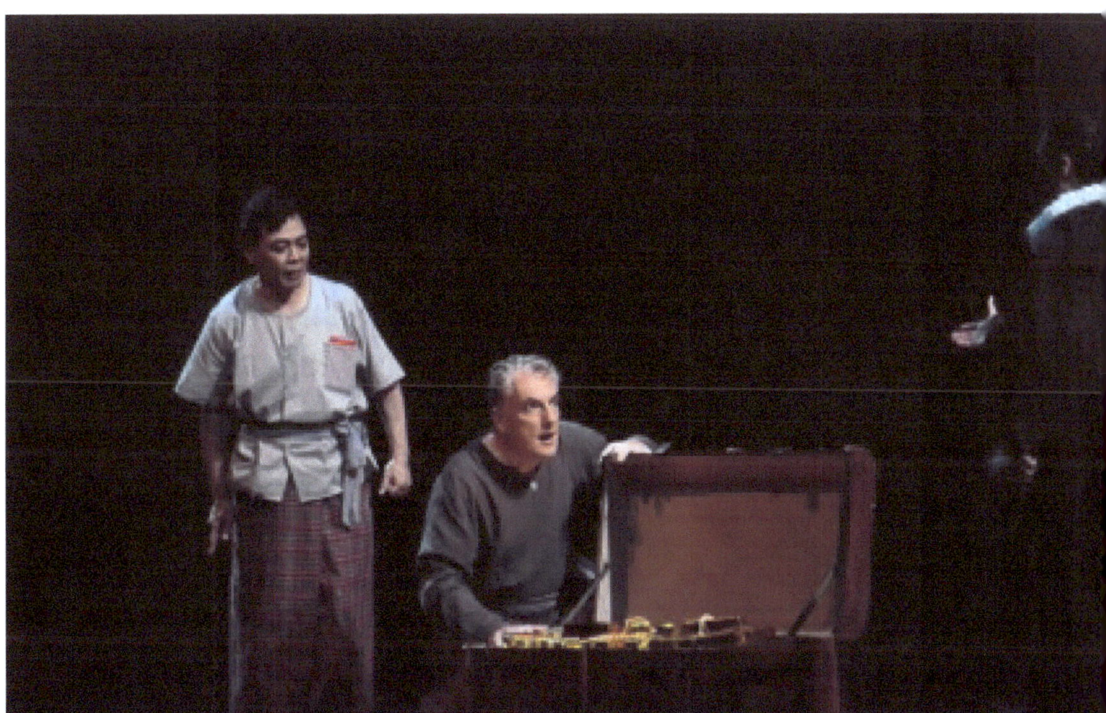

39. JEUX 3 (2014)
WORLD PREMIERE

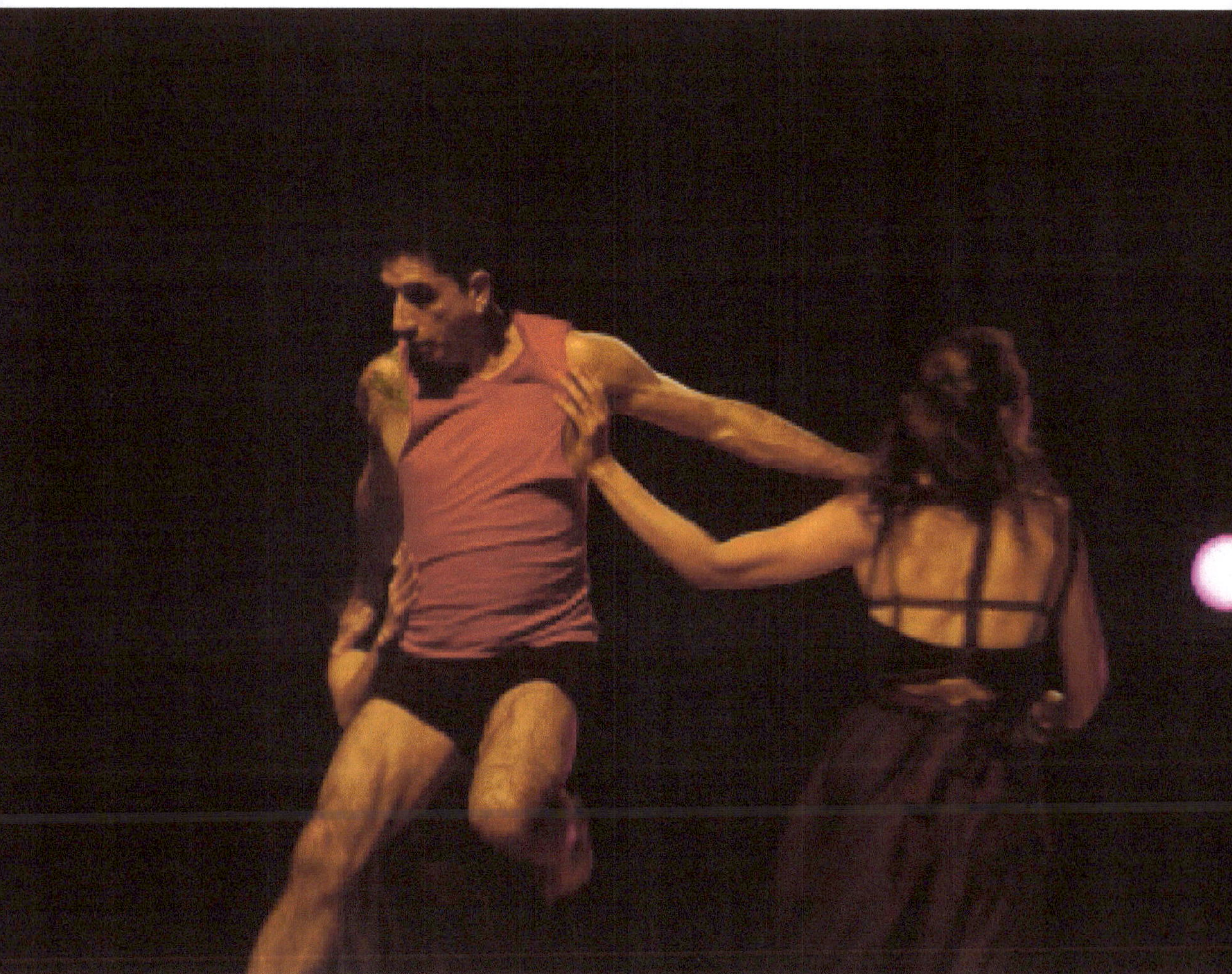

This ballet was created by Philippe of the Urban Bones Dance Company and is perhaps a contemporary commentary on the Debussy and Stravinsky pieces for the Ballets Russes. The music used was excerpts from Somtow's composition *Starscapes* which was premiered in Florida in 1979. The ballet was created as an opening to the one-hour-long *Mahajanaka* ballet.

40. LA CALISTO (2014)
THAILAND PREMIERE

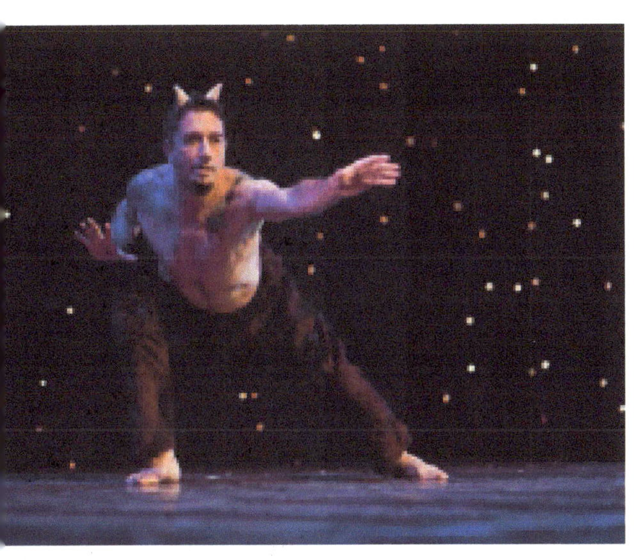

The first semi-staged show of Opera Siam's Young Soloists Program (YSP), established to train young Thai singers to become professionals. Also the first work by Cavalli to be performed in Thailand. Richard Harrell directed and Trisdee na Patalung conducted from the harpsichord.

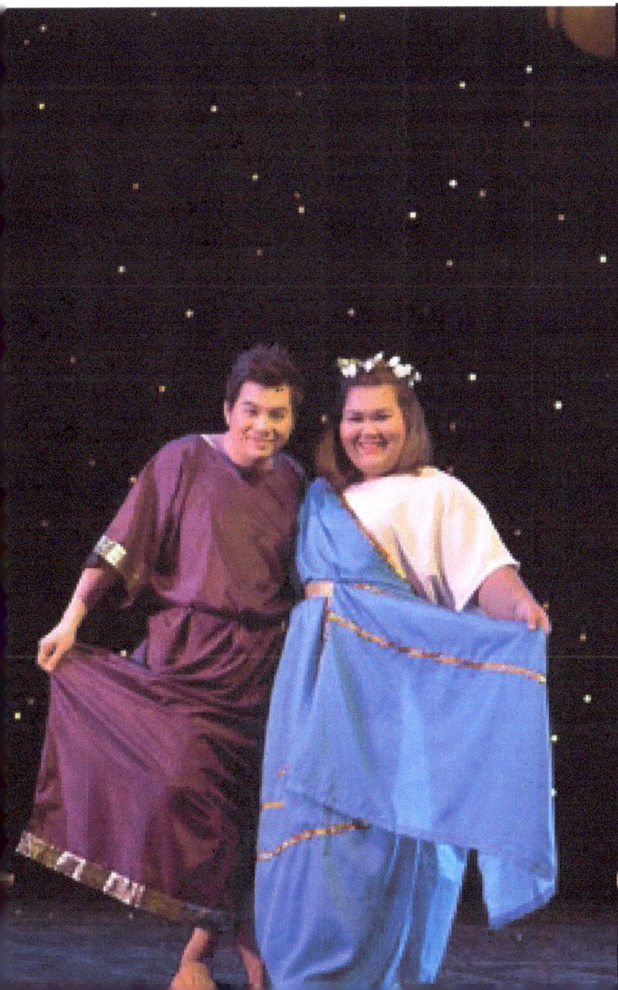

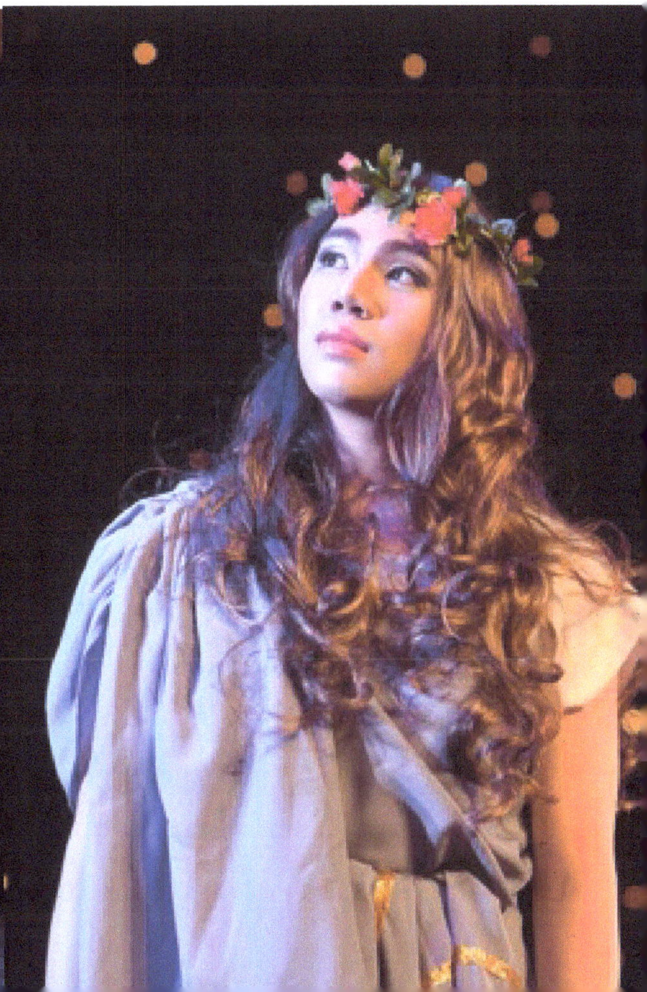

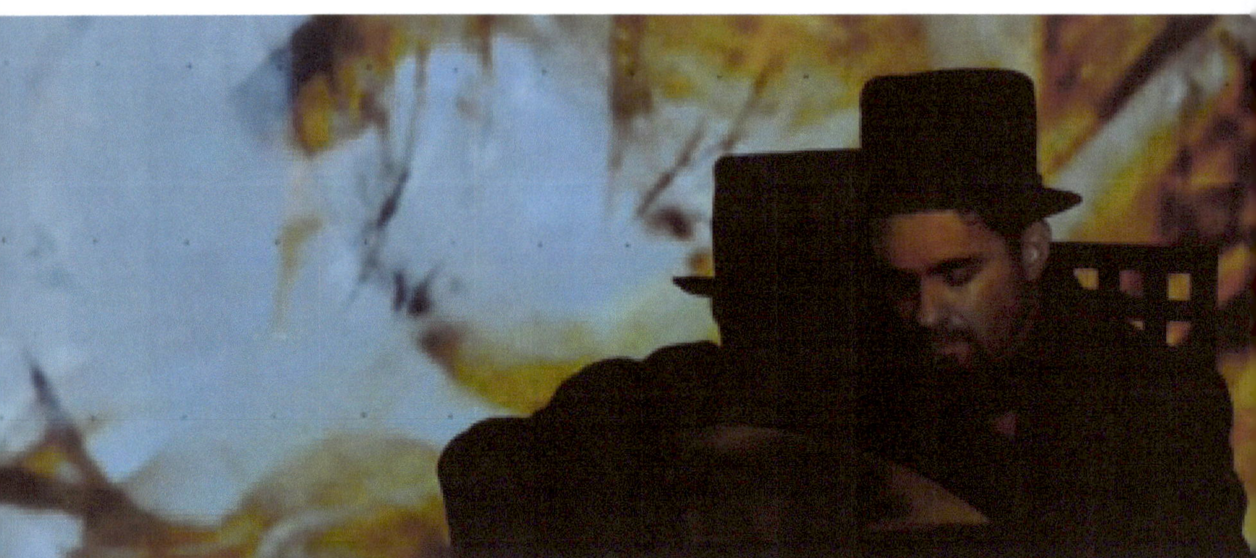

41. LUX IN TENEBRIS (2014)
THAILAND PREMIERE

A theater piece by Somtow Sucharitkul who read a series of poems, meditations on the paintings of Caravaggio, and improvised music by Jacopo Gianninoto, the lutenist who pioneered many early music performances in Thailand.

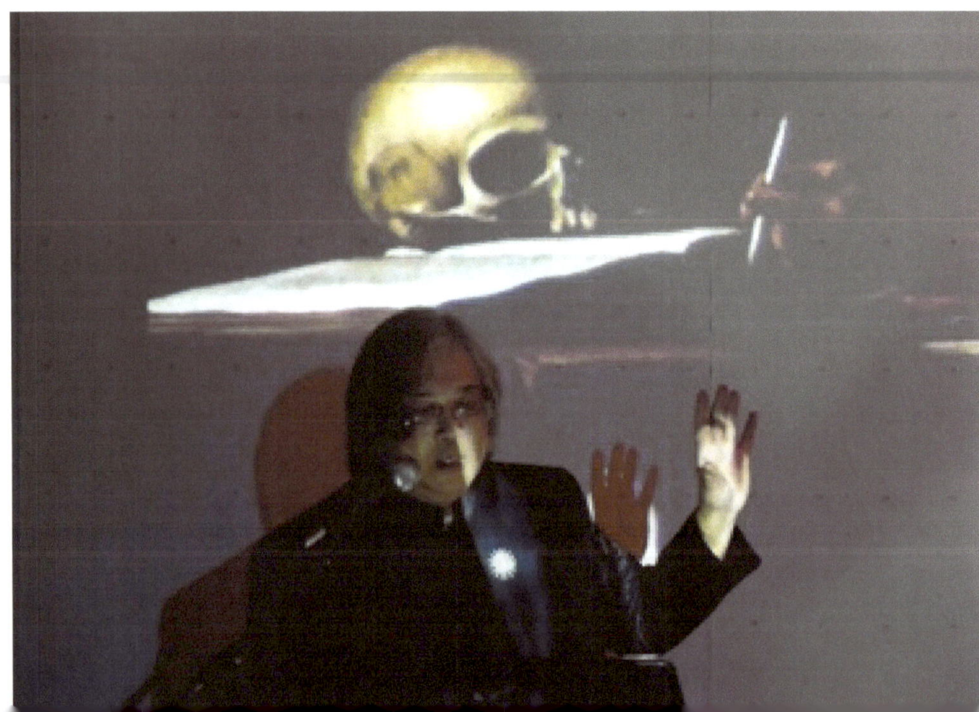

42. MAHAJANAKA (2014)
WORLD PREMIERE OF STAGE ADAPTATION

Somtow composed this work in 1998 as a symphony, inspired by *Mahajanaka* by H.M. King Rama IX, on the occasion of the King's Sixth Cycle celebration. For the premiere of the stage version, Somtow composed additional music to fill out the narration.

Stacey Tappan, who recorded the solo part in 1997 for a recording that made No. 4 in the Thai pop charts, reprised her role as the goddess Mekhala. Puwarae Wongatichat created the choreography and the scenic design was directly inspired by the artwork of Chalermchai Kositpitat, who had illustrated the first edition of the King's book.

The ship seen below, for example, was modelled on one of Chalermchai's paintings.

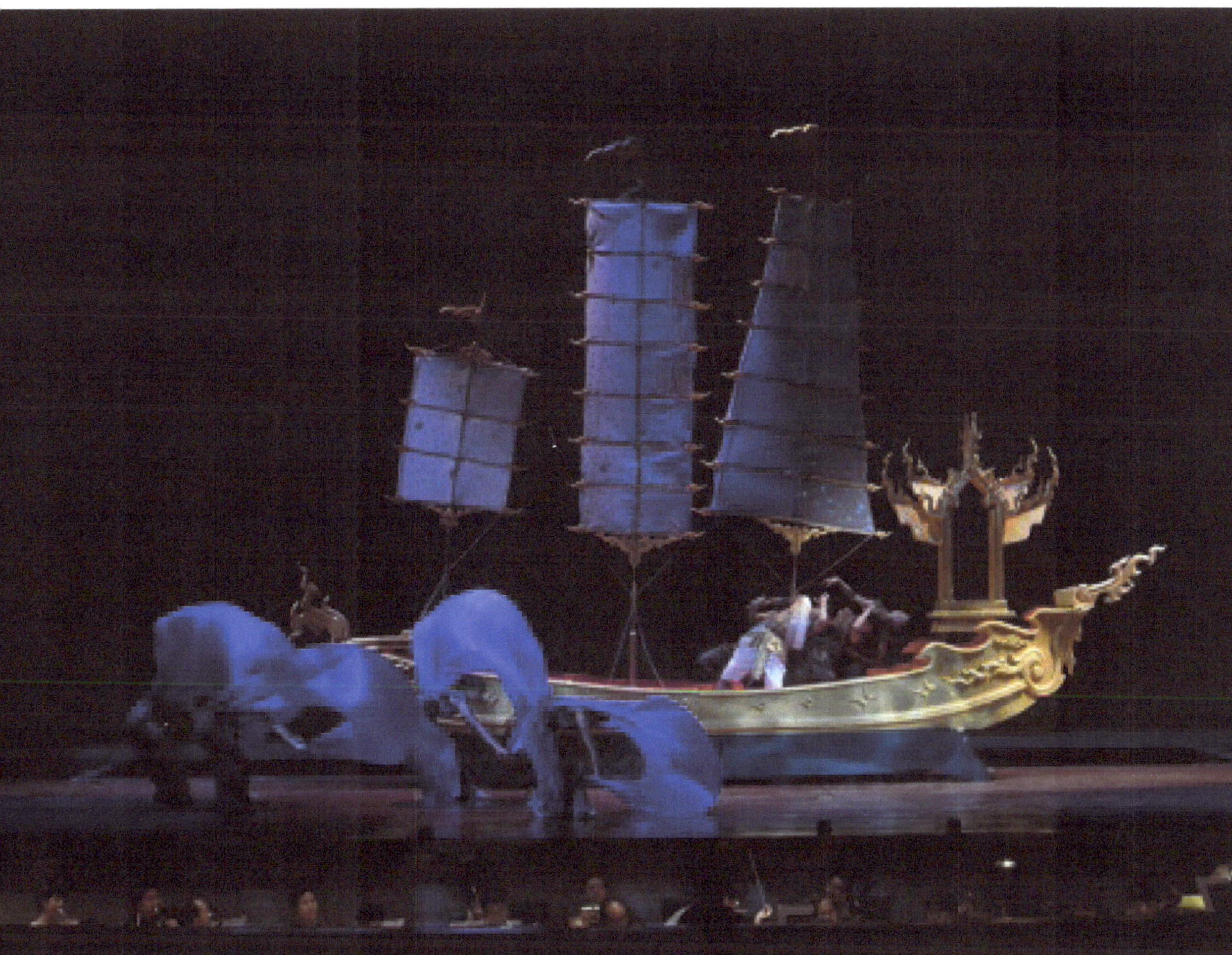

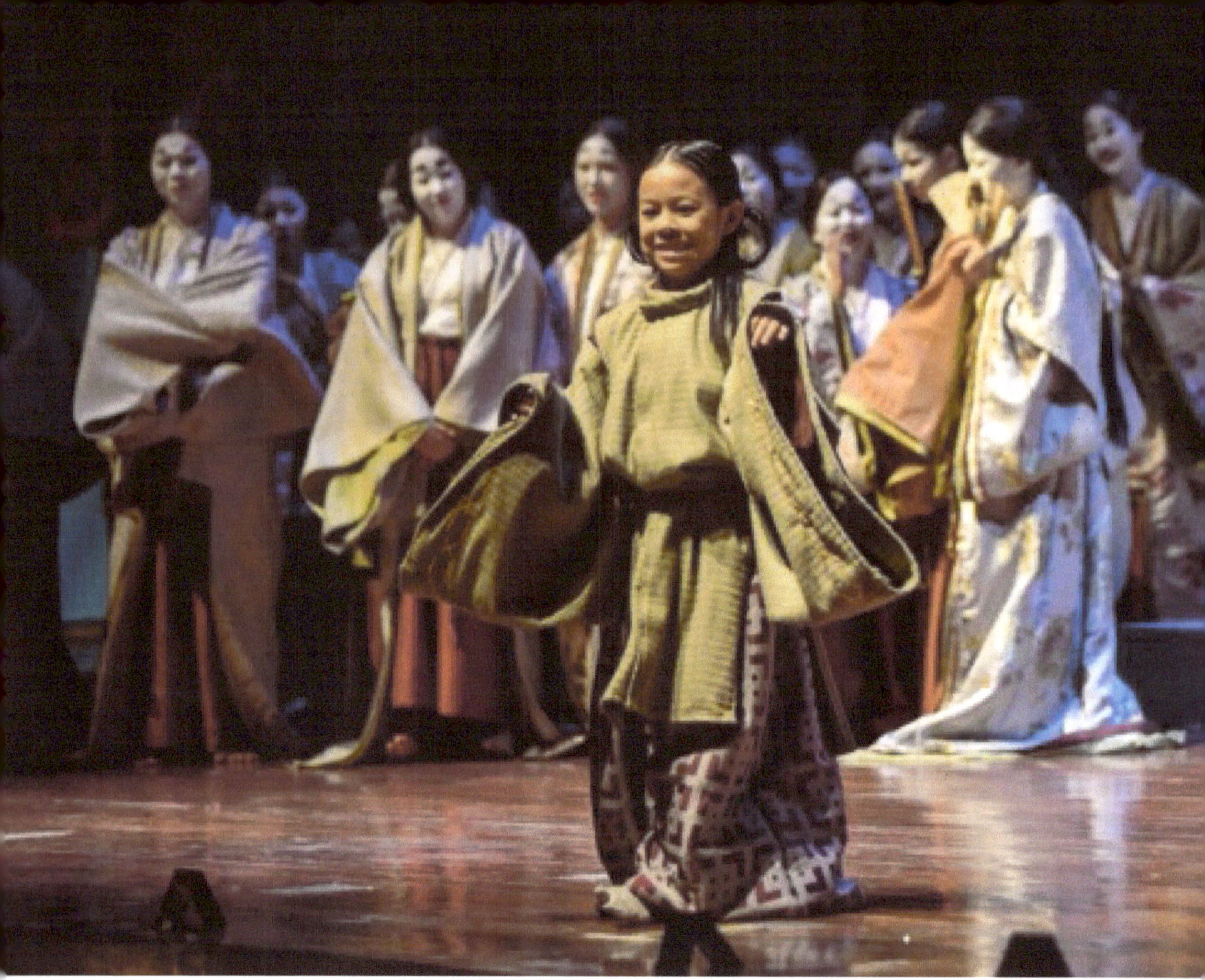

43. DAN NO URA (2014)
WORLD PREMIERE

Somtow Sucharitkul spent many years composing *Dan no Ura,* which earned much international acclaim. The story which comes from the classic *Tale of the Heike* is an iconic piece of Japanese history. The production took over a year to prepare, with the date having to be postponed owing to some elements not being ready. Astonishing cast which was designed to accommodate all the regular Opera Siam stars and as many of the Young Soloists as possible. The performance had many in tears, especially members of the Japanese community at the grandmother's aria whose words were directly taken from the original Japanese text.

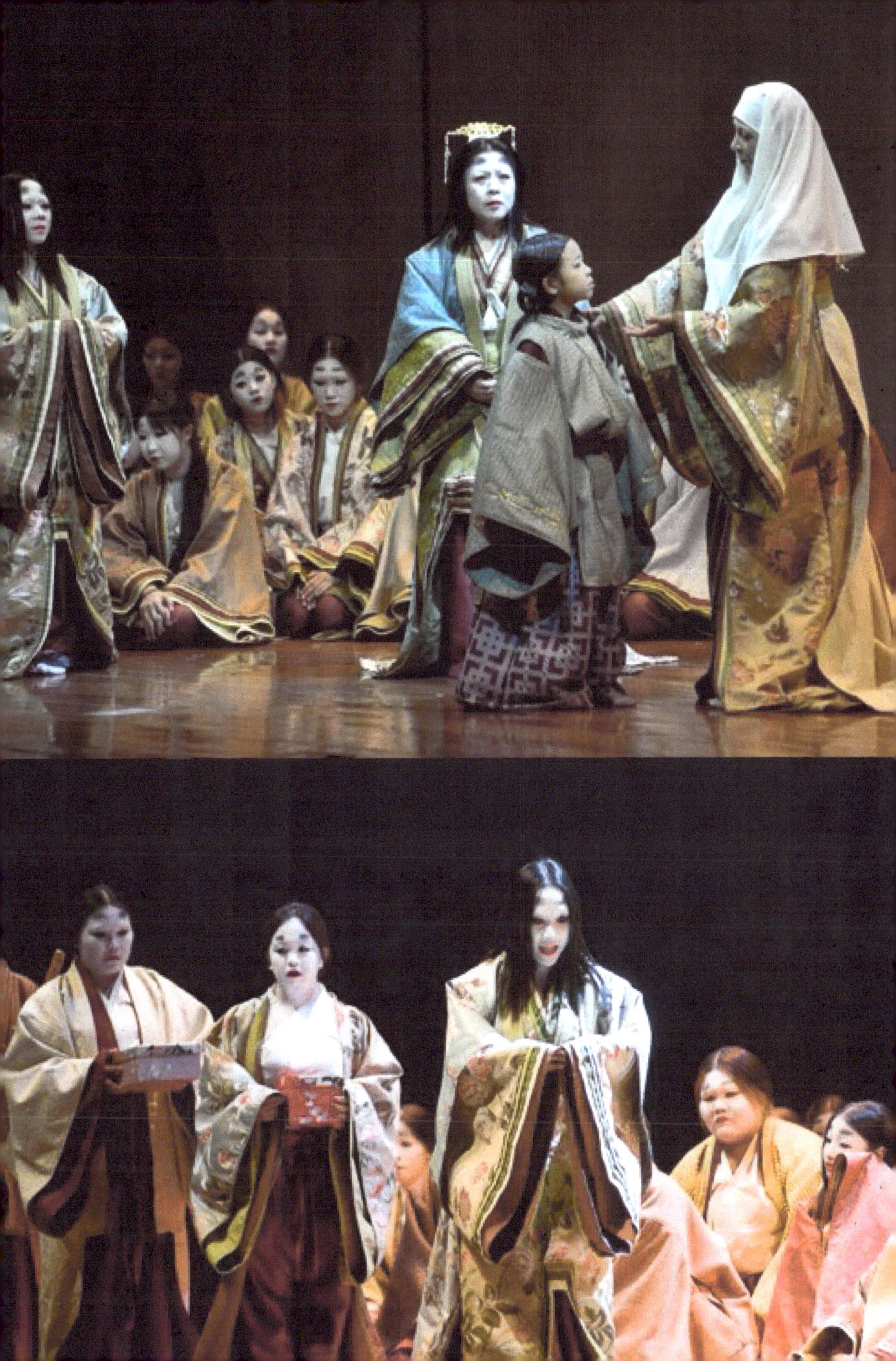

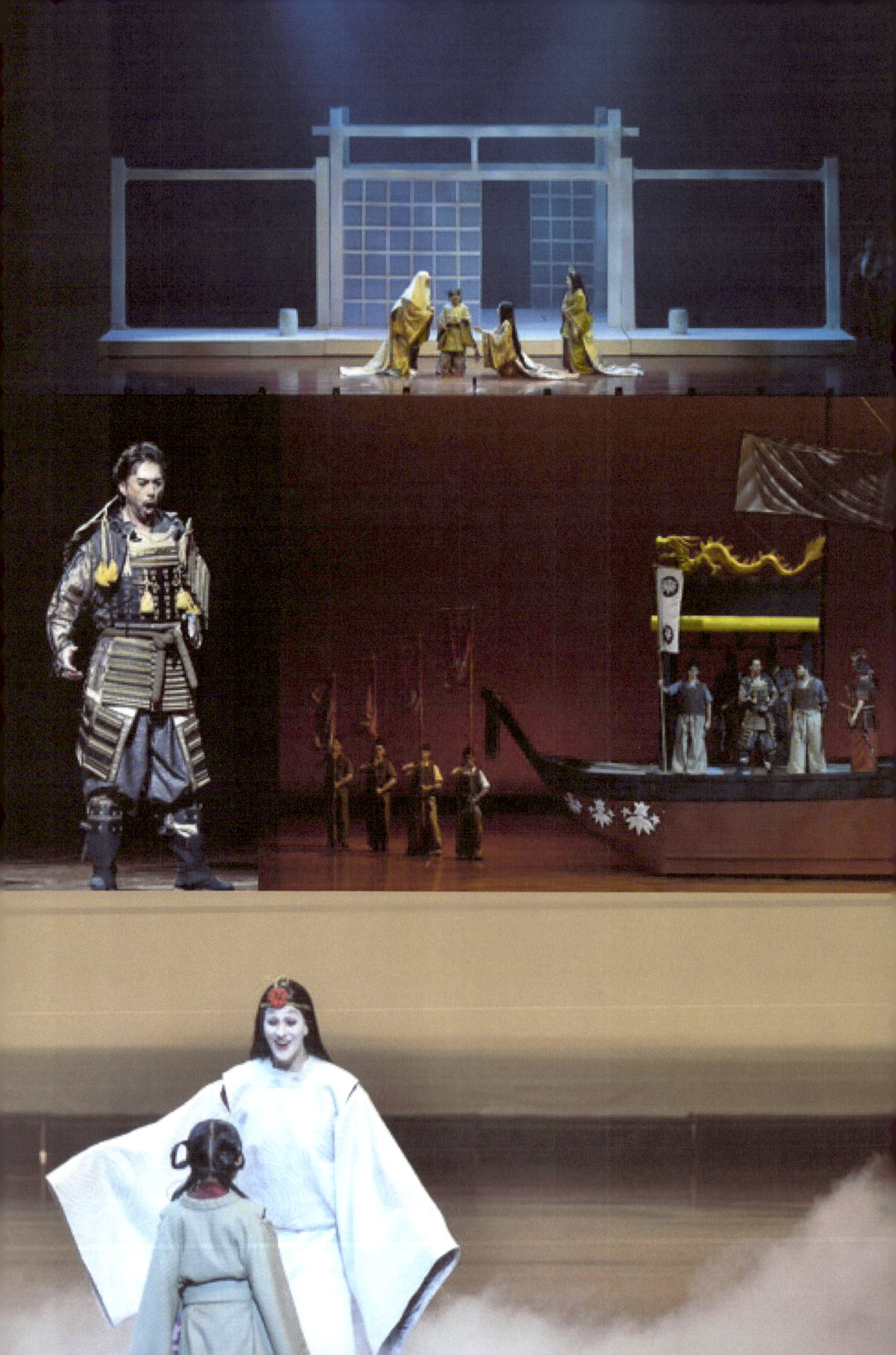

The World Premiere performances of Somtow Sucharitkul's "Dan no Ura" in Bangkok on 11th and 12th August confirmed Sucharitkul as one of the most intriguing of contemporary opera composers. It is a wonderful piece that should have the world's major companies lining up to stage.

It is written for large orchestra and multiple soloists. While not a pastiche of Japanese music, there are Japanese touches, such as extensive use of flute and wooden blocks. The opera is, however, completely suffused with a Japanese aesthetic, including both the spare elegance of the sets (designer, Dean Shibuya) and the gorgeous costumes (Nattawan Santiphab).

Film-like and episodic in construction, it is a continuous two-hour Act of constantly shifting scenes. It is rhythmically complex and demanding for both singers and orchestra, but easily accessible, with many passages of deeply romantic lyricism.

There was not a weak link in the international cast. The powerful and defiant matriarch, grandmother of the boy Emperor, who is prepared to sacrifice everything for the sake of honour and family, was imperiously sung by the Mexican mezzo Grace Echauri. She personified an unbending sense of duty, her voice soaring gloriously above even the loudest orchestral passages. Nancy Yuen as her daughter engagingly expressed a mother's protective love for her child. The major role of the Emperor was taken with winning charm and dramatic poise by nine year old Rit Parnichkun, who caught exactly both the Emperor's innocence and, at the same time, his acceptance of his fate.

The Emperor is helped to understand his destiny by two ghosts. The first is the ghost of his beloved cousin and playmate, Lord Atsumori, sung with ethereal beauty by the counter tenor Jak Cholvjarn. Atsumori tells the Emperor not be afraid – "It is only death". The other ghost is the Goddess of the Sun, Amaterasu, ancestor of the divinely-descended Imperial line. The American Stacey Tappan sparkled brilliantly in Amaterasu's extraordinary coloratura scene – the Queen of the Night meets Zerbinetta – hitting stratospheric heights, including a top F, with nonchalant ease.

Damian Whiteley as Yoshitsune captured the conflicted general's complex character: the war hero who nevertheless realises "the mighty fall at last, They are as dust before the wind". Korean baritone Kyu Won Han stirred profound emotions in the role of the Teiran Lord Kumagae, wracked with remorse at having killed Atsumori, and sang the heart-breaking music with great power, style and beauty. The Taiwanese-American tenor Joseph Hu as one of the Emperor's uncles was ringingly clear and sweet-toned, and the young Thai baritone, Saran Senavinin, impressed as another uncle. Nadlada Thamtanakom was movingly expressive as the Emperor's nurse.

Sucharitkul was himself the director of this spectacular production. Trisdee na Patalung, Thailand's star international conductor and Sucharitkul's ideal interpreter, brilliantly guided the orchestra and singers through the tricky score. Thailand should be proud of the jewel that is Opera Siam. This production and their 'Flying Dutchman' last December are the match of those of any European opera company.

— from London's Opera *magazine*

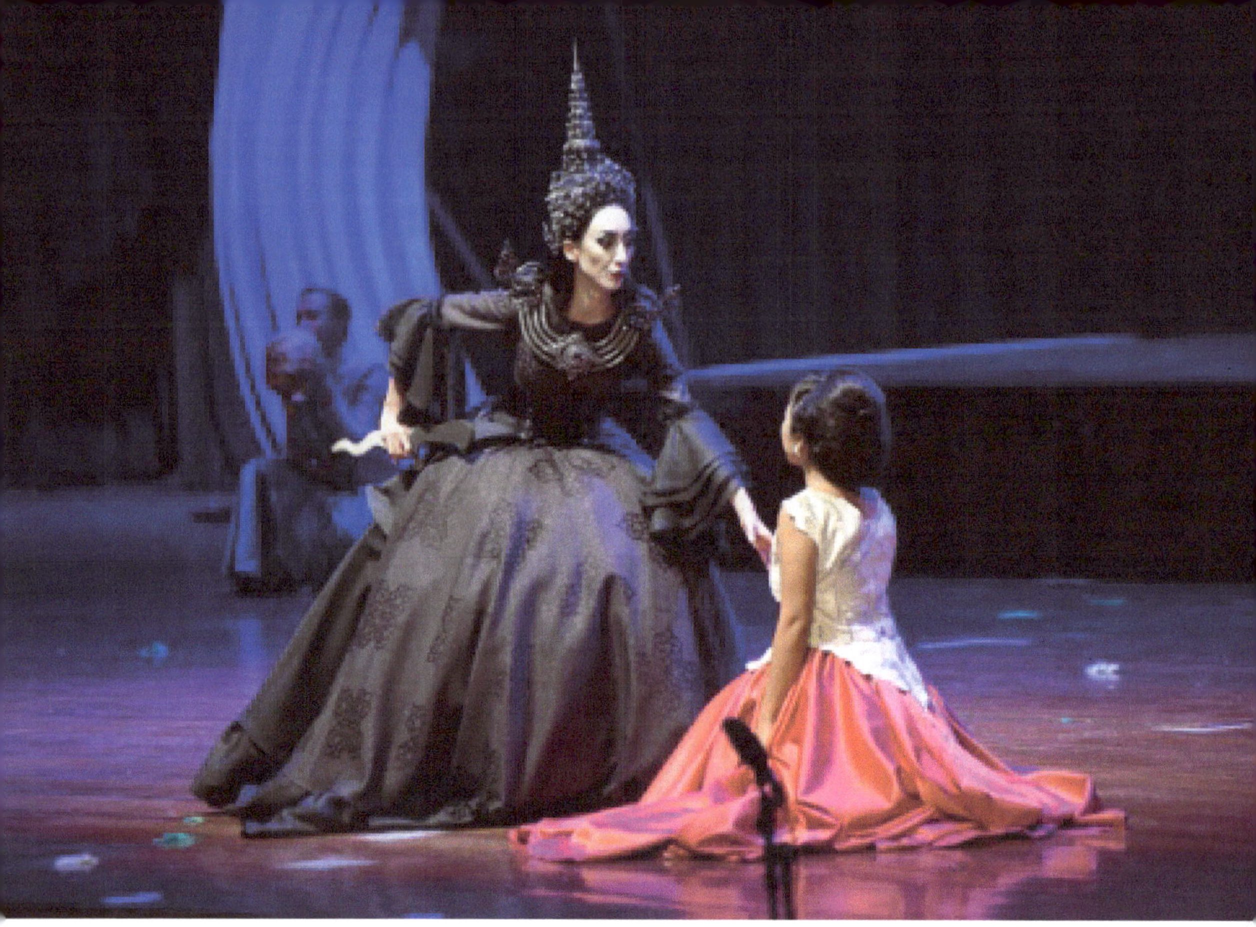

44. THE MAGIC FLUTE (2014)
NEW PRODUCTION

The third *Magic Flute* to be done by Opera Siam was originally planned as a revival of the 2006 production, but soon evolved into a completely new concept. Set in Opera Siam's trademark "Thai-Sci-Fi" milieu, this version showed (during the overture) a number of normal people in an office building, each with his own very contemporary problems to work through. As the overture ends, they participate in a kind of mass hallucinatory experience in which they live out their fantasy lives — and through which they are able to work out who they really are and come to terms with their identities in their real-life existences. It was an interpretation that actually created a logic for the plot's many much-made-fun-of inconsistencies.

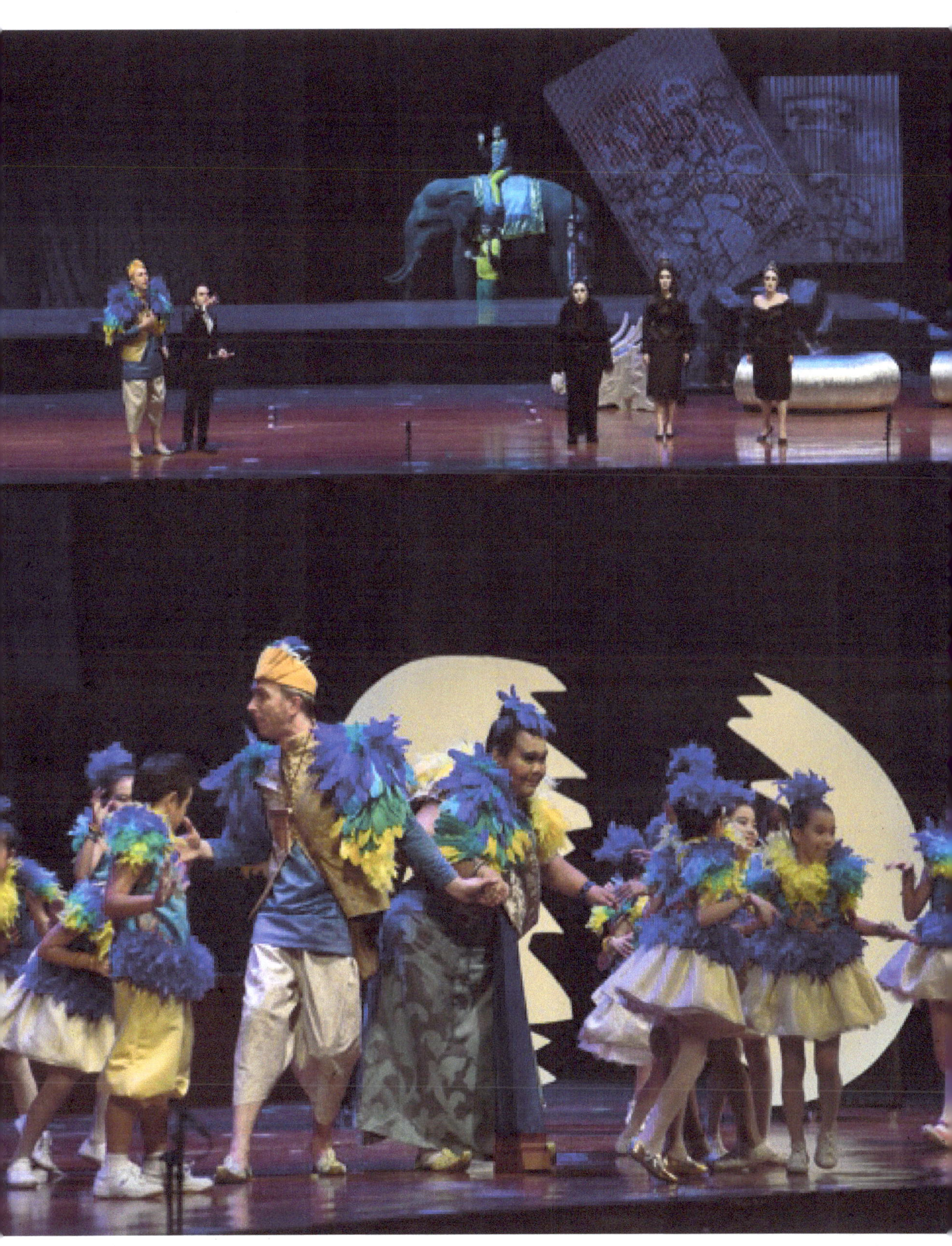

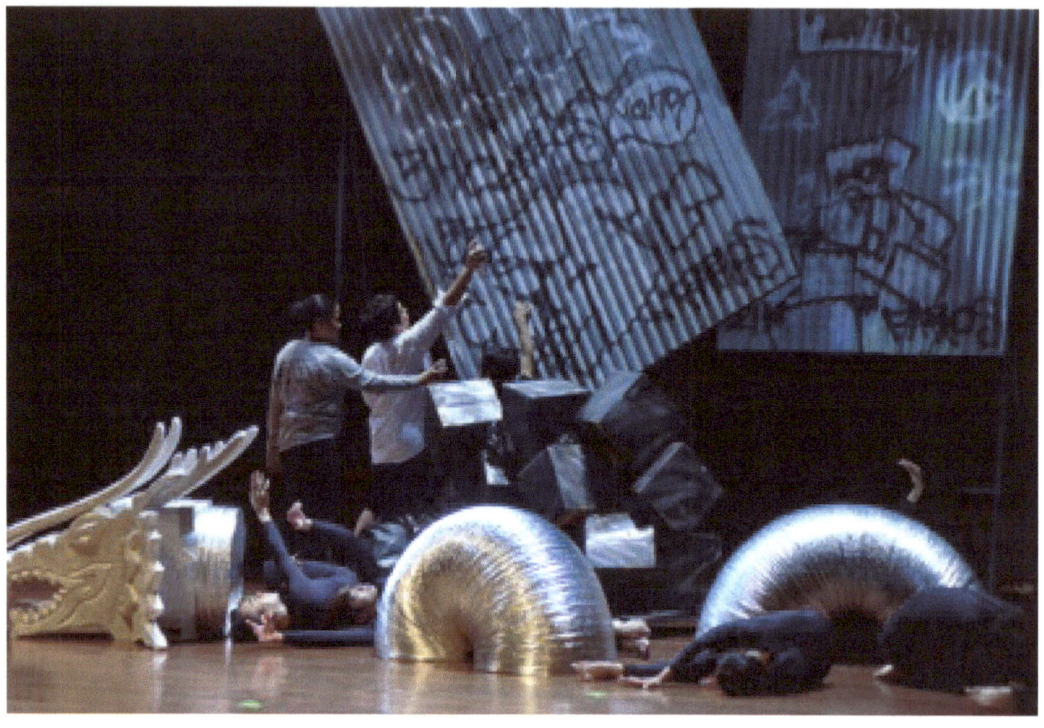

— Main Cast: Nadlada Thamtanakom, Emilio Pons, Falko Hönisch, Damian Whiteley, Dag Schantz, Arreya Rotjanadit, JC Manar, Monique Klongtruadroke

— Puwarate Wongatichat, choreographer
— Somtow Sucharitkul, director
— Siam Philharmonic Orchestra, conducted by Trisdee na Patalung

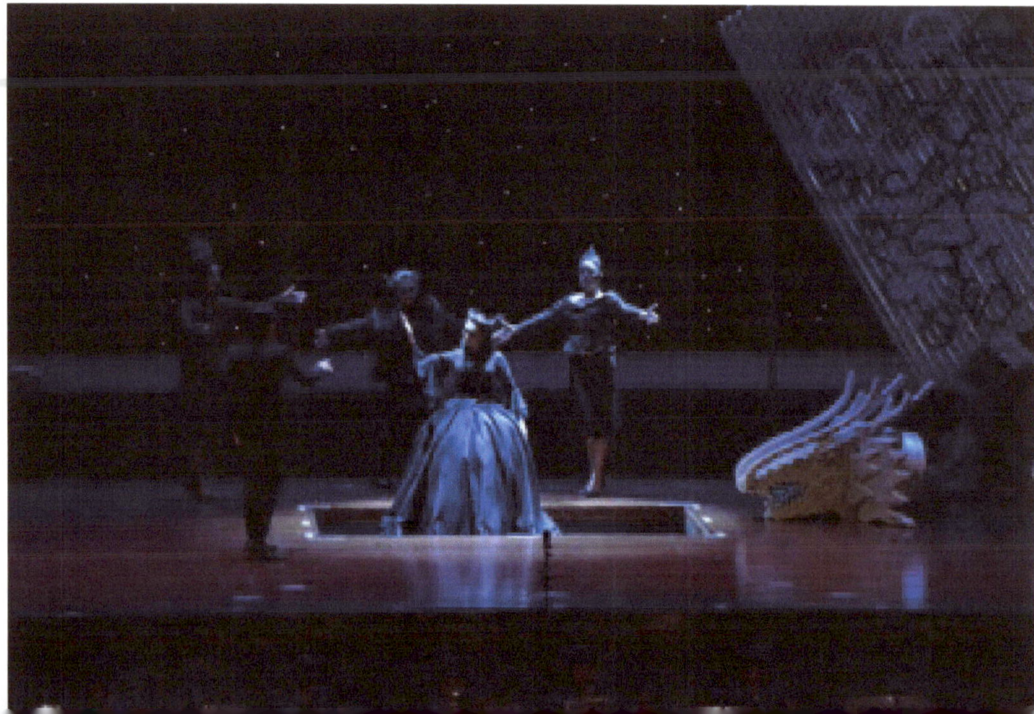

"How to present The Magic Flute? The problem is that it combines some of Mozart's most sublimely beautiful and profound music with an absurd plot containing what seem inexplicable contradictions. In Opera Siam's wonderful new production in December at the Thailand Cultural Centre, director Somtow Sucharitkul imaginatively reconciles the contradictions of the plot by seeing the potential for both good and evil in all of us, at least within our imaginings. He presents the opera as a fantasy which a group of ordinary people jointly entertain. They appear first, during the Overture, in their everyday clothes, working in an office, and, in mime, an argument develops between them.

"Then, as Act I starts, they are transformed into their fantasy avatars - Princes, Princesses, Priests and so on. In the course of the opera they work through their petty quarrels. Reconciled, they, and the audience, return to their real lives, happy that friendship and love have eventually triumphed.

"The opera was sung in German, with the spoken dialogue a mixture of English and Thai. There were surtitles, in English, Thai and Japanese, which sometimes got out of phase, and, in their English version, employed a weirdly old-fashioned translation – "To your goal leads this road, still you must, young one, manly win". The chorus were rather thin on the ground, and sometimes, too, in voice.

"Overall the standard not only equalled but actually exceeded what one would expect to experience in a typical European Opera house. Mexican/German Emilio Pons, Tamino, has a clear, rather Italianate tenor, with great emotional expressiveness (a touch of Gigli). The Australian Damian Whiteley has the powerful and generous basso profondo necessary for Sarastro, while Italian/Thai Monique Klongtruadroke as Queen of the Night looked terrific as a wicked witch (think Cruella de Vil in '101 Dalmatians'), and sang her two famously fiendish arias effortlessly, hitting top Fs with élan.

"There were three outstanding performances. The German baritone Falko Hönisch gave a hugely energetic and entertaining performance as Papageno. He sang strongly and mellifluously. Schikaneder would surely have approved! The scenes between him and Papagena (Areeya Rotjanadit the first two nights and JC Manar the final night), were the comic highlights, enlivened at the end by their family of tiny Papagenos and Papagenas, played with huge enthusiasm and flapping of wings by a flock of young children.

"The young Thai soprano Nadlada Thamtanakom was a sensational Pamina, a radiantly beautiful fairy-tale princess. She sang gloriously with great purity of tone and deeply affecting lyrical warmth – simply the best Pamina I've ever seen.

"The third outstanding performance was by the young Thai conductor Trisdee na Patalung. It was Opera Siam's 2006 production of Magic Flute that marked the operatic debut of the then 20 year old Trisdee, to rave reviews. It led to Trisdee being invited to conduct at the Rossini Festival in Pesaro, to equal acclaim, and further engagements in Italy, and in the Netherlands and the UK. In this production, Trisdee achieved miracles with the very young Orchestra, in a performance of great sensitivity and warmth, bringing out the sublime nature of Mozart's amazing score. Opera companies around the world should be looking to snap him up."

— *Auditorium Magazine, Berlin*

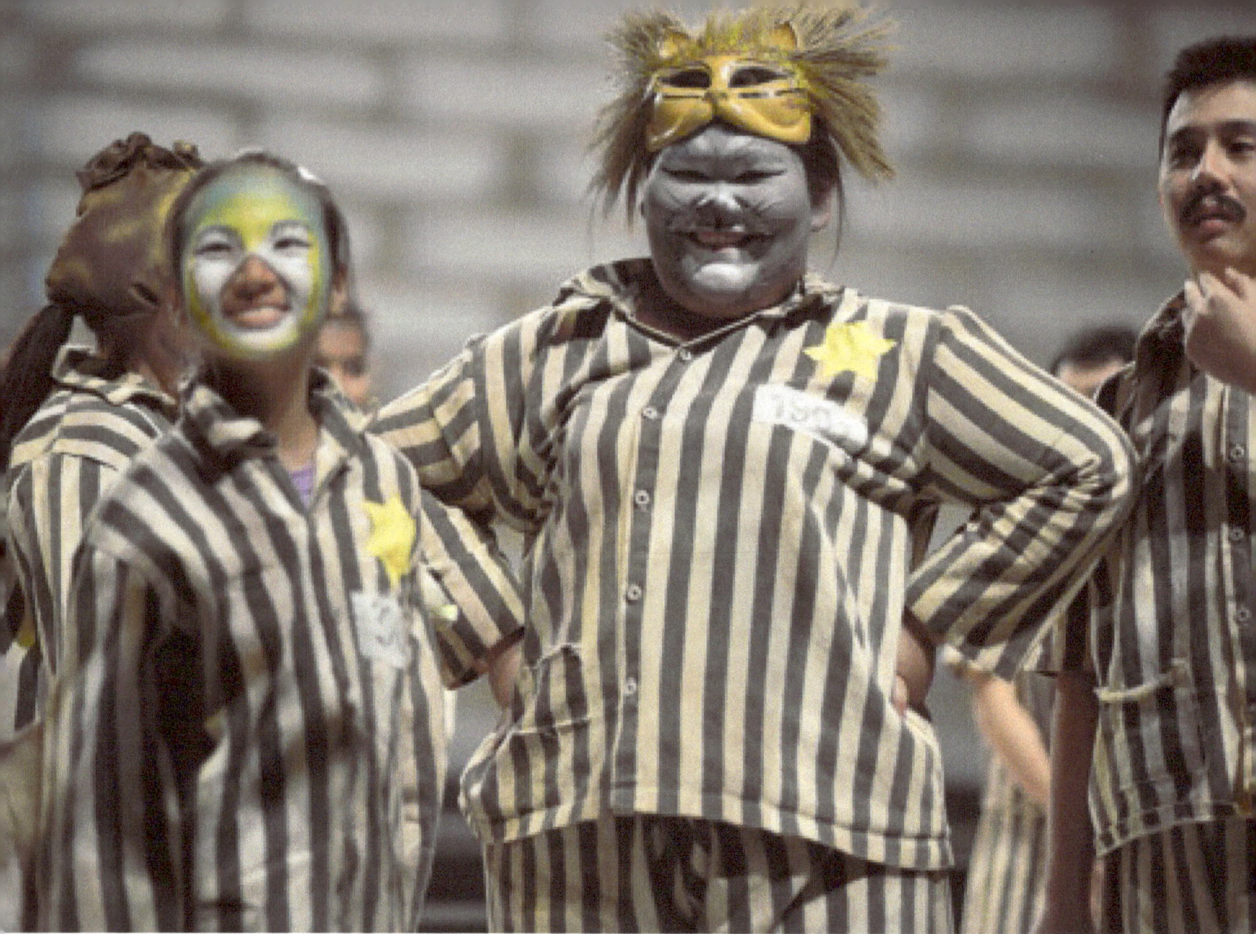

45. BRUNDIBAR (2015)
THAILAND PREMIERE

The premiere of *Brundibar* was the first official collaborative effort between Opera Siam and local embassies to put on an event memorializing the Holocaust each year. It was also an occasion to involve children and young people so the opera that was chosen was *Brundibar* by Hans Krasa. This children's opera was performed 55 times at the Terezin Concentration Camp; the Nazis used a propaganda film of the opera to delude the outside world about their treatment of the Jews. Most of the children, along with the director and the composer, were sent to Auschwitz.

The production, which also included a concert performance of other music created by composers who were imprisoned in Terezin, in the words of *The Nation*, "made for an almost unbearably poignant occasion"

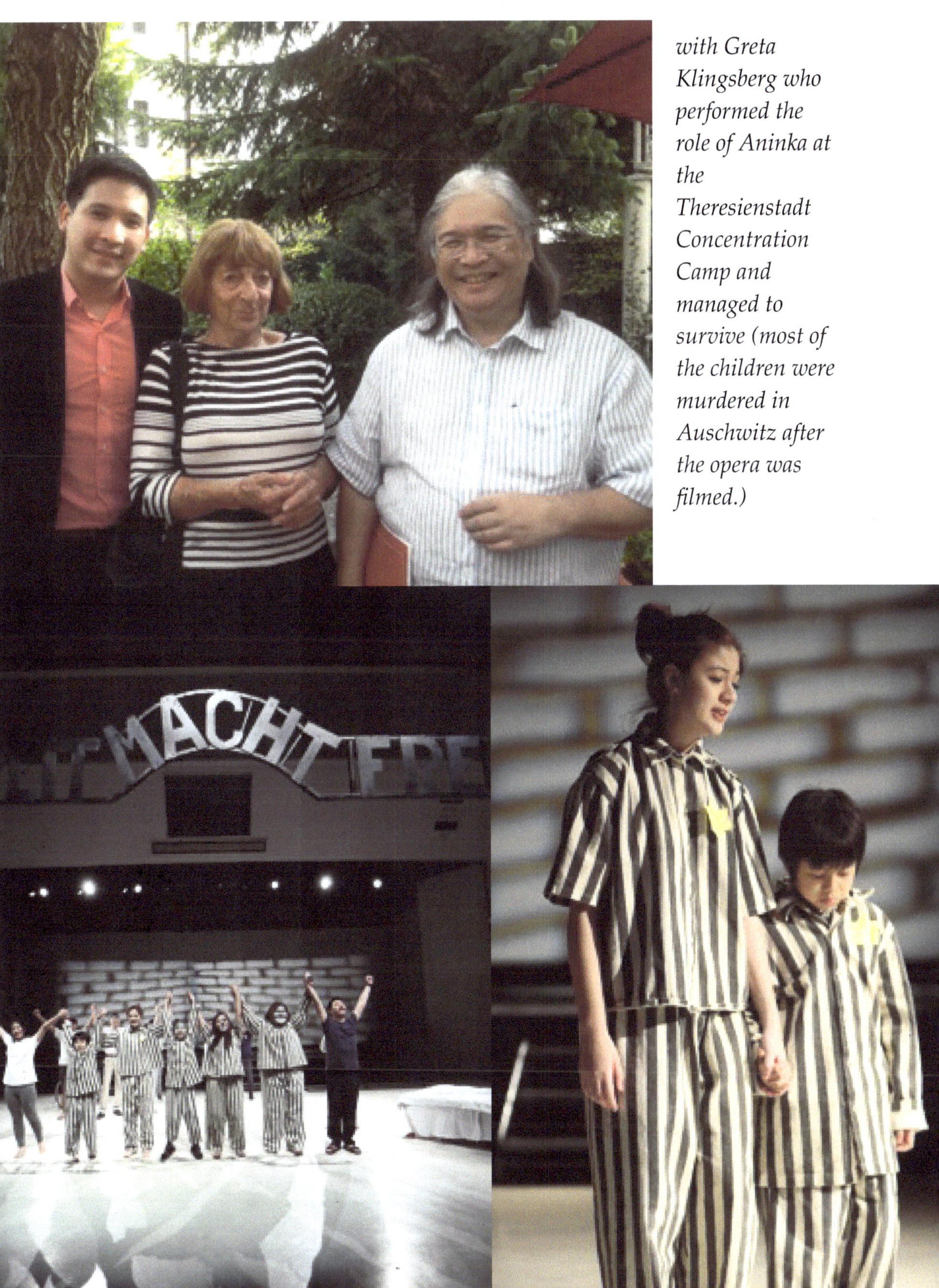

with Greta Klingsberg who performed the role of Aninka at the Theresienstadt Concentration Camp and managed to survive (most of the children were murdered in Auschwitz after the opera was filmed.)

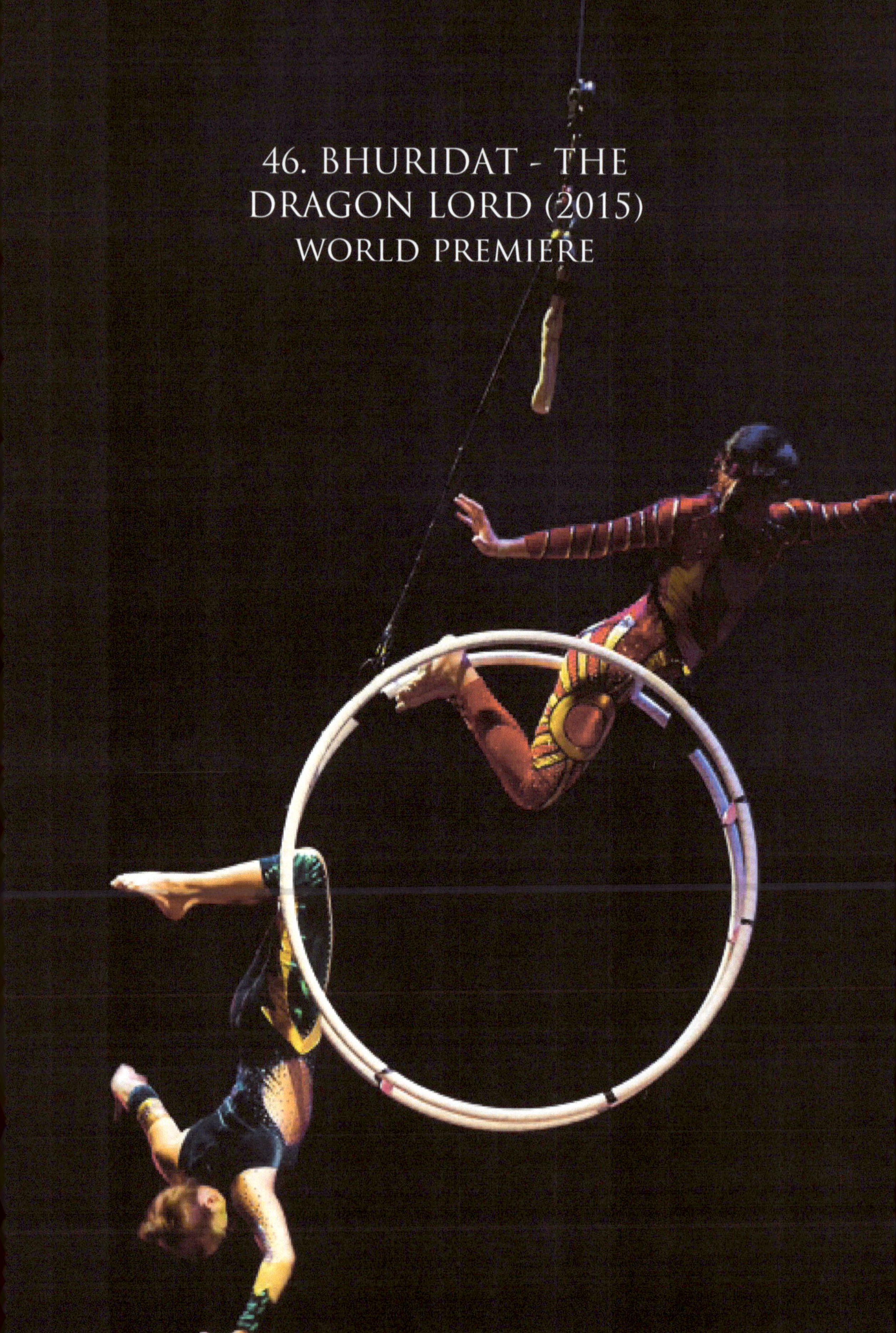

46. BHURIDAT - THE DRAGON LORD (2015)

WORLD PREMIERE

It was really with *Bhuridat* that the idea of *DasJati* was born. The fact is that *The Silent Prince* is an adaptation of the first of the ten iconic tales and that *Mahajanaka* is the second of the stories. Somtow said, "I became drawn to these tales and was casting around for one that I could do into another opera. It was in the middle of composing *Bhuridat* that it hit me like a bolt of lightning: why not do all ten?"

It was a shocking concept because Wagner's *Ring* only has four operas and is the reigning work of "epic" in opera. A series of ten operas, whether or not it was actually longer in terms of minutes, would automatically be the greatest magnitude of integrated classical work in history. Somtow began researching all ten of the *DasJati* stories. As of 2018, five have been performed. In the coming season, two more are planned for release.

Bhuridat was the first Opera Siam production to make extensive use of aerial ballet. The opening battle between a garuda and a naga, the dragon lord's levitating dances, were a radical new dimension for Opera Siam's productions.

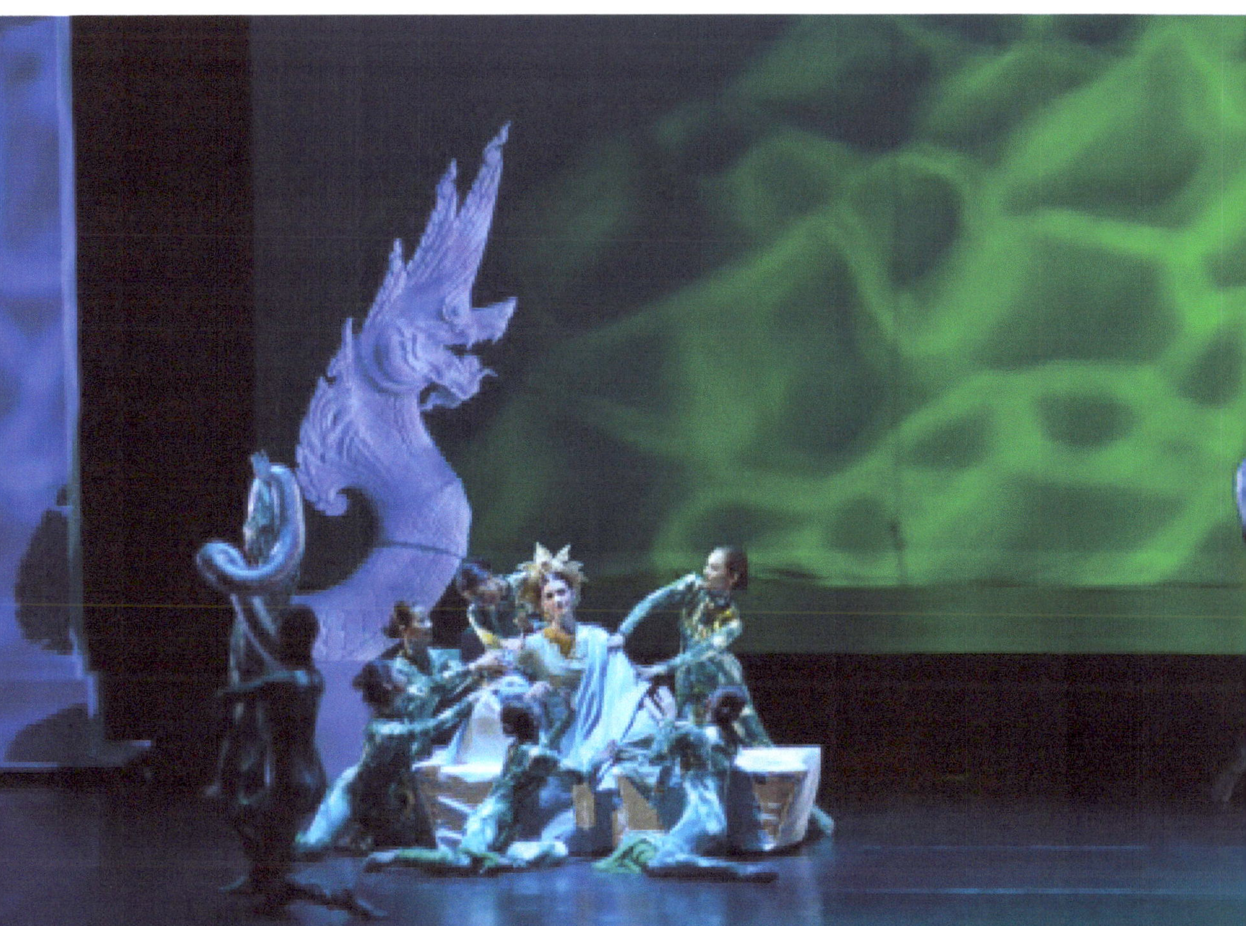

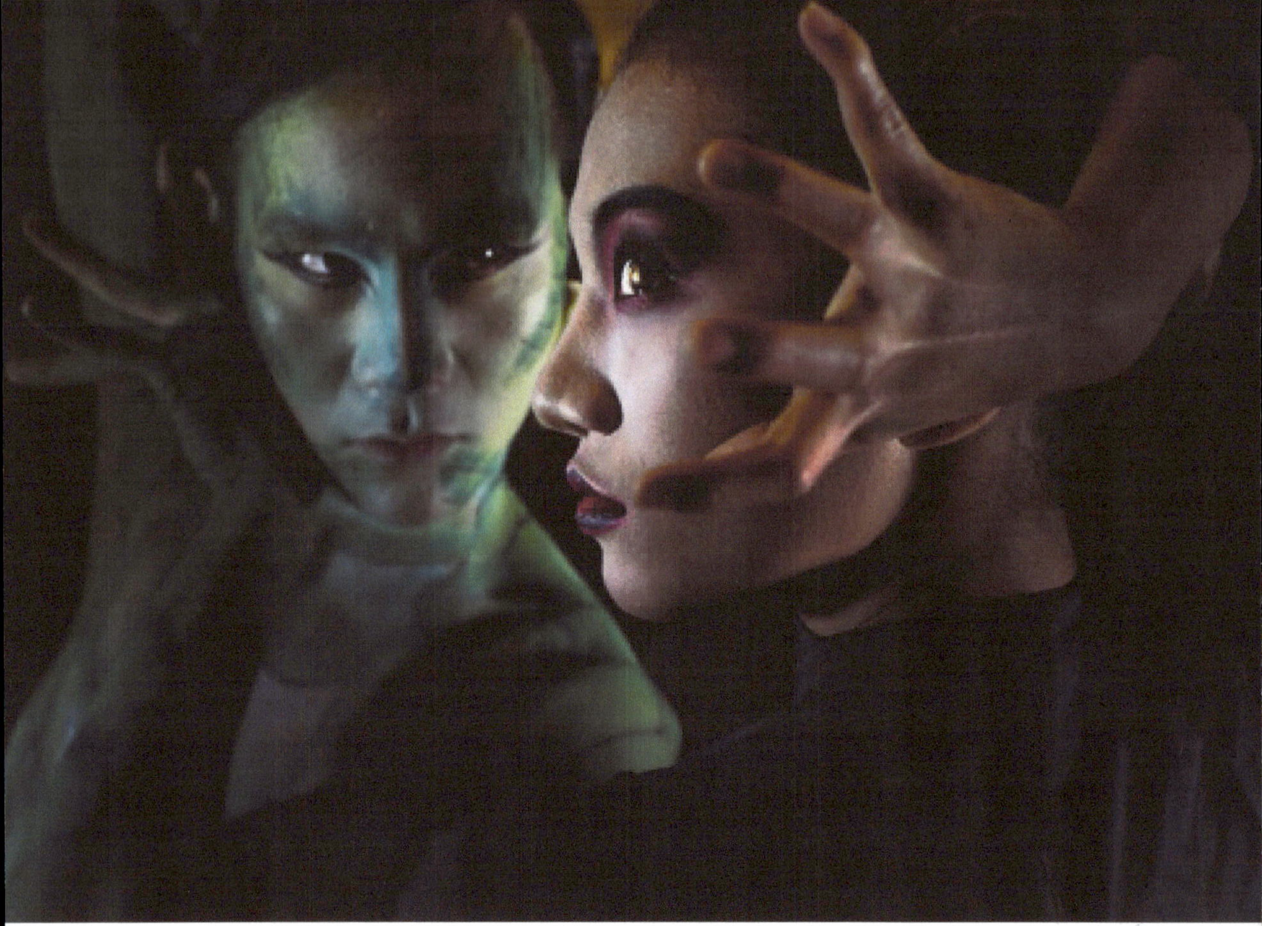

— Main Cast: Jak Cholvijarn, Damian Whiteley, Stacey Tappan, Chaiporn Puangmalee, Puntwitt Asawadejamethakul, Kyo Won Han, Dag Schantz, Monique Klongtruadroke

— Puwarate Wongatichat, choreography

— Somtow Sucharitkul, director

— Siam Philharmonic, conducted by Trisdee na Patalung

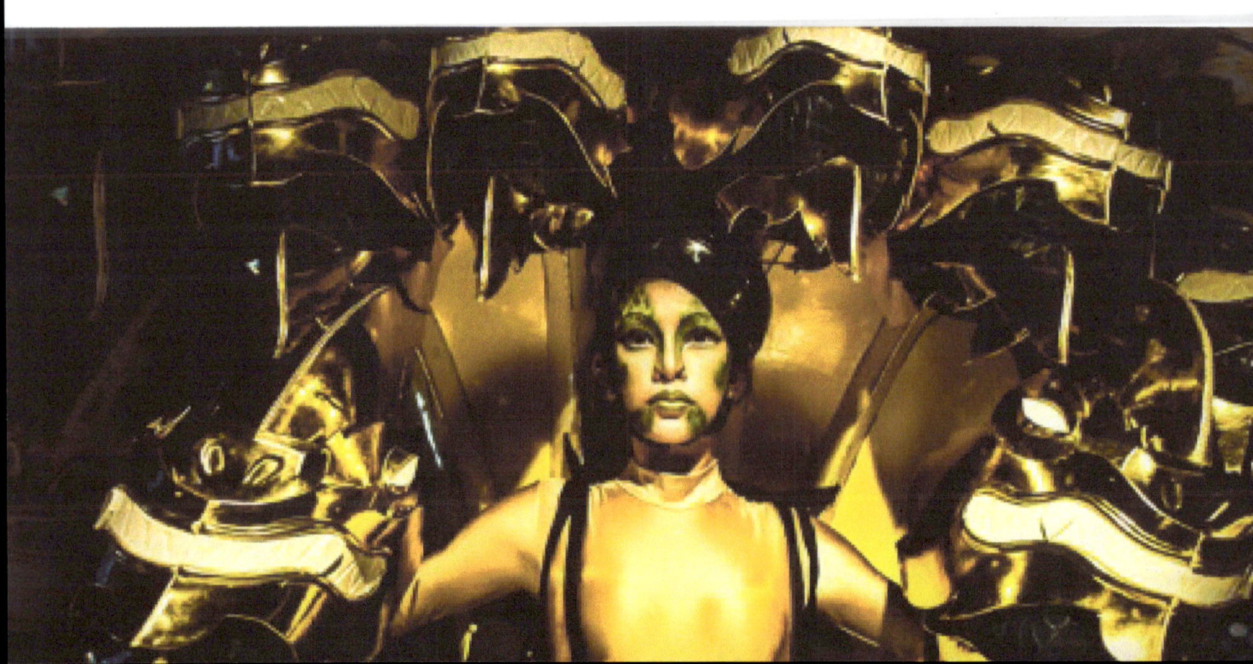

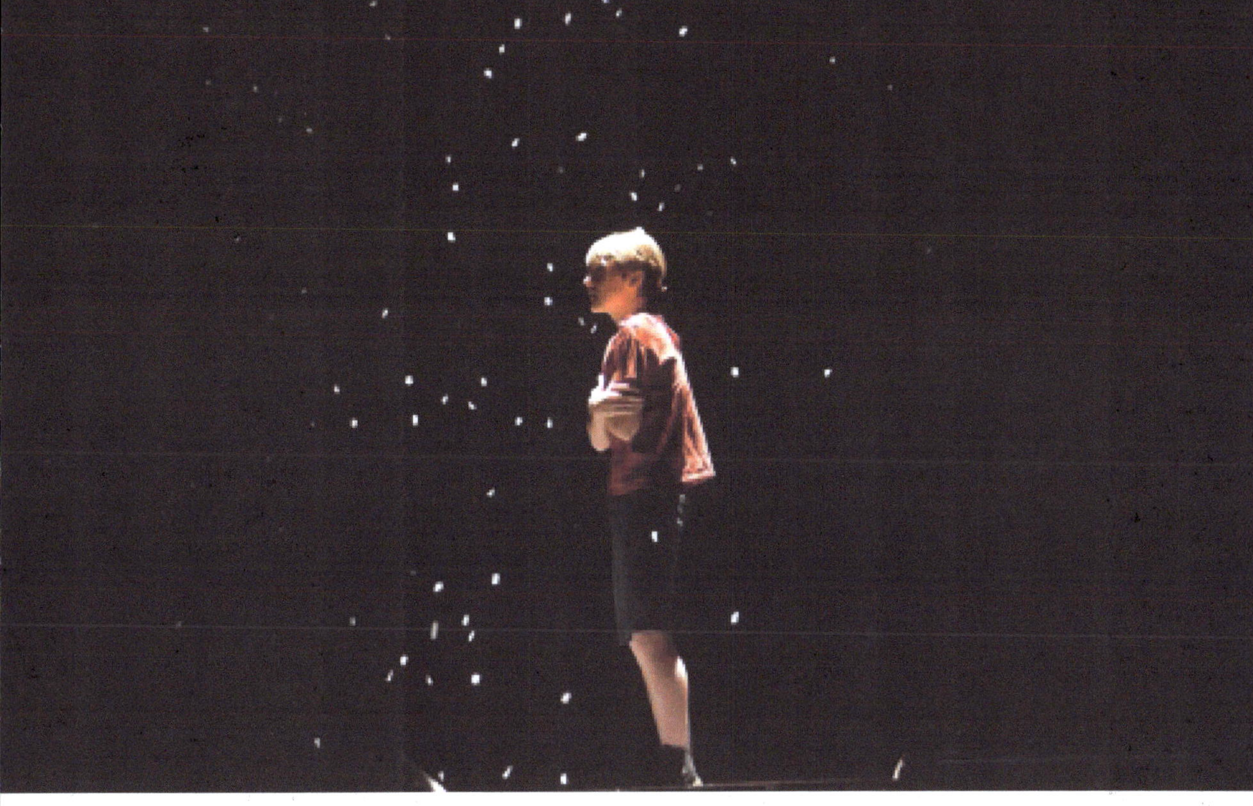

47. THE SNOW DRAGON (2015)
THAILAND PREMIERE

The Snow Dragon is adapted from Somtow's 1979 short story *The Fallen Country.* Commissioned by the Skylight Theater in Milwaukee, the opera premiered there under the baton of Viswa Subbaraman. Matthew Ozawa directed. The Bangkok production was basically the Milwaukee version, adjusted for a much larger stage, with members of the Siam Philharmonic in the orchestra. Dealing with a painful contemporary subject, that of an abused child who escapes into a fantasy world that is even more perilous than his real life, and a tormented psychiatrist who has lost her way, this is a short but searing work.

It is accessible and enjoyable music that, along with the sensitive handling of the difficult subject-matter, helped audiences on the first two nights, which I attended, to respond with standing ovations.

They were reacting, too, to some powerful performances on stage. Luke Brotherhood, like Billy, a 12 year old, was a wonderfully convincing Billy, flinching from human contact, both real and metaphorical. His voice, sensibly amplified, was clear and gained in confidence. Colleen Brooks convincingly portrayed Dora's own emotional journey, with a firm and radiant mezzo. Cassandra Black was magnificently Wagnerian as the soprano Snow Dragon. Erica Schuller magically transformed from Billy's foster mother into a fantasy princess, and blended beautifully with Brooks and Black in the final trio. The imaginative direction, drawing on both Eastern and Western elements, was by Matthew Ozawa.

— *Auditorium Magazine, Berlin*

The music and imagery are more than sufficient to tell the story clearly, move the heart and may actually engage the mind more. *The Snow Dragon* is a remarkably important stretch in the concept of opera!

— *Dial Urban, Milwaukee*

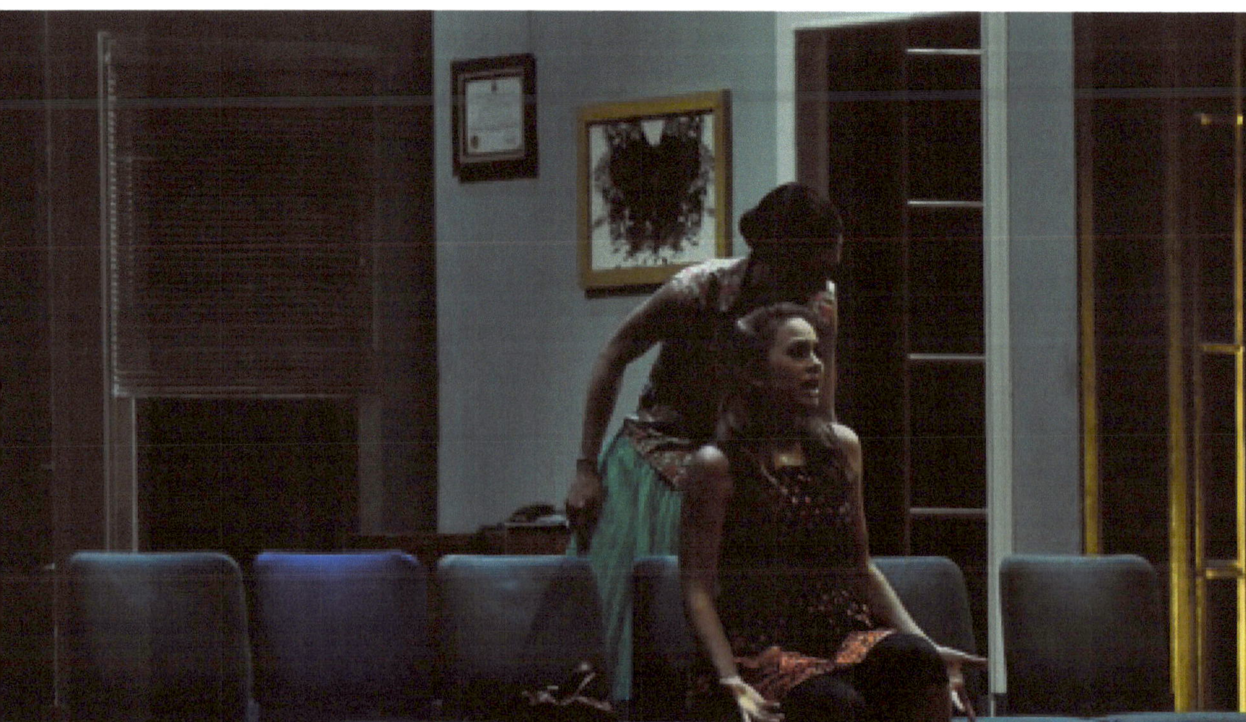

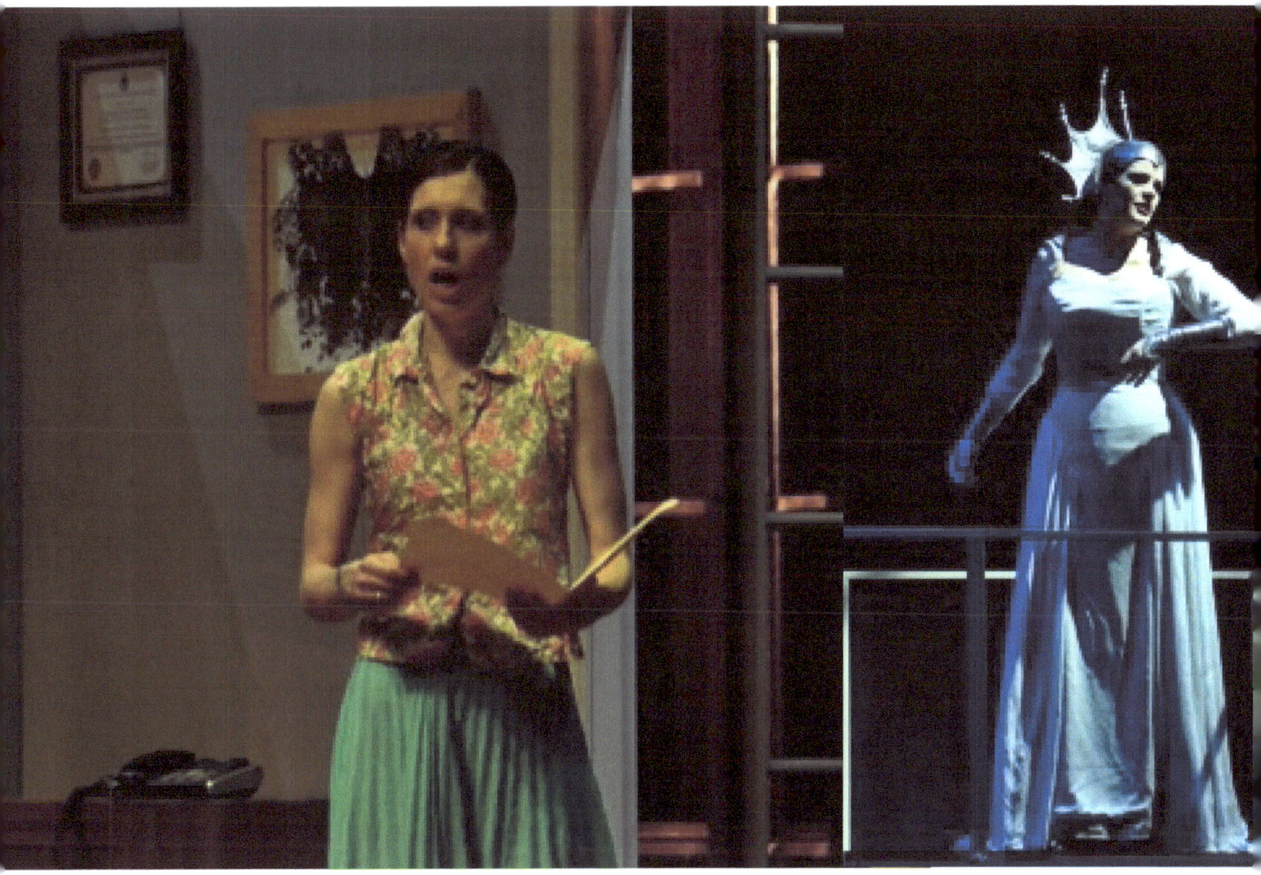

— Main Cast: Luke Brotherhood, Colleen Brooks, Erica Schuller, Damian Whiteley, Cassandra Black

— Matthew Ozawa, director

— Siam Philharmonic Orchestra, conducted by Viswa Subbaraman

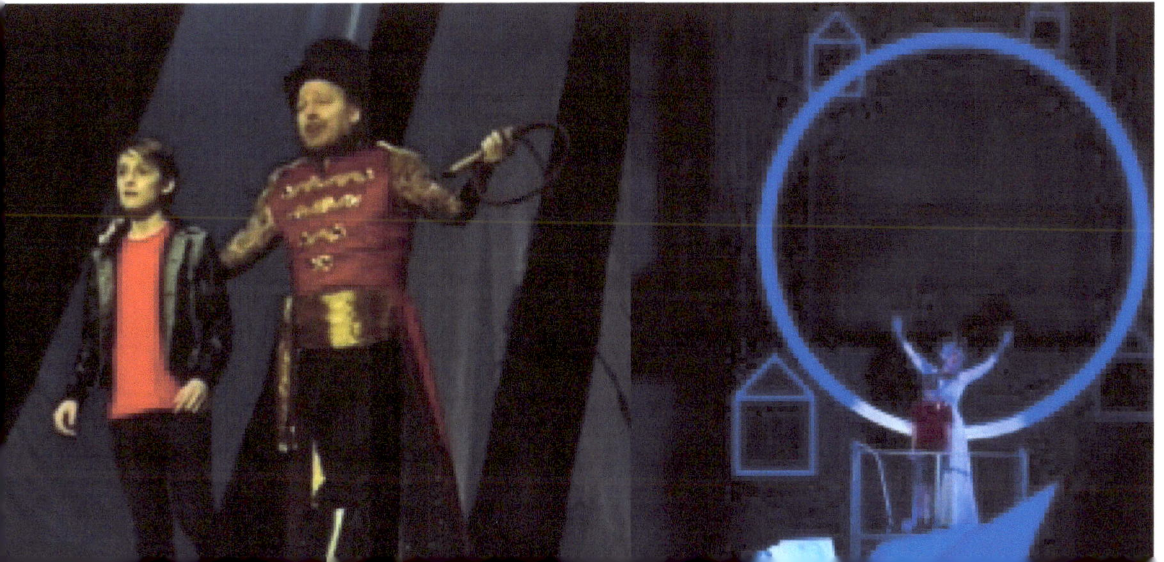

48. SAMA - THE FAITHFUL SON (2015)
WORLD PREMIERE

With the idea of *DasJati* firmly in place, *Sama* was the fourth opera to be written and produced, though it is actually No. 3 in the standard sequence. This is because the idea of doing all ten only came to Somtow in a flash while he was in the *middle* of composing *Bhuridat,* which is No. 6 in the official list.

Whereas *Bhuridat* is an ornate and complex tale that goes through several generations of a family saga, *Sama's* story is very simple, rather folkloric. It required a different approach; dealing always in dualities, the composer scored it for two symmetrical chamber orchestras.

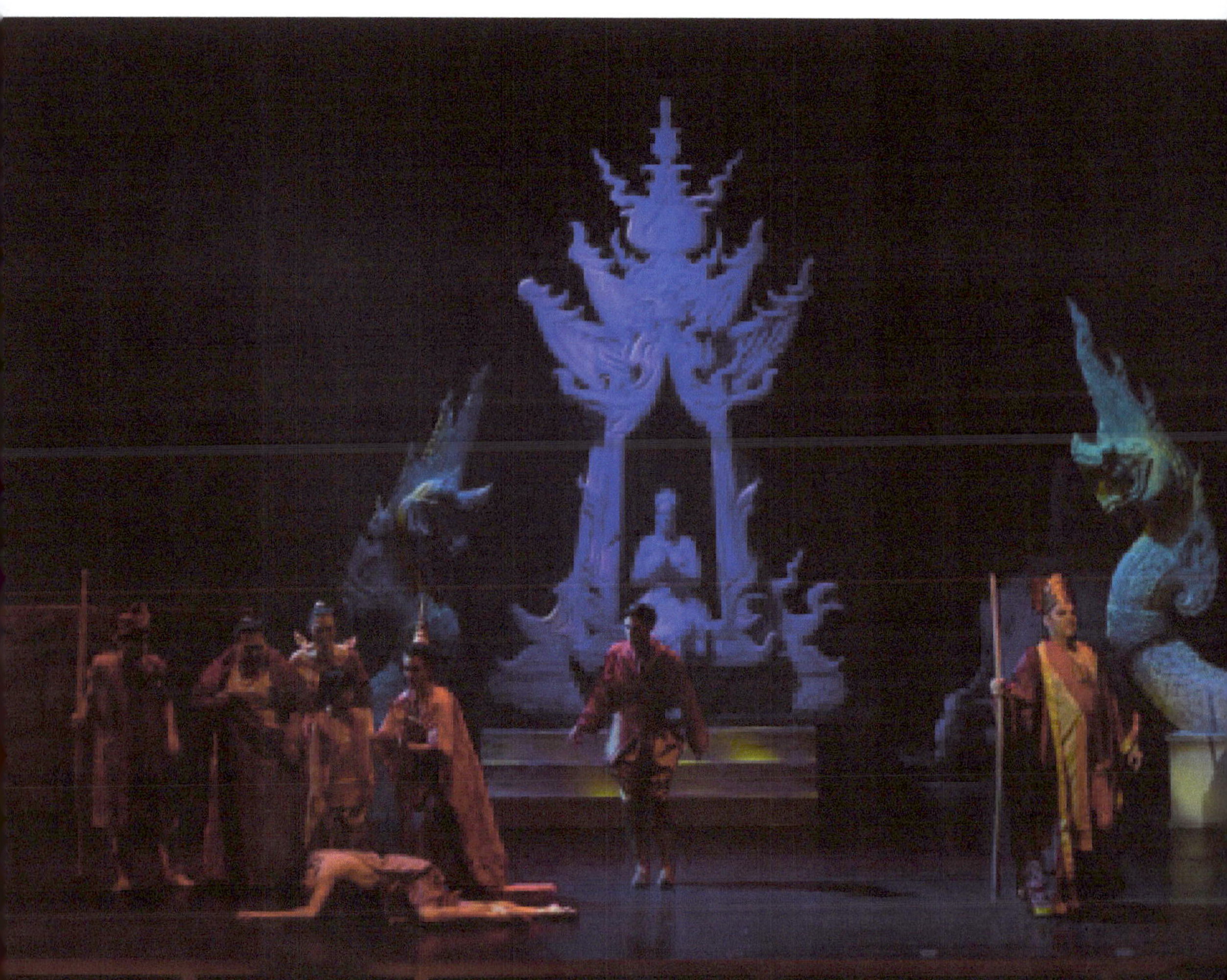

The opera was premiered in the new state of the art theater in Rangsit, the Suryadhep Hall, and took advantage of its brilliant acoustics.

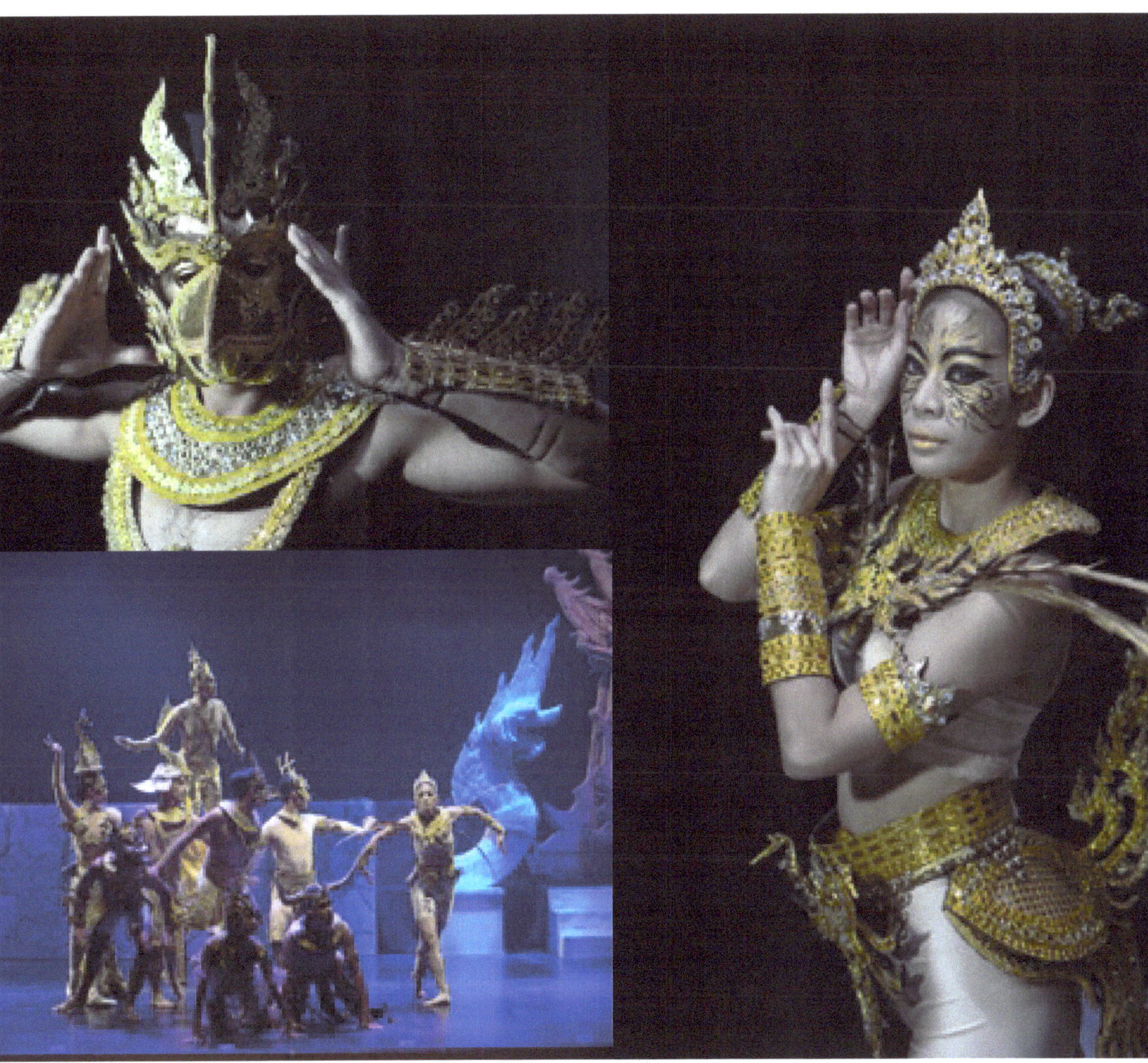

— Main Cast: Cassandra Black, Jak Cholvicharn, Damian Whiteley, Kaleigh Raw Gamaché
— lighting by Ryan Attig
—costumes by Nathawan Santiphab
— directed by Somtow Sucharitkul
— Siam Philharmonic Orchestra, conducted by Trisdee na Patalung

49. MOZART AND ME (2016)
THAILAND PREMIERE

An engrossing one man show, acted, sung, and produced by Australian bass Damian Whiteley, absolutely riveted the small but intense audience at the Siam Society.

Truly a virtuoso performance: Whiteley changed costumes on stage several times, accompanied himself at the piano, and acted with a manic energy. He plays the role of Lorenzo da Ponte, Mozart's great collaborator, somehow managing to survive to hang around in Hollywood in modern times.

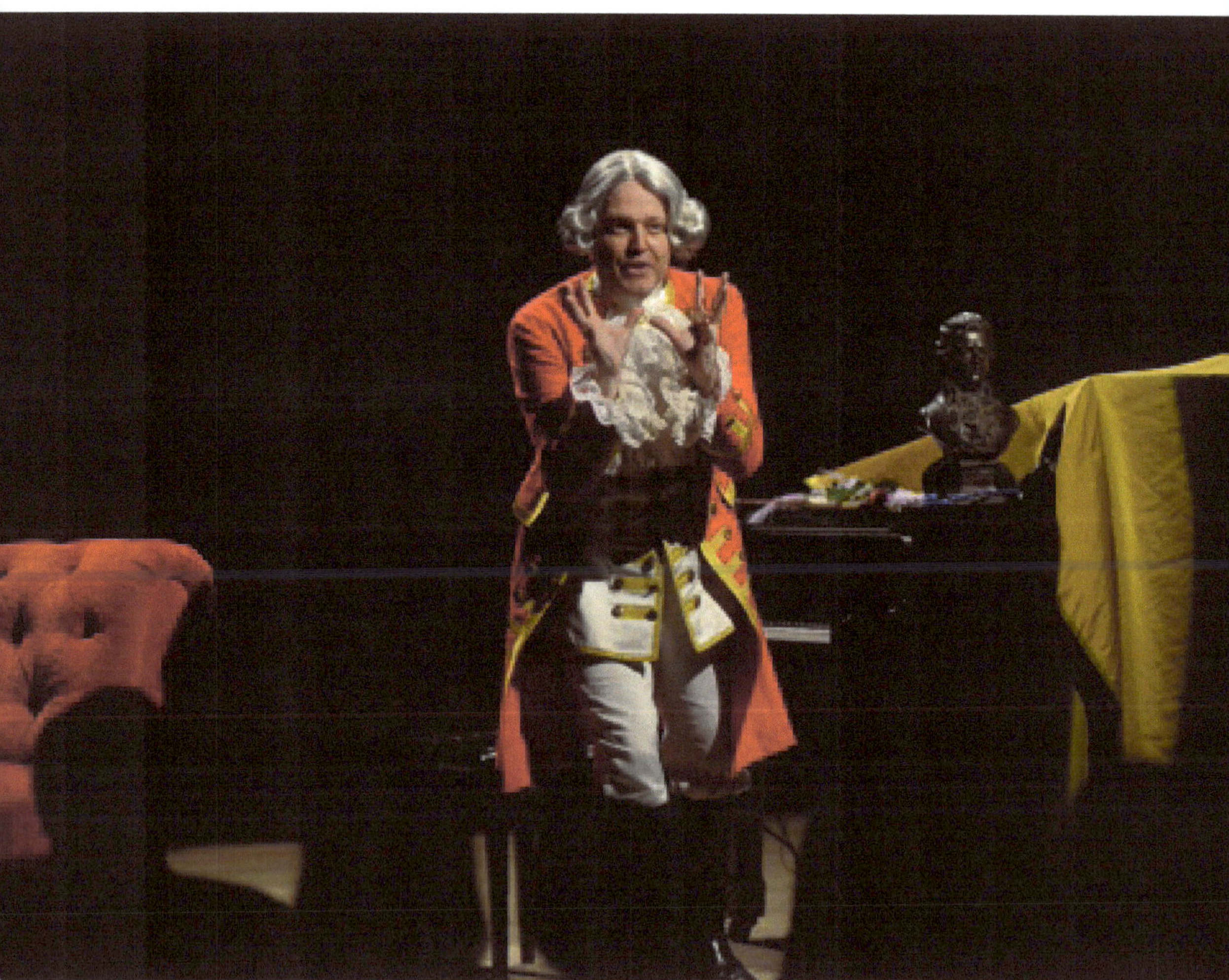

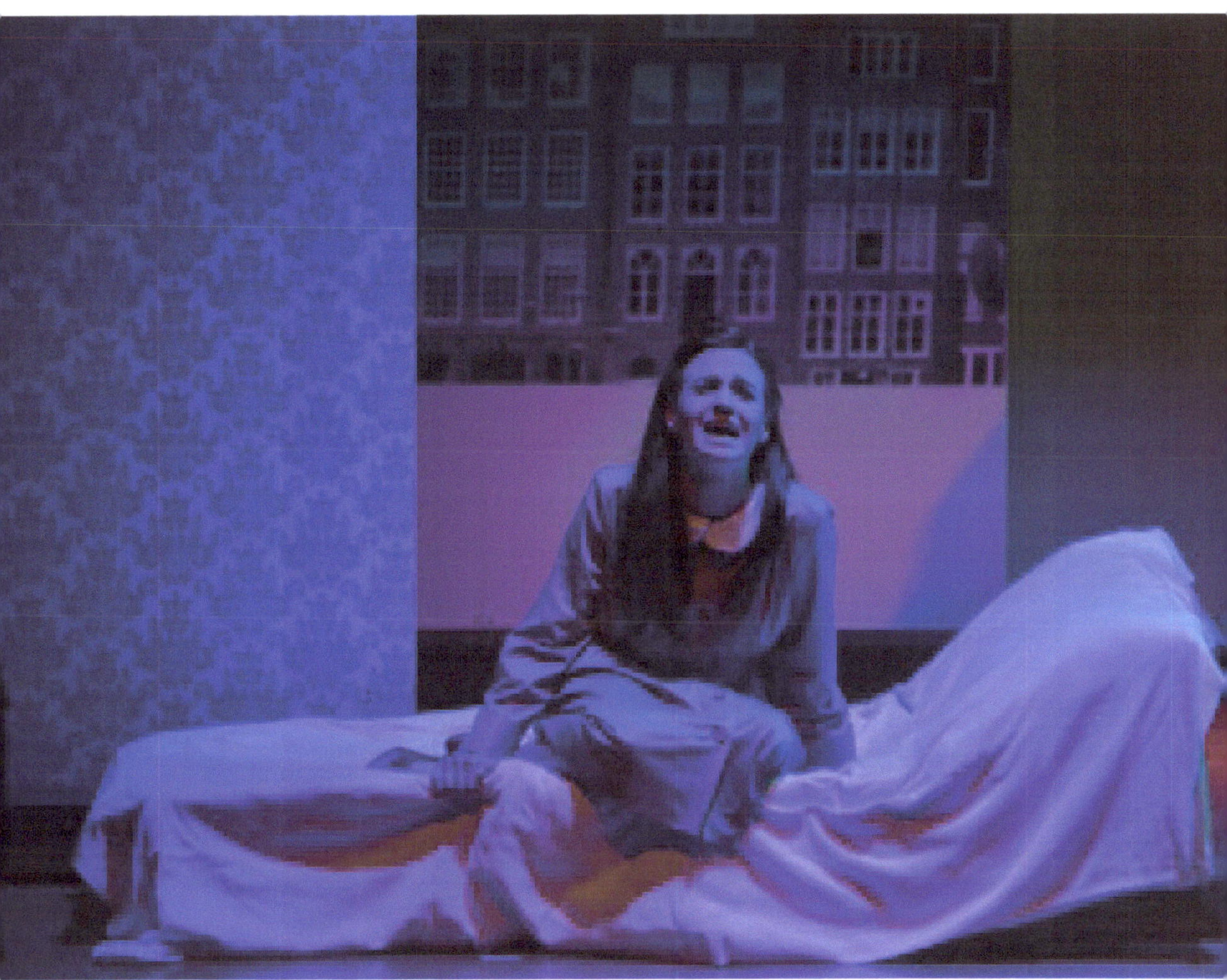

50. THE DIARY OF ANNE FRANK (2016)
THAILAND PREMIERE

This production was introduced to Opera Siam but Singaporean conductor and producer Adrian Tan, who conducted the Thai premiere. Somtow, in a last minute director's role, opened up the drama, having non-singing actors portraying the roles alluded to in this normally one-man show.

— Main Cast: Kaleigh Rae Gamaché
— directed by Somtow Sucharitkul
— Siam Philharmonic Orchestra, conductor Adrian Tan

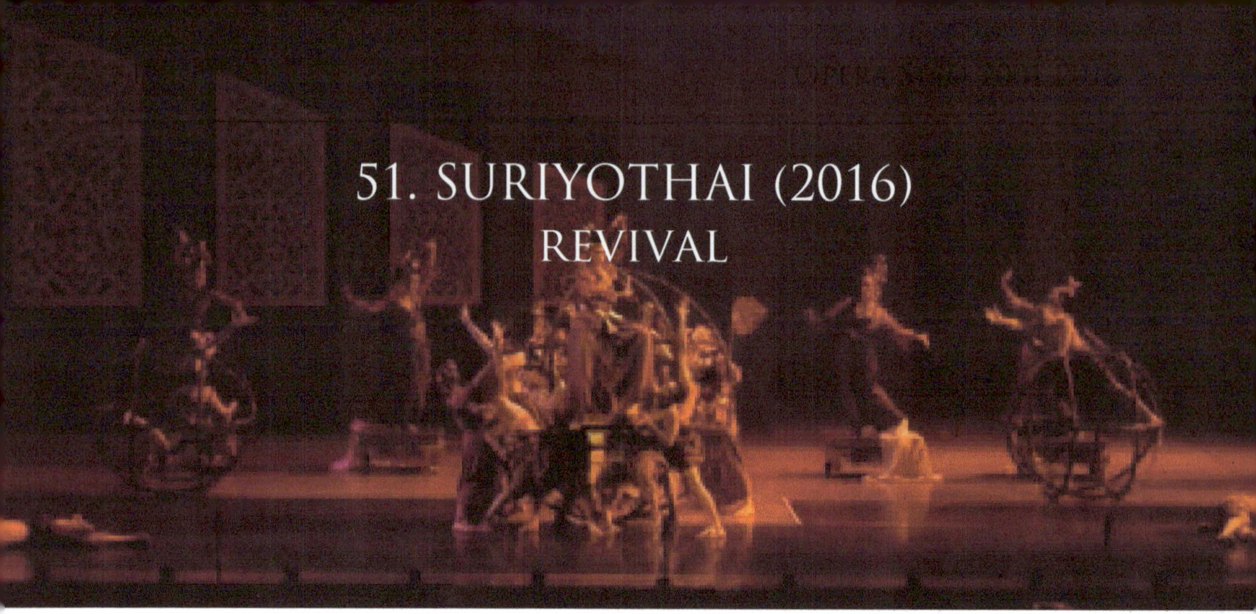

51. SURIYOTHAI (2016)
REVIVAL

Popular as ever, the performances of *Suriyothai* in the 2016 revival were as packed as the first performances. Once again, Trisdee na Patalung conducted and the original cast returned.

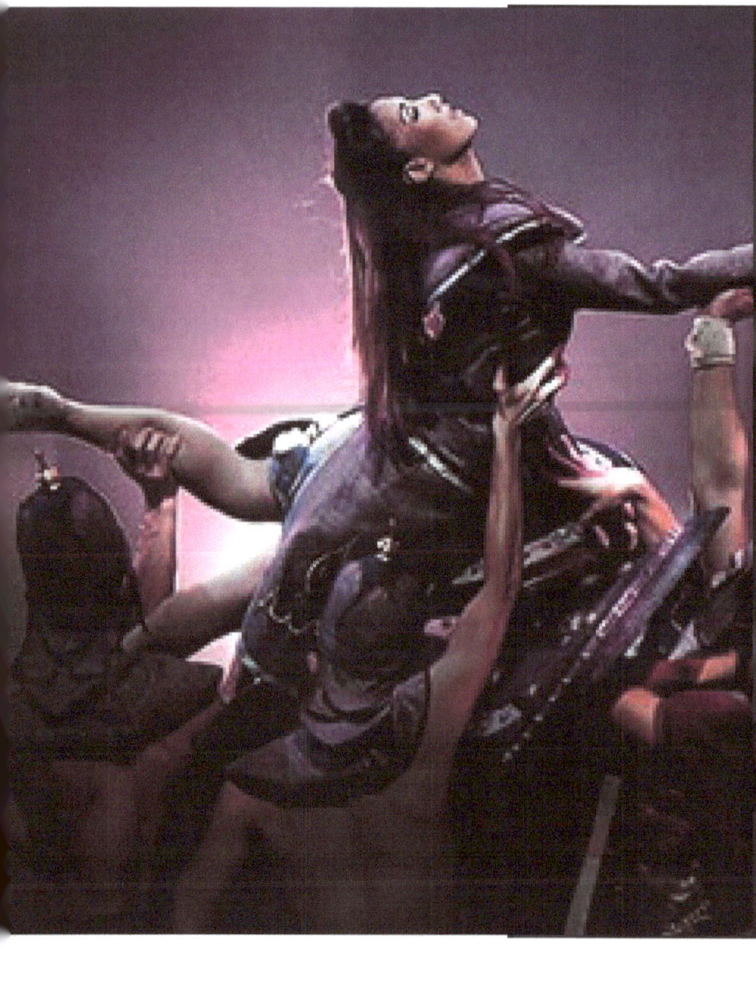

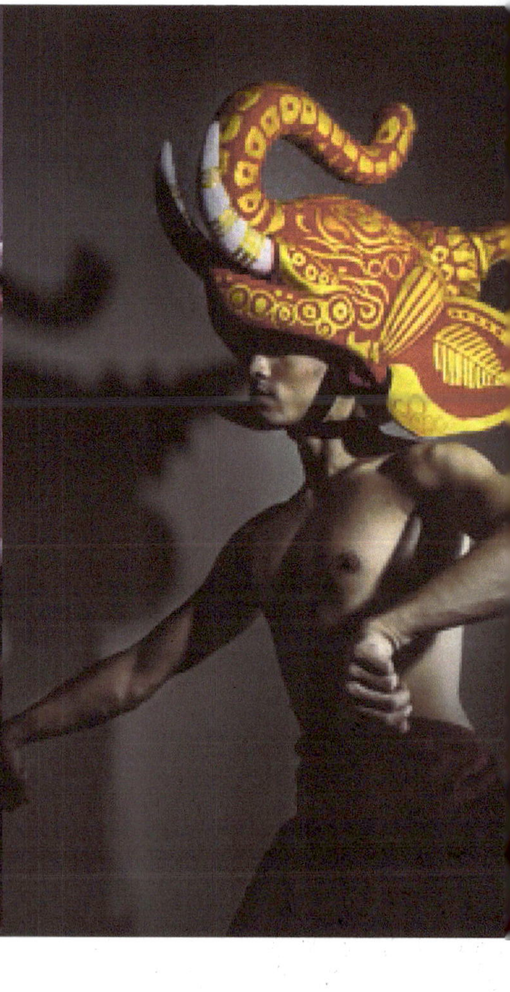

52. TEN LIVES OF THE BUDDHA (2016) COMPILATION

A collection of scenes from all the *DasJati* operas composed so far, and some from the then unfinished *Nemiraj,* was an indication of where the project stood at that time. The evening included a sneak preview of the 33 Gods scene from *Nemiraj,* the first ensemble for 33 distinct characters in the history of opera.

Khun Ploypailin Jensen, granddaughter of HM King Rama IX, appeared as one of the thirty-three gods.

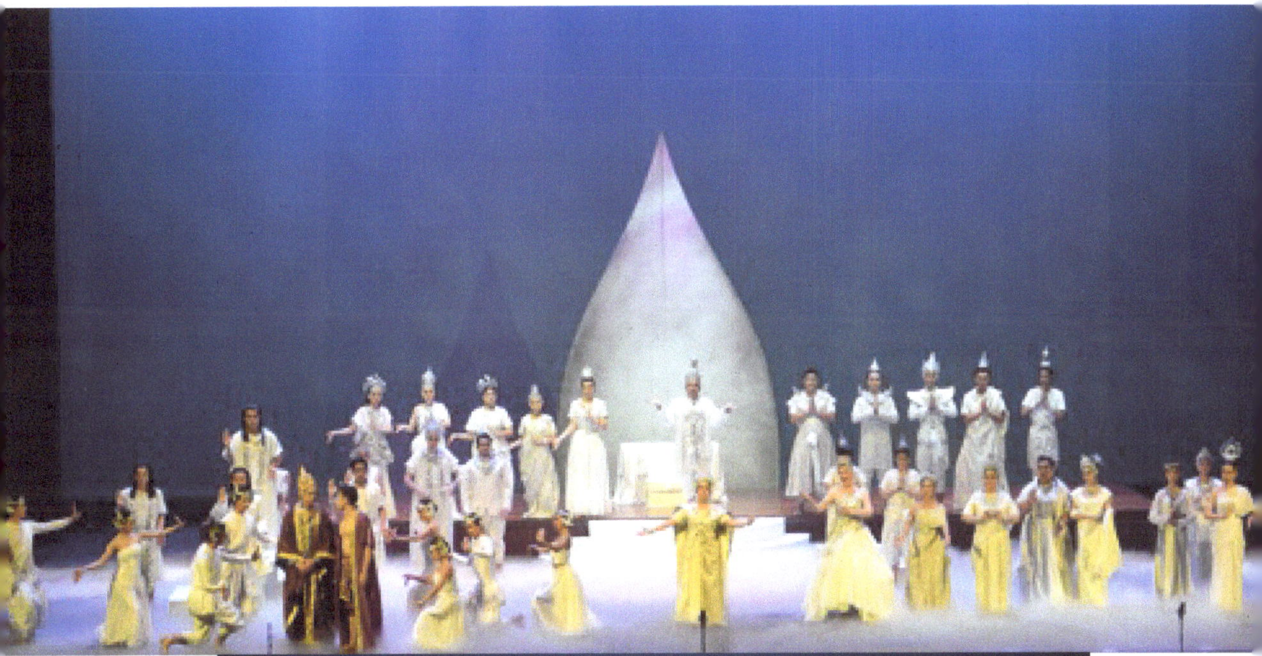

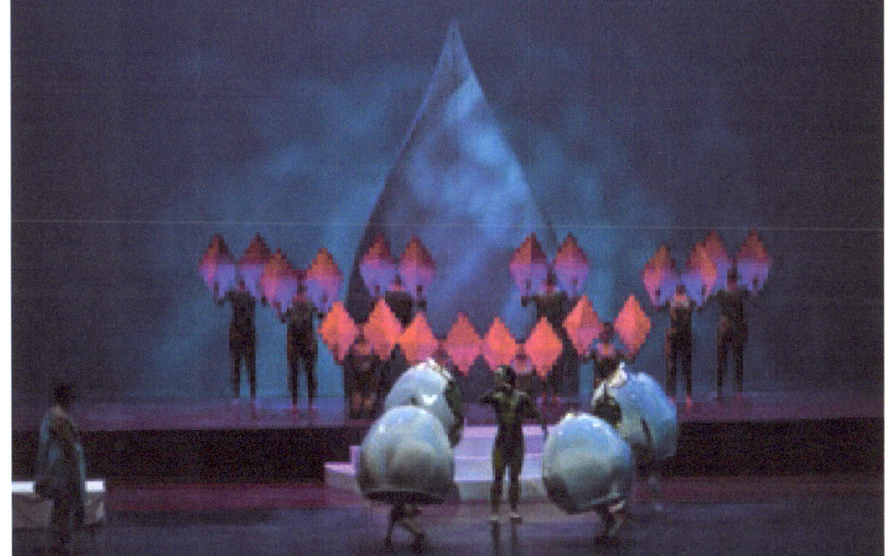

53. THE SILENT PRINCE (2016)
EUROPEAN TOURING PRODUCTION

The 2016 European tour, taking the production of *The Silent Prince* to Bayreuth, Brno, and Prague, was an important breakout event in the history of Opera Siam. Reviews in the German and Czech press were thoughtful, and lent weight to the idea that Opera Siam had truly come of age and was truly ready to take on Europe.

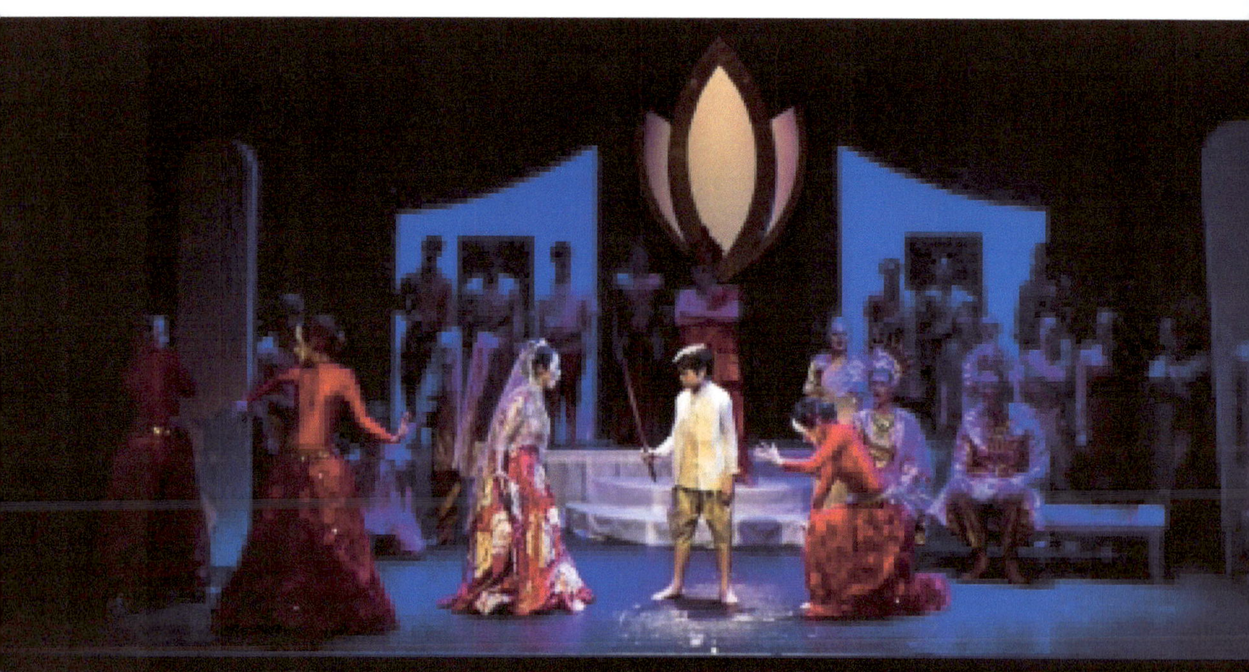

"based on traditional Southeast Asian aesthetics, but subtly adapted to the comprehensibility of a western audience."

— *Opera Plus, Czechia*

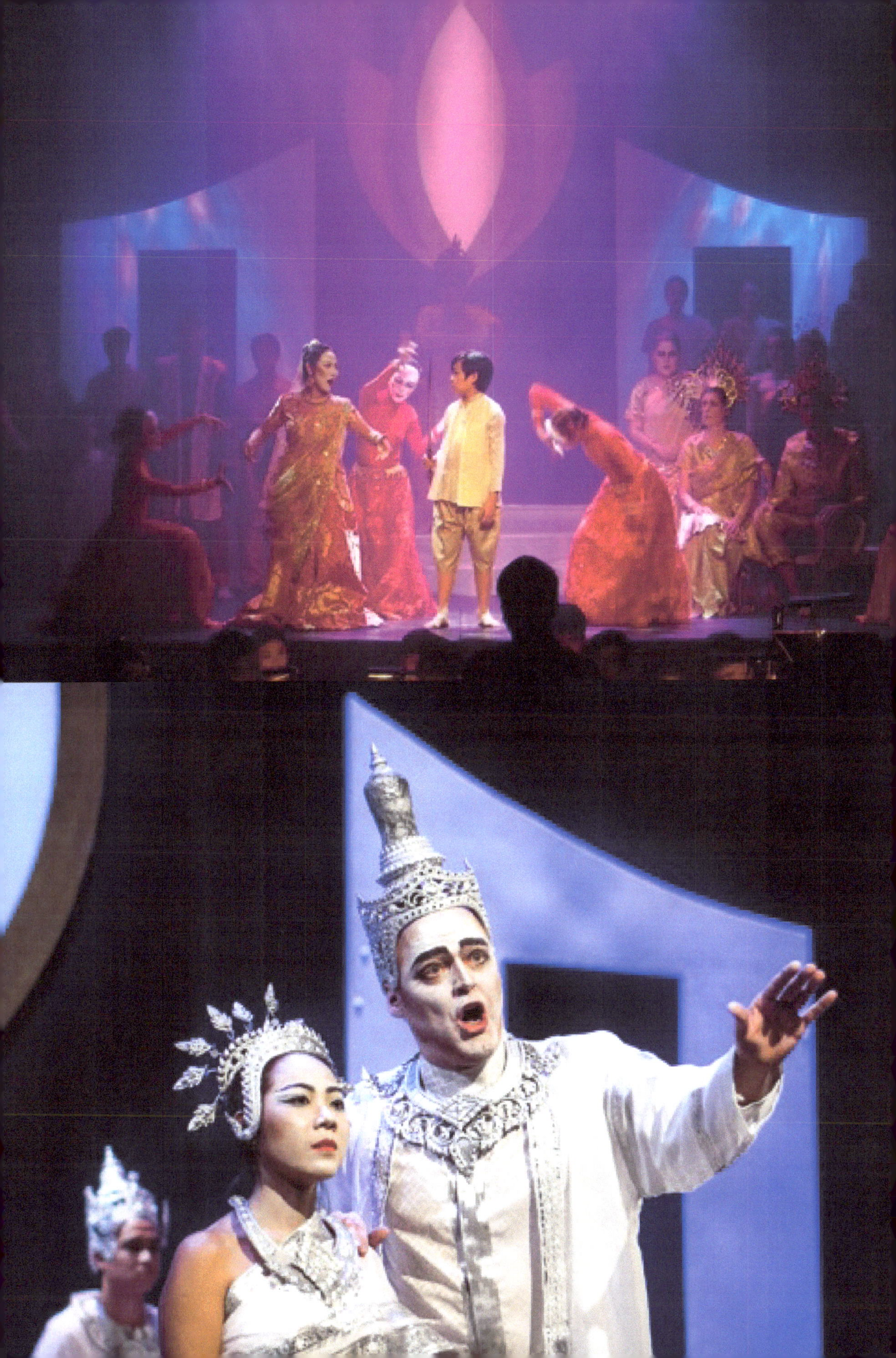

"the composer truly knows his craft. This is a joyful and technically very accomplished syncretism. The stylistic collage conflates highly coloristic and saturated melodic lines with simple rhythms in the manner of the refined musical worlds of Franz Schreker (Vienna 1920), Leonard Bernstein and Steven Sondheim ... Western tonalities are overlaid with Southeast Asian melodies. But rather than creating a confused chaos of sound, Sucharitkul has fashioned an exciting score in which - and this is what is so modern about it - East and West are united in harmony yet with their differences clearly audible — partaking fully in the spirit of this festival."

— *North Bavaria Courier*

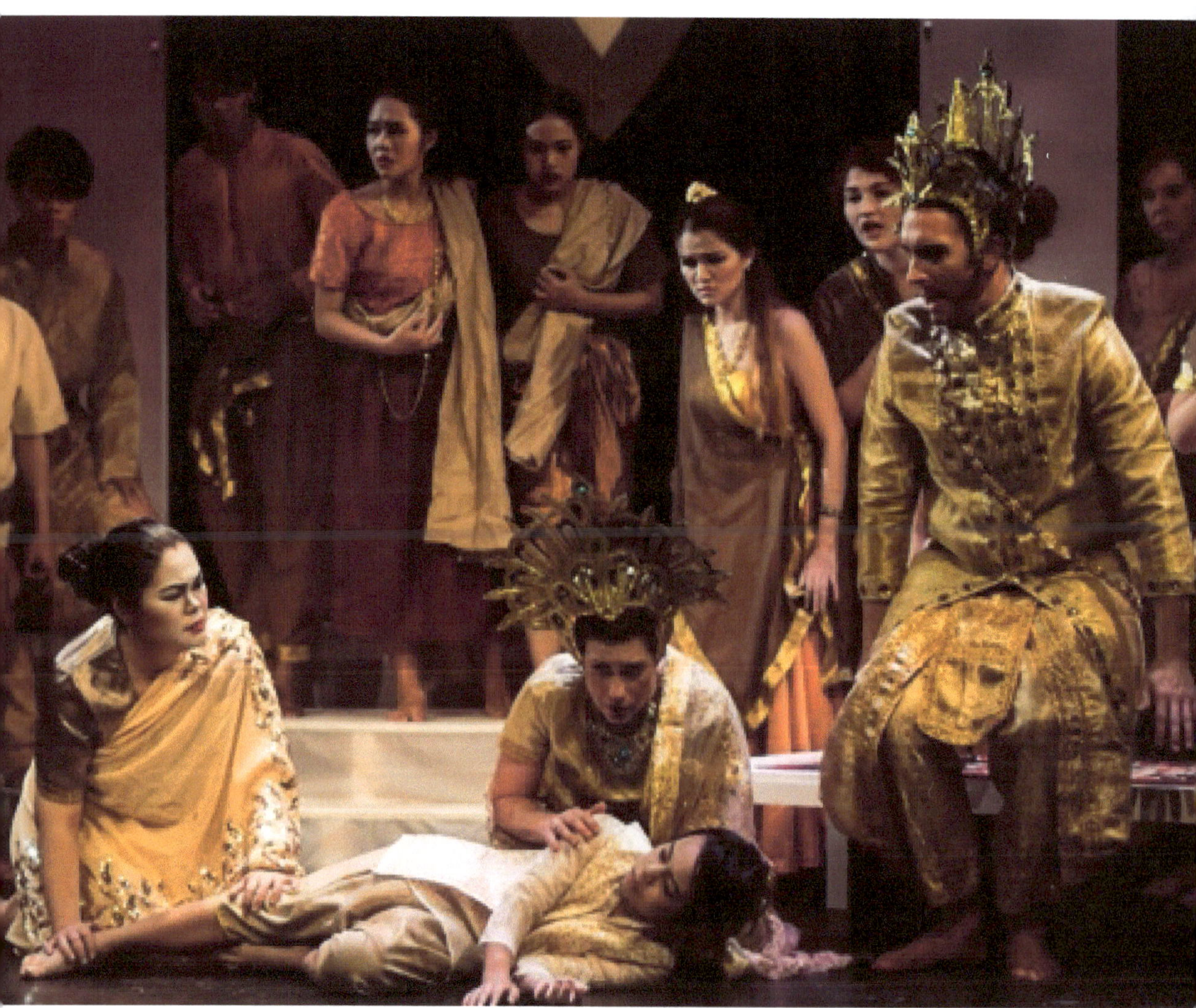

54. NEMIRAJ - CHARIOT OF HEAVEN (2017)

WORLD PREMIERE

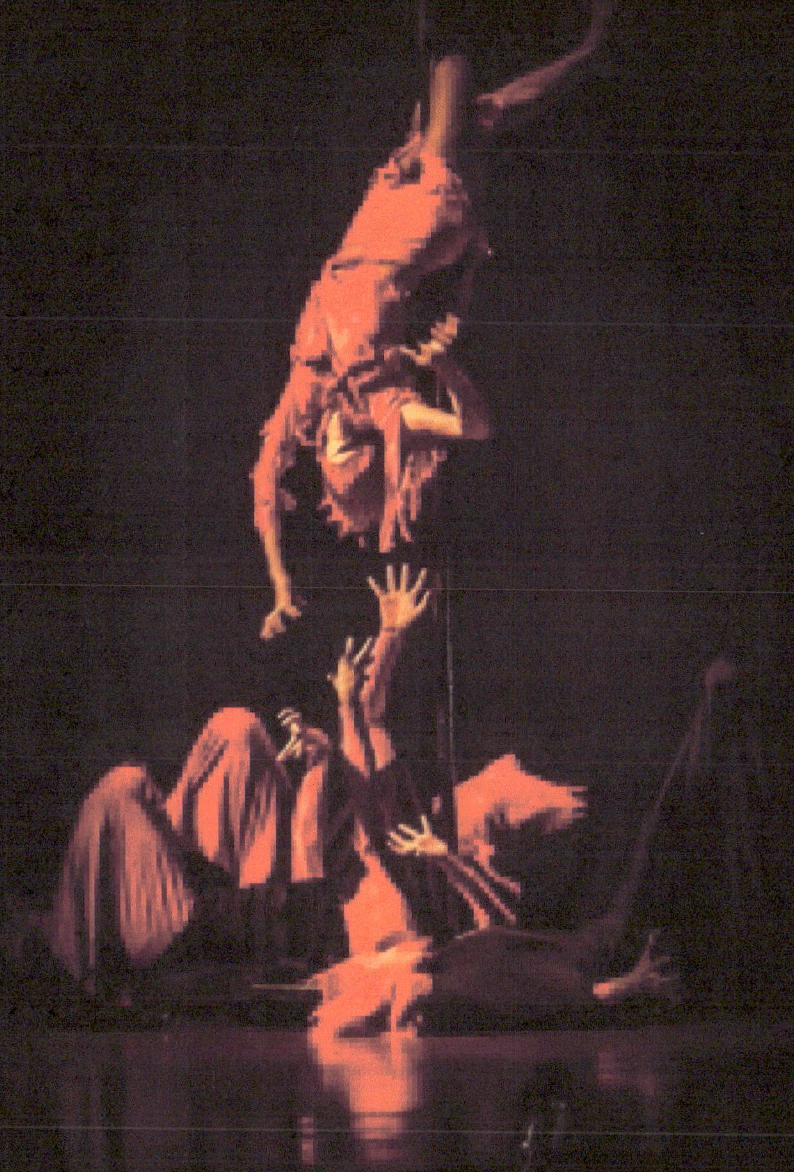

After some logistical problems forced delays in its premiere, the fifth *DasJati* opera to be composed finally made it to the stage. Each of the five operas composed so far contains one or more exotically divergent elements and *Nemiraj* was no exception. First there was the ensemble number for thirty-three distinct voices, an operatic first, in the heaven scene. Equally a first was the necessity to have 82,000 generations of time go by between the first and second scene. Allowing twenty years for each generation this meant that 2 million years would pass, more than the entire recorded history of human existence

Somtow's solution was the entertaining *March of Time* ballet, a parade of music and dance constantly moving in time to encompass all of civilization, culminating in a nuclear holocaust and beginning all over again, with variations.

Unlike *Bhuridat,* with its convoluted plot, *The Chariot of Heaven* had virtually none, and depended on impressive, static tableaux and great singing and musicianship for its effects.

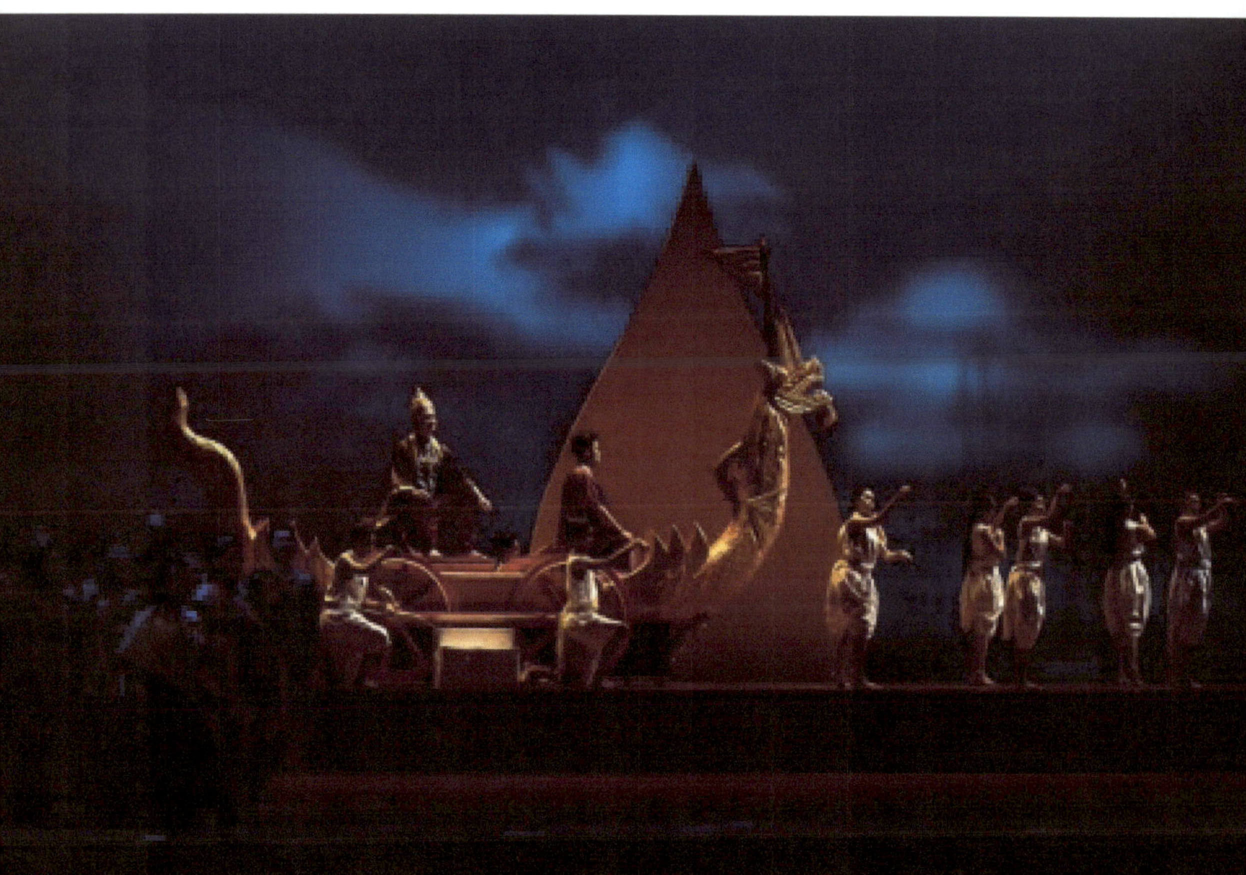

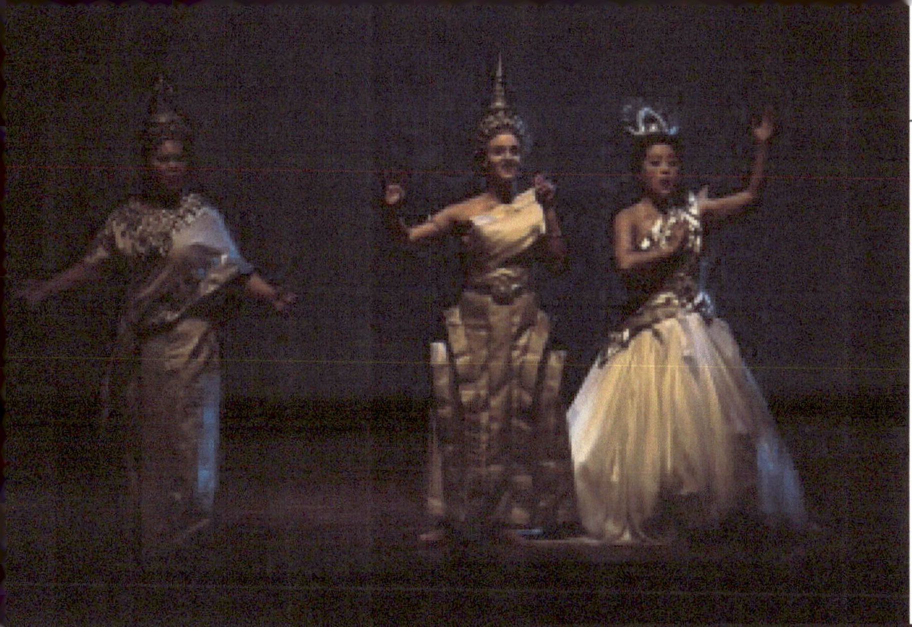

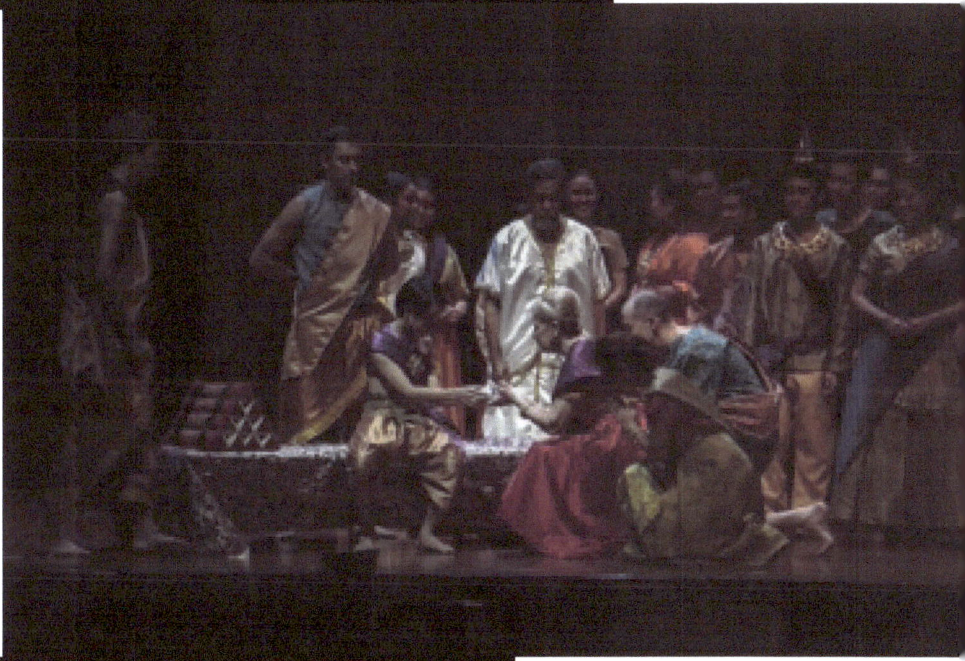

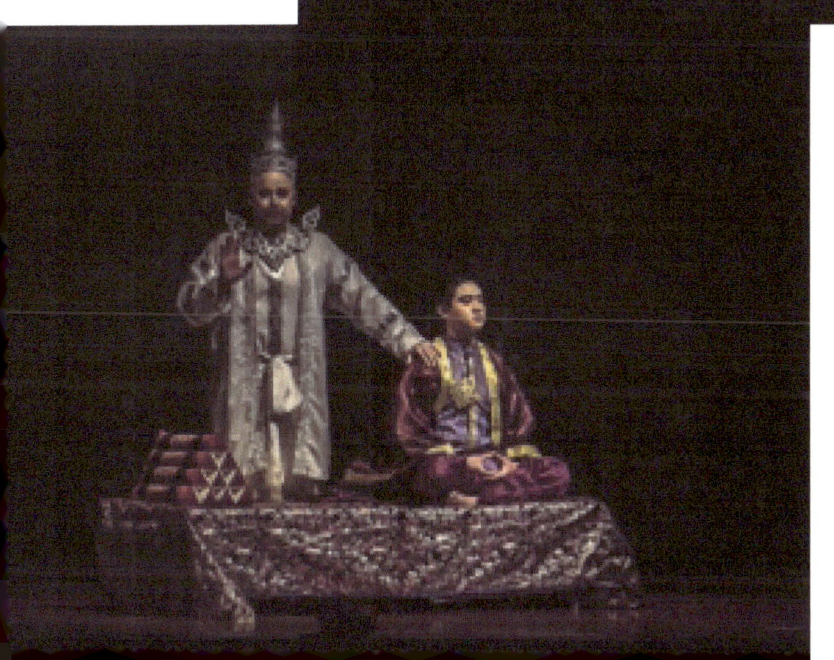

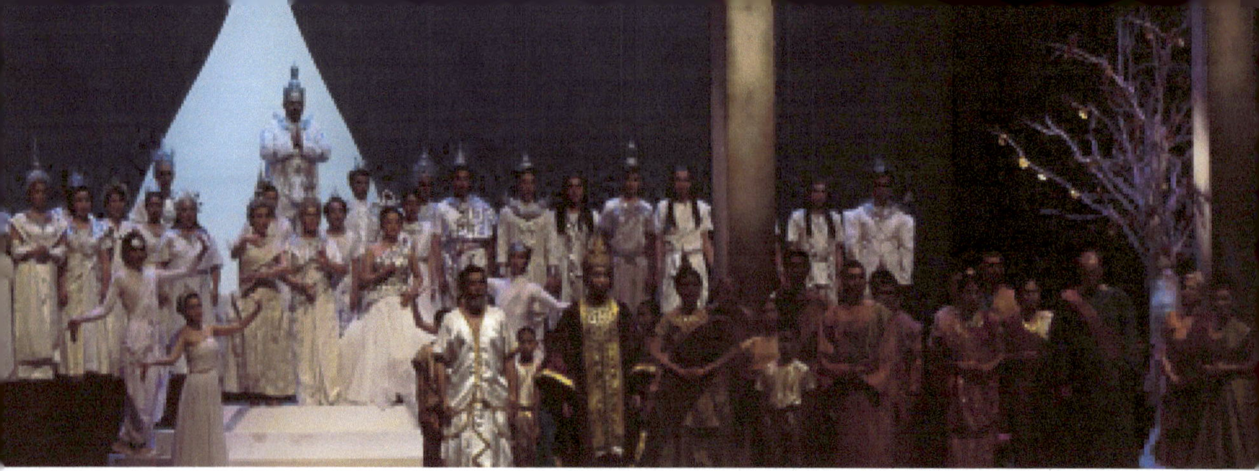

— Main Cast: Jak Cholvijarn, Puntwitt Asawadejmetakul, Damian Whiteley, Kaleigh Rae Gamaché, Zion Daoratanahong, Sen Guo, Raphael Ayrle, Rit Parnichkun
— Siam Philharmonic Orchestra, conducted by Trisdee na Patalung
— directed by Somtow Sucharitkul

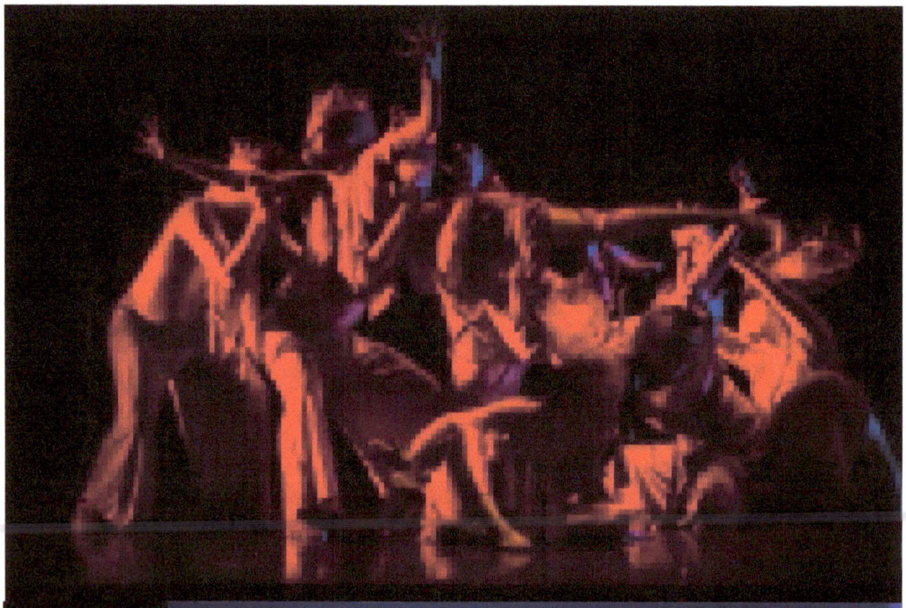

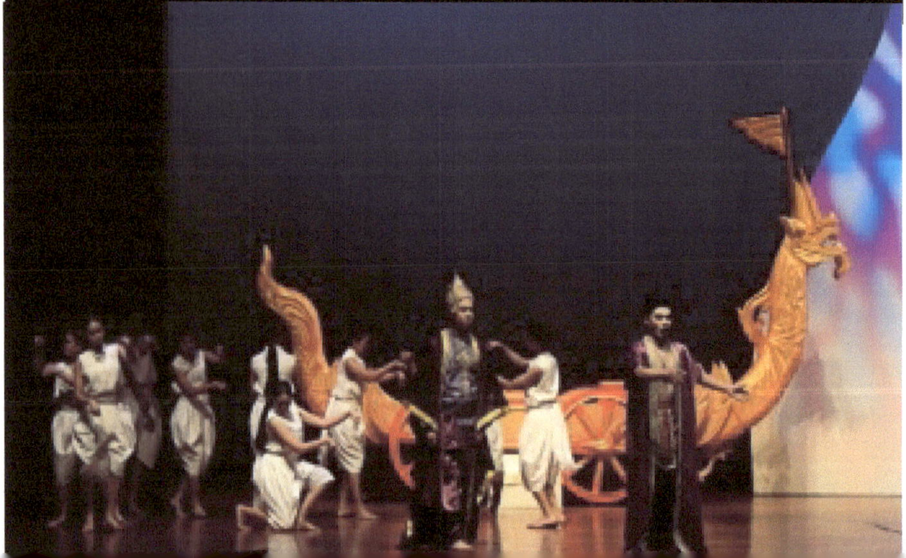

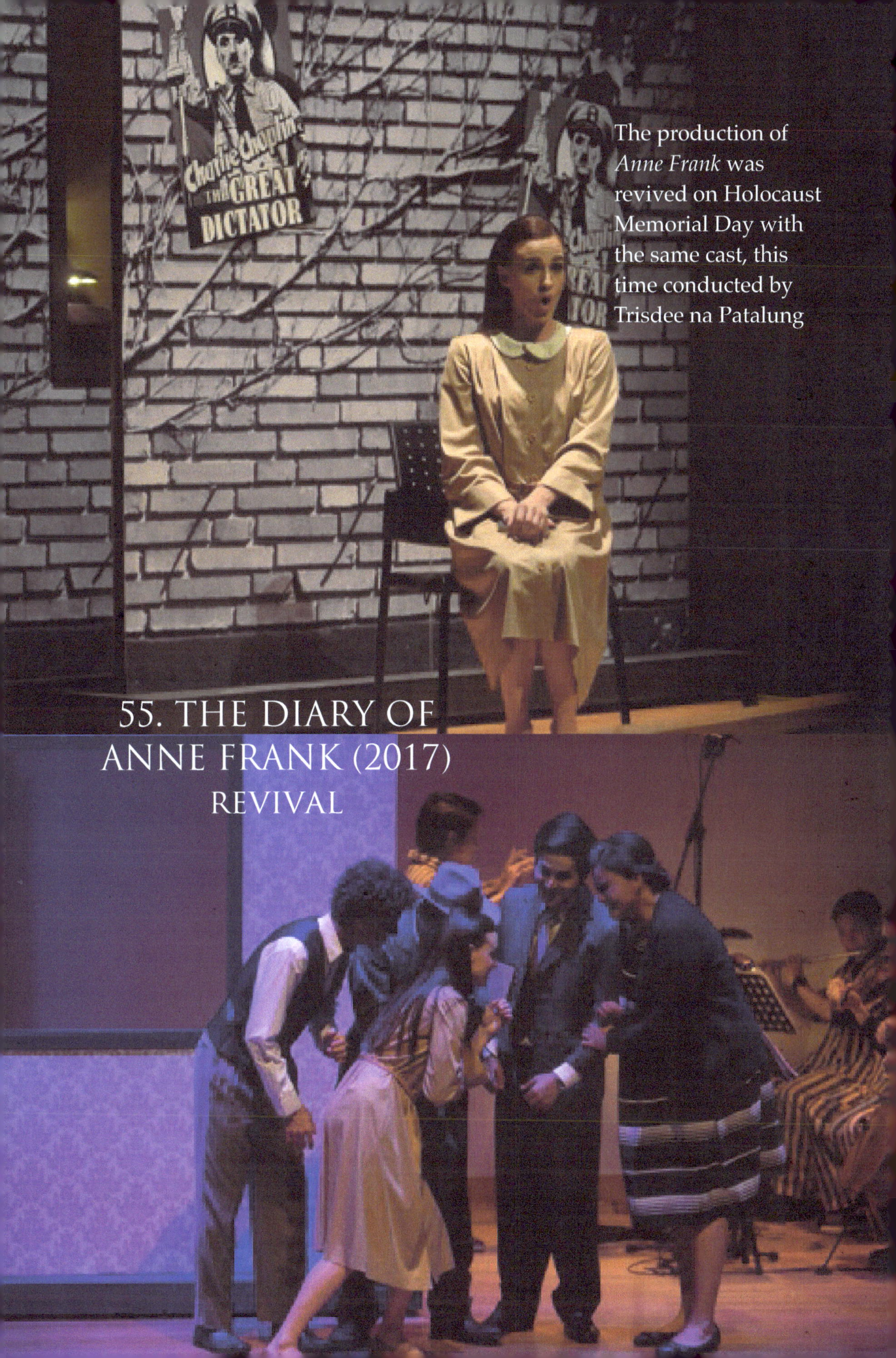

The production of *Anne Frank* was revived on Holocaust Memorial Day with the same cast, this time conducted by Trisdee na Patalung

55. THE DIARY OF ANNE FRANK (2017) REVIVAL

56. THE HAPPY PRINCE (2017)
THAILAND PREMIERE

The Happy Prince, an adaptation of Oscar Wilde's classic fairytale by Malcolm Williamson, is a perfect miniature opera and was Opera Siam's selection for the next children's opera.

The debut in a leading operatic role of Tölz Boys' Choir veteran Ralph Ayrle, it was unfortunately also his last role as a boy soprano as his voice changed shortly afterwards.

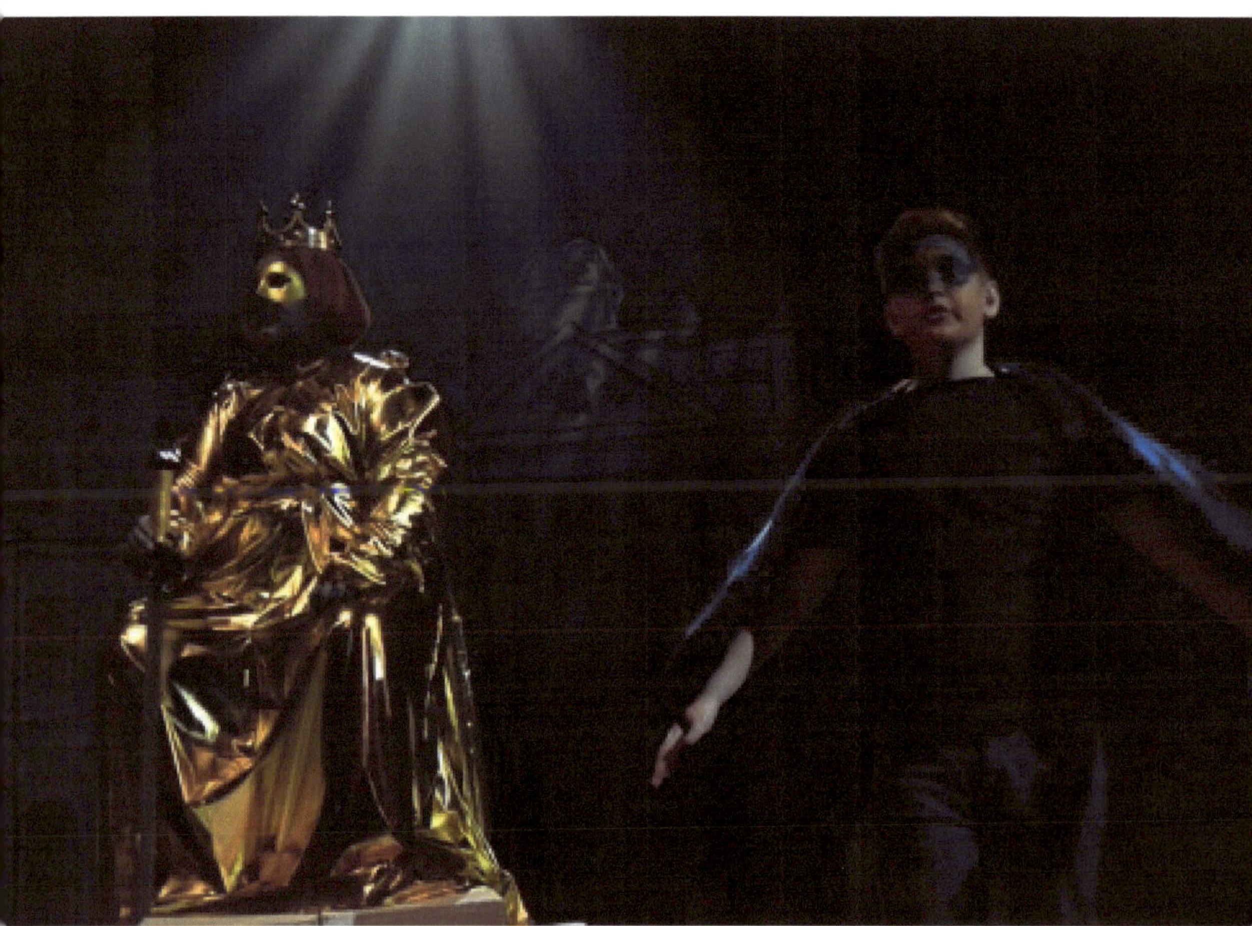

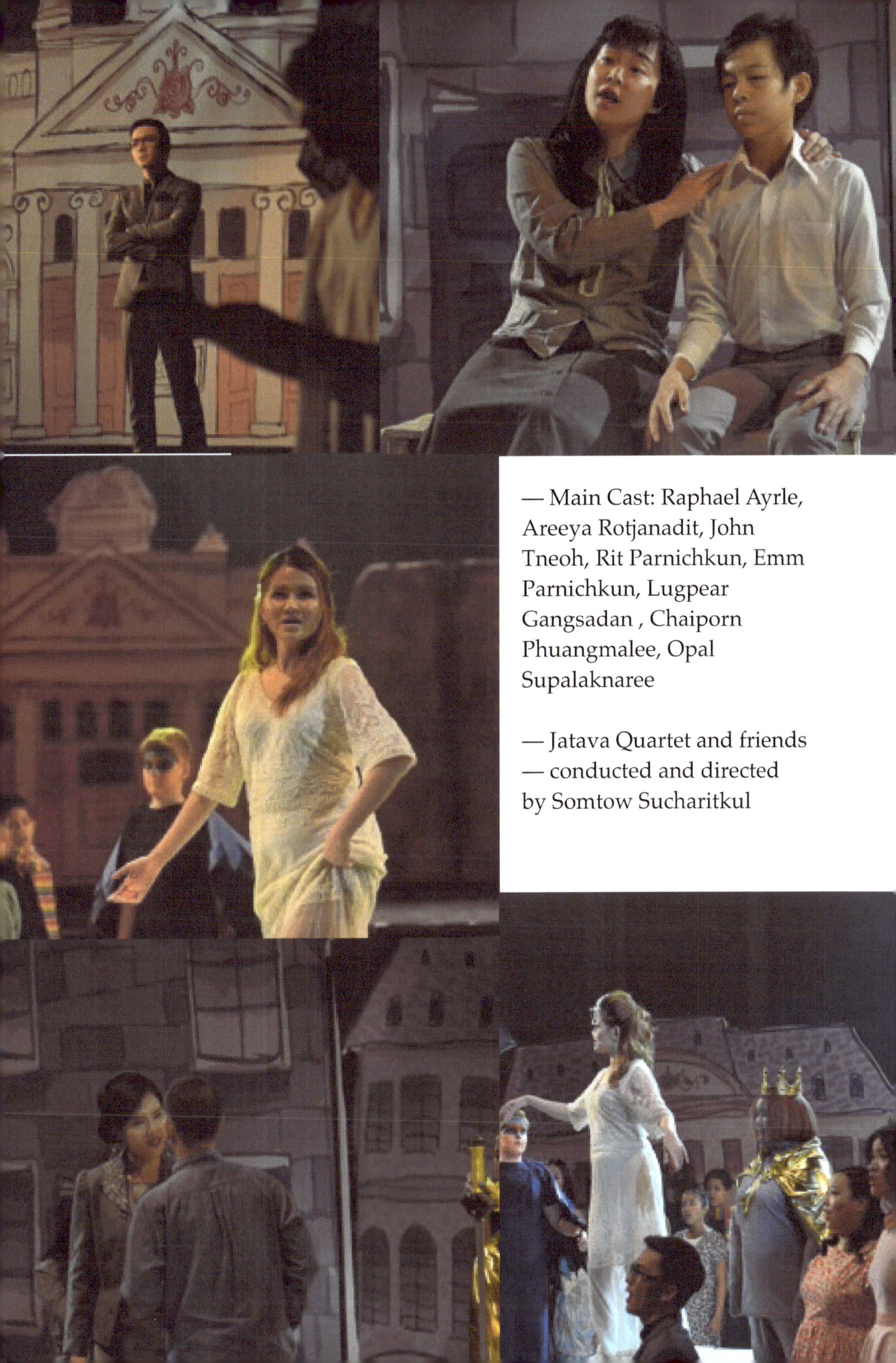

— Main Cast: Raphael Ayrle, Areeya Rotjanadit, John Tneoh, Rit Parnichkun, Emm Parnichkun, Lugpear Gangsadan , Chaiporn Phuangmalee, Opal Supalaknaree

— Jatava Quartet and friends
— conducted and directed by Somtow Sucharitkul

57. SAMA - THE FAITHFUL SON (2017)
REVIVAL

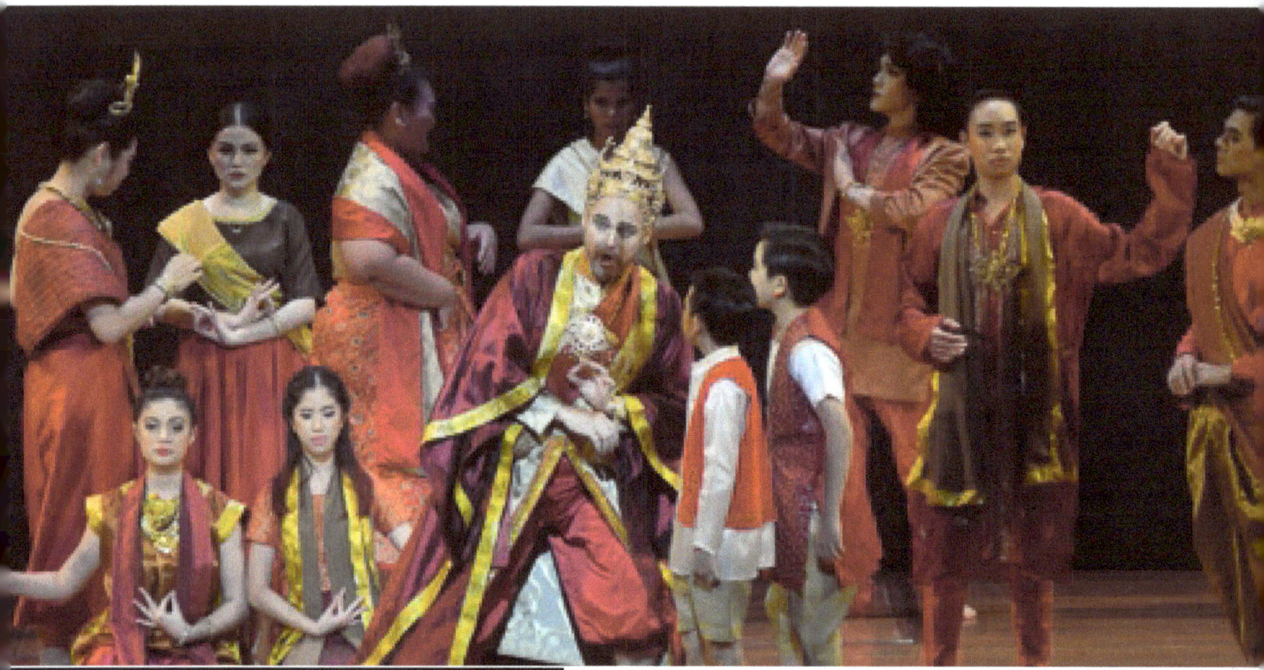

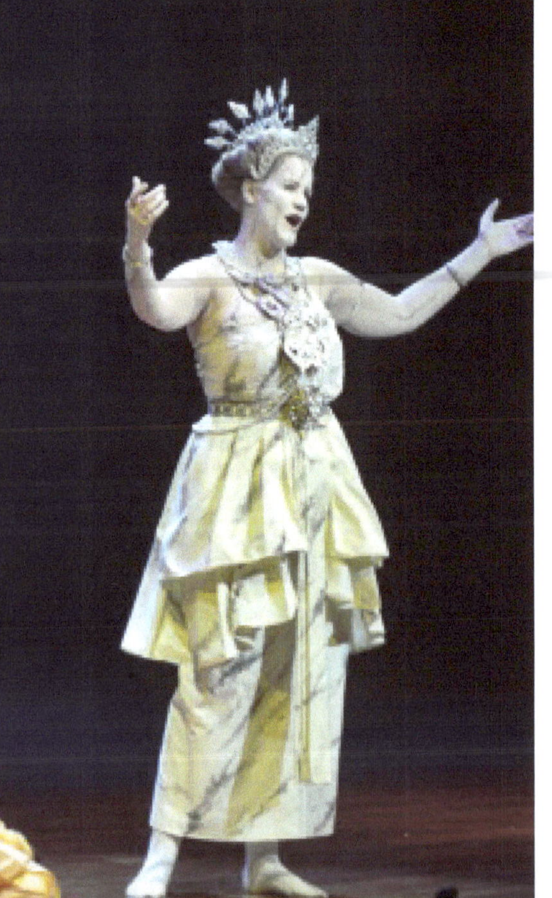

The Faithful Son returned, this time to the Cultural Center. After a year of almost certain financial collapse, crowdfunding enabled Opera Siam to finish its Sixteenth Season, though its Seventeenth brought the opera to a state of near-death. Many changes are coming in the near future.

— Main cast as first production, with the remarkable Stacey Tappan instead of Kaleigh Rae Gamaché

— Trisdee na Patalung conducting and Somtow Sucharitkul directing

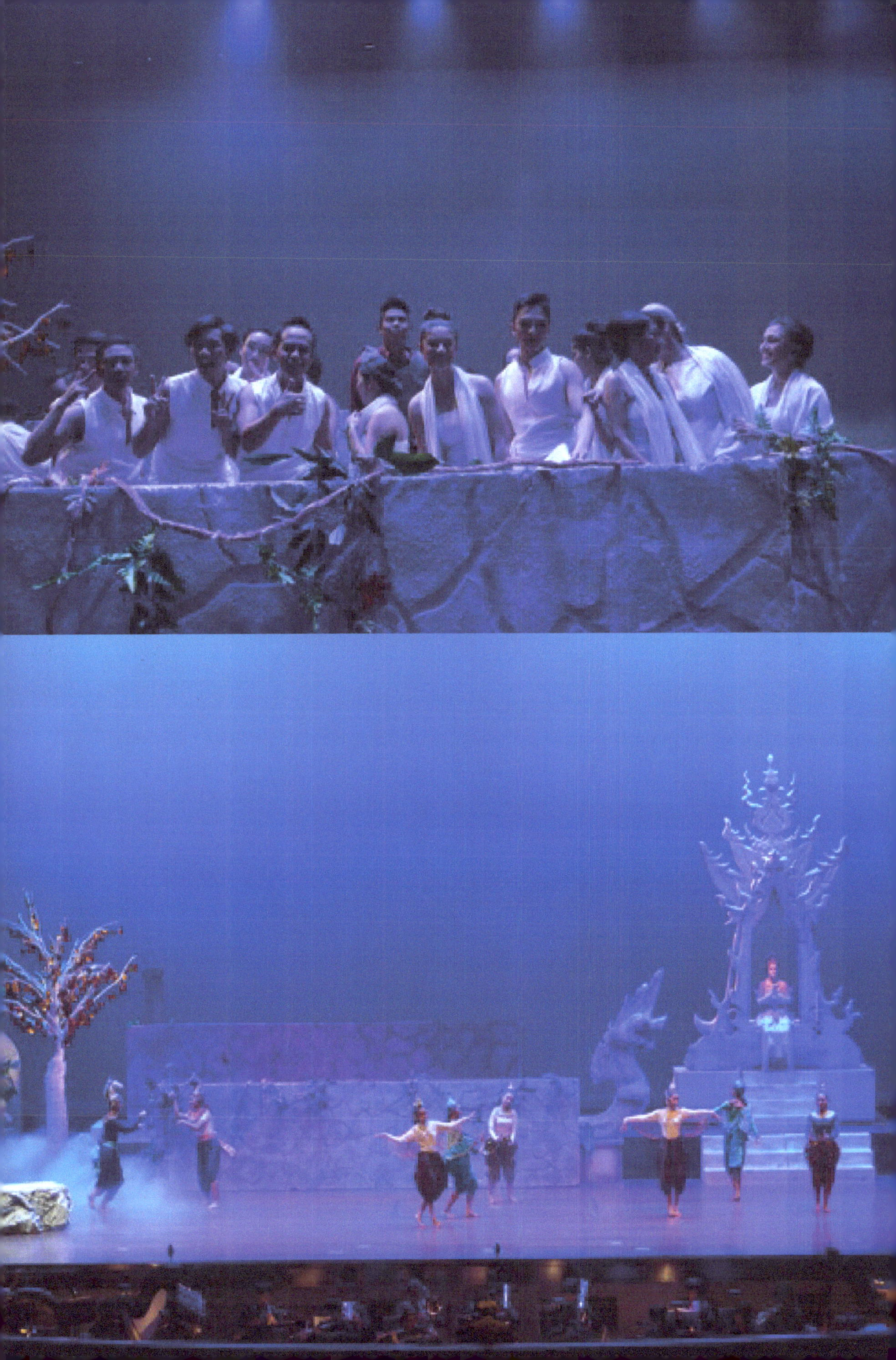

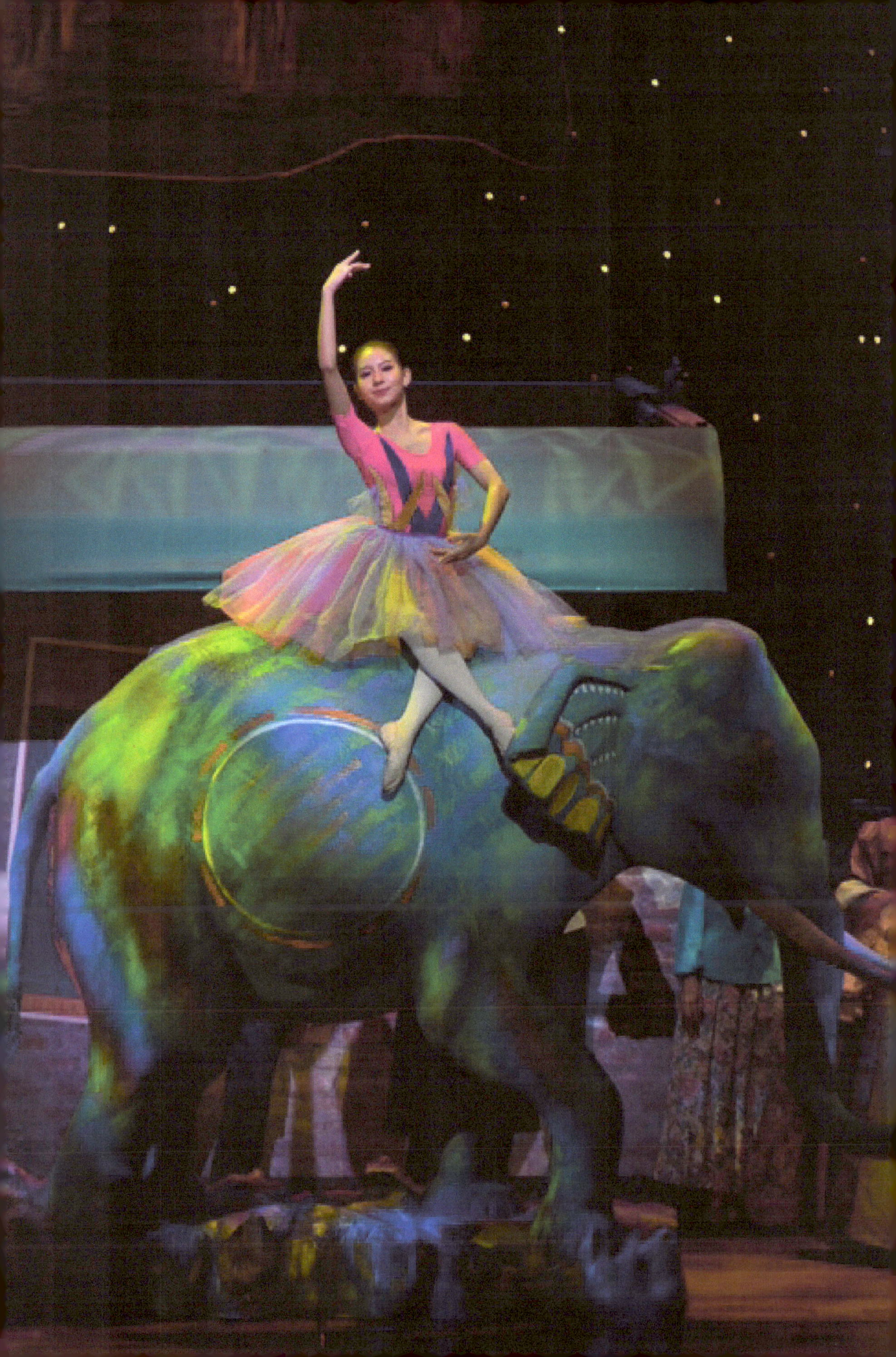

58. LA BOHEME (2017)
NEW PRODUCTION

Designed to appear as though the audience were trapped inside a phantasmagorical painting of Chagall's Paris, Somtow's new production of *La Bohème* received more critical acclaim than any previous production of a standard repertoire work. As one of the most frequently performed works in the operatic repertoire, this unusual new presentation took the audience by storm and was a stunning kickoff for Season Sixteen and for the planned Puccini Project — intended to produce all of Puccini's operas over the next few five or ten years.

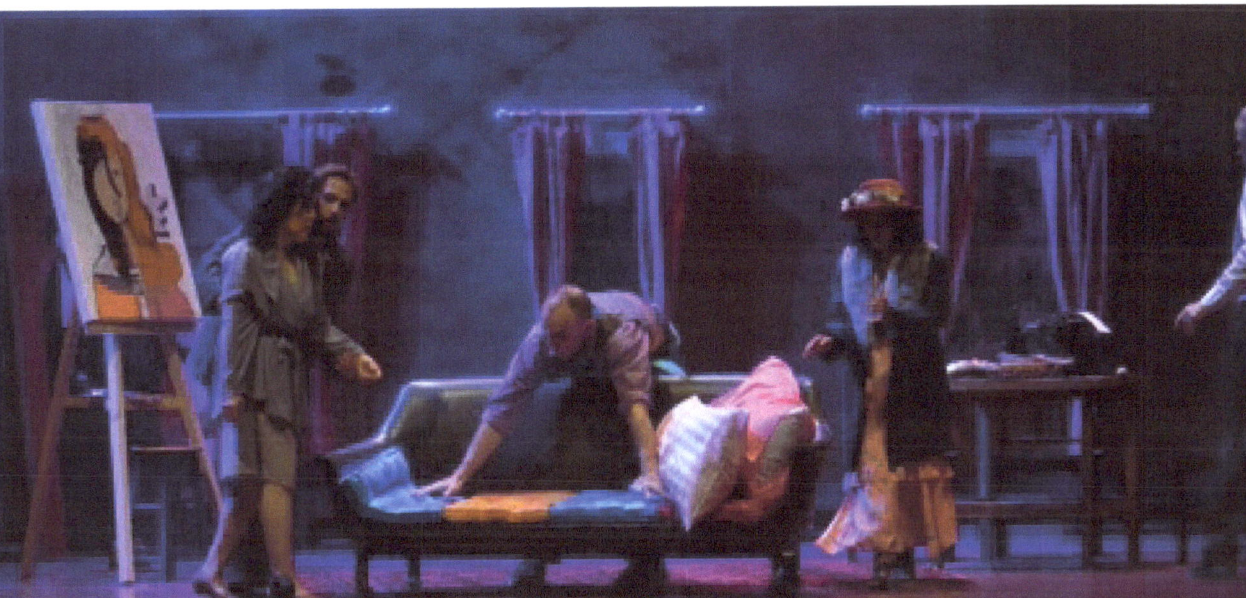

"a completely fresh, energetic take on Puccini's score, blowing away the cobwebs of convention and pulling a glorious rush of sound from the Orchestra."

— *The Bangkok Post*

"Nadlada Thamtanakom was a sensational Musetta!"

— Michael Proudfoot, reviewer for *Opera Now*

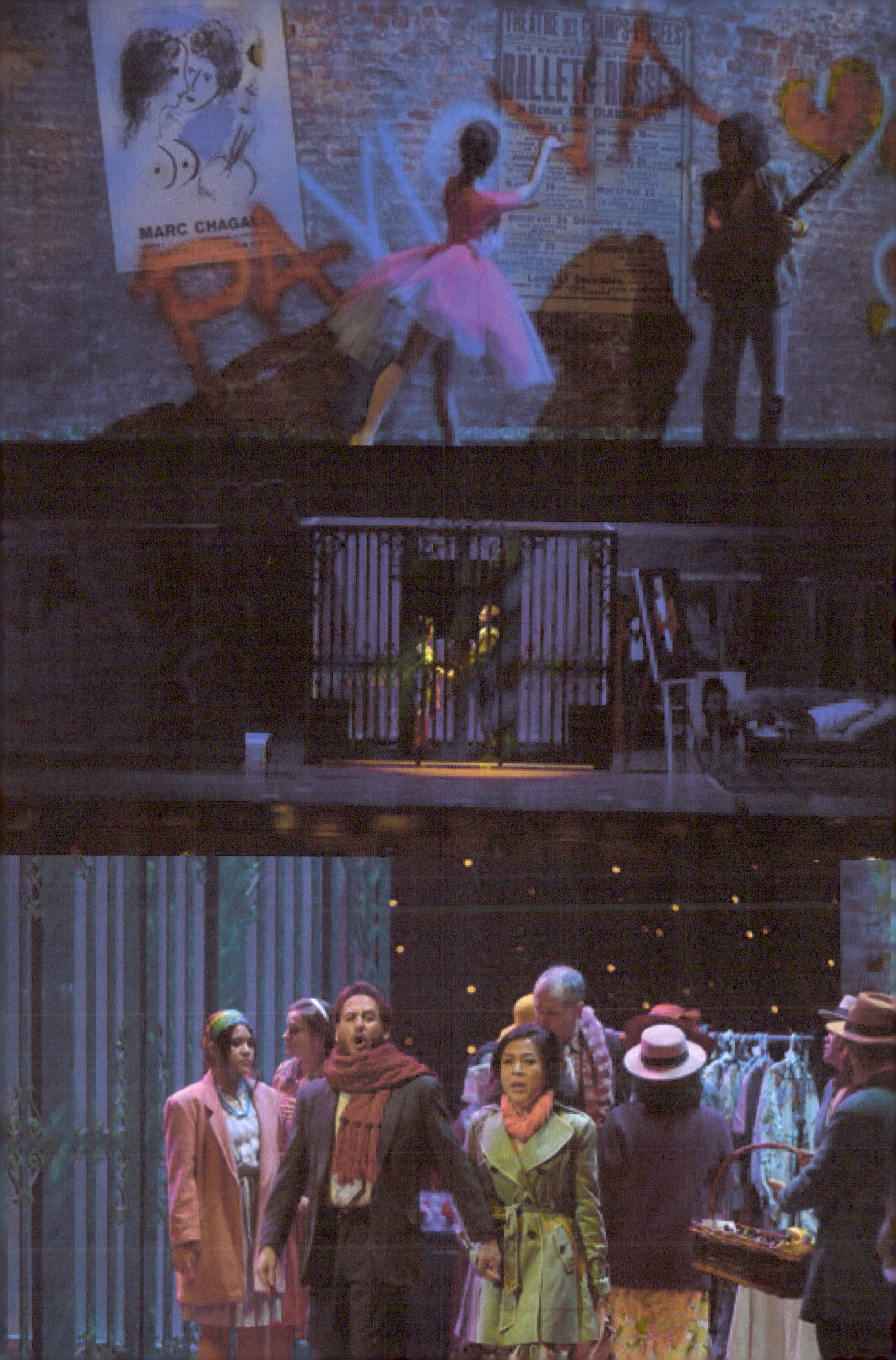
MARC CHAGA

— Main Cast: Nancy Yuen, Israel Lozano, Nadlada Thamtanakom, Simon Meadows, Krittahad Pusitiwong, Panuwat Phiensa, Nicholas Malakul, Damian Whiteley

— designed and directed by Somtow Sucharitkul

— Siam Philharmonic Orchestra

— conducted by Trisdee na Patalung

Opera Siam launched what is intended to be the first of a run of the complete Puccini operas over the next few years with *La Bohème* at the Thailand Cultural Center (December 23 and 24) . The company had previously staged Boheme in 2009, and the same two principals, Israel Lozano as Rodolfo and Nancy Yuen as Mimi, reprised their roles in a new production by Somtow Sucharitkul, who placed the opera roughly a couple of decades alter its 1896 premiere.

Imaginatively lit by Ryan Attig, the Chagall-inspired set provided a colourful background: a cold but sparkling Christmas Eve in sweltering Bangkok.

The stars of the evening were the Siam Philharmonic Orchestra and its young conductor Trisdee na Patalung who is best known for his Baroque, Mozart and Rossini performances, was conducting his first Puccini opera. It was a revelation.

Lozano gave full-throttle, whole-hearted performances as Rodolfo, Yuen was affecting as Mimi. a slight and slender figure, full of pathos. but rising to the heights. especially in the duets With Lozano. There were strong performances from the other Bohemians, Simon Meadows (Marcello) providing some of the best singing of the evening along with his fellow Australian Damian Whiteley (Colline). There was an Impressive professional debut from the 20-year-old Thai singer Panuwat Phiansa, in a comic vignette as a gangly Schaunard. Another Thai singer, Nadlada Thamtanakom, now basedin Belgium With Operastudio Vlaanderen, was a delightful Musetta. Her 'Quando m'en vo' was wonderfully sung.

The crowd scenes in Act 2 were very effectively managed. With the chorus singing and acting well. The parade that followed the marching soldiers —in this production, an excellent children's marching band — included the inevitable elephant, a signature of Opera Siam.

Somtow Sucharitkul sees La Bohème as a 'joyous' opera, with Mimi's death redemptive, bringing out the best in her friends. It was another near-miracle produced by Siam Opera. with its modest budget and limited rehearsal time — a production as good as any by a European company.

— *Opera Magazine, London*

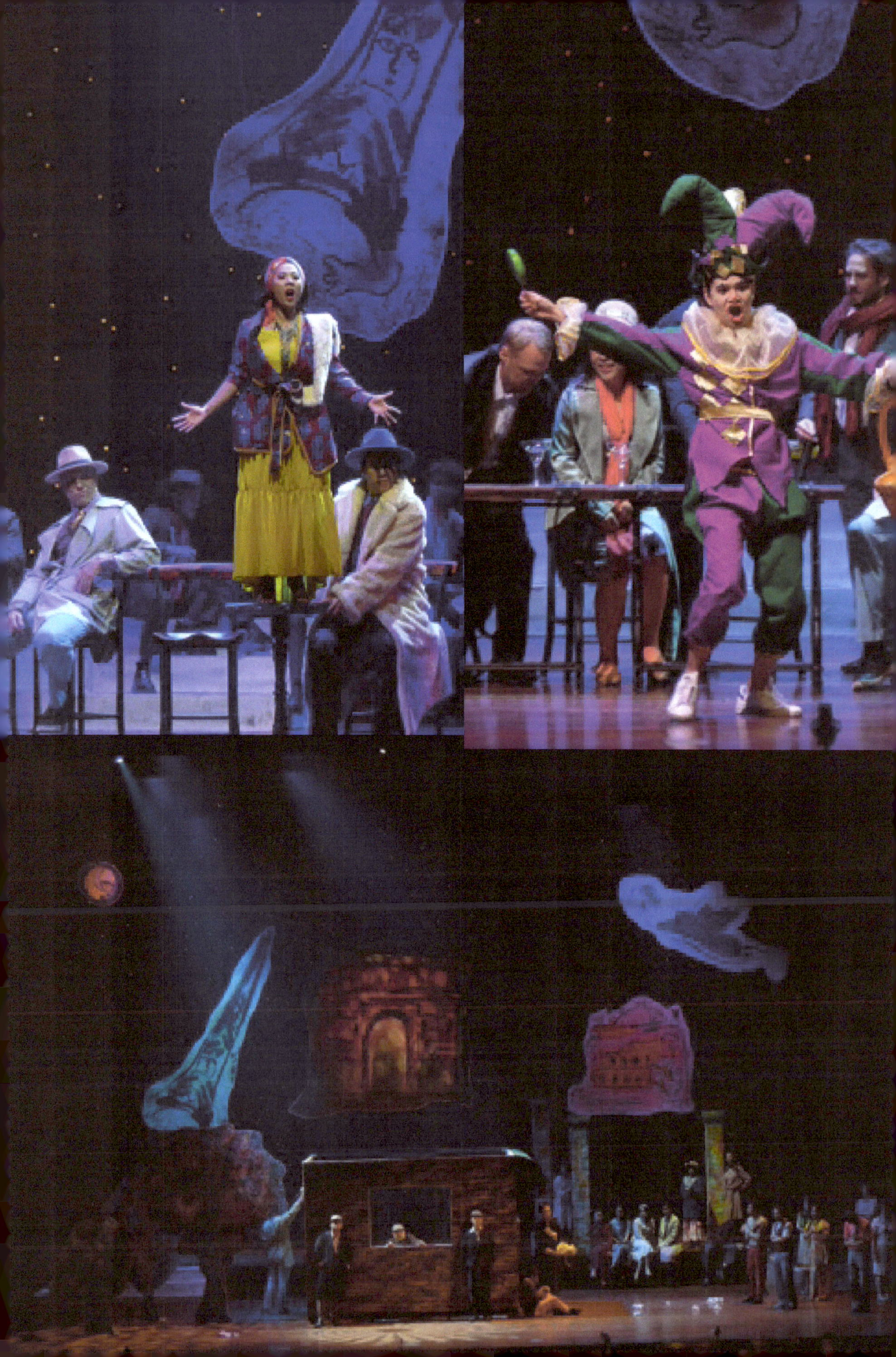

59. LA SERVA PADRONA (2018)
SEMI-STAGED PRODUCTION
COLLABORATION WITH THE DEUTSCHE OPER BERLIN

A long and fruitful friendship with the Deutsche Oper Berlin and its orchestra representative Daniel Draganov led to this visit in which the opera orchestra members came to Bangkok and worked with young Thai musicians of the Siam Sinfonietta to produce a number of events including this memorable performance of *La Serva Padrona,* Pergolesi's entertaining one-act comedy, at the Arnoma Hotel in downtown Bangkok.

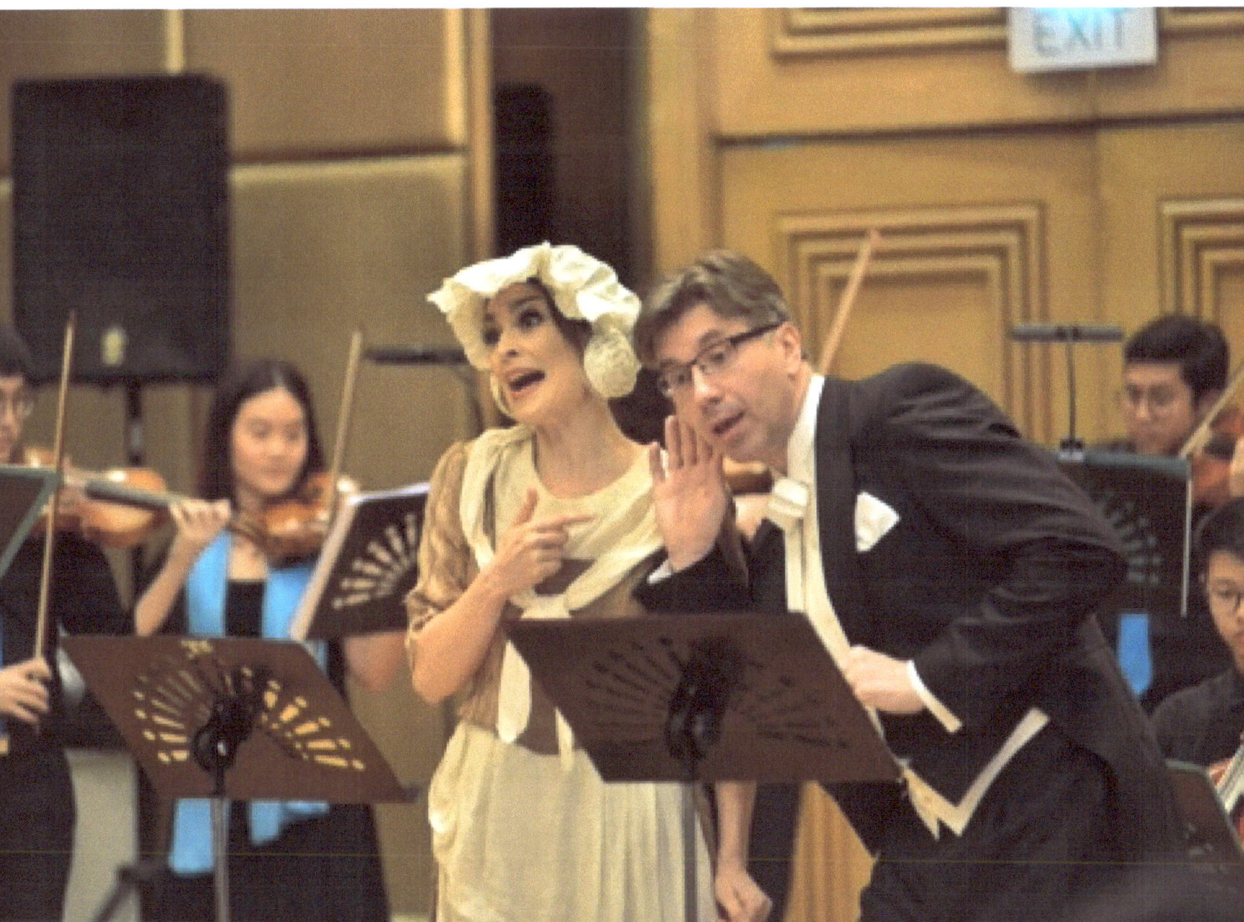

— Main Cast: Tadeusz Milewski, Natali Buck
— DOB Chamber Orchestra / Siam Sinfonietta

60. MADAMA BUTTERFLY (2018)
NEW PRODUCTION

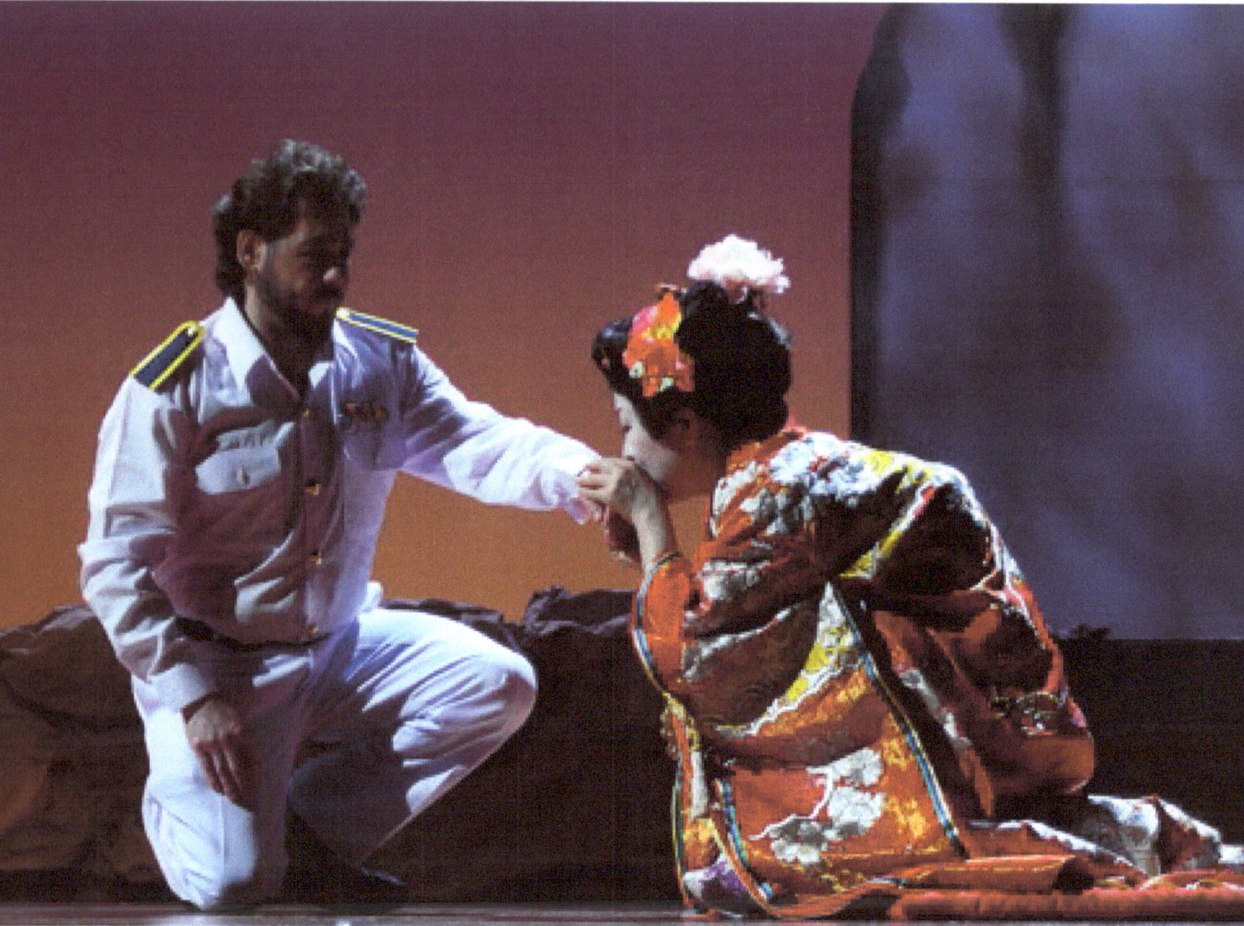

Opera Siam's season concluded with one of its most-praised productions, a new version of *Madama Butterfly.* Somtow's design was based on Japanese aesthetic principles and in particular on *sumie* paintings. The production incorporates a more contemporary viewpoint, not shying away from the undercurrents of exploitation and human trafficking that can be glossed over in more romantic versions. The cast consisted of some of the finest interpreters of their roles, but the Siam Sinfonietta, Thailand's internationally acclaimed youth orchestra, experienced its operatic debut in this challenging score.

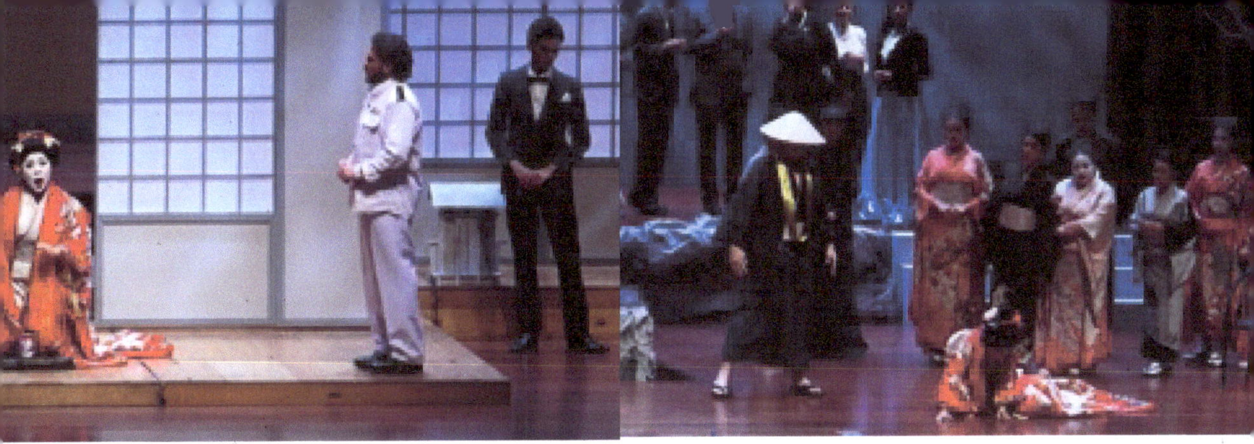

— Main Cast: Nancy Yuen, Israel Lozano, Phillip Joll, Emanuela Barazia, Damian Whiteley, Chaiporn Phuangmalee, Steve Ang, Barbara Zionm, Ilona Gruchot, Krittahad Pisuttiwong, John Tneoh, Charin Sumakka, Chayut Makarasut

— Siam Sinfonietta

— Ryan Attig, lighting

— Natthawan Santipab, costumes

— designed, conducted and directed by Somtow Sucharitkul

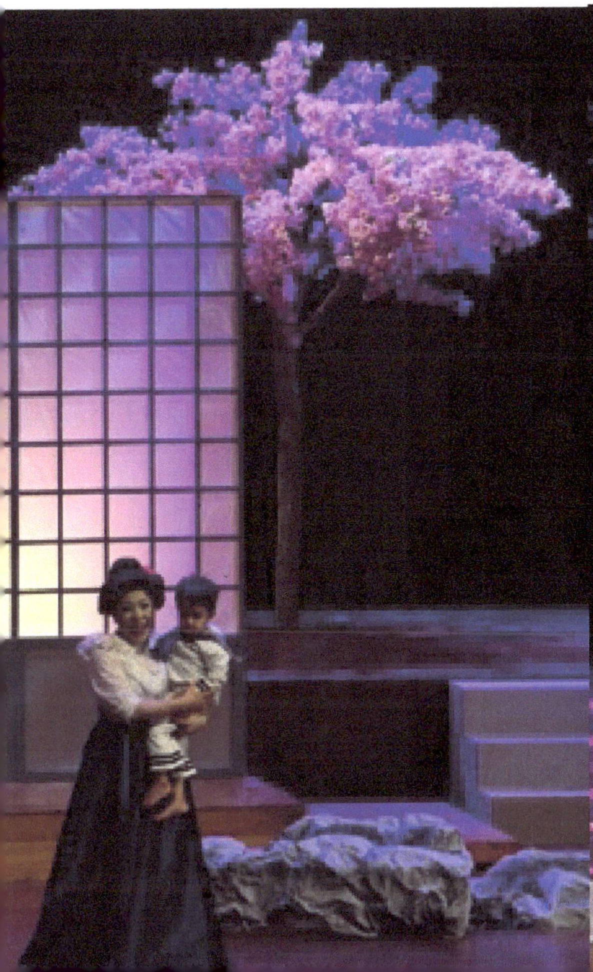

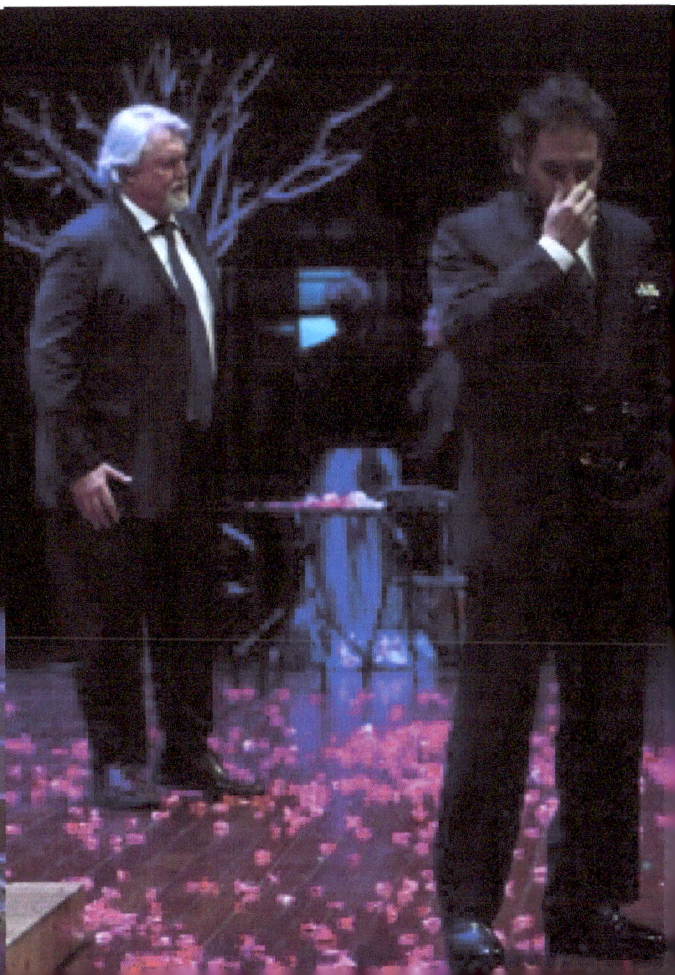

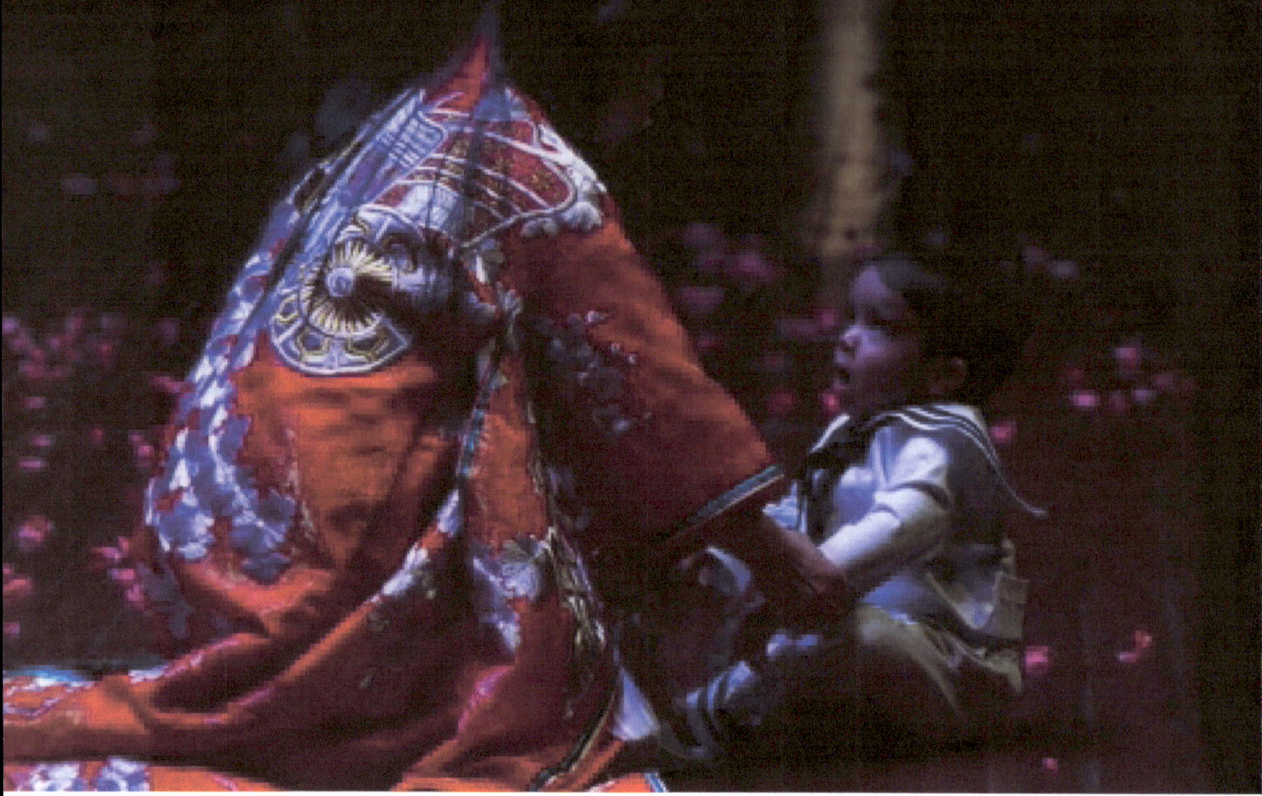

Review

"Surprise" is rarely a word associated with a production of such a popular opera as Giacomo Puccini's *Madama Butterfly*, a staple of the operatic repertoire around the world. But indeed, many delightful surprises were in store for those who attended Opera Siam's *Butterfly* on July 11-12 at the Thailand Cultural Center.

First, it was probably Siam Sinfonietta's debut in undertaking an opera. Under Maestro Somtow Sucharitkul's tutelage, the young musicians displayed unexpected musical prowess, ravishing and alluring. The texture and phrasing sounded fresh and new, whether in the restrained delicate sounds or the

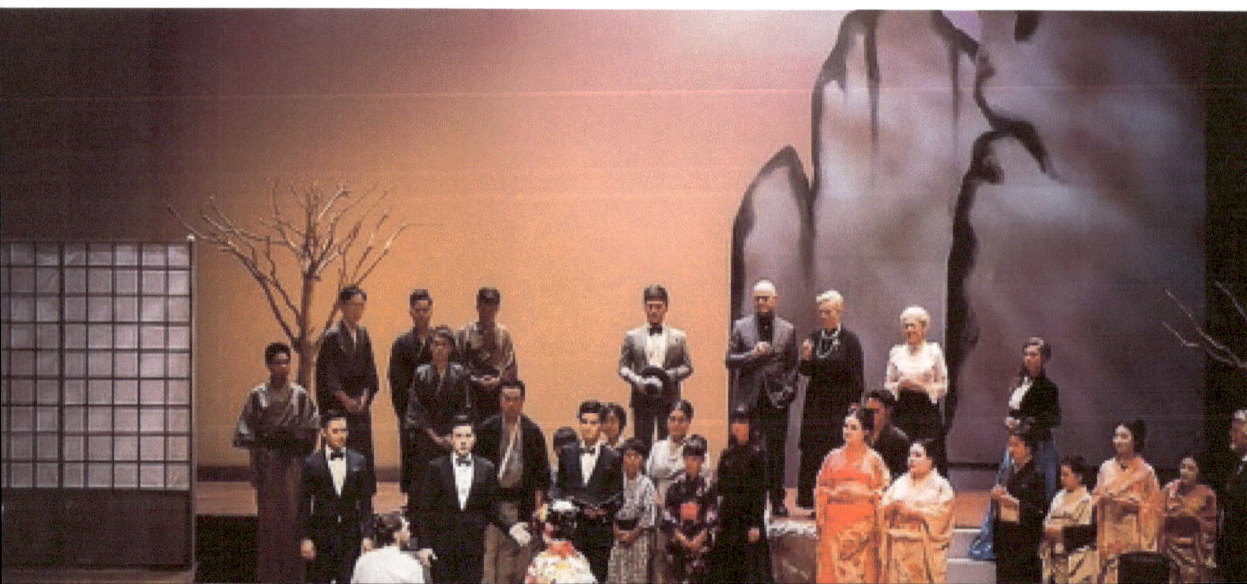

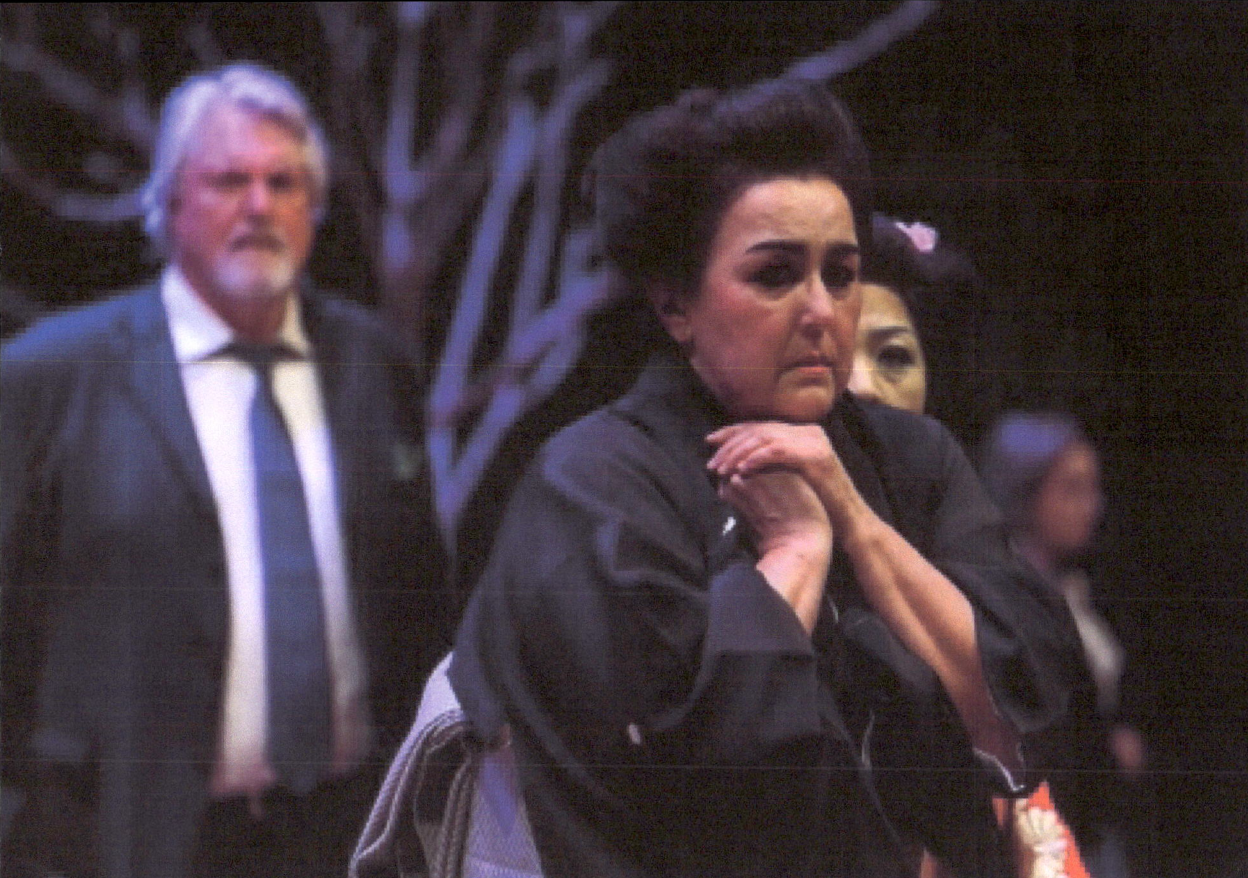

climactic crescendo. The music, with a slow-burning intensity, flowed flawlessly throughout the evening.

This is an amazing accomplishment for a youth orchestra whose first concert together was only less than a year ago. The contribution of Maestro Somtow Sucharitkul to classical music education in Thailand cannot be over-emphasized.

Singaporean Diva Nancy Yuen is exquisite in her signature role as the ill-fated heroine Cio-Cio-San. Her powerful spinto quality brings electric vibrancy to the spine-tingling 'One Fine Day' (*Un bel dì vedremo*), one of opera's most beautiful arias. There are elements of surprise here for those who haven't seen her recently.

Israel Lozano's performance as the American naval officer Pinkerton is also sterling. Covent Garden star Phillip Joll (the American consul Sharpless), Italian mezzo-soprano Emanuela Barazia (Butterfly's maid, Suzuki), Australian bass Damian Whiteley (Butterfly's uncle, the bonze), and Thailand's Chaiporn Phuangmalee (the devious marriage broker cum trafficker, Goro), with their refined musicality, are all superb in their roles.

The set is a triumph of simplicity, with Japanese shoji screens and sliding doors and a few cherry trees. The simple set, free from clutter and distraction, draws us relentlessly into the opera's unsettling world, making this production extremely intimate and profoundly moving.

— *The Bangkok Post*

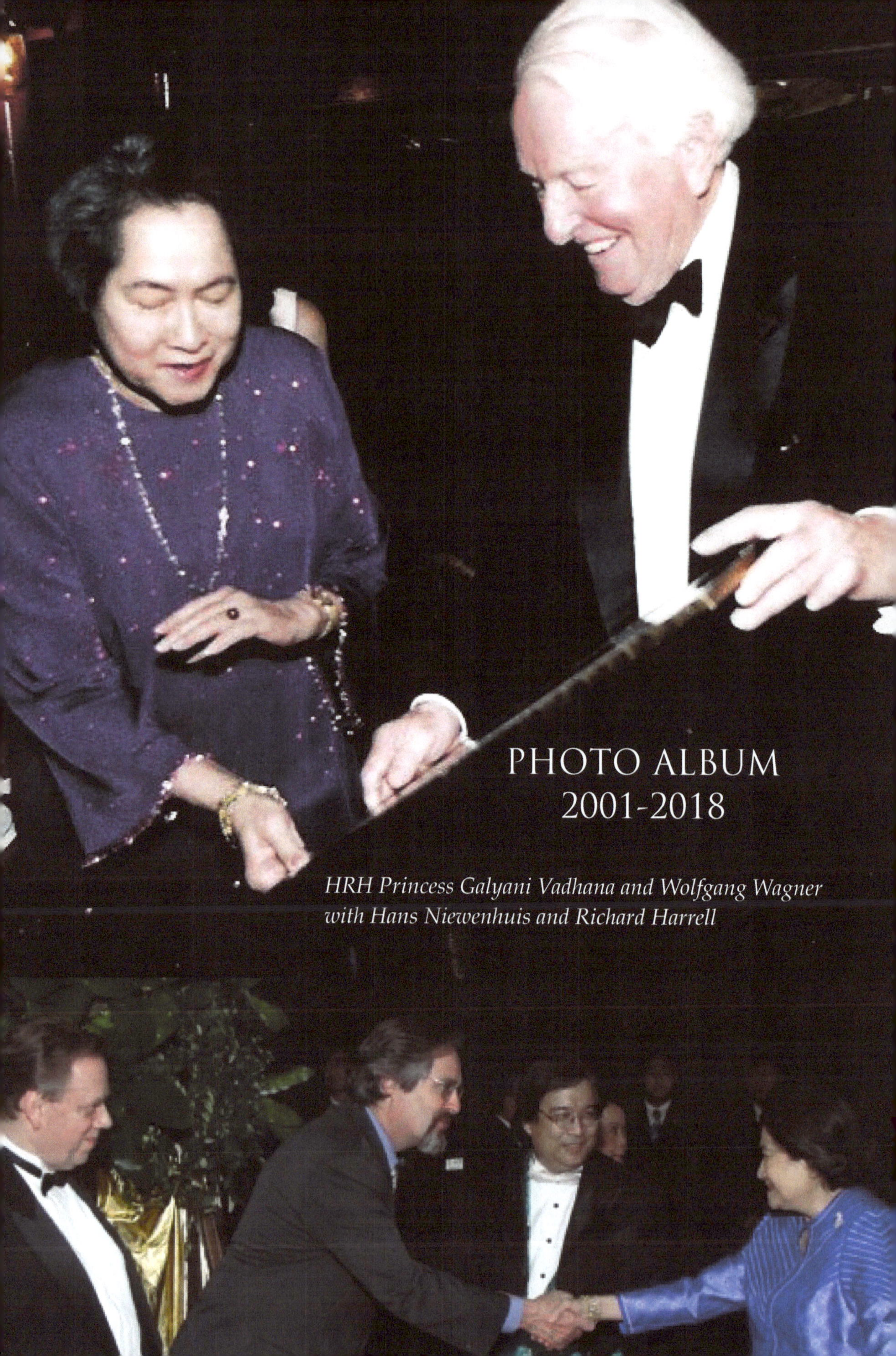

PHOTO ALBUM
2001-2018

HRH Princess Galyani Vadhana and Wolfgang Wagner with Hans Niewenhuis and Richard Harrell

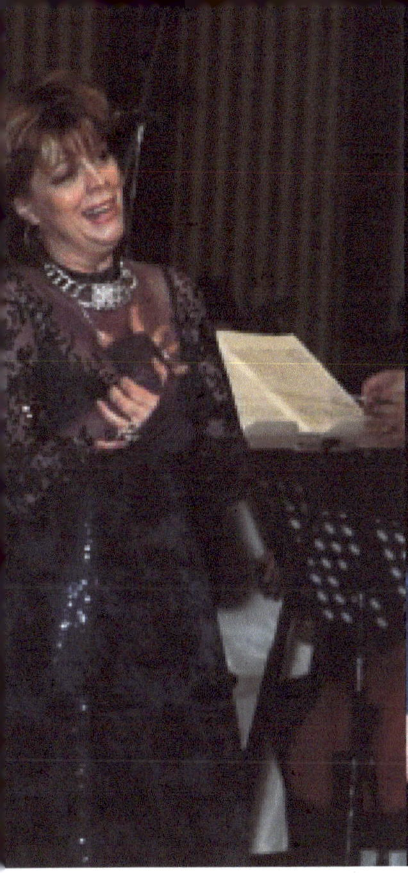

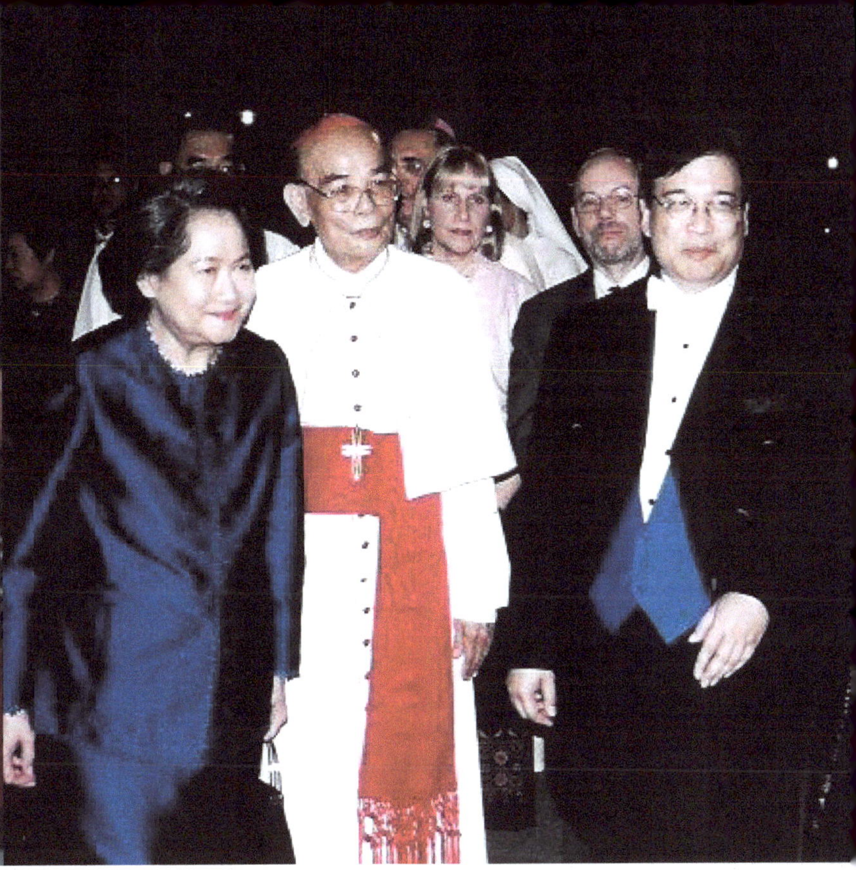

Lyuba Kazarnowskaya at Opera Sam Fifth Birthday Party; HRH Princess Galyani Vadhana, H Em. Cardinal Meechai, Mr. and Mrs. Botwick of Chevrolet; Jessye Norman, Nancy Yuen at A Voice For Peace concert

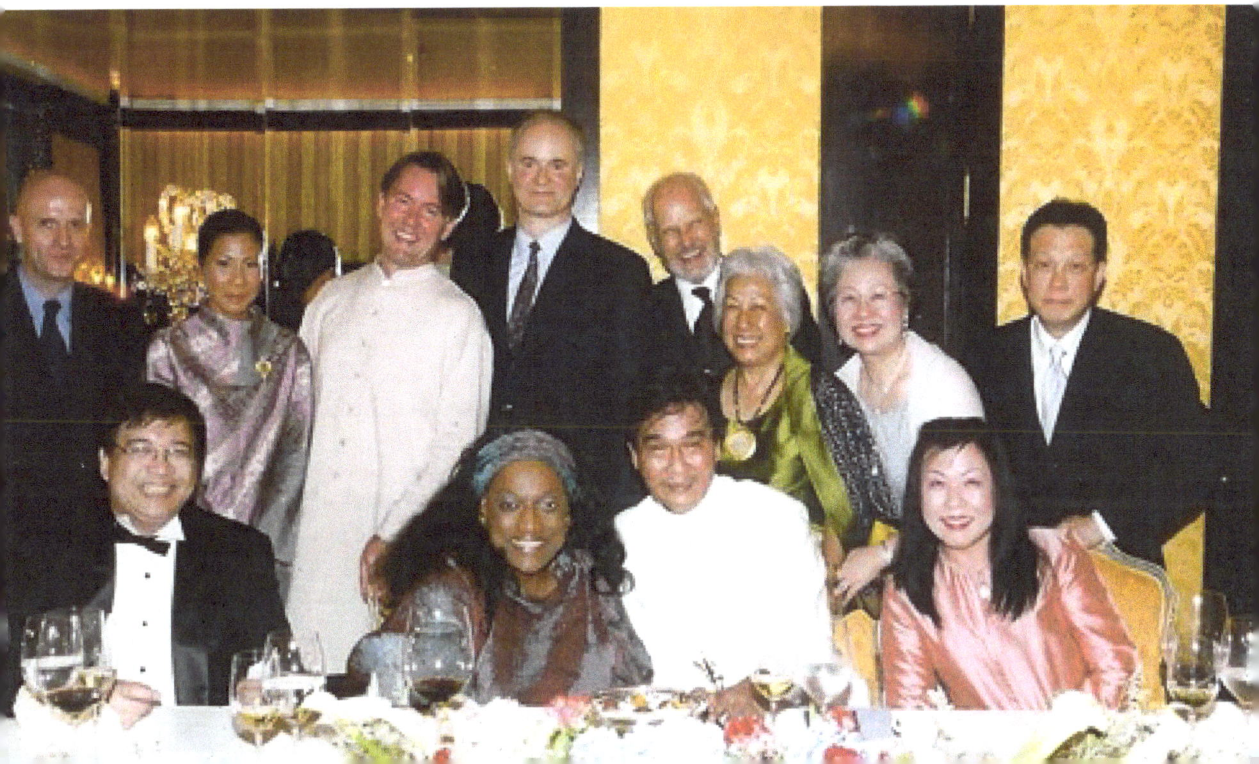

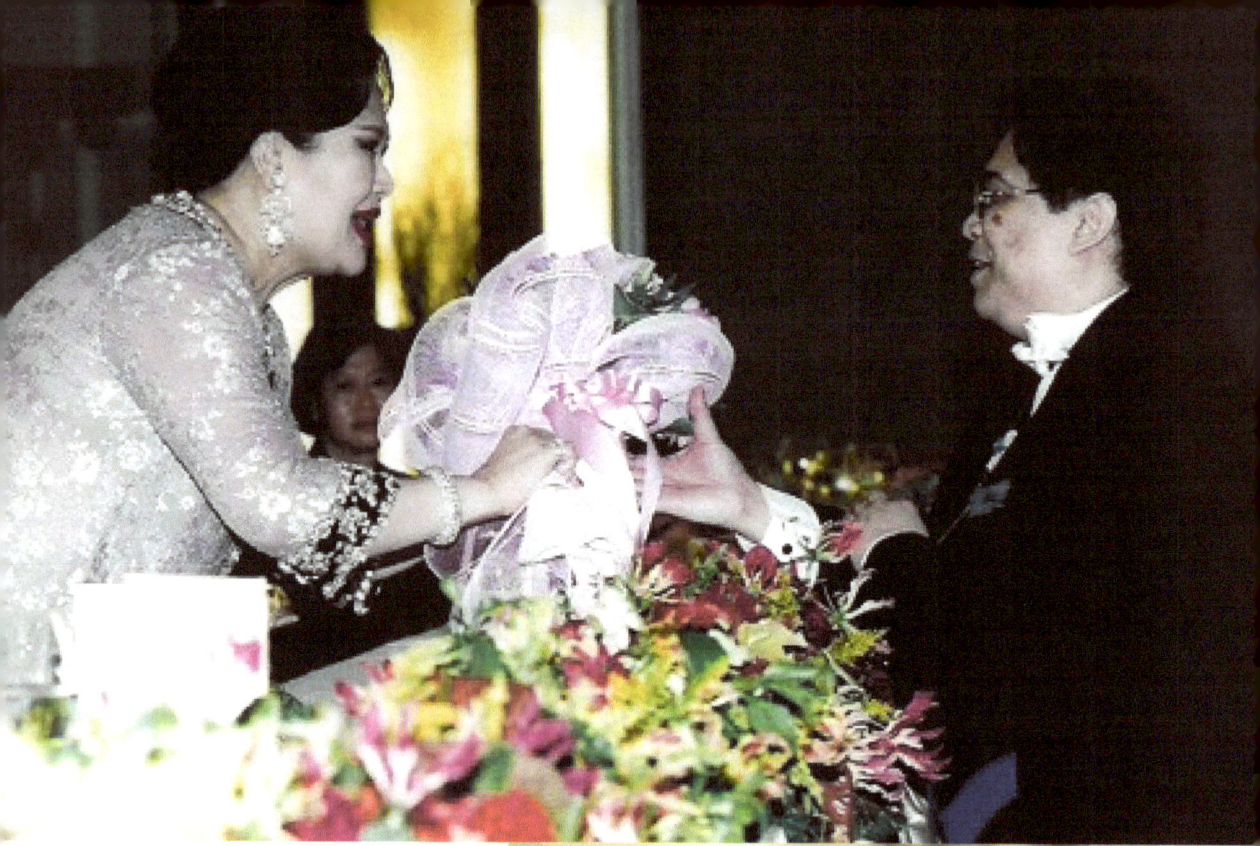

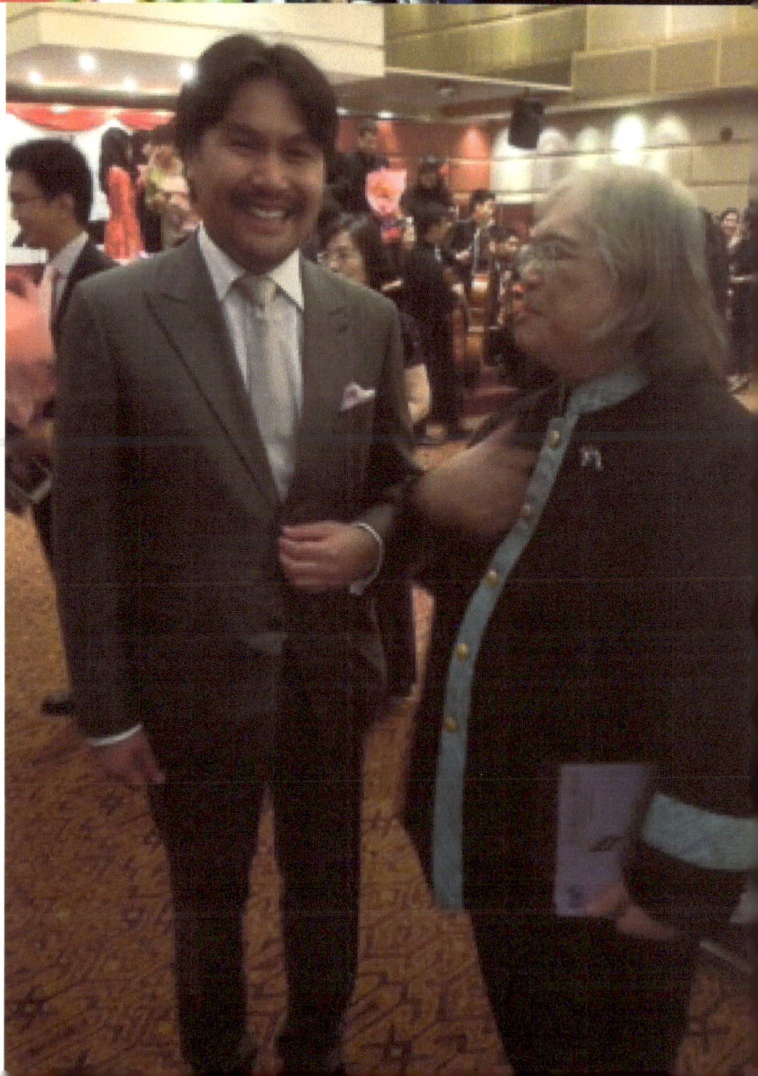

above

HM Queen Sirikit of Thailand presenting flowers to Artistic Director Somtow at Sirikit Concerto premiere

right

Crown Prince Ali of Negeri Sembilan, Malaysia, at Festival opening EuroAsia

above: at Turandot premiere, HRH Promcess Galyani, Thaithow Sucharitkul, Khunying Wanna and Khun Charoen of ThaiBev

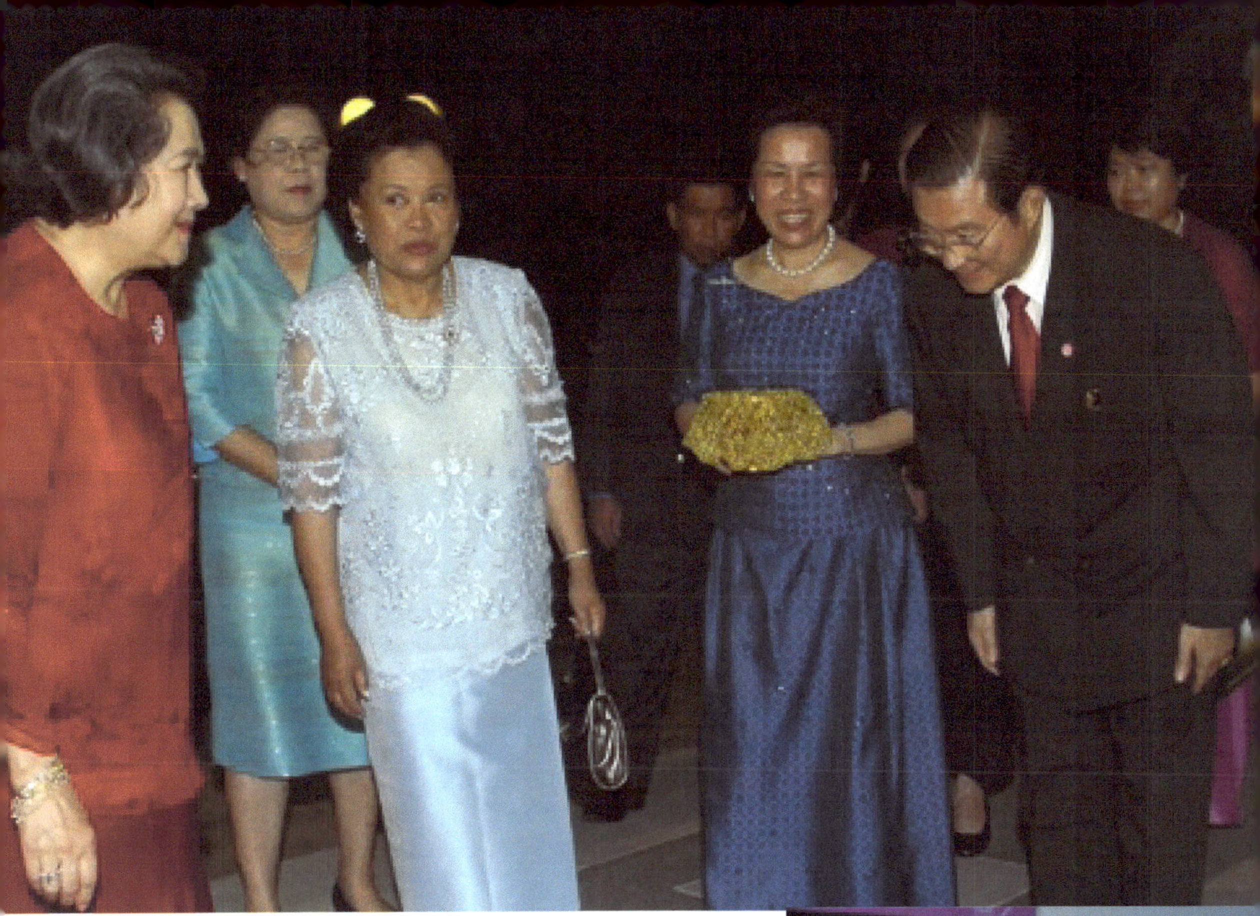

right: Prime Minister Anan Panyarachun

below: Vanessa Mae

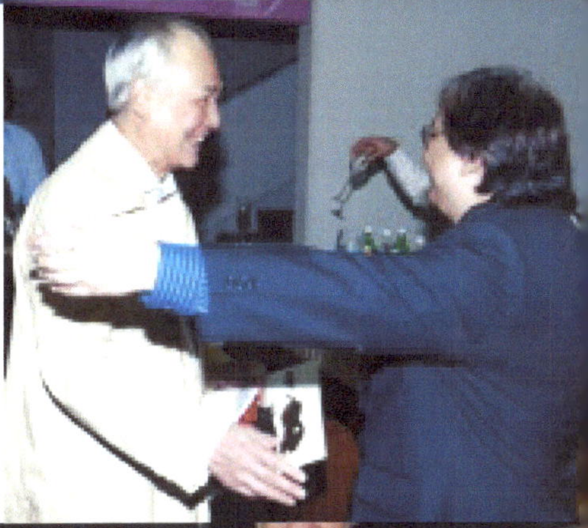

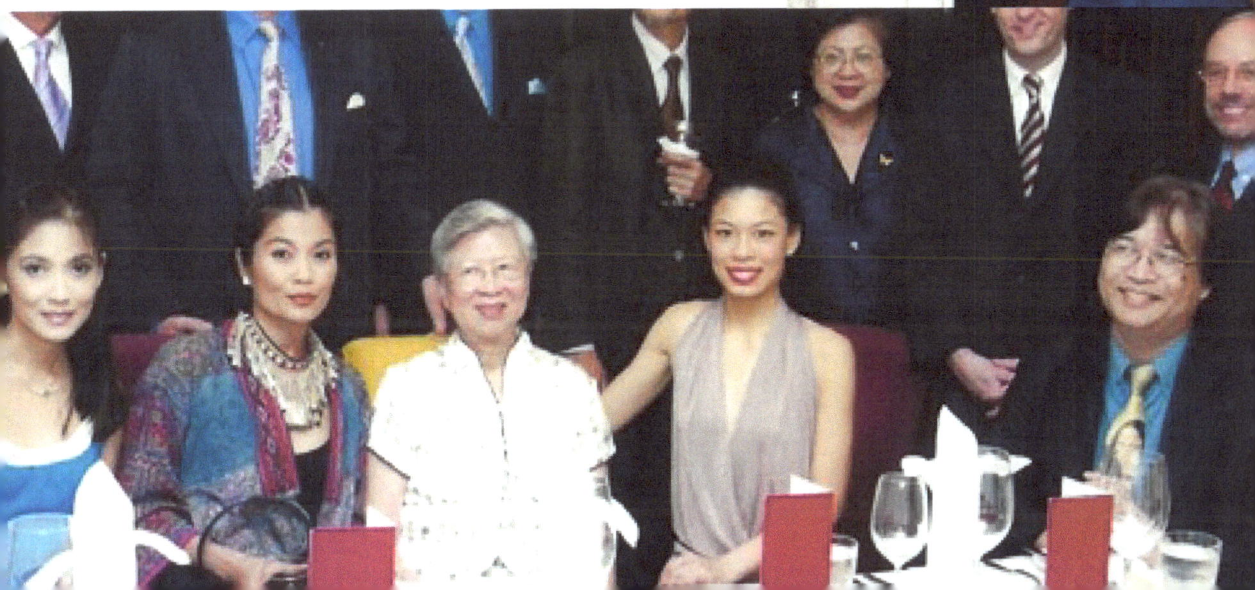

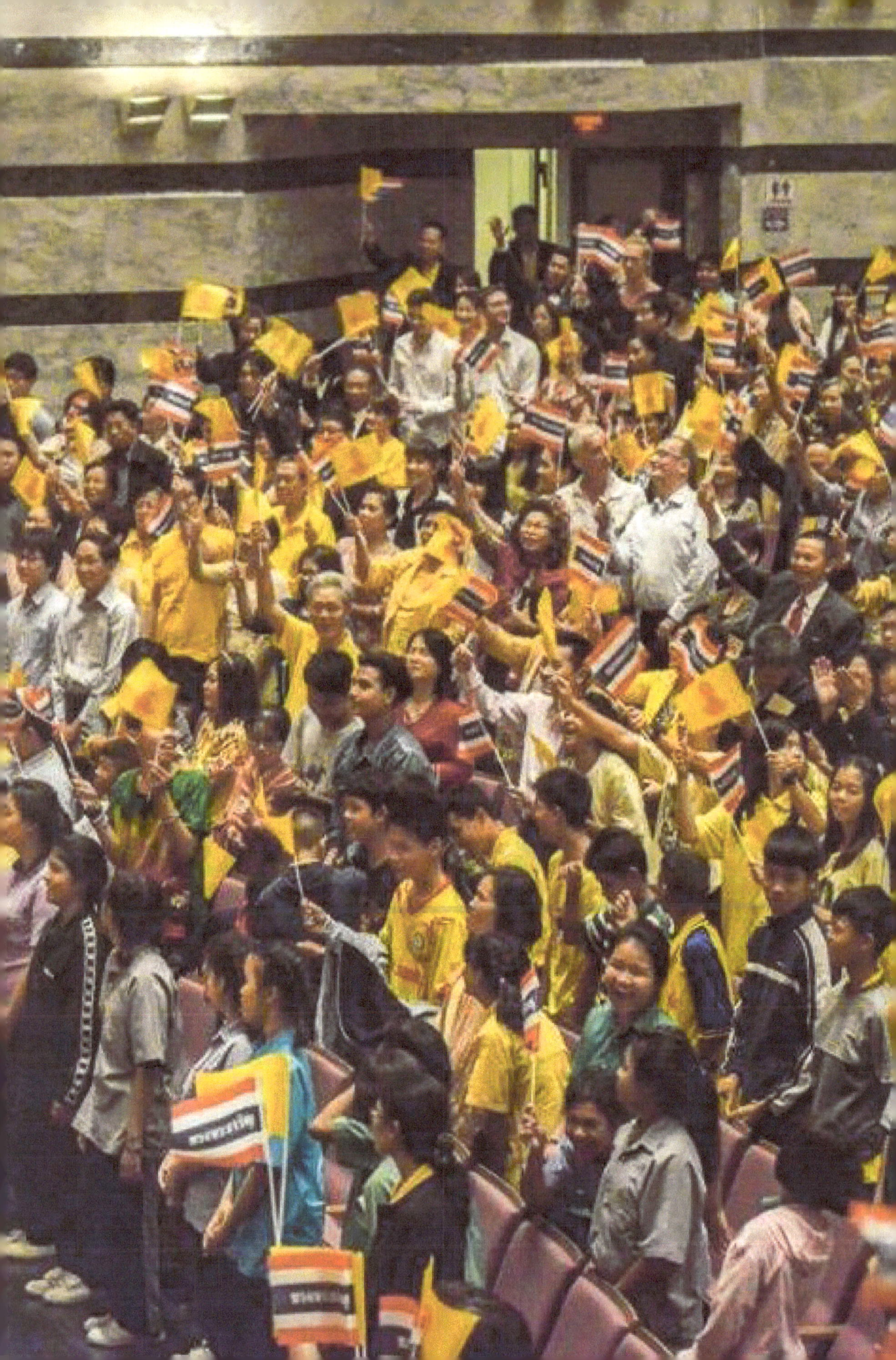

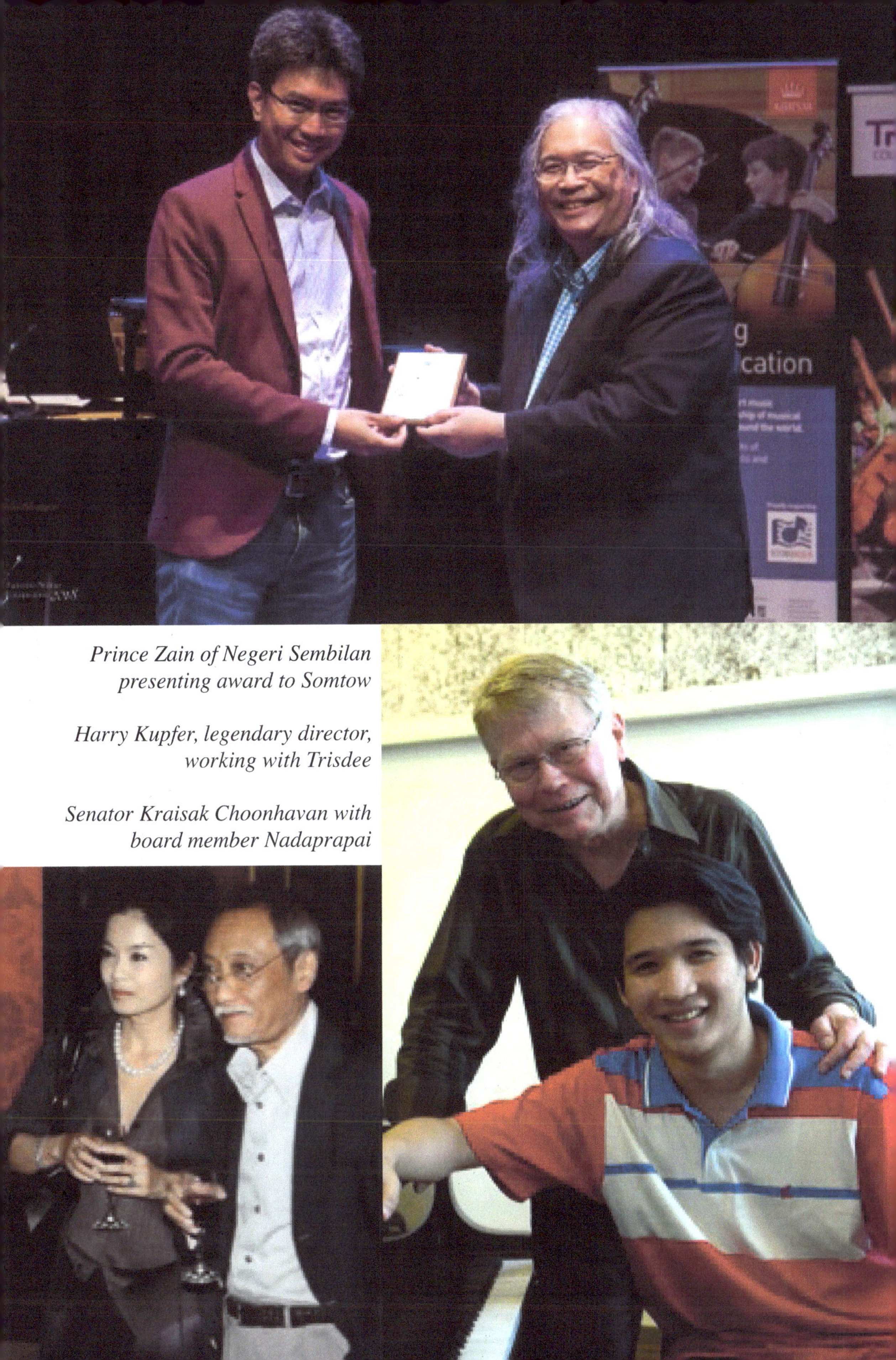

Prince Zain of Negeri Sembilan presenting award to Somtow

Harry Kupfer, legendary director, working with Trisdee

Senator Kraisak Choonhavan with board member Nadaprapai

EUROPEAN CULTURAL ACHIEVEMENT AWARD - ACCEPTANCE SPEECH

In 2017, the Artistic Director of Opera Siam, Somtow Sucharitkul, became the first Asian to win the European Cultural Achievement Award and the only composer, after Hans Werner Henze, to do so. He was cited for his work in creating bridges between East and West through art and culture. In his acceptance speech, Somtow spoke of how Thailand has come of age as a true player in the international cultural world. Opera Siam is proud of the major role it has planned in this coming of age. This pictorial history reflects the evolution.

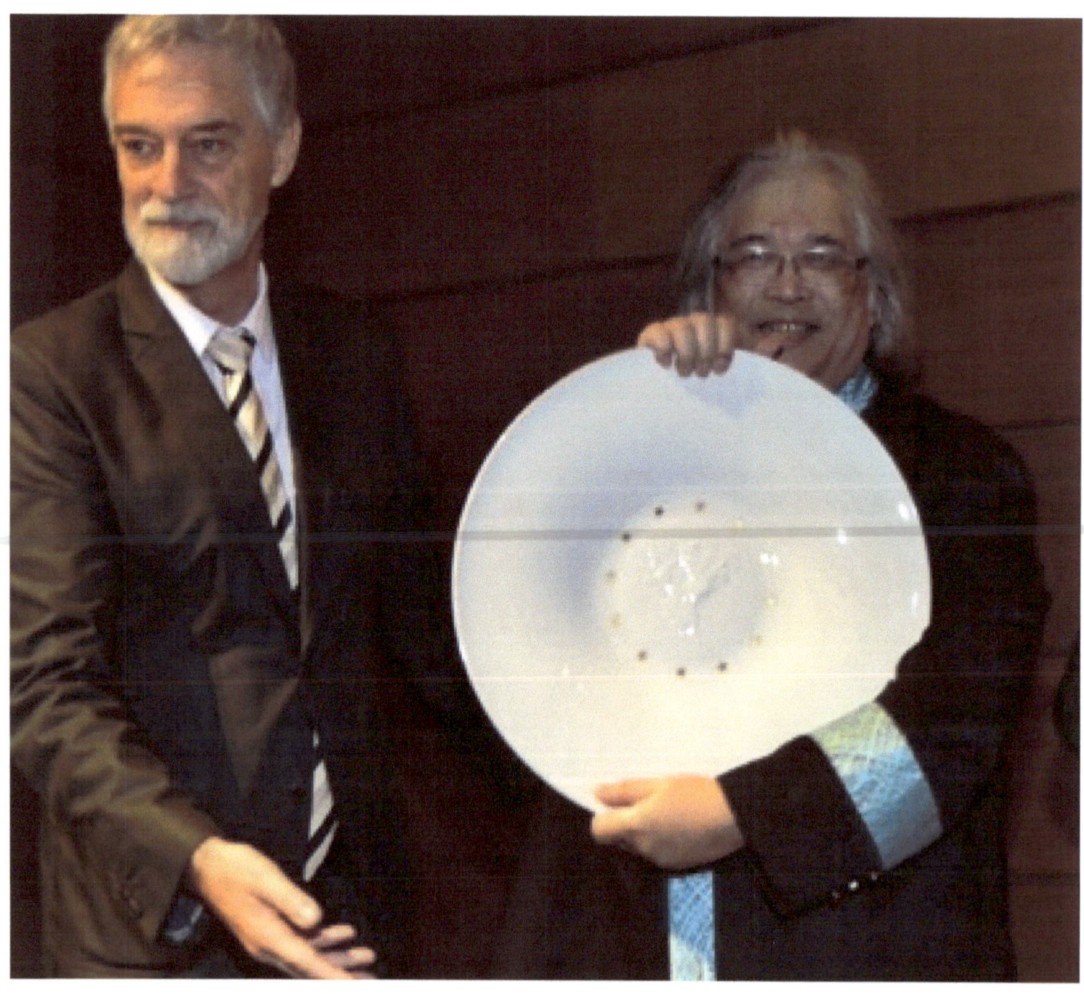

ACCEPTANCE SPEECH

Your Excellencies, Ladies and Gentlemen:

Mr. Topp, the president of the European Culture Forum, has painted a glowing picture of my achievements. I will be long dead before we find out if history will validate his praise.

But, as the first winner of the European Cultural Achievement Award to come from a place once quaintly known as "The *Far* East", I feel that the award is less about what I have done, but about how far *we* have come, as a nation, as a region, in taking our rightful seat at the table of the world's culture.

When I was a child growing up many European countries, I would sometimes see performances from Thai or other Asian artists. I could sense that though these performances were greeted with respect and interest, there was always a sense that what we did was something *other,* outside the mainstream. "How charming! These clever little natives are playing our music!"

But in only the last few years, there has been an absolute and permanent change in how the world views us. When Siam Sinfonietta, created using a radical educational theory, became the first Thai symphony orchestra to win the first prize in any major international competition, five years ago, interpreting the music of Austria to a panel consisting entirely of Austrian judges, the foreman of the jury said, "We have heard the message from the young people of Thailand. We have heard it loud and clear." Last year, when part of my *DasJati* series toured in Europe, a Czech reviewer said, "This was by no means an ethnographical curiosity, but a fully professional display of contemporary Thai culture in fusion with European traditions."

There was a time when the west saw us as unformed, as pristine vessels ready to receive western culture as a divine gift. But those days are over. The west has come to understand that our relationship is no longer only about what can learn; it is now equally about what we can teach.

There are many people who have made today possible, and I would like to thank some of them who are in this hall.

I would like to thank my family, who defied the conventions of society by allowing me the freedom to follow a different road, illumined by a different light.

Many countries have welcomed me and let my voice be heard. In particular, tonight I thank Germany, represented this evening by Dr. Prügel, the ambassador the first European country to embrace my work.

I would like to mention some of the educational institutions of this country, who have tolerated my out-of-the-box methods and allowed my holistic approach to flourish. In particular, I would like to mention Dr. Arthit Ourairat, whose visionary approach has conjured up a new performing arts center where once there was nothing, appearing like a magical oasis in a suburban desert.

And I would like to thank my fellow artists, who have been with me on this thrilling journey. It's been a hard journey.

But we have come to understand that we too are participants in the great drama of the world. That we too may stand on the stages of the world and show its audiences truths that they would have remained unseen, had we not been there to show them. Whether it is in theater, film, the visual arts, dance, or, now, in classical music, the artists of Thailand now dare to hold up the mirror to the world.

We have inherited many great forms of expression from western culture — among them film, television, and opera. But these gifts are no longer shiny trinkets from another land. They are our inheritance. They belong to us, and we have new things to say about them.

We may now dare to show the audiences of the world who they are, because we have finally dared to understand who we are.

As to the question of who we are, I would like to draw your attention to the quintessentially Thai thing I know. This is not some architectural marvel, or some arcane dance, but something ubiquitous, and known throughout the world: the simple Thai salad, or *yam*.

This is the most amazing invention. The great secret of *yam* is that every ingredient retains its original texture, its original identity. And yet, this dish has a gestalt that is unmistakably Thai in every bite.

Our culture is like that salad. There's a nibble of India, a crunch of China, a sprinkle of Hollywood, and you can see all the pieces, each disparate, each unique. But the whole thing could never be anything other than Thai.

This is the culture that transformed a pile of broken pottery into the Temple of Dawn.

In this regard, I am so happy the cultural world is beginning to notice what I'm trying to do in creating the *DasJati* series. Of course a lot of people are hung up on its 'giganticism' — you see a lot of commentators mentioning it's the "biggest integrated work of classical music in history" and that sort of thing.

But the canvas needs to be big, because the strands being woven together are so multitudinous and so diverse. Buddhism as music drama, told in a language drawn as much from film as from theater and in a musical idiom that bridges Europe and Asia; it's not just the story of a religion, but a story about all of us, the people in today's world.

It's a project that will bring together creative individuals from many fields, and which, I hope, can be interpreted and reinterpreted by the ever-widening viewpoints of future artists.

Since returning to Thailand almost two decades ago after several decades of searching for identity and meaning, I've learned a simple truth that is difficult to learn; that home is not a place, but a feeling; that to know the world you must first dare to know yourself.

It is therefore as a Thai artist, and in the name of Thailand's many great artists on whose shoulders I stand, and on behalf of this great country that has brought me to this moment, that I accept, with humility, the 2017 Award for European Cultural Achievement.

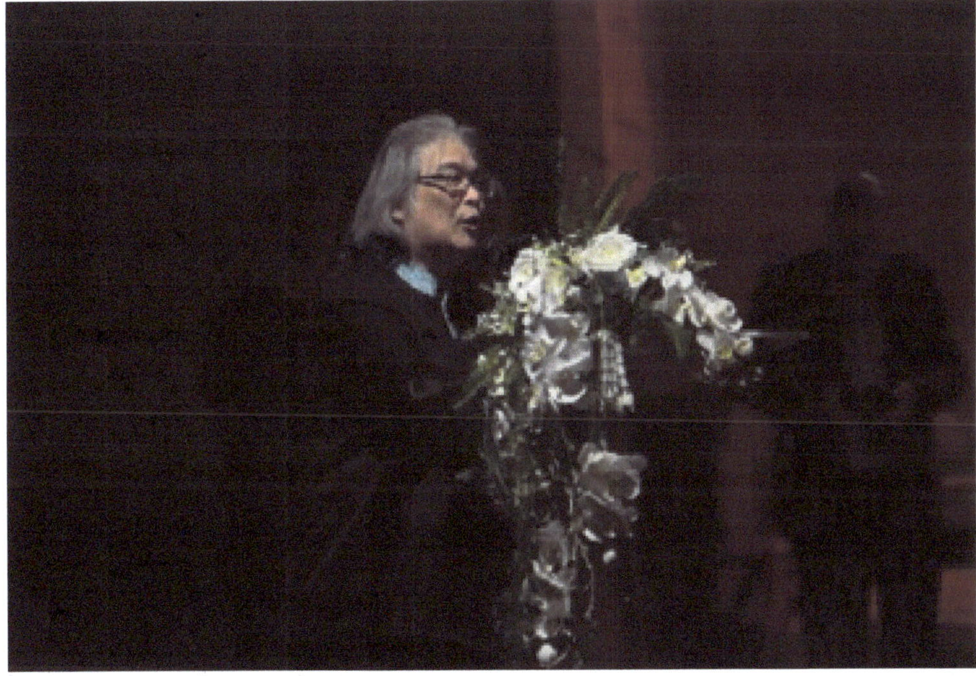

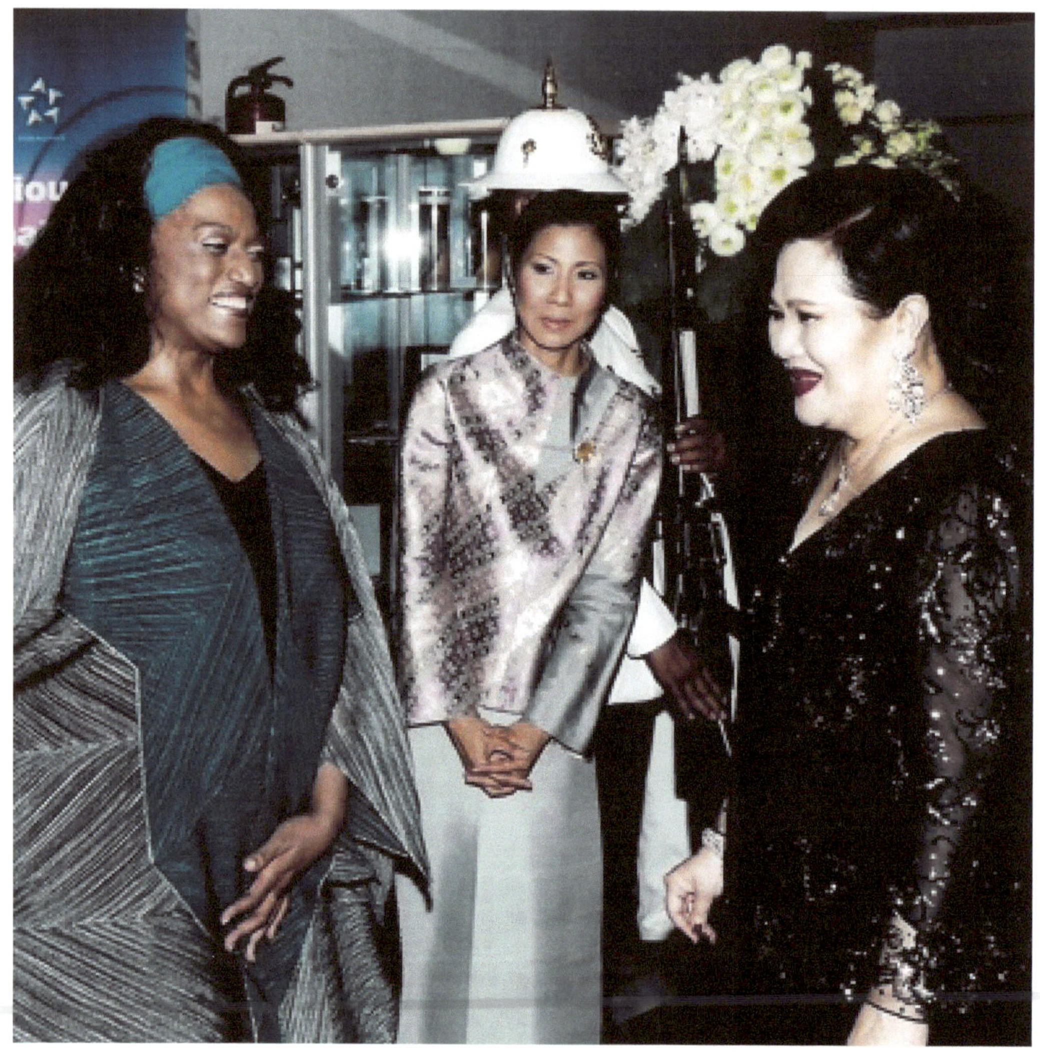

Jessye Norman, Korbkarn Wattanavrangkul, former Minister of Tourism and head of Toshiba Thailand, HM Queen Sirikit of Thailand

Opera Siam

www.operasiam.com

34 Soi Piphat 2
Silom Road
Bangkok 10500
Thailand

created by the Bangkok Opera Foundation
a registered nonprofit educational and cultural entity

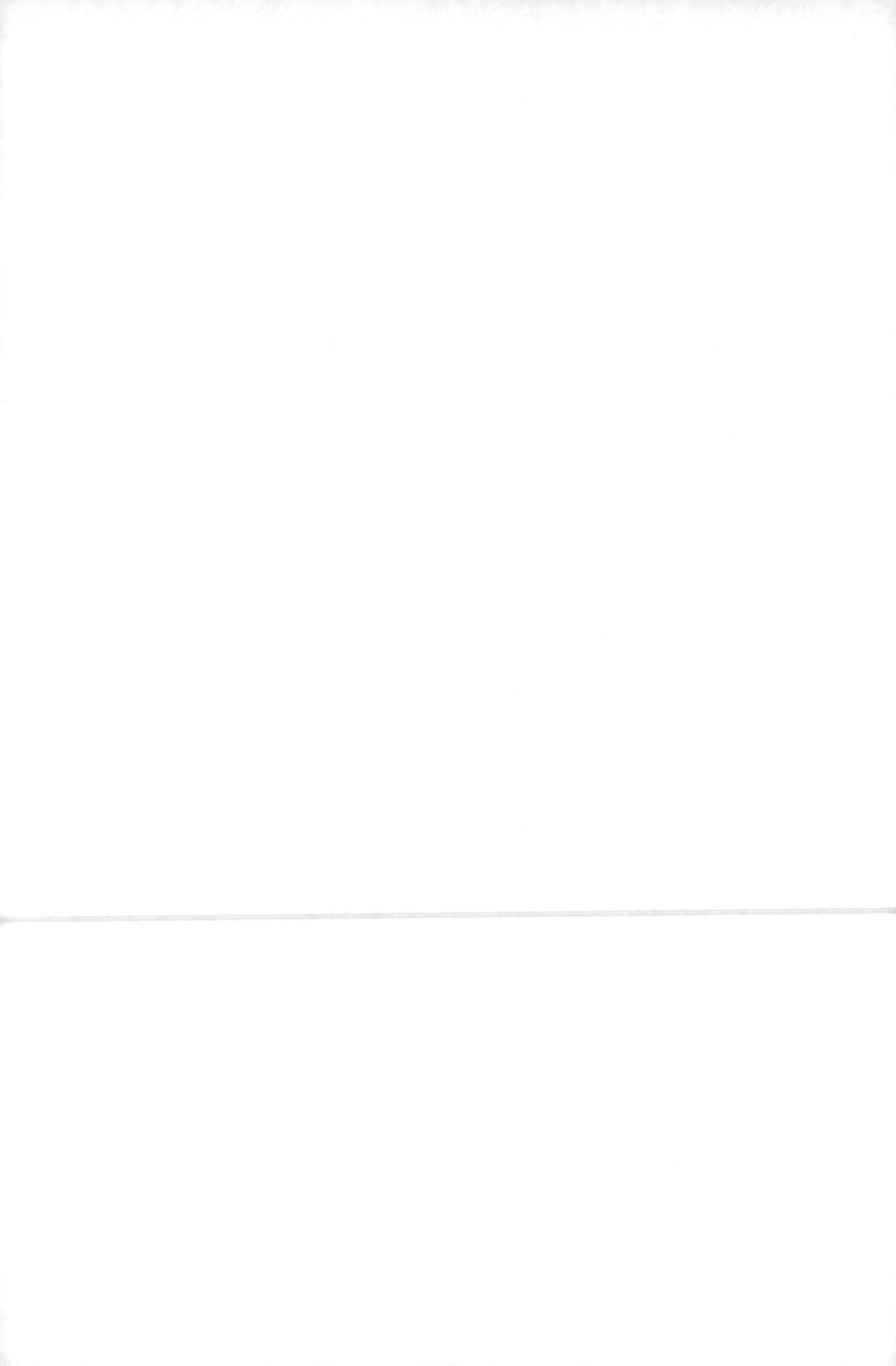

www.ingramcontent.com/pod-product-compliance
Lightning Source LLC
LaVergne TN
LVHW070122110826
845147LV00002B/170